The Form of Cities

For Jean

THE FORM OF CITIES

CITIES

Political Economy
and
Urban
Design

Alexander R. Cuthbert

Blackwell Publishing

BLACKWELL PUBLISHING
350 Main Street, Malden, MA 02148-5020, USA
9600 Garsington Road, Oxford OX4 2DQ, UK
550 Swanston Street, Carlton, Victoria 3053, Australia

First published 2006 by Blackwell Publishing Ltd

1   2006

Library of Congress Cataloging-in-Publication Data

Cuthbert, Alexander R.
   The form of cities: political economy and urban design /
   by Alexander R. Cuthbert.
      p. cm.
   Includes bibliographical references and index.
   ISBN-13: 978-1-4051-1639-8 (hardback: alk. paper)
   ISBN-10: 1-4051-1639-0 (hardback: alk. paper)
   ISBN-13: 978-1-4051-1640-4 (pbk.: alk. paper)
   ISBN-10: 1-4051-1640-4 (pbk.: alk. paper) 1. City planning.
   2. City planning – Philosophy. 3. Cities and towns – Philosophy. I. Title.

HT166.C885 2006
307.1′216–dc22

2005022741

A catalogue record for this title is available from the British Library.

Set in 10.5/12.5pt Sabon
by SPI Publisher Services, Pondicherry, India
Printed and bound in Singapore
by Fabulous Printers Pte Ltd

For further information on
Blackwell Publishing, visit our website:
www.blackwellpublishing.com

Contents

Figures

Tables

Preface

This book concludes four years of research into the theoretical basis for urban design, a project conceived in two stages, namely the publication of a reader, followed by a text that elaborated on the same basic structure. The first two years of the research process therefore resulted in *Designing Cities* (Cuthbert 2003), which accomplished four basic tasks: first, to assemble critical readings in the field that I felt had been largely ignored by urban designers in general; second, to suggest that mainstream 'urban design theory' be redirected towards critical theory and spatial political economy; third, that the adopted form of both books would suggest a structure and organisation of material that would reflect this ideological shift and, at the same time, make it accessible to individuals in a variety of fields – professionals, postgraduate students and an educated lay audience; and fourth, the adopted form for the articles contained in the reader would be the same one used in the planned text, so that anyone reading the first volume would already be familiar with the principles guiding the second volume, as well as its structure and organisation.

This current volume, *The Form of Cities*, is the text that completes another two years of research. It uses the same structure as *Designing Cities* to elucidate in significantly greater detail the parameters for an appropriate knowledge in urban design. Both volumes were conceived as part of the same project and are meant to be used together. When articles in Volume 1 are referenced, I have used the prefix *DC* to indicate that the article can be sourced from *Designing Cities*, so the first volume acts as a generic information base for Volume 2.

In writing this text (Volume 2), it was not my intention to propose any new *theory* of urban design. As we shall see, several writers have fallen into this trap and all have failed. While some may have generated quite admirable and credible models of various aspects of urban design, each has done so at the cost of vastly oversimplifying essential interactions between social relationships and design processes. In addition, any author writing on theory today has to walk a tightrope between two antagonisms. On the one hand, postmodernist criticism rejects any attempt to promote an integrated theory, one that will automatically be labelled structuralist, totalising and therefore unacceptable. On the other hand, postmodernism, in rejecting the idea of structure, easily falls into an intellectual anarchy composed of myriads of separate and competing discourses, voices and nebulous 'others'.

Using the intellectual grid of spatial political economy, I hope to demonstrate a fabric of interconnected principles that will guide the evolution of theoretical knowledge in urban design. As I discovered in researching *Designing Cities*, knowledge, like national economies, is subject to uneven development. In certain areas, for example history, the concept of political economy is widely utilised, while in others, such as aesthetics, it is weakly developed. So each chapter unfolds based upon an overall evaluation of available discourses within each subject area, the extent to which spatial political economy is used and useful, and an assessment of how the uneven development of urban design knowledge may be rectified.

Since the first draft of this book was 32,000 words over the limit set by the publisher, I was faced with the problem of how to retain the integrity of the work while having to eliminate every fourth word. I decided to drastically reduce chapter 1, which formed an extended and detailed critique of the central texts and actors in traditional urban design, with an in-depth explanation of the philosophical basis for spatial political economy, my chosen method of approach throughout this book.

There were three basic reasons for this choice. *Designing Cities* already contains a significant overview of urban design theory in the extended introduction to that work. I am assuming that many readers will either have purchased or will have access to this companion text, and will be familiar with the important debates. Next, chapter 1 still contains the substance of my argument. Political economy is explained in some detail in chapters 2 and 3, and is deployed in all of the remaining chapters. Finally, the 30,000-word original chapter 1 is available to anyone who wishes to access it on my website at http://www.fbe.unsw.edu.au/staff/Alexander.Cuthbert/. This allows me to explore the nine remaining essential elements of urban design knowledge in significantly greater depth than would otherwise have been possible.

In greater detail, *The Form of Cities* offers everyone involved in the built environment a framework for study. The book is structured so it will have wide application to tertiary education, professional practice and for the educated layperson who might wish to delve deeper into the design process. Since urban design is taught universally at Master's level to graduates in a variety of disciplines, it assumes a pre-existing level of critical thinking. It is written for graduate students, particularly those studying architecture, landscape architecture, cultural studies, urban planning, urban geography, urban sociology and other disciplines (engineering, real estate, etc.), and offers a multidisciplinary theoretical approach to the art of designing cities.

While the intellectual scaffolding derives from spatial political economy, the text is not blind to other paradigms. I am very aware in adopting this position that most of the material written to date about designing cities has avoided this

perspective. Why this is so forms a large part of chapter 1. Some other considerations also need to be made clear at the outset. Probably the most important
point is that this book is deliberately 'Western' in focus, dealing principally with
Europe and North America as prime sites.

The central reason for distinguishing between East and West is because the
whole development paradigm has been different. The Industrial Revolution of
the eighteenth and nineteenth centuries in the Western world spawned the
economic basis for capitalist imperialism and the ensuing process of urbanisation. The expansionism which resulted saw vast tracts of Asia come under
colonial rule in one form or another. The planet was carved up by the great
powers of the time, resulting in the first great imperialist war of 1914–19. Prime
among these were the British in India, Malaysia and China, the French in
Vietnam, Laos and Cambodia, the Dutch in Indonesia, and the Japanese also
in China. Imperialism and colonisation were predicated on the basis of Western
development strategies, not Asian.

Whereas the Western system of development was built on a vast industrial
surplus, colonisation and imperialist practices, Asia was on the receiving end of
this process as a fundamentally agrarian society, to be plundered by Western
nations for raw materials and markets. This is not to say that economic imperialism did not occur in the East – the 'stealth imperialism' of the Chinese in south-
east Asia is legendary, and China still exerts enormous influence throughout the
region today. Nonetheless it is difficult if not impossible to encompass the
production of urban form as a process common to both East and West, based
on dissimilar developmental histories. Having lived and worked in Asia and
Australasia for the last twenty years, I accept the limitation that both regions
cannot be encompassed in the same text, and I have another project on the
drawing board to deal with this omission.

Acknowledgements

In completing this work I must express a great debt to two institutions and to the many individuals who have made this book possible. The London School of Economics and Political Science offered me the opportunity to transform my thinking about society and space over the course of my doctoral studies, and the University of New South Wales, Faculty of the Built Environment, supported me financially with two grants over the course of this project. Four friends and colleagues in particular deserve special mention, all of whom encouraged me to push the boundaries of my own abilities and interests. In this regard I wish to honour the debt I owe to Professor Manuel Castells for the many conversations we had in Hong Kong, and to my friends Professor Allen Scott of UCLA, Professor Jeffrey Henderson of Manchester University and Professor Harry Dimitriou of University College London for twenty years of banter, intellectual stimulation and friendship.

Many others have supported me, with camaraderie, recognition and sometimes just 'being there'. Those that come immediately to mind are Keith McKinnell of the University of Hong Kong, and one tragic but wonderful human being, the late, great Brian McLoughlin, formerly Professor of Planning at Melbourne University. My friend and colleague Peter Murphy at the University of New South Wales has always provided much-needed support and encouragement. Dr Bruce Judd and Professor Jon Lang have also been there for me on countless occasions, helping to create a sterling urban design programme. My other good friends Chris Abel, Rob Samuels, and John Zerby reviewed several chapters in the course of writing, and Deepak George offered his valuable computing skills to me when it really mattered. Andrew Covell arrived at precisely the right time to assist me with editing the text. The staff of Blackwell Publishing have carried out all the difficult tasks of production with their usual professionalism, and I wish to thank everyone involved in this process, particularly Kelvin Matthews, Joanne Cartwright and Valery Rose who kept me on track at different times over the last two years. But special thanks must go to Jolyon Phillips for the exceedingly difficult and rigorous task of copy-editing the entire text. Needless to say, all imperfections in the text are mine and I take full responsibility for any errors or omissions.

I also wish to thank Ayu for her affection, fortitude and grace, and to honour my dearest and oldest friend, Dr Jean Cavendish, who saved my life on more than one occasion with her insight and compassion. For a lifetime of selfless sacrifice and dedication to the welfare of her fellow travellers, it is to her that I dedicate this work.

Introduction

Thinking people search for truth in matter because they
are aware that there is nowhere else for them to search
                                                    Tariq Ali

Urban Design Origins

Urban design is the study of how cities have achieved their physical form and the
processes that go into renewing them. Urban design is not merely the art of
designing cities, but the knowledge of how cities grow and change. It is the study
of how civilisations have chosen to represent themselves in spatial form, and the
processes through which specific urban forms come about. Cities are not simply
physical containers of social processes any more than languages are solely a
functional method of transmitting information. Languages are symbolic representations of the world we inhabit, evolving gradually over historical time. They
embody entire philosophies, ideologies, conceptual systems, and many ways of
seeing. The same is true of cities. Since all human action is infused with meaning,
so the spaces we inhabit are also replete with symbolic values, collective memory, association, celebration and conflict. Ultimately, urban design is about the
transmission of urban meaning in specific urban forms. For this reason we must
go beyond abstract social science into the realm of human experience and the
creative process in order to fully understand why cities are how they are. As
Andrew Sayer (1984: 148) comments, 'social processes do not occur on the head
of a pin', meaning that people by definition live and breathe *in* and *through* space.

The design of cities has been going on as long as civilised life, and to a certain
extent is a measure of it. Many ancient civilisations had various kits of component
parts that were used in organising social space. The Greeks for example had the
agora, the theatre, the polis and the stadium, and many cities, particularly in Asia
Minor, used the organising framework of the gridiron. Usually architects designed
the buildings and spaces, and in Greece, as in other cultures over the centuries,
there was no need for a separate concept of 'urban design'. In most regions of
the world, urban form had to pay some respect to nature, both in the organisation
of social space and in domestic architecture. Cities evolved in accordance with

1

certain natural laws in regard to location, climate, defence and other considerations. Beyond that point, functional, economic, political and religious factors generated enormous complexity in the way cities worked and how they developed.

While cities continued to grow physically, real knowledge of their social organisation had to wait until the development of modern social science in the nineteenth and early twentieth centuries, when the full consequences of capitalist development was exposed in such epic writing as Marx's three volumes of *Capital* (1894), George Simmel's *The Philosophy of Money* (1900), Freud's *Civilisation and its Discontents* (1930) and Max Weber's *Economy and Society* (1968). Taken together, the penetrating analysis of society that emerged categorically demonstrated that urban life in its full complexity could only be explained through the invisible web of economic and social processes. With such immense intellectual activity taking place in the social sciences, it became undeniable that the physical world was an ephemeral product of much deeper and enduring forces. It was also true that none of these great thinkers were concerned with space or cities, let alone urban form. Nonetheless, many considerations inherent to these treatises were symbolically represented at the *fin de siècle* when Vienna became the intellectual epicentre of European thought.

The conflict between two great Viennese architects, Camillo Sitte and Otto Wagner, over the design of the city centre enclosed by Vienna's Ringstrasse, symbolically represented two alternative visions of the twentieth century. Almost exactly one century ago, the concept of the public realm expressed in urban design became directly linked with emergent concepts of the modern world. The inception of urban design as social process therefore became condensed as praxis, something different from architecture, but also something different from the profession of town planning which did not become institutionalised until 1914 as the Royal Town Planning Institute in London. From the *fin de siècle*, architecture and urban planning progressed as independent professions, and urban design was born as a process of major social consequence. In addition, the seminal textbook on urban design was brought into existence by Camillo Sitte in 1889, namely *The Art of Building Cities: City Building According to its Artistic Fundamentals*. Although Marcus Pollio Vitruvius had written his ten books on architecture (*De Architectura*) in Rome in the first century BC (first published in 1471), it had taken some 2000 years for a text of overwhelming consequence to emerge regarding the built form of the city.

Despite this new awareness of urban form as social process, the organisation of cities was still conceived as the sole domain of architects well into the twentieth century. Indeed Otto Wagner's classic textbook *Modern Architecture* written in 1898 was the original stimulus for much of this, whereby 'the architect would have to liberate himself from the enslavement to history, to the tradition of "Stilarchitecture" ' (Schorske 1981: 83). Over the next century, architects did not prove very successful at doing this, and cities continued to be seen as an extension of building design, with little or no recognition of the added complexities involved in urban structure. The dynamiting of the

Pruitt-Igoe housing estate in St Louis, USA, on 15 July 1972 inspired Charles Jencks to announce the symbolic death of modernism and the rise of a new ethos – postmodernism. By that time it had become obvious that the physical determinism of modern architecture could not be relied upon to resolve complex social issues. Many disasters had followed from this approach in other countries, for example the entire system of 'new towns' in Britain, abandoned as government policy after three-quarters of a century, and the failure of high-rise, high-density residential development in social housing from the late 1950s (Dunleavy 1981). Other great planning disasters (which in most cases were actually architectural disasters) have been documented in a book by the same name by Peter Hall (1982). At that point it became abundantly clear that cities, the public realm and projects beyond the level of a few related buildings lay well beyond the reach of an architectural education, and that a different kind of knowledge was required in order to accommodate the design of cities.

Synopsis of the book

In trying to obviate the inherent physical determinism of architectural and urban design, I have adopted a particular approach outlined in the preface. In order to make my aims explicit, I also need to be clear about the content of this book and its particular orientation. This can be done by locating it in relation to four levels of knowledge that are required by urban designers.

1   The theoretical, philosophical and contextual foundation of the discipline and the meta-programmes that both inform and legitimise practice.
2   The legal, financial and administrative context within which the discipline operates.
3   Technologies of space and form.
4   Case studies of urban design practice.

This book is categorically about the first of these levels, for a variety of reasons. It adopts the position of how to understand urban design rather than how to do it. So while this volume is a text, it is one that deals with theory rather than practice in the context of 'Western' urbanisation. It does not, for example, try to suggest how we should incorporate non-sexist processes into design. Instead, it lays out the foundation for gendered practices within capitalist society, and how this has affected the spatial and symbolic structure of our cities. Thus the book suggests one possible structure for acquiring meta-theory and meta-knowledge, the substrate that relates all subsequent learning and practice into an intellectually coherent discipline. No doubt there are other ways to accomplish this task. The central reason for this position is that while the other three levels mentioned above are reasonably well covered, the first remains completely problematic. In following this framework, I will step back from the apparent substance of the discipline in levels 2 to 4, to a basic structure of concepts that might reasonably form its deeper structures. In chapter 2, which deals with history, my concern will not be to recount (yet again) the chronological sequencing of urban design products from Miletus to the Docklands, but to show how history itself is socially constructed and to demonstrate how various histories have been assumed in order to explain essential knowledge in the field. While a dialectic exists to some degree between theory and practice, the latter will continue regardless, since it is driven in most cases by financial and administrative expediency. In order for the discipline to move forward, a new discourse needs to be set in place with ideas derived from a significantly wider compass.

It is therefore in the realm of theory that advances need to be made, and this has been my focus throughout. As I have made clear in *Designing Cities*, the actual administrative, financial, legal and formal foundations for the practice of urban design is not my concern in undertaking this project, although the formation of cultural capital is considered in depth in chapter 10. Another reason for this focus is that there are already a great many books and reports dealing with level 3, the technologies of urban design practice, namely design and development control, historic conservation, land valuation, planning law, site analysis, standards for residential development and layout, formal typologies and standards for open space, facilities provision and the rapidly shifting world of geographic information systems (GIS), and systems for computerised graphic design and representation. These are so well developed that the discipline is being undermined by its own dependence on applied technologies of all kinds, ignoring in the process the intellectual and theoretical considerations that might lend it credibility and integrity as an independent region of practice. Similarly, at level 4, case studies abound, for example my colleague Jon Lang (1994) has written the definitive text on the public realm in his exhaustive *Urban Design: The American Experience*, with privatised public space extensively documented in Kayden (2000). The key factor that distinguishes a profession from other forms of practice is that its acts are based in theory. If urban design as a social process is not to be degraded into a series of displaced technologies, then it must be reoriented onto a new trajectory where substantial theoretical engagement is part of the overall process of educating (designing) urban designers. How this process might be represented is the purpose of this volume.

With regard to the organisation and categorisation of substantive material into chapters, the trade-off in any taxonomy is that one sacrifices continuity to convenience. There is no linear 'story' being told. Each chapter is to some degree independent of the others. The underlying theme of spatial political economy provides an intellectual and critical reference point throughout the text. This position is new to urban design, but it is not a new paradigm. Nor is it immune to critical self-reflection. In fact it has a long history, originating as the political economy of Adam Smith during the Scottish Enlightenment in the latter half of the eighteenth century. I also stress that spatial political economy will be used thematically, as a reference point or baseline, rather than a pragmatic position. This is the central reason why a chapter is not included on the subject of economy since an 'economic' perspective is inherent in the entire work.

Consequently, the text has been organised in basically three sections. Theory, history and philosophy are directly interconnected and are the most encompassing categories. Similarly, politics, culture and gender deal with the social dimension. The next three categories, environment, aesthetics and typologies, deal with questions of form, while chapter 10 ('praxis') addresses some of the necessary relations between education, research and practice. Therefore the book is both limited by, and benefits from, this structure. There will always be a significant degree of overlap between categories, for example between history and theory, or between culture and politics This is not a problem of the text but a problem of knowledge in general. In fact, every attempt has been made to cross-refer theories, concepts, subject matter and references. The purpose of each chapter and the interconnections between them is described in greater detail below.

Chapter 1 performs three tasks: first, it gives an overview of mainstream urban design theory; second, it traces where political economy and critical theory have been most active to date in offering a different viewpoint; and third, it suggests how we should consolidate a framework from spatial political economy that can use various components derived from the mainstream position, and at the same time, offer it a coherence that it presently lacks. The chapter addresses problems of definition and context: what exactly is it we are trying to encapsulate in the concept 'urban design'? A taxonomy of classic texts is offered, with a clear exposition of the differences between the intellectual territories claimed by architecture, urban design and urban planning. This is followed by a brief discussion of political economy as a concept, and the more recent spatial political economy of the social sciences. The chapter concludes by arguing for the use of this paradigm as a framework for urban design knowledge.

Chapter 2 addresses the idea of history in relation to urban design. It begins by asking the question 'What is history?' in order to contextualise urban design practice. Next I look at the idea of history from the ideological position of professional intervention, a process that has significantly influenced how urban design has been configured as an intellectual product. The two main influences here, as one would expect, are from architecture and urban planning. In both cases, history has frequently been used as a vehicle for legitimating professional solidarity, rather than for its capacity to enlighten us about humanity. I then discuss four ways in which urban design history has been enunciated, via chronologies, typologies, utopias and fragments/collage. An alternative historical perspective is then given, based in materialist theory. In the process I discuss the work of many scholars whose writing supports a concept of urban design as the dynamic product of society's need to generate material and symbolic capital from space.

Chapter 3 (Philosophy) overlaps extensively with the previous chapter, to the extent that it is impossible to separate the content of history from some conception of the overall process. Here the implications of philosophy are discussed, prior to a detailed consideration of key philosophies of urbanism in the twentieth century. These paradigms reflect particular locations at the epicentre of intellectual debate in their time: from Vienna at the *fin de siècle*, to the Frankfurt School of the 1920s, to Chicago and the Bauhaus in Weimar in the 1930s and 1940s, to Paris in the 1960s and 1970s, and arguably to Los Angeles today, with a significant body of contemporary urban theory emanating from that location. A detailed account of the central philosophical paradigms that have informed urban design is then suggested: semiotics (semiology), phenomenology and Marxian political economy. While all of the chapters in this text are designed to interact and overlap, the first three chapters on theory, history and philosophy have particularly strong connections.

Chapter 4 tackles the difficult subject of politics. For most urban designers, politics, like philosophy, is a topic that has no significant bearing on their education. In order to demonstrate why this should not be the case, the relationship between politics and ideology is discussed, since they are inseparable parts of the same process. Mao Tse-tung once described politics as 'war without guns', and in the theatre of the built environment, urban politics is influential at all levels of engagement in design. Also intimately connected is the idea of power, and how the built environment is the theatre where power expresses itself through the medium of political ideologies that configure, and are embedded within, spatial configurations, architectonic space and the expression of symbolic capital. Continuing from this point, the central ideological construct of capital, namely the legal system, is discussed in relation to the concept of right, which has ultimate authority over the public domain and therefore of urban design as its custodian. The state's legitimating control over urban design in the form of urban planning is then discussed. This has two aspects: theories that begin with an a priori concept of society, and those that somehow view urban planning as an independent factor in the overall process of urbanisation. The core concept defining urban design, that of the public realm, is then contextualised within this defining framework.

Chapter 5 investigates the interdependence of urban design and culture, accepting that urban design is also a physical expression of cultural processes and aspirations. I then discuss the relationship between modernism and postmodernism in the context of global culture and posthistory. Two central concepts and two emergent manifestations in the built form of cities are outlined. Authenticity and symbolic representation form key processes in the expression of urban form within first-world countries, with the New Urbanism fast becoming the dominant design paradigm. The chapter concludes by suggesting that while the New Urbanism reflects the engrained ideologies of capitalist society, a New Ruralism contains a greater capacity for resistance and change in the developing world.

Chapter 6 deals with the relationship between gender and design. Gender is almost wholly absent as a referent within all urban design programmes, despite the fact that after capital it is the largest single influence over the design and use of urban space. In order to obviate this situation, it is important to examine all related concepts, as well as the meanings and significance that the concept of gender has for the built environment. Also important is the fact that traditional political economy ignored gender entirely, as it did with ethnicity, language, lifestyle and sexuality. The chapter therefore deals in turn with the four building blocks of gender theory, namely society, patriarchy, capital and space, before looking at the overall impact of gender on urban design.

Chapter 7 (Environment) analyses the origins, theoretical development and practical realisation of sustainability in urban design, not from a technical point of view but from the perspective of political and economic progress. The history of the environmental movement is first discussed, beginning in the middle of the twentieth century and continuing until today. Attitudes to nature are then delineated as the source of ongoing dilemmas of the fundamental unsustainability of so-called 'sustainable development practices'. These ideas then segue into a discussion of the relationship between sustainability and development, on the basis of the inherent contradictions of the capitalist world order. Within these parameters, the ideology of sustainable cities is interrogated in three aspects: first, in relation to capital accumulation; second, in terms of social justice; and third, in relation to the material problems of urban space and sustainable urban design. As in the first three chapters, chapters 4, 5, and 6, on culture, politics and the environment have significant interactions.

Chapter 8 (Aesthetics) has probably been the dominant element in the *Weltanschauung* of urban designers, since most have undergone training in architecture defined either as art or technic. Paradoxically, however, there is so little written on the subject by urban designers that their learning in this respect must have been through osmosis. The chapter begins by examining aesthetic theory and the intersection between object and experience. The aesthetics of urban form are then discussed, reviewing the three articles selected in *Designing Cities* as paradigmatic of particular approaches, namely aesthetic philosophy and cognition, the production of the aesthetic object, and the mediation of symbolic form. To these I add a fourth dimension, namely the relationship between aesthetic production and commodity production, focused on Paul Clarke's article 'The economic currency of architectural aesthetics' (*DC* 2), one which was in fact included in the first section on theory. Three dominant paradigms are then outlined, namely mathematics and the divine order, contextualism and rationalism, and three forms of aesthetic production in the realms of symbolic capital, state regulation and theming.

Chapter 9 (Typologies) is concerned with the manner through which urban design understands itself and constructs models, appropriate or otherwise, to its own social formation. One way or another, the idea of typology lies at the heart of the discipline, since it allows designers to encapsulate key concepts and processes in a compressed and accessible form. As a method of introducing the concept, distinctions are made between four related ideas: typology, taxonomy, morphology and system. These concepts are explained using examples from a range of different disciplines such as science, anthropology, psychology and semiotics. I then enunciate three typological forms: those which emerge from disciplines closely related to urban design, those directly derived from urban design, and others evolving out of spatial political economy. In so doing it is possible to demonstrate influences on urban design awareness, how the existing conceptual framework is encapsulated, and how it might be transformed with access to a more critical perspective based in urban social theory.

Chapter 10 (Pragmatics) looks at the two most significant (ideological) processes that affect the production of cultural capital: the training of urban designers and their relationship to tertiary education and to the professions. My analysis begins with the role of professional service within the capitalist system of production, and how they interact in the reproduction of surplus value and the maintenance of class barriers. I then move onto the role played by professions in the production of knowledge systems, and the nature of their authority. In greater detail, professional intervention and influence over the construction of urban space is discussed, concentrating on its ideological role in implementing planning law, and how the exacting ideologies of form so produced serve to reinforce the reproduction of capital from space. I conclude the chapter, and the book, with an extended analysis of the relationship between the two professions of architecture and planning, predicated on the absence of any independent profession of urban design, with an extended assessment of the actual content of urban design education.

Chapter One
Theory

It is the theory that determines what can be observed.

Albert Einstein

Introduction: The Problem

What is understood as urban design 'theory' is anarchistic and insubstantial. This is a situation which has been ongoing for the best part of fifty years and needs to be corrected. Urban design is a discipline where, almost without exception, its major 'theorists' have failed to engage with any substantial origins in the cognate disciplines of economics, social and political science, psychology, geography or the humanities. We can push this idea even further and say that it has not even embraced what today would be recognised as significant subdisciplines, such as urban geography, urban economics, urban sociology or cultural studies, the latter only recently emerging as a major force in critical theory. This effectively situates urban design as several realms removed from any substantial theory at all. At its weakest it could be seen as merely an extension of the architectural imagination or the physical consequence of state planning policies. Both of these are heavily constrained attitudes that ignore the fact that the organisation and design of our physical world cannot be so narrowly drawn. They suggest a theoretical dependency on architecture and planning, focusing narrowly on their function as social technologies. What constitutes the theoretical object of urban design remains in question, one upon which the foundation for any substantial theory is predicated. In order to do this we must begin by defining what we mean by 'urban design', its relationship within a hierarchy of practices, from architecture through urban design into urban and regional planning, and its social function within a larger and more embracing social context.

Urban Design: Definitions

The term 'urban', apart from the fact that it originates in the Latin word *urbs* meaning city, has contained significant added value since Lewis Wirth first wrote his legendary paper 'Urbanism as a way of life' in 1938. The term 'urban' also

formed the basis for one of the most meaningful interrogations of urban structure, that of Manuel Castells' now iconic book *The Urban Question*, first
published in French in 1972. After its English debut in 1977, it set in motion a
debate lasting the next ten years over the idea of a conceptually valid 'urban
sociology', one that still resonates today, although much of the territory has now
been captured by urban geography. So I will continue to deploy the term 'urban'
since it remains a more relevant and conceptually challenging term than either
'civic' or 'city' when applied to design, one whose meaning will hopefully
become clearer over the remainder of this chapter.

Progress towards developing some substantial theory of urban design in the
form of a satisfactory hypothesis, a set of guiding constructs or principles, or a
reasoned manifesto of ideological practices has been absolutely glacial. Virtually
all definitions begin and end in dogma, and 'the crisis in urban design', like the
endless 'crisis in urban planning' continues, fuelled by a dearth of critical and
dialectical thinking, an *emballage* of anarchistic practices, an obsession with
skill-based learning and a continuing belief in physical determinism. Here two
papers stand out simply because of their titles: David Gosling's 1984 paper
'Definitions of urban design' and Alan Rowley's paper of the same name exactly
ten years later (more recent examples are represented in Punter 1996 and
Schurch 1999). In his paper, Gosling has adopted a wholly architectural perspective, as if only architects had any right to define the discipline. While it may
seem unfair to criticise this paper, now twenty years old, it remains significant
precisely because it represents the most powerful and enduring ideologies still
dominating the field of urban design. The paper is an articulate manifestation of
a wholly one-sided, ideologically biased and atheoretical example of the genre,
alienating every major theorist concerned with urban development, structure
and form. Similarly, potential models of urban design (e.g. as a definition of the
public realm, as a spatial matrix, as inversion, revitalisation, iconography) are
wrapped and made accessible only in and through the work of architects and
their critics.

Similar criticisms can be applied to Alan Rowley's paper. On the first page
(twenty years after the huge debates about the term 'urban' raged within urban
sociology, involving some of the best social theorists of the time) we are still
presented with a definition of 'urban' as something (we know not what) in
contrast to 'rural' development. Quoting Ruth Knack, we are informed that
'Trying to define urban design is like playing a frustrating version of the old
parlor game, twenty questions' (Rowley 1994: 181). In 'Definitions of urban
design', Rowley concludes with ten definitions, by which point it should be
apparent to the intelligent reader that the discipline is in serious trouble. The
last of these notes that urban design education demands literacy in the social
sciences, law, economics, public policy and business administration, none of
which are deployed in the paper. The problem with all of these attempts to
define urban design is that they are depthless and incapable of moving us
forward, except perhaps into another set of so-called basic values, functional
qualities, descriptive properties, performance dimensions or other qualitative

groupings that are usually claimed to have universal significance. Such an approach is akin to running on the surface of a sphere. At some point, and on a random basis, you have to arrive back where you started. So the overall problem remains. In the absence of any substantial theoretical framework that links urban design activity to the historical process, to social development and to other professions, the same basic positions and approaches will be endlessly recycled.

Urban Design: 'Theory'

It is not my intention here to write a normative history of urban design but to selectively illustrate some of the more influential and prototypical discourses that legitimise traditional theory from forty texts. All are classics in their own right, and constitute significant markers in the journey towards an improved understanding of urban design (see table 1). Historically, each text represented a major attempt to correct what was considered a dominant problem at the time it was written. Despite what I have said above, much practical criticism contained between their covers will remain valid for years to come, for the simple reason that even basic principles remain widely ignored decades after they were presented, as in Gordon Cullen's *Townscape* for example. As we approached the end of the second millennium, however, three things became very clear.

The first was that the positions represented in the collective corpus traditionally associated with urban design had lost most of their explanatory power. Many of these marked, in a very real sense, the last significant breath of the modernist position, twenty years after postmodernism had started to flourish in urban design. Second, over the last ten years, a new era in urban design theory has surfaced, although this remains to be articulated in any significant manner. Nan Ellin's book *Postmodern Urbanism* (1996) and Ross King's *Emancipating Space* (1996) are among the few memorable texts written in the intervening period, the latter being notable due to its rare dialectical relationship to theory. Third, the upsurge in things urban in disciplines that had previously been wholly disconnected to the design of cities began to produce a significant corpus of work. Urban sociology, economics and geography, cultural studies, art history, landscape architecture and other disciplines from anthropology to philosophy were all involved. Urban sociology and human geography have been the two key players since the early 1980s.

This progression results in the inevitable observation that more significant theoretical paradigms about the shape and form of urban space are originating from outside the discipline of urban design rather than from the inside. It also offers a partial explanation as to why so few key texts on urban design have emerged. The old paradigm has withered away and the new has not yet taken hold. In *Designing Cities*, I therefore made a clear distinction between what I consider to be normative theory *in* urban design over the thirty-year period from 1960 to around 1990 and the other more significant theory *of* urban design

Table 1   Forty classic texts in urban design.

Chermayeff & Alexander (1960) *Community and Privacy: Toward a New Architecture of Humanism*

Lynch (1960) *The Image of the City*

Mumford (1961) *The City in History*

Jacobs (1961) *The Death and Life of Great American Cities*

Cullen (1961) *Townscape*

Webber (1963) *Explorations into Urban Structure*

Halprin (1963) *Cities*

Buchanan (1963) *Traffic in Towns*

Rudofsky (1964) *Architecture without Architects: An Introduction to Non-pedigreed Architecture*

Sprieregen (1965) *Urban Design: The Architecture of Towns and Cities*

Bacon (1967) *The Design of Cities*

McHarg (1969) *Design with Nature*

Rudofsky (1969) *Streets for People*

Sommer (1969) *Personal Space: The Behavioural Basis for Design*

Halprin (1969) *The RSVP Cycles: Creative Processes in the Human Environment*

Proshansky, Ittelson & Rivlin (1970) *Environmental Psychology: Man and His Physical Setting*

Lynch (1971) *Site Planning*

March & Steadman (1971) *The Geometry of Environment*

Newman (1972) *Defensible Space*

Banham (1973) *Los Angeles: The Architecture of Four Ecologies*

Rapoport (1977) *The Human Aspects of Urban Form*

Venturi, Scott-Brown & Izenour (1977) *Learning from Las Vegas*

Alexander (1977) *A Pattern Language*

Rowe & Koetter (1978) *Collage City*

Norberg-Schulz (1979) *Genius Loci: Towards a Phenomenology of Architecture*

Krier (1979) *Urban Space*

Lynch (1981) *A Theory of Good City Form*

Barnett (1982) *An Introduction to Urban Design*

Hillier & Hanson (1984) *The Social Logic of Space*

Trancik (1986) *Finding Lost Space: Theories of Urban Design*

Alexander (1987) *A New Theory of Urban Design*

Gehl (1987) *Life Between Buildings: Using Public Space*

Broadbent (1990) *Emerging Concepts in Urban Space Design*

Katz (1994) *The New Urbanism*

Lang (1994) *Urban Design: The American Experience*

Hillier (1996) *Space is the Machine*

Ellin (1996) *Postmodern Urbanism*

Madanipour (1996) *Design of Urban Space*

Dovey (1999) *Framing Places: Mediating Power in the Built Environment*

Gosling & Gosling (2003) *The Evolution of American Urban Design: a Chronological Anthology*

and urban form that addresses urban spatial theory, beginning with Castells'
seminal study *The Urban Question*.

In addressing mainstream theory, we must briefly look at the key relationships
between architecture, urban design and urban planning. Table 2 gives a systems
view of the three related disciplines, couched in terms of Herbert Simon's
irreducible elements of systems referred to in his book *The Sciences of the
Artificial* (1969). Like all attempts to create a simple table of relationships,
one has to resort to some fairly pragmatic statements. Nonetheless, significant
differences between these activities soon become transparent. Architecture is
constrained to the design of individual buildings, which are governed by the
parameters imposed by artificially controlled environments. The term 'artificial'
used in this context does not connote false but man-made. The essential function
of architecture is defensive, predominantly from the weather and from other
people; hence buildings generally operate as closed systems with human, electronic or physical means of surveillance used to mediate external relations.
Urban design on the other hand is represented as an open system that uses
individual architectural elements and ambient space as its basic vocabulary.
Whereas architecture is predominantly concerned with social closure and pro-
tection, urban design is by its very nature focused on social interaction and
communication in the public realm. Urban planning is then conceived as something fundamentally different again, as the agent of the state in controlling the
production and reproduction of profit from land development, in allocating
sites for the collective consumption of social goods such as hospitals, schools,

Table 2 A systems view of professional boundaries.

Element	Architecture	Urban design	Urban planning
Structure	Statics + human activity	Morphology of space and form (history + human activity)	Government bureaucracy
Environment	Three dimensional (closed system)	Four dimensional (open system)	Political economy of the state
Resources	Materials + energy + design theory	Architecture + ambient space + social theory	Systems of legitimation and communication
Objectives	Social closure/ physical protection	Social communica- tion and interaction	To implement the prevailing ideology of power
Behaviour	Design parameters: artificially controlled environments	Dynamics of urban land markets	Dynamics of advanced capitalist societies

religious buildings, and in providing space for the production, circulation and eventual consumption of commodities.

Oren Yiftachel's paper 'Towards a new typology of urban planning theories' (1989) investigates the relationship between urban planning and urban form, where he delineates the three debates of planning theory, variously outlined as the analytical debate (What is urban planning?), the urban form debate (What is a good urban plan?) and the procedural debate (What is a good planning process?). While Yiftachel draws a fairly big picture of the positions that con-figured urban planning at the end of the 1980s, more mainstream urban design-ers were also doing the same thing within what he termed the 'urban form debate' (see also chapter 10). There have been a few influential articles within this paradigm that suggest a typology, synthesis or theory of urban form, for example Chris Abel's 'Analogical models in architecture and urban design' (1988), Anne Vernez Moudon's epistemological map for urban design (*DC* 28), Ali Madanipour's *Design of Urban Space* (1996a), and the New Urbanism, explained at length in a special issue of the *Journal of Urban Design* (Duany and Talen 2002). More importantly, we can make three fundamental distinctions in regard to theory.

1   There are claims to primacy. By this I mean some claim to a theory of urban design by individuals. Prime among these are Kevin Lynch's *A Theory of Good City Form* (1981), Rob Krier's *Urban Space* (1979b) and Christopher Alexander's *A New Theory of Urban Design* (1987).
2   There have been four courageous attempts to synthesise the entire field of urban design, the most notable being Rowe and Koetter's *Collage City* (1978), Gos-ling and Maitland's *Concepts of Urban Design* (1984), Roger Trancik's *Finding Lost Space: Theories of Urban Design* (1986) (see figure 1), and Bill Hillier and Julienne Hanson's *The Social Logic of Space* (1984) (see figure 2).
3   There is a new generation of writers approaching urban design from a variety of different academic backgrounds and critical perspectives (Aravot 2002, Inam 2002 and Gospodini 2002). While many of these retain attachments to mainstream theory, they also incorporate certain new forms of learning into their analysis. Although these do not appear to emerge from any unitary perspective at all, even an opaque postmodernism, they do indicate a trend towards very different sources than their predecessors.

Overall, however, there is little coherence among or between these various paradigms and approaches. Exhibited here is postmodern deconstruction with-out the intentionality or the conceptual framework. On the other hand, it is also unreasonable given the limitations of structuralism to return to a wholly prag-matic and inflexible framework for the discipline. A new and encompassing theory is not the answer either. The rationale I have expressed in the introduction suggests that an appropriate foundation for urban design should be located within spatial political economy rather than architectural determinism, policy planning or a generalised anarchy of ideas within mainstream urban design.

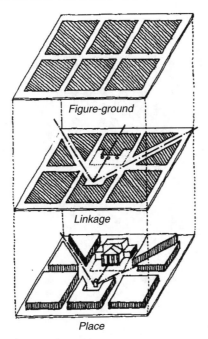

Figure 1   Three urban design theories.
Source: R. Trancik, *Finding Lost Space: Theories of Urban Design.* New York: Van Nostrand Reinhold, 1986. © 1986 by Van Nostrand Reinhold. Reprinted with permission of John Wiley and Sons, Inc.

Spatial Political Economy and Urban Design

Spatial political economy can be considered a meta-language or meta-narrative. It constitutes a loose coalition of ideas with a powerful intellectual base that goes back to Adam Smith, Hegel and Marx. Today it incorporates the spatial interests of social science, geography, cultural studies, economics, architecture, art history and other disciplines, and existential positions such as feminism, and sustainability. In other words it offers urban design the credibility it now lacks, without the attached dogma. Another property of spatial political economy is its wholesale rejection of any division of knowledge based upon professional and academic boundaries. Taking the profession of urban planning as an example, McLoughlin says, 'One of my main conclusions is that the dominance of the town planning tradition in the academy is a serious and ideologically driven limitation on our ability to understand urban problems and policies which might improve our cities and the lives of their people' consisting in what he refers to as 'the sheer intellectual incoherence of the whole business' (McLoughlin 1994: 1113; see also Huxley's elaboration and critique, 1997). His position is that the core–periphery relationship currently existing in urban planning and to a large degree throughout tertiary education should be reversed. The ideological role of professional influence and the somewhat arbitrary nature of academic programmes should be relegated to the periphery, with a focus on social-scientific

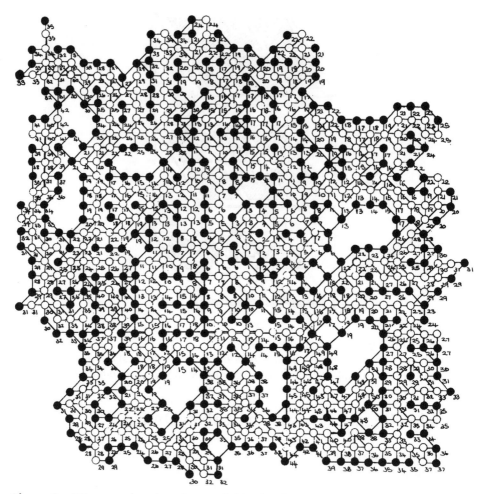

Figure 2 Diagram showing the spatial logic of encounters.
Source: W. Hillier and J. Hanson, *The Social Logic of Space*. Cambridge: Cambridge University Press, 1984. Reprinted by permission of Cambridge University Press.

perspectives. This argument would of course encompass the built environment disciplines, including urban design. McLoughlin maintains that the discipline occupying a key role at the centre of spatial political economy must be human geography since it is the core of what has been called the 'socio-spatial dialectic' (Soja 1989), part of a coalition discourse 'which is multi-faceted and includes (at least) insights which are drawn from (critiques of) positivist geography and neoclassical economics, as well as neo-Marxist and neo-Weberian social theory, feminist geography, the "Green" movement, and much else. It is a puzzling, contradictory and sometimes conflictual set of discourses' (McLoughlin 1994: 1114).

The position of spatial political economy has been much more highly articulated in the realm of urban planning than it has been in architecture or urban design, most likely because of its closer proximity to social science (keeping in mind the considerable overlap between these somewhat arbitrary professional realms). Indeed, many of the key scholars driving what was called the New Urban Studies, whose task was to reconstruct urban social theory during the 1980s, concerned themselves with urban planning as part of the state apparatus because of its role in the social control and regulation of urban space; see Castells (1977, 1978), Harvey (1973, 1982), Mingione (1981), Scott (1980), Saunders (1986), Pahl (1970, 1975, 1983), Dear (1986) and many others. Over the same period, the critical extension of social theory into the arena of architectural and urban form, what has been called the 'powers of architecture', began to develop (Knesl 1984).

To this end, seminal papers by Scott and Roweis (1977) and Harvey (1979a) cannot be underestimated, as well as influential writing by Tafuri (1976), Maxwell (1977), Korilos (1979), Rubin (1979), Dickens (1979, 1981), Frampton (1980), Knox (1982), Knesl (1984), King (1984) and King (1996). Several of my own papers collectively provide an in-depth study of Hong Kong from this perspective around the same period (Cuthbert 1984, 1987, 1989, 1991, 1992a,b). The general trajectory of this writing is exemplified in extracts from Castells' 'The city and the grassroots' (DC 1), and in Sharon Zukin's 'Postmodern debate over urban form' (DC 3). Castells (1983: 303) frames the fundamental question 'on the basis of the fundamental concepts of historical materialism, how can we grasp the specificity of the forms of social space?' In concert with this question, he offers by far the most encompassing and theoretically rigorous definition of urban design to date, one which informs this entire text:

> We define urban meaning as the structural performance assigned as a goal to cities in general (and to a particular city in the inter-urban division of labour) by the conflictive process between historical actors in a given society.
>
> We define urban functions as the articulated system of organisational means aimed at performing the goals assigned to each city by its historically defined urban meaning.
>
> We therefore define urban form as the symbolic expression of urban meaning, and of the historical superimposition of urban meanings (and their forms), always determined by a conflictive process between historical actors.
>
> We call urban social change the redefinition of urban meaning. We call urban planning the negotiated adaptation of urban functions to a shared urban meaning. *We call Urban Design the symbolic attempt to express an accepted urban meaning in certain urban forms* [my italics].
>
> (Castells 1983: 303–4)

Rather than resort to definitions of urban design such as those previously discussed, where the various qualities, properties and dimensions of cities are used to delineate urban design as praxis, Castells' great contribution was to define it theoretically as an embedded part of other urban functions and processes (notwithstanding the fact that what exactly constituted 'urban' remained unresolved). Importantly, Castells also assigns the term 'meaning' (not 'economy' as one might expect) as the ultimate measure of the performance of cities. He associates such meaning with the outcome or representation of urban conflict.

In this regard, Paul Walker Clarke's article 'The economic currency of architectural aesthetics' (*DC* 2: 28) also provided a relatively rare synthesis of this general *Weltanschauung* at the end of the 1980s: 'It is a simple assertion that architecture costs money and occupies space. It is therefore integral to the production of space and to the spatial configurations of the urbanism of our political economy.' The mystification of the connectivity between urban processes is what Clarke seeks to dispel, bringing together the work of Harvey, Rowe, Tafuri, Knesl and others previously mentioned. At the same time, Sharon Zukin's article 'The postmodern debate over urban form' (*DC* 3: 45) summarised what had taken place during the 1980s, where disciplines such as architecture, social science, philosophy, cultural studies and human geography had been maturing on the basis of structural economic and social change (Harvey 1989). I have tried to encapsulate the move to postmodernity and postindustrialism in relation to their various characteristics and spatial outcomes (see table 3). Zukin points to the significance of culture in the creation of urban form when she says, 'the liminal space of postmodern urban forms is socially constructed in the erosion of autonomy of cultural producers from cultural consumers'. Despite this, Zukin (*DC* 3: 47) remains convinced that certain fundamentals remained unaltered:

> The constant rebuilding of cities in core capitalist societies suggests that the major condition of architectural production is to create shifting material landscapes. These landscapes bridge space and time; they also directly mediate economic power by both conforming to and structuring norms of market driven investment, production and consumption.

While it is impossible to prioritise texts in relation to the general field of spatial political economy over this period as they relate to urban space and form, some typify or otherwise encapsulate the critical issues of the time. In this regard, honours for the most encompassing text must be shared between *Postmetropolis: Critical Studies of Cities and Regions* (Soja 2000) and *Postmodern Urbanism* by Nan Ellin (1996). The latter is a brilliant summary of the overall development of the period. The same is true of Claudio Minca's edited collection *Postmodern Geography: Theory and Praxis* (2001). The volume provides a beginning of millennium statement of the concerns of human geography, with contributions from luminaries such as Michael Dear, Dennis Cosgrove, Cindy Katz, Ed Soja and Neil Smith. Landmark texts have also been written in many areas, for example Doreen Massey's *Space, Place and Gender* (1994), Scott Lash and John Urry's *Economies of Signs and Space* (1994), Sharon Zukin's *Landscapes of Power* (1991), Mike Davis' *The Ecology of Fear* (1998), Castells' trilogy beginning with the *Rise of the Network Society* (1996), Allen Scott's *The Cultural Economy of Cities* (2000a), Michael Dear's *The Postmodern Urban Condition* (2000) and David Harvey's *Spaces of Hope* (2000).

Table 3 Properties of industrial and cultural forms and practices.

Industrialism	Postindustrialism	Modernism	Postmodernism
Qualities			
Regulation	Deregulation	Order	Anarchy
Rigidity	Flexibility	Control	Chance
Fusion	Diffusion	Direction	Indeterminacy
Standardisation	Diversification	Need	Desire
Material base	Information base	Product	Process
Hierarchies	Grids and networks	History	Destiny
Legitimation	Discretion	Function	Signification
Properties			
State power	Corporate power	Construction	Deconstruction
Class politics	New class politics	Society	Ethnicity
Mass production	In-time production	Community	Locality
Strategic planning	Contextual planning	Monoculturism	Pluralism
Development	Adaptation	Class culture	Commodity culture
Nationalism	Ethnic fission	Permanence	Transience
Economies of scope	Economies of scale	Similarity	Diversity
Welfare statism	Ind. accountability		
Specialisation	Synergy in labour		
Unionisation	Individual bargain		
Philosophical attributes			
Scientific rationality	Neo-Darwinism	Structuralism	Poststructuralism
Keynesianism	Functionalism	Realism	Hyperreality
Taylorism	Flexible specialisms	Romanticism	Mysticism
Fordism	Diversification	Formalism	Imagery
		Narrative	Discursive
		Contiguity	Difference
Spatial effects and implications			
Massification	Demassification	Urban functions	Urban landscape
Concentration	Diffusion	State symbols	Corporate symbols
Centralisation	Dispersal	Arch 'styles'	Arch rhetoric

Continues

Table 3 *Continued*

Industrialism	Postindustrialism	Modernism	Postmodernism
Community base	Locality based	Paradigmatic	Eclectic
Zoning	Complex integration	Syntactic	Metaphoric
Suburban focus	Urban focus	Design	Codification

Source: A. R. Cuthbert, 'An agenda for planning education in the nineties (part 2), *The Australian Planner* 32, no. 1, *Journal of the Royal Australian Planning Institute*, 1994. Reprinted by permission of Planning Institute Australia.

This small list is an injustice to the many other phenomenal texts in the area of spatial political economy, urban geography, feminism and culture. However, there is a marked contrast when we come into the specific compass of main-stream urban design. Here we are dealing with a fairly rarified field. Nonetheless, Christine Boyer's *The City of Collective Memory* (1994) is an original contribution to the history of urban form, followed two years later by Ross King's *Emancipating Space* (1996), an intellectual tour de force subtitled *Geography, Architecture and Urban Design*. Kim Dovey's *Framing Places: Mediating Power in Built Form* (1999) explores how the built environment mediates and represents the social practices of power. Joseph Rykwert's *The Seduction of Place: The City in the Twenty First Century* (2000) is badly titled because we have to wait until chapter 8 to arrive at considerations of the new millennium, but until that point the book is a fascinating account of the creation of place in the twentieth century. *Gender Space and Architecture: An Interdisciplinary Introduction*, edited by Rendell, Penner and Borden (2000), demonstrates exactly how many different disciplines, and therefore different perspectives, now focus on urban and other spaces (a text that should be read in concert with Colomina's *Sexuality and Space*, 1992).

From the above discussion of theory in urban design, several things are evident. First, the relationship to architecture remains paramount and consequently the development of significant theory in urban design remains deterministic, weakly developed and compromised in scope. The cult of the individual architect and of the architect as master planner, which dominates architectural design, has been carried over into urban design. Urban design theory is then seen to be determined by whichever individual perspective one adopts. Consequently, the nature of theory that emerges is altogether fractured since there are few shared theoretical constructs, ideologies or paradigms. Kevin Lynch offers his own eclectic combination of aesthetic choices as to how city design should take place. Christopher Alexander's ideas are utopian, utterly impractical and require society to be reinvented. Roger Trancik presents us with choices between various elegant patterns, and Hillier's models require doctoral-level mathematics to understand them. As a result, the major theorists in the discipline present us with concepts of urban form that are unrelated, largely devoid of any social content and alienated from any serious socio-economic and political base. There is no recognition, except in some rare instances, that the production of the built environment, its form and symbolic content are part and parcel of the material production of society.

In the following pages I hope to demonstrate that urban design can indeed be viewed as the social production of space in its material and symbolic dimensions. Instead of adding yet another theory to the one's presented above, I will concentrate on revealing the necessary features of such a theory rather than its contingent qualities – the fundamentals we can share rather than the differences that keep us apart, commonality rather than ownership. In so doing, my main effort is oriented towards more integrated explanations of urban form as a basis for establishing the credibility of urban design as an independent discipline, proceeding in each chapter from an evolutionary assessment and critique of each intellectual region to the place of urban design within a political economy of space.

Chapter Two
History

L'histoire, ce mélange indécent de banalité et d'apocalypse.

Jean Amery

Introduction: What is History?

There is no more encompassing field of study than history, since it involves the process of human evolution in its entirety. It is also difficult, if not impossible, to separate history from the preceding section on theory, or indeed the subsequent one on philosophy. Many writers such as Amery and Joyce view history as fundamentally tragic, an ongoing catastrophe or nightmare respectively. This is a position we will find echoed in several histories of urban form. Not only is history nightmarish in many respects, it is also constituted in a vast maze of philosophical perspectives and paradigms. There is no such thing as an unassailable philosophy of history, and a brief glance through some of the captivating literature surrounding the topic is sufficient to ensure absolute confusion about such terms as 'facts', 'truth' and 'progress' as a precursor to debates on the relationship between history and philosophy (Cohen 1978, White 1980, Carr 1987, Heller 1993, Thompson 1995, Hobsbawm 1997, Evans 1997, Burns and Rayment-Pickard 2000, Fulbrook 2002). Some basic questions that guide historical enquiry have been given as follows (Jenkins 1991: 27).

What is the status of truth in the discourses of history?

Is there any such thing as an objective history (are there objective 'facts' etc.) or is history just an interpretation?

What is bias and what are the problems involved in trying to get rid of it?

What is empathy? Can it be done? How? Why? If it cannot be achieved, why does it seem so important to try?

What are the differences between primary and secondary sources (traces) and between 'evidence' and 'sources'? What is at stake here?

What do you do with those couplets (cause and effect, continuity and change, similarity and difference) and is it possible to do what you are asked to do through using them?

Is history an art or a science?

22

In Mary Fulbrook's book *Historical Theory*, she notes the impossibility of detatching historical investigation from theory and maintains that all writing on history, even by default, is nonetheless theoretical since it has adopted a specific viewpoint, even if this is solely a chronological rendition of 'the facts'. Another simple but difficult point to accept is that history can be reinvented *post facto*, in the sense that new theories can be applied to a reading of historical events that took place centuries or even millennia before the theory itself existed. Some theorists are more comfortable in following an explicit body of knowledge, such as classical historicism, hermeneutics, narrativism, structuralism, discourse theory or feminism. Then there is the problem of method: would you rather follow Hegel, Weber, Marx, Popper, Foucault or Dray, or what has been referred to as 'post history', which includes the work of Michel Foucault, Jean Baudrillard and Francis Fukuyama? Each of these histories is decomposable into several layers or levels of interest. Within narrativism for example, Rayment-Pickard notes that the historiographical style may be represented in three specific modes of operation that cannot be combined arbitrarily in a given work:

Mode of emplotment	Mode of argument	Mode of ideological implication
Romantic	Formist	Anarchist
Tragic	Mechanist	Radical
Comic	Organicist	Conservative
Satirical	Contextualist	Liberal

Burns and Rayment-Pickard (2000: 295) note that these relationships must not be construed as necessary relations

> for example, a comic emplotment is not compatible with a mechanistic argument, just as radical ideology is not compatible with a satirical emplotment. There are, as it were, elective affinities among the various modes that might be used to gain an explanatory effect on the different levels of composition. And these elective affinities are based upon the structural homologies which can be discerned among the possible modes of emplotment, argument and ideological implication.

The mode of ideological implication is particularly germane in society as a whole, particularly in how courses are taught in universities. For example, Jenkins (1991) raises the idea that it would be quite possible and properly historical for a syllabus to be presented from a black, Marxist, feminist perspective but that this would be an exceedingly unlikely occurrence because of the lack of an appropriate power base. Hence there is the tendency to write histories in terms of dominant discourses, meaning they are ideological constructs, many of which focus on societal self-regulation. To this extent, Jenkins suggests that it is better not to ask 'What is history?' but instead to ask 'Who is history for?'

So in order to acquire a mere foothold in understanding history, we must adopt some conceptual lens through which some key features of the historical process come into focus (DC 4, 5). Every discipline from philosophy to science and literature has its own vision as to the meaning and content of history. Hence it can be viewed as the development of the productive forces (Marx), as the evolution of the species (Darwin), of the human psyche and the collective unconscious (Freud), or even though the history of ideas, as Peter Watson (2000) does in *A Terrible Beauty: A History of the People and Ideas that Shaped the Modern Mind*. Foucault (1977) has called his study of the history of the last 400 years *The Archaeology of Knowledge*, likening history to an excavation of human consciousness over that period. History may then be better termed 'histories' since any one history does not necessarily devalue other discourses. Foucault's writings, for example, are an appropriate counterpoint to Marx.

Foucault denies most of the central tenets of classical Marxism, for example of the concept of domination being rooted solely to social class, of a teleological (as opposed to a genealogical) approach to history, of domination existing purely in the labour process, of a base–superstructure model of society, etc. Foucault himself was forced to address Marx early in his career, as most great theorists inevitably do, and although he ended up in a diametrically opposite camp, Foucault's work is a direct intellectual extension of Marxist theorising. They do not *have* to be read in opposition to each other, despite the fact that for Foucault, classical Marxism

> cannot be the basis for a critical theory of history, because the modes of domination in the twentieth century cannot be perceived from the limited vantage point of the subject. Instead, domination today takes the form of a combination or structure of knowledge and power which is not external to the subject, but still intelligible from his or her perspective. Critical theory cannot present history as the transition from abusive aristocrats to exploiting capitalists, because domination is no longer centred in or caused by subjects.
>
> (Poster 1984: 80)

Histories also have differing destinies. In Christianity, history is considered finite, supposedly ending with Parousia, associated with the second coming of Christ, after which divine rule will prevail. The Renaissance introduced the idea of development, that progress was in fact inherent to the historical process, an idea that still continues to inform the developed economies of the world. The idea that history will end, expressed most recently in Fukuyama (1992), is not new. Fukuyama believes that history has come to an end because liberal democracy contains the ultimate promise of a free and democratic society, retaining the delusion that somehow this principle will ultimately be shared by everyone. However, a recent text called *Straw Dogs* (Gray 2002) challenges the idea that humanity has some place to progress *to*, and that the Enlightenment idea of progress is self-destructive to our species. No prior age has in fact viewed history as a series of developmental stages as in Marxian ideology for example. Foucault on the other hand dismisses the principle of continuity and with it a facile relationship to diachronic concepts of time:

> Foucault is not a historian of continuity, but of discontinuity. Foucault attempts to show how the past was different, strange, threatening. He labours to distance the past from the present, to disrupt the easy, cosy intimacy that historians have

traditionally enjoyed in the relationship of the past to the present...Foucault unmasks the epistemological innocence of the historian. He raises the discomforting question: What does the historian do to the past when she or he traces its continuity and assigns its causes?

(Poster 1984: 74–5)

Jean Baudrillard holds yet another position with respect to history, referred to as 'posthistory', based on the hyperreality of contemporary life, where he argues that semiotics is a more appropriate lens through which history can be observed than Marxism. Due to the impact of mass media on social life, Baudrillard contends that we are now in a period where reality has been transformed into hyperreality, where individuals become the products of the mass media rather than mere consumers, as for example in Debord's *Society of the Spectacle*.

In the last instance, all historical perspectives are flawed as ideological constructs, since subjectivity, rationality and time cannot be suspended. When I visited the lost cities of the Incas in 1975, I learned that they had official scribes whose job it was to rewrite their history as they would have liked it to appear. Rather than being unusual, it seemed to me that this was the normal process in every society, that history is largely an invention, and the most convincing invention is the one that has the largest audience.

History and Urban Design

In looking at history from the point of view of urban design, as distinct from architecture and urban planning, I maintain my adopted definition of the subject, that urban design is fundamentally about the purposive production of urban meaning in certain urban forms. Overall I prefer the phrase 'production of urban form' to 'production of urban design', and conflate one to the other. Urban design can easily be taken to mean only professional design projects undertaken by architects over the last forty years that the term has been in widespread use, as in for example Battery Park City in New York, Canary Wharf in London or Potsdamer Platz in Berlin. The term 'urban form' applies more appropriately to the whole of history. What this suggests is that all urban space is designed, and that our concept of design should not be limited to commodified services. The idea that any urban design should be either defined by, or confined to, professional legitimation is unacceptable. So I will continue to use the terms 'urban design' and 'production of urban form' synonymously, applying to the totality of the built environment. By minimising professional intervention in this manner, two things become possible: first, to see the production of the physical world without the limitations imposed by professional categories; and second, to allow a larger range of material to be considered than might otherwise be possible, since there is no text published to date entitled 'A History of Urban Design'.

Taking the above comments into account, the task of defining which texts constitute a significant history of urban form becomes even more difficult. A narrow functionalist viewpoint prevails across much of mainstream urban design theory and history, promoting the idea that urban design is an exercise in pure form and not much else. Furthermore, definitions, theories and histories are subscribed to the formal properties of space, with little knowledge of its production, and that the relationship between urban form and globalisation, national economic and political systems, cultural forms, class conflict, ideological structures and technical change is marginal to an understanding of history in urban design. Over the last fifty years, some of the more important texts that bear on the question of urban design may be situated chronologically as shown in table 4.

Notably, only five of these histories mention the word 'design' and most are written by architects. On this basis it is fair to assume that the first comprehensive history of urban design remains to be written. This begs two major considerations. First, any comprehensive text would probably have to rely on some totalising discourse in order to capture the territory, which in today's intellectual

Table 4 Thirty classic urban design histories.

Geddes (1915) *Cities in Evolution*
Childe (1935) *Man Makes Himself*
Gibberd (1953) *Town Design*
Korn (1953) *History Builds the Town*
Tunnard (1953) *The City of Man*
Hilberseimer (1955) *The Nature of Cities*
Mumford (1961) *The City in History*
Gutkind (1964) *The International History of City Development*
Sprieregen (1965) *Urban Design*
Reps (1965) *The Making of Urban America*
Bacon (1967) *Design of Cities*
Benevolo (1967) *The Origins of Modern Town Planning*
Moholy-Nagy (1968) *The Matrix of Man*
Tafuri (1976) *Architecture and Utopia*
Rowe and Koetter (1978) *Collage City*
Morris (1979) *The History of Urban Form*
Boyer (1983) *Dreaming the Rational City*
Roseneau (1983) *The Ideal City*
Fogelson (1986) *Planning the Capitalist City*
Tafuri (1987) *The Sphere and the Labyrinth*
Hall (1988) *Cities of Tomorrow*
Kostoff (1991) *The City Shaped*
Kostoff (1992) *The City Assembled*
Benevolo (1993) *The European City*
Boyer (1994) *The City of Collective Memory*
Hall (1998) *Cities in Civilization*
Eaton (2001) *Ideal Cities*
El Khoury & Robbins (2002) *Shaping the City: Studies in Theory, History and Urban Design*
Gosling & Gosling (2003) *The Evolution of American Urban Design*

climate would be unacceptable. Alternatively, if we adopt a postmodern approach, we may as well stick with what we have – a minimum of 30 different 'discourses' all of which address the built form of the city in a variety of different ways. Second, the problem of professional ideology addressed above highlights the issue as to the coherence of urban design as a discipline, one for example that could be taught at undergraduate level with its own 'history' and 'theory', identifiably separate from architecture and urban planning (DC 6). Overall, the texts listed in table 4 are all classics, but remain dominated by architectural interpretations and the architectural imagination. Nonetheless, there are many different perspectives involved. This makes classification difficult, but it is possible to organise most of these into five basic categories with all the limitations that this involves.

Chronologies: Mumford, Sprieregen, Gutkind, etc.
Typologies: Kostoff, Moholy-Nagy, Hall, Krier
Utopias: Eaton, Tafuri, Doxiadis, Roseneau
Fragments: Boyer, Hall, Koetter and Rowe, Kostoff
Materialist theory: Korn, Tafuri, Frampton, Boyer, Knesl, Dickens

Chronologies

The simplest way to present any history is through a diachronic commentary of what happened over time, sticking to 'the facts' as closely as possible. This method has been followed by many scholars in some manner or another (Mumford 1961, Gutkind 1964, Benevolo 1967, Morris 1979, Roseneau 1983). In this sense *Urban Design: The Architecture of Towns and Cities* by Paul Sprieregen was the first book to claim the territory of urban design on behalf of the architectural profession since it was commissioned by the American Institute of Architects. Sprieregen opens his introduction by describing the book as a challenge and a guide 'to those who would save the city and the metropolis from itself during the fateful decades of explosive urbanization which lie just ahead' (1965: v), a view of history which seemed to prevail at the time, that somehow the present needed to be saved from the future. Importantly, Sprieregen's book only deals with urban design history directly in the first two chapters, although case studies of contemporary projects of the time are included throughout the book. Here we find an interpretation of history that is diachronic, atheoretical and focused on the architectural (and landscape architectural) object. History begins with ancient (i.e. classical) Greece and the Athenian Acropolis in 400 BC. We then proceed through ancient Rome, the medieval period in Europe, the Renaissance and a summary of events between 1600 and 1850, ending with the Parisian boulevards of Napoleon III and the commencement of the Ringstrasse in Vienna in 1850. The modern period is treated likewise, commencing around 1800 and concluding about 1950. The central problem with this, the dominant paradigm, is encapsulated by the quotation that 'the city is as much a physical object in three dimensions as it is anything else. As a physical object it can be designed – perhaps as artfully as the gardens of Versailles, as practically as the town of Ferrara, and as humanely as the towns of the ancient Greeks' (Sprieregen 1965: 48). On the surface this statement is perfectly sensible, but it embodies the whole philosophy of physical determinism. It assumes that designing today's cities can be carried out in the same fashion as French landscape gardens, Italian hill towns or ancient Greek settlements (apart from the impossibility of comparing these three typologies).

Lewis Mumford is another great commentator on the form of the city, writing thirty books over fifty-five years from 1922, beginning with *The Story of Utopias* and ending with *My Works and Days* in 1979. The majority of this prodigious output dealt with the form and culture of cities, the most famous being *The Culture of Cities* (1938), *The City in History* (1961) and *The Urban Prospect* (1968). Peter Hall, in a massive tome *Cities and Civilisation*, says 'Mumford was fundamentally a brilliant polemical journalist, not a scholar' (Hall 1998: 6). Despite this comment, Mumford had iconic status in his time and was widely recognised as one of the most significant commentators on urban form, influencing several generations of architects, planners and others environmentalists. Like Sprieregen, Mumford's classic text *The City in History* is also a chronological rendition of sequential historical stages, and he held similar views about the future: that metropolitan civilisation was inevitably drawn to what he called 'Necropolis', the city of the dead, a position he predicted in his earlier work *The Culture of Cities*, which he called 'A Brief Outline of Hell' (1961: 556). Given that *The Culture of Cities* was written in 1938, Mumford's claims in *The City in History* that his predictions were correct are difficult to dispute, since the nuclear and human holocausts of the Second World War occupied much of the intervening space. Without doubt, Peter Hall's description of Mumford's work as polemical is valid, and one could even go further and describe the prose as Gothic: 'The monstrous gods of the ancient world have all reappeared, hugely magnified, demanding total human sacrifice. To appease their super-Moloch in the nuclear temples, whole nations stand ready, supinely, to throw their children into his fiery furnace' (Mumford 1961: 572). The only alternative to this situation of economies driven by military production would require the replenishment of the human personality: 'once the sterile dreams and sadistic nightmares that obsess the ruling elites are banished, there will be such a release of human vitality as will make the Renascence <sic> seem almost a stillbirth' (Mumford 1961: 574).

Throughout *The City in History*, Mumford pays homage to many scholars, but none more so than the Scottish philosopher Patrick Geddes who was his mentor. Geddes, himself a biologist, had a profound influence on the development of planning thought, and between 1914 and 1924 was involved in the design or revision of plans for fifty cities in India and Palestine (see chapter 9). This influence remains today, since the fundamental concept of the New Urbanism, the transect, is a direct transposition of both the logic and formal implications of Geddes' valley section, which first appeared in his book *Cities in*

Evolution in 1915. In consequence, Mumford's approach to the form of the city is humanist-organic, symbolised in his frequent use of such natural terms as predation (or parasitism), symbiosis and commensalism, three words derived from biology to describe specific relationships within the natural world, as well as the anthropomorphic use of psychological terminology (pathology, sublimation, regression, trauma, etc.) applied to cities.

Similarly, parallels with the human body abound in terms of both function and form. This emerges in the frequent use of similes, metaphors and analogies to human biology. Rome, for example, 'contained a greater number of pathological cells than any healthy body should tolerate' (1961: 237), and he sums up Rome's capital achievements by analogy 'with words used by a great scientist about a flatulent architectural interpretation of his highly revolutionary concepts of space and time, as "poorly digested but splendidly evacuated".' Nonetheless, Mumford's conception of urban form is properly focused on the economic, social and political development of cultures, and the manifestation of these processes in institutions, spaces and places that together compose the urban text. While *The City in History* in its entirety is about the form of the city, Mumford is totally aware of the complexity of forces which produce it. This understanding can probably best be summarised in his own words about the Hellenic polis, that in order to understand the form of the city, 'one must take one's eyes off the buildings and look more closely at the citizen' (1961: 165).

Mumford and Sprieregen apart, many other historians have similarly adopted a chronological approach to an understanding of urban form (Gutkind 1964, Bacon 1967, Morris 1979, Benevolo 1980). Overall, no theoretical position is followed in any of these, although clearly the concept of teleology, of significance attributed to successive phases of development over time, is dominant. Another adopted method in urban design has been to look at the historical process as a series of typologies, in terms of both the form of the city and the generation of subtypes, building groups, urban spaces and nature.

Typologies

Many historians have chosen to look at the city not as a time-series but as a form-series. This goes back to a concept common to the contextualists, for example Rob Krier mentions in chapter 1 of *Urban Space* that the vocabulary of potential urban forms is for all practical purposes complete. The history of the city can therefore be investigated in terms of how and when various typologies of urban form came into existence, whether specific typologies always shared the same function, or whether the form was the same but the function changed over historical time (Moholy-Nagy 1968, Kostoff 1991, 1992, Hall 1998). In this interpretation, the chronological sequence becomes subordinated to both form and function. Urban history is then reduced to the evolution of its superficial physical organisation, with meanings read into, and associated with, specific urban forms.

For mainstream urban designers, the key text is arguably *The Matrix of Man: An Illustrated History of the Urban Environment* by Sybil Moholy-Nagy (1968), one of the few books I know that is dedicated to a city (Manhattan). In the spirit of the age, like Mumford, her vision of urban growth is again organic, anthropomorphic and oriented to death and dissolution:

> Cities, like men, are embodiments of the past, and mirages of unfulfilled dreams. They thrive on economy and waste, on exploitation and charity, on the initiative of the ego and the solidarity of the group. They stagnate and ultimately die under imposed standardisation, homogenised equality, and a minimum denominator of man-made environment. Most decisive of all, cities like mankind, renew themselves unit by unit in a slow, time bound metabolic process.
>
> (Moholy-Nagy 1968: 11)

Moholy-Nagy rails against what she calls 'the scientific approach' of people such as architects Buckminster Fuller, Christopher Alexander and Constantinos Doxiadis, the iconic planner of the 1960s, and the British Archigram Group's plug-in cities of the same period. Against this position she argues for the idea that individual responses to the environment are largely irrational, based on emotional attachments to family, religion, art, etc. Her argument borders on a rejection of any kind of rationality in design or human organisation, or even explanations driven by reason. She argues that organisation of the built environment is a representation of our need for tradition. Since these traditions share basic principles, or what she terms 'eternally recurrent constellations of matrix and content' (1968: 17), the outcomes are archetypal and conform to certain basic and distinctive patterns that can be described in five basic types.

1   Geomorphic: interrelated growth between landscape and building.
2   Concentric: ideological, deriving from a commitment to a supramundane ideal.
3   Orthogonal: connective (linear cities). Pragmatic, adjusting the city to constantly changing requirements of communication and expansion.
4   Orthogonal: modular (linear cities).
5   Clustered.

The purpose of *The Matrix of Man* was to use this typology to classify human settlements. Curiously, Moholy-Nagy uses a famous quotation from Marx to underscore the idea that imagination must triumph over science:

> A bee puts to shame many an architect, in the construction of her cells. But what distinguishes the worst architect from the best of the bees is this, that the architect raises his structure in the imagination before he erects it in reality. At the end of the labour process we get a result that already existed in the imagination of the labourer at its beginning.
>
> (Moholy-Nagy 1968: 18)

Had Moholy-Nagy stuck to Marx's original concept of tracking the relationship between the imagination and the labour process, it is likely that a much more satisfying explanation of urban form would have emerged. However, the choice of looking for what she terms 'applicable meaning' solely on the basis of these five types was doomed from the beginning, since it would seem a fruitless task to search for any generalisable conclusions purely on the basis of similarity in urban form, particularly over diachronic time. Overall it is almost impossible to understand the differences between these types from the examples given, particularly so for categories 3 and 5. Some of the causes given for urban development are quite astounding, for example that the emergence of the orthogonal–linear environment in the merchant cities of the Middle Ages 'shaped the physical image of the city in the likeness of the middle stratum of society which has, ever since been the determining factor in urbanization' (1968: 198). After having condemned 'the scientific' high-tech approach, Moholy-Nagy incorporates many such examples as potential solutions to future development, and the book's focus on typologies is abandoned without further mention.

Spiro Kostoff's two-volume study of the history of urban form also adopts a typological approach, and includes an astounding array of illustrative material that adds significant depth to our understanding. In the first volume, *The City Shaped*, urban form is studied as a totality. In the second volume, *The City Assembled: The Elements of Urban Form Throughout History*, the city is studied in terms of its composite elements:

1 the city edge;
2 urban divisions;
3 public places;
4 the street;
5 the urban process.

Unlike Krier's *Urban Space*, or even Paul Zucker's treatise of 1959 *Town and Square*, there is no 'system' presented, other than what is inferred from these five major sections that make up the volume, two of which (2 and 5) do not fit well with the others. Streets, public places and the city edge all contain immense formal variation, but 'urban divisions' and 'the urban process' by definition are not 'elements of urban form'. Each of these is further divided into subsections. For example, some street types are given as waterways, the bridge street, the boulevard and covered streets. Michael Webb's *The City Square* (1990) is a singularly more coherent rendition of the development of public places than Kostoff's. Both volumes nonetheless constitute a tour de force in terms of the content and illustrative material, and while each detailed study is informative and fascinating, wholesale confusion reigns in Kostoff's *Weltanschauung* as to any comprehensible urban process, linked in some manner to a coherent theoretical explanation.

Peter Hall adopts an entirely different typological approach in *Cities in Civilisation*, his 1160-page masterwork of 1998. On his own admission, the work is 'shamelessly pillaged and borrowed' in that it does not contain primary research (Hall 1998: 8). However, the book's purpose was not to unearth new facts but to generate new interpretations of what is called the *belle époque* or the golden age of cities: why these arise at all, what forces drove them and why cities seldom repeat their success. The single volume is subdivided into five books: the city as cultural crucible, as innovative milieu, as the marriage of art and technology, as the establishment of urban order and as the union of art, technology and organisation. Each book is organised chronologically, book 5 being a significantly shorter concluding chapter. Despite the virtual absence of illustrations, there is infinitely greater clarity in Hall's book than in the two volumes of Kostoff discussed above. Unlike Kostoff, on the surface, the work has nothing to say about urban design. On the other hand, there is infinitely more to learn about the production of urban form in *Cities in Civilisation* than in most urban design textbooks that purport to deal with the subject directly. For example, in chapter 18 of *Cities in Civilisation*, 'The dream factory', Hall describes the impact of Hollywood on the development of urban form in Los Angeles, and in chapter 24, 'The city of perpetual public works', Hall enunciates how the development of public works in Paris from 1850 to 1870 stimulated a tradition that remains to this day, and how the built form of one of the world's most beautiful cities evolved into the twenty-first century.

Other histories can also be viewed as typological, for example Christine Boyer's *The City of Collective Memory* (1994), which describes a series of visual and mental models and three major 'maps' or typologies of the traditional city (works of art), the modern city (as panorama) and the contemporary city (the city as spectacle). Similary Eaton (2001) uses the concept of utopia as a typological base for exploring the ideal city, and covers the influence of utopian typologies over two millennia, demonstrating the significant influence of utopian ideals and concepts on the design of cities. While typologies qua history provide significant and interesting insights into the creation of urban form specifically in the realm of culture, they also mask the dominant role of political and economic forces in the generation, signification and expression of urban form. Christine Boyer beautifully sums up the limitations of the typological approach in *Dreaming the Rational City* when she says 'to begin to unravel the process where building typology and spatial morphology confront one another and transform urban development, we must return to the economic and political, cultural and social context that are important to both the spatial morphology and building typology of the city' (Boyer 1983: 288).

Utopias

Utopias, being the earthly manifestation of paradise, have been part of our conception of society, and hence our conception of urban form, at least since the time of Plato, Aristotle and Zeno in the fourth century BC. The word was first coined by Sir Thomas More in his book *Utopia* in 1516. Utopia is derived from two Greek terms, *ou* meaning not or no, and *topia* meaning place. Hence u-topia literally means no-place. The original word does not carry today's connotation of some place better or more beautiful than what already exists. Plato sketched out his basic ideas on the form and institutional arrangements of his ideal city in *The Laws*, and fully developed his ideas in *The Republic*, where he called for an ideal city of around 5040 citizens. Since Plato's idea of utopia was based on the organisation of the Greek state of the time, with a structure of second-class citizens, of women slaves and metics (foreigners not entitled to vote), this figure implied a total population of around 30,000, a number also favoured by Ebeneezer Howard for his Garden Cities. Hippodamus, a Greek city planner who created the archetypal urban design plan for Miletus in Asia Minor, conceived of his ideal city on the basis of triads. Quoting from Aristotle, Mumford states that the city

> was composed of 10,000 citizens divided into three parts – one of artisans, one of husbandmen, and a third of armed defenders of the state. He also divided the land into three parts, one sacred, one public, the third private: the first was set apart to maintain the customary worship of the Gods, the second to support the warriors, the third was the property of the husbandmen.

Mumford notes caustically that on this basis, the working classes, as in Marx's concept of labour power, would have to remain forever in grinding poverty if they had to support the idleness of the upper class by handing over two-thirds of the wealth (Mumford 1961: 173), and his *The Story of Utopias* (1922) remains a classic for all urban designers.

Since the time of classical Greece, the concept of utopia has been part of every generation, and possibly of every society, and there are countless examples of utopian ideas and places, for example in systems of belief, literature and the cinema, as well as in urban planning and design (figure 3). Sir Thomas More was the originator of the utopian novel in 1516, later emulated by thousands, the classics among these being J.V. Andrea's *Christianopolis*, Francis Bacon's *The New Atlantis* (1626), Etienne Cabet's *Voyage en Icarie* (1848), William Morris' *News From Nowhere* (1891), B.F. Skinner's *Walden Two* (1948), Aldous Huxley's *Brave New World* (1960) and *Island* (1962), and George Orwell's *Nineteen Eighty Four* (1948). *Brave New World* and *Nineteen Eighty Four* are better termed dystopias rather than utopias since they contain bitter warnings about the future, Orwell's future now being twenty years old. Since their publication there has been an explosion of novels and films all trying to conceptualise urban life at some future point, both good and bad, and Richard Lehan's *The City in Literature* (1998) is central to this understanding of the intellectual and cultural history of cities, utopian, dystopian and all the variations in between. Adopting the postmodern genre, Lehan introduces the city as text, moving through the Enlightenment, modernist urbanism, and American representations of the city. It is clear that in the design of cities, the vast treasure trove of literature is largely ignored as a source of inspiration for urban designers, and is not even considered in academic programmes. This loss is immense, simply because literature has the ability to replicate the experience, organisation and design of cities in a manner alien to most of the literature on urban design. Much

Figure 3   William Robinson Leigh: utopian visionary city (1908).
Source: Courtesy of Mary Evans Picture Library.

better to read Dickens' *Oliver Twist* or Emile Zola's *Germinal* if we want the most intense portrayal of industrial landscapes than to gaze at sterile plans and charts; better to read James Joyce's *Ulysses* so you can actually feel and smell Dublin at the turn of the century than to pore over a land-use map of Dublin (table 5). This no doubt overstates the problem, but the case in point is that literature, particularly fiction, represents a massively underrated resource to those involved in the design of cities. It allows us to recreate in a manner impossible to the designer, the actual lived experience of cities, and to more effectively project into the future the costs and benefits of our decisions.

The same is true of the cinema. The archetypal film about the future form of the city and urban life is undoubtedly Fritz Lang's expressionist masterpiece *Metropolis* (1926; see figure 4), a movie that was not emulated for many years, possibly not until Ridley Scott's *Blade Runner* of 1982. The best history of the city in cinema is given in David Clarke's *The Cinematic City* (1997), while Shiel and Fitzmaurice (2001) provide a brilliant collection of essays in *Cinema and the City*. Notable among these are the authors' own introductions, 'Cinema and the city in history and theory' (Shiel) and 'Film and urban societies in a global context'. Shiel and Fitzmaurice's text contains not only a complex selection of articles about the city and cinema in terms of direct visual content, but also a significant amount of commentary and critique on global cities, the urban landscape, capital flows, urban redevelopment, capital infrastructuring, airports, public space and other issues. Germane to the idea of utopias, Geoffrey Nowell-Smith's essay 'Cities: real and imagined' (2001) explores the important point that the cinema, via the medium of film, has generated a powerful tool through which the nature, design and consequences of urban life can be examined.

The actual design and building of our utopias (and dystopias) has also taken many forms, from the great Pyramid cities of Egypt, to Filarete's Sforzinda, the first ideal city of the Italian Renaissance, to Walter Burley Griffin's plan for Canberra, the new capital city of Australia. Ideal cities have been conceived from a multiplicity of perspectives, religious, ideological, political, defence, art and technology (Rosenau 1983, Eaton 2001). Many great (and some not so great) architects have felt compelled to present their own egomaniacal visions for posterity. Some classics in this regard are Soria y Mata's Ciudad Lineal for Barcelona (1894), Tony Garnier's Cité Industrielle (1901), Antonio Sant'Elia's The New City (1914), Ludwig Hilberseimer's Hochhaustadt, Berlin (1928), Le Corbusier's Plan Voisin for Paris (1925), La Ville Contemporaine (1930) (see figure 5) and Fort L'Empereur for Algiers (1931), Frank Lloyd Wright's Broadacre City (1934), and Peter Cook and Archigram's Plug-in City (1964, see Fishman 1987). The quality that distinguishes all of these, and virtually every other ideal city or utopian city concept, is geometry. Circles, octagons, hexagons, squares, triangles, grids, mandallas, every possible geometric alternative to the forms actually adopted by most cities subject to the rules of capitalist or pre-capitalist development. Closer to reality, utopian concepts do not have to remain in the realm of fantasy, since each of us lives to some degree in our own personal utopia, realised or otherwise. Manfredo Tafuri's ground-breaking work was

Table 5 Basic structural components of James Joyce's novel *Ulysses*.

Title	Scene	Hour	Organ	Art	Colour	Symbol	Technic
1. Telemachus	The Tower	8 a.m.		Theology	White, gold	Heir	Narrative (young)
2. Nestor	The School	10 a.m.		History	Brown	Horse	Catechism (personal)
3. Proteus	The Strand	11 a.m.		Philology	Green	Tide	Monologue (male)
4. Calypso	The House	8 a.m.	Kidney	Economics	Orange	Nymph	Narrative (mature)
5. Lotus-eaters	The Bath	10 a.m.	Genitals	Botany, chemistry		Eucharist	Narcissism
6. Hades	The Graveyard	11 a.m.	Heart	Religion	White, black	Caretaker	Incubism
7. Aeolus	The Newspaper	Noon	Lungs	Rhetoric	Red	Editor	Enthymemic
8. Lestrygonians	The Lunch	1 p.m.	Oesophagus	Architecture		Constables	Peristaltic
9. Scylla and Charybdis	The Library	2 p.m.	Brain	Literature		Stratford, London	Dialectic
10. Wandering Rocks	The Streets	3 p.m.	Blood	Mechanics		Citizens	Labyrinth
11. Sirens	The Concert Room	4 p.m.	Ear	Music		Barmaids	*Fuga per canonem*
12. Cyclops	The Tavern	5 p.m.	Muscle	Politics		Fenian	Gigantism
13. Nausicaa	The Rocks	8 p.m.	Eye, nose	Painting	Grey, blue	Virgin	Tumescence, detumescence
14. Oxen of the Sun	The Hospital	10 p.m.	Womb	Medicine	White	Mothers	Embryonic development
15. Circe	The Brothel	Midnight	Locomotor apparatus	Magic		Whore	Hallucination
16. Eumaeus	The Shelter	1 a.m.	Nerves	Navigation		Sailors	Narrative (old)
17. Ithaca	The House	2 a.m.	Skeleton	Science		Comets	Catechism (impersonal)
18. Penelope	The Bed		Flesh			Earth	Monologue (female)

Source: S. Gilbert, *James Joyce's Ulysses*. Harmondsworth: Penguin, 1963, p. 23.

Figure 4   Fritz Lang's vision of the future: from the film *Metropolis* (1926).
Source: D. B. Clarke (ed.), *The Cinematic City*. London: Routledge, 1997, p. 37.
Reprinted by permission of Routledge.

called *Architecture and Utopia: Design and Capitalist Development* (1976), a text totally immersed in problems of the relationship between ideology and utopia. His focus is on the tasks that capitalist development has removed from the realm of architecture, or what Tafuri calls ideological prefiguration, pure architecture, architecture without utopia, or in the most famous of his quotations, a state where architecture is reduced in function to that of 'sublime uselessness' (Tafuri 1980: ix). Closer to daily life is Robert Fishman's reification of the suburb as a utopian concept, which it undoubtedly is, in *Bourgeois Utopias: The Rise and Fall of Suburbia* (1987), probably the most realisable of all utopian ideals.

Fragments

The preceding approaches to history, i.e. the chronological, typological or utopian interpretations, are all largely dependent on externally imposed rules of order. Each approach reflects an inescapable teleology, specific generic forms or idealistic concepts which somehow bring order to the passage of time. In

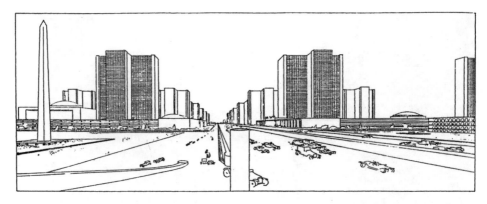

Figure 5   Le Corbusier: La Ville Contemporaine.
Source: Reprinted by permission of Le Corbusier Foundation and the Design and Artists Copyright Society. Copyright © 2005 by FLC/ADAGP, Paris and DACS, London.

contrast, there is another stream of thinking running through interpretations of urban form that tries to deal with the chaotic assembly of urban fragments represented in contemporary cities. The logic behind this approach can be stated simply: as a general rule, our entire built environment is not a coherent, logical and comprehensible structure that has been designed by any kind of rational process. So superimposing our preconceptions upon it will get us nowhere. Instead, it can only be understood if it is viewed as a composite of millions of separate fragments, the assembled detritus of wars, pestilence, fire, earthquake, floods, redevelopment and the largely uncontrolled expansion of cities since the Industrial Revolution. Despite the actions of contemporary planning to 'control' development, cities largely mirror the inchoate, chaotic and random processes of social evolution. However, this randomness does not imply that the process cannot in some way be represented or theorised in reverse. In other words, the city can just as well be explained through processes of *de*construction as they can from *con*struction.

This concept is even embedded in the philosophy of history, with Kierkegaard writing a treatise entitled *Philosophical Fragments* as early as 1844. Agnes Heller in her work *A Philosophy of History in Fragments*, points out that it

> . . . is not a book on history. It is a philosophy of history after the demise of grand narratives . . . Postmoderns inherited historical consciousness, but not the complacency of the grand narratives. The confidence in an increasing transparency of the world is gone. This is not a good time for writing systems. On the other hand it is quite a good time for writing fragments.
>
> (Heller 1993: 8)

Ludwig Wittgenstein adopted this style, for example in *Philosophical Grammar* and in *Zettel* (Anscombe and Wright 1970), a genre continued by Jean Baudrillard some fifty years later. Baudrillard became a cult figure for architecture students, first in *America* and then through his three popular volumes on philosophy called *Cool Memories I*, *Cool Memories II* and *Cool Memories III: Fragments* (Baudrillard 1986, 1990, 1996, 1997).

One of the central tenets/analytical tools of postmodernism embodies this very idea of fragmentation and deconstruction, a concept derived from the French philosopher Jacques Derrida (1976, 1978, see also Soltan 1996). Inseparable from this is his concept of 'difference' which derived from his work on semiotics and language (see also chapter 3). Derrida's position was that the Saussurian legacy (named after the French philosopher of linguistics, Ferdinand de Saussure) had been largely ignored, despite the fact that Saussure had demonstrated that language, instead of being constructed as a system of meanings based in nouns (that is positively in phenomena), could best be understood as a system of differences *without* positive terms. Derrida recognised the revolutionary potential in this idea, which had not been developed in any meaningful sense by Saussure himself or indeed by his American counterpart, Charles Sanders Pierce: 'With Derrida, difference becomes the prototype of what remains outside the scope of Western metaphysical thought, because it is the latter's very condition of possibility' (Lechte 1994: 107). Important also is the use of the French spelling of the word *differer*, which has two meanings, 'to differ' and 'to defer', combining meanings of deferment (time and history) and distinction (matter, ideas, values, etc.).

Postmodernist thinking therefore assumes that because totalising discourses cannot accommodate this concept of difference, they must be rejected, not merely on the basis of function but also on the basis of politics, since 'there is a necessary relationship between conceptual apparatuses and political institutions' (Ryan 1982: 8). Also, in relation to historical studies in general, and for our purposes in particular, Derrida notes that 'We shall designate by the term *differentiation*, the movement by which language, or any code, any system of reference in general, becomes *historically constituted* as a fabric of differences' (quoted in Ryan 1982: 15); and again, 'If one accepts that the historical world is produced as a process of differentiation, in which specific events are subsumed by larger chains, series, structures, and sequences, then one must also acknowledge that all knowledge of it which isolates self identical entities or events from that differential seriality is necessarily institutional, that is conventional and constructed' (Ryan 1982: 25).

Out of these concepts comes a series of metaphors, prime among which is the idea of the city as text that can be read as a system of differences or fragments that bear a loose or indeterminate relation to each other. Since these texts are all constructions following certain laws, it follows that they can also be deconstructed and therefore understood. While this idea is now well established in architecture, where the principle of deconstruction has been explored in building design for some twenty-five years, it has had a small but significant effect on urban history. Bernard Tschumi in his book *Architecture and Disjunction* (1996: 4) comments that the essays which it contains describe the condition of architecture at the end of the twentieth century, and 'While their common starting point is today's disjunction between use, form and social values, they argue that this condition, instead of being a pejorative one, is highly "architectural"...architecture being defined as the pleasurable and sometimes violent confrontation between spaces and activities'. Later he argues in an essay on his most famous work, the Parc de la Villette in Paris, that 'If the new mediated world echoed and reinforced our dismantled reality, maybe, just maybe, one should take advantage of such dismantling, celebrate fragmentation, by celebrating the culture of differences, by accelerating and intensifying the loss of certainty, of center, of history' (Tschumi 1996: 237; see figures 6 and 7).

This idea, of urban design history as a process of assembling and integrating fragments, and of the assumption of discontinuity rather than order, had been initiated at least twenty years previously in early work by Colin Rowe and Fred Koetter's *Collage City* (1978). The authors refer to the process of urban design as 'collage', an image derived from expressionist painting but applied in this instance to urban morphology (see figure 8). Here, fragments of materials, usually containing pre-existing images were assembled into a single pastiche which nonetheless read as a unified work. The reference to the idea of collage, however, is not merely a reference to the abstract patterning of the evolutionary outcome. It also refers to the social and psychological processes that informed it, questioning the possibility that urban form could ever be conceived 'in the abstract' as many urban designers would believe. Echoing Tschumi, Rowe and

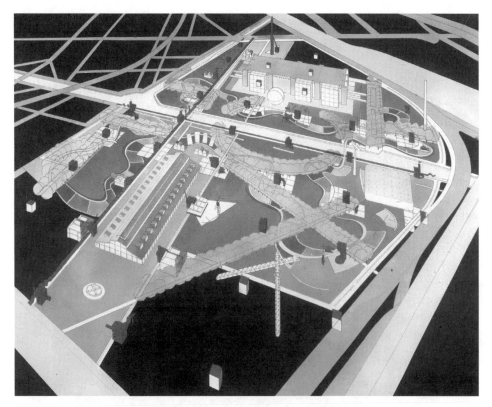

Figure 6   Bernard Tschumi: Parc de la Villette, aerial view (1985).
Source: Courtesy of Bernard Tschumi Architects.

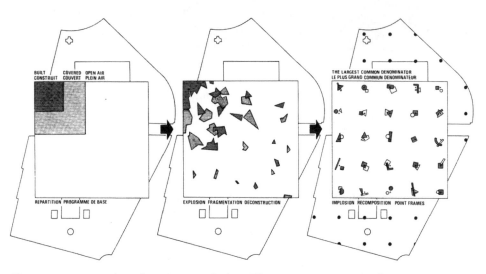

Figure 7   Bernard Tschumi: Parc de la Villette, programmatic deconstruction (1983).
Source: Courtesy of Bernard Tschumi Architects.

Figure 8   Example of Dadaist collage: Hanna Hoch's *Cut with the Dada Kitchen Knife through the Last Weimar Beer Belly Cultural Epoch of Germany* (1919). *Source:* Courtesy of the Staatliche Museen Preussischer Kulturbesitz, Nationalgalerie, Berlin.

Koetter prescribe their work as 'A proposal for constructive dis-illusion, it is simultaneously an appeal for order and disorder, for the simple and the complex, for the joint existence of permanent reference and random happening, of the private and the public, of innovation and tradition' (1978: 8). In many ways a similar conceptual base is present in Rob Krier's *Urban Space*, since his proposed typology of urban space revives a basic vocabulary of 'bits' that can be used to organise any such collage city. While Krier would insist on using a vocabulary of pre-existing forms, their use would be analogical, since the old meanings and associations would be redundant to new circumstances. The principle of using collage as a metaphor is therefore as good as far as it goes, but there remains the need for a contemporary method of integrating the necessary geometries and articulations of the contemporary city.

Materialist Theory

In urban design, discernible approaches to history appear as eclectic as they were in the previous chapter on theory, resulting in a wholesale anarchy of competing discourses. None of the positions presented to this point either share, or emerge from, any substantial theoretical position. Somehow the vast powerhouse of economic production that underpins social life has become mysteriously detached from the production of urban form. The physicality of urban space and its configurations are not seen as products of social processes, political strategy and economic policy, but instead come about as a result of utopian wish fulfilment, normative spatial concepts, professional influence or a series of somewhat random and arbitrary aesthetic choices. We are forced to conclude that either the majority of interpretations informing urban design bear no relationship to social production like most mainstream interpretations would suggest, or something substantial is missing. Fortunately, a small but significant number of scholars have recognised this omission, adopting the standpoint that indeed the symbolic and material production of urban space and form which results in the totality of our 'designed' environment must relate in some substantial manner to social life as a whole. Most of these scholars are, in one way or another, influenced by the Marxian dialectic.

Historical materialism is based on the fundamental assumption that life as we know it is predicated on human beings coming together to manufacture the material necessities of life that cannot be created solely by individuals. Hence the productive process becomes transformed into a social event:

> In the social production of their life men enter into definite relations that are indispensable and independent of their will, relations of production which correspond to a definite state of development of their material productive forces...at a certain stage of their development the material productive forces of society come in conflict with the existing relations of production, or, what is but a legal expression of the same thing – with the property relations within which they have been at work hitherto.
>
> (preface to Marx's *Critique of Political Economy*)

The built environment may therefore be seen as a mirror of production (borrowing a phrase from Baudrillard), since this collective process cannot be abstracted away from the actual production of specific urban forms. As society reproduces itself, a set of social and property relations are similarly established and reproduced over time based upon the private ownership of or control over land, property and the means of production. This fact cleaves society into two divisions: those who possess capital in its various forms and who are therefore in a position to purchase labour power, and those who are forced to sell their labour in order to survive.

Owing a great debt to the Scottish Enlightenment, German philosophy and French socialism, Marx's philosophy of history is fundamentally teleological. In other words, it is based on a necessary diachronic sequence of modes of production tied to specific forms of class domination. Both before and after this period,

> society existed in a form of undifferentiated unity, and that after the demise of class society, there will again be unity, but now in a differentiated form that allows full scope for the development of the individual. True, this view need not be based on a priori assumptions. One might well argue on empirical grounds that the advent of a communist society is highly probable, given certain trends in capitalism.
>
> (Elster 1985: 107)

Karl Popper (1986) offers the opposite point of view in *The Poverty of Historicism*, where he argues against the idea of historical laws or trends. Popper refers to these somewhat scathingly as 'prophecies', implying that it is quite impossible to predict the future and that there is no necessary relation between future states and past history. This denies Marx's prediction for example that communism is the logical outcome of the stored wealth of capitalist development, which provides the surplus required for true socialism to occur. As Marx states in *The German Ideology*, 'Communism is not a *state of affairs* to be established, an ideal to which reality will have to adjust itself. We call communism the real movement, which abolishes the present state of things. The conditions of this movement result from the premises now in existence' (Marx 1981: 57). It is clear from this that no socialist state has ever existed in the form he anticipated. Inherent to the idea of modes of production (Asiatic, ancient, feudal, modern, bourgeois, etc.), as definitive of the forms of material life, is the principle that they also condition the social, political and intellectual life-process. In other words, consciousness itself emerges from the social relations of production. These relations are dependent on the amount of his/her own labour power 'owned' by the individual, as Cohen says:

> Unlike the slaveholder, the lord of the manor has only some ownership of the labour power of the producer subordinate to him. He is entitled to tell the serf what to do with his labour power only some of the time. Unlike the proletarian, the serf has only some of the rights over his labour power, not all; but whereas the proletarian has no rights over the means of production he uses, the serf does have some.
>
> (Elster 1985: 65)

He goes on to note that these relations can be represented as:

1   ... is the slave of ...
2   ... is the master of ...
3   ... is the serf of ...
4   ... is the lord of ...

5   ...is hired by...
6   ...hires...
7   ...owns...
8   ...does not own...
9   ...leases his labour power to...
10 ...is obliged to work for...

The material relation between capital and labour can then be stated in terms of the degree to which one owns one's own labour, and the means of production that are used in the generation of surplus value. For example, a slave owns neither his or her own labour nor does he or she own any means of production. Marxian theory therefore maintains that history progresses on the basis of particular modes of production, which are defined by these specific social relations. Land and property ownership, institutional forms and their symbolic representation all emerge from this process, and are inherently interlinked in the social production of urban form, towns, cities, conurbations, as well as the location and expression of places, spaces, monuments and buildings. Since each mode of production also develops its own forms of consciousness, these surface in literature, art and architecture, the latter inscribing the aspirations, dreams, systems of repression, nightmares, fears and accomplishments of civil-isation in both mental and material space.

Post-Marxist theory has developed not only from inconsistencies and faulty deduction in the original exposition but also from the inability of orthodox interpretations to explain the dynamic complexity of contemporary capitalist development. This reformulation is due in part to the empirical evidence, which was available to Marx during his lifetime, and to the actual historical evolution of society over the last 150 years, which has contradicted many of his original assumptions. Marx's concentration on productive forces derived from industrial capitalism does not for example reflect the dominance of service economies within advanced capitalist societies and the functions of management and infor-mation as major economic activities. As labour productivity increases, the reproduction of the social relations of production has become increasingly complex, and hence a change of emphasis is required from production to consumption and to social conflict related to the reproduction of labour power. This change of emphasis demands not merely a reorientation towards the social wage, but the actual material circumstances of labour in regard to the spatial forms within which consumption processes come about, and therefore to the spatial construction of urban life – to the deployment of the consumption fund; to the increasing complexity of social structure and the competing interests that exist between classes and class factions; of problems related to the function-ing of the state; of urban planning and urban social movements; and to conflict centred around the political allocation of urban space.

While few scholars concerned with urban history have adopted historical materialism in its entirety, most have had to address the conceptual system it embodies, if for no other reason than it offered them the best opposition in working through their own ideas. Some have touched on Marxian thinking momentarily, some use it as a whipping post, while others have adopted it as a lifetime project. Bernard Tschumi for example begins his book *Architecture and Disjunction* by begging the question 'Is space a material thing in which all material things are located?...Does the Hegelian end of history mean the end of space as a material product?...On the other hand, if history does not end, and historical time is the Marxist time of revolution, does space lose its primary role?' (Tschumi 1996: 53–62; see table 6). Most scholars of the left would agree to the principle of a dialectical relationship between theory and practice, allowing space for new concepts and ideas to be accommodated. Foremost among these are Tafuri (1976), Dickens (1979, 1980, 1981), Boyer (1983), Cosgrove (1984), Knesl (1984), King (1984, 1988, 1996), Harvey (1989), Davis (1990, 2002) Zukin (1991), Ward (1996), Tschumi (1996), and Frampton (2002). In addition, most would also be sympathetic to the type of critical thinking exhibited by the intellectual nexus represented in the new urban studies of the late 1970s and early 1980s; Harvey (1973, 1982), Castells (1977, 1978), Saunders (1979), Scott (1980) and Mingione (1981), as well as in related areas of intellectual development such as human geography, cultural studies and urban sociology since that time. Probably the best overall interpretation is G.A. Cohen's outstanding work of 1978 *Karl Marx's Theory of History*, although many other commentaries are available, from Boudin's *The Theoretical System of Karl Marx* (1907) to Bober's *Karl Marx Interpretation of History* (1950) or John Elster's *Making Sense of Marx* (1985). While Marxian thought will be one of the

Table 6   Bernard Tschumi: extracts from 'Questions of Space'.

1.0	Is space a material thing in which all material things are located?
1.1	If space is a material thing, does it have boundaries?
1.2	If space is not matter, is it merely the sum of all spatial relations between material things?
1.3	If space is neither matter nor a set of objective relations between things, is it something subjective with which the mind categorises things?
1.4	If, etymologically, 'defining' space is both making space distinct and stating the precise nature of space, is this an essential paradox of space?
1.5	Architecturally, if defining space is making space distinct, does making space distinct define space?
1.6	Is architecture the concept of space, the space, and the definition of space?
1.7	If Euclidean space is restricted to a three-dimensional lump of matter, is non-Euclidean space to be restricted to a series of events in four-dimensional space-time?
2.0	Is the perception of space common to everyone?
3.0	Is there a language of space (a space-language)?
4.0	Is space a product of historical time?

Source: B. Tschumi, *Architecture and Disjunction*. Cambridge, MA: The MIT Press, pp. 53–62. Reprinted by permission of The MIT Press and Bernard Tschumi Architects.

dominant paradigms represented in the next chapter on philosophy, I will limit my comments here to explaining a few elementary points regarding any Marxian interpretation of history and concentrate on the implications for urban form and design.

Taking but a few examples from the literature, the first serious attempt to connect materialist theory to the development of urban form was Manfredo Tafuri's *Architecture and Utopia: Design and Capitalist Development* (1976). The book was a reworked and much expanded version of a paper he published in 1969, and was criticised on at least three levels unrelated to its content: the quality of the translation, Tafuri's adopted use of language and the opacity of the arguments presented. Tafuri's argument is ideological, particularly in regard to what he terms the bourgeois intellectual's obligation in relation to architectural ideology.

Tafuri begins by stating his focus thus

> What is of interest here is the precise identification of those tasks which capitalist development has taken away from architecture, that is to say what it has taken away in general from ideological pre-figuration. With this, one is led almost automatically to the discovery of what may well be the 'drama' of architecture today; that is to see architecture obliged to return to pure architecture, to form *without* utopia; in the best cases to sublime uselessness.
>
> (Tafuri 1976: ix; my italics)

Here he is referring to the idea of architecture as a pure sign in semiotic terms, that is, a sign that is purely self-referential, or a building that contains no referents whatever. In postmodern terminology, this would imply that the buildings do not contain any 'text' and therefore no symbolic references to urban politics. The supra-material function of architecture would therefore be expunged, eliminating all reference for example to class domination or to resistance, to dominant ideologies or forms of power. The archetypal example of this kind of urban form is that of Aldo Rossi, whose struggle to produce an ideologically pure architecture (one that represents nothing at all) lasted much of his life. In relation to Rossi's famous design for the Gallaretese Quarter in Milan (figures 9 and 10), Tafuri says 'Rossi sets the hieratic purism of his geometric block, which is kept aloof from every ideology, from every utopian proposal for a new lifetime' (Tafuri 1974: 157). Tafuri was a leading theorist in the Italian School of Architecture and Urbanism called *La Tendenza* whose work has been summed up in the context of a materialist interpretation of history by Bernard Huet (2000: 512) as 'an ideological deconstruction and re-evaluation of the history of architecture as an integral part of the history of labour. The typological criticism developed by Carlos Aymonino and Aldo Rossi attempted to situate architecture as a typical production in the historical process of the formation of cities'.

While Tafuri, Aymonino and Rossi focus on the centrality of ideological production to the history of urban design, Cosgrove concentrates on the significance of modes of production. However, he also recognises the extent to which

Figure 9   Aldo Rossi: Gallaretese Quarter, loggia.
Source: Aldo Rossi, *Architect.* London: Architectural Press, 1987, p. 85.

Marxian concepts are interlinked when he says, 'Landscape, I shall argue, is an *ideological* concept. It represents a way in which certain classes of people have signified themselves and their world through their imagined relationship with nature, and through which they have underlined and communicated their own social role and that of others with respect to external nature' (Cosgrove 1997: 15; my italics). He concentrates in particular on the transition between feudalism and capitalism, and on the connections between social formation and symbolic landscape in a book of the same name (1984). In materialist terms, each specific mode of production outlines the manner in which collective social life is reproduced (Althusser and Balibar 1970, Banaji 1977, Bottomore 1983). While Cosgrove is sensitive to criticisms of interpretations that rely upon a dominant narrative, he views the deconstructivist philosophy of recent times as a positive force, where the inclusions of alternative realities strengthen rather than weaken historical interpretation. He also acknowledges that the term 'social formation' in the title of his book derives from a Marxist formulation.

Figure 10 Aldo Rossi: Gallaretese Quarter, elevation.
Source: Courtesy of the Courtauld Institute of Art. Copyright © Courtauld Institute of Art.

Peter Dickens also recognises the weakness in traditional architectural and urban theory in a seminal article called 'Marxism and architectural theory' (1979), a theme pursued in 'The hut and the machine: towards a social theory of architecture' (Dickens 1981). Dickens adopts, on the one hand, a Marxist perspective on architecture as social closure and ideological production, while railing against simple-minded misinterpretations of Marxian theory, one of his targets being Tafuri: 'Thus Tafuri's historical account involving the use of much Marxist jargon ("the working class", "the bourgeoisie", "the always outdated level of ideology", "the capitalist use of land", and so forth) becomes, when examined in any historical detail, almost entirely lacking in analytical and political value' (Dickens 1979: 111). He criticises architectural and urban theory as pseudo-science because of its habit of plundering social theory in order to gain credibility at no cost to itself. Dickens says that the opposite needs to happen, that we have to move inwards from social theory to architecture, viewing the production of architectural and urban form as an integral part of all other social production. He attacks the rationalists and in particular *Collage City* for its

superficiality. The theory that Rowe and Koetter propose, based on reifying
additive structure and a perpetually incomplete urban form, exhibits low levels
of refutability in the classic Popperian sense, 'It is a proposal for a liberal
democratic society, but, since we are not told what the social environment is
within which Collage City is being tested, we can never know in Popper's terms
whether it is a "success" or a "failure" ' (Dickens 1981: 1).

Dickens is also critical of the Marxian thinking in Krier's *Urban Space*, not
because it is misplaced but simply because it is a distortion of Marxist thinking
on the relationship between culture and society. He argues that the critical
required reversal from the continuing architectural rip-off of social science, to
a placement of architecture *within* social science, hinges around the concept of
ideology. Clearly the left is its own worst critic, and one wonders what
Tafuri would have to say about the capital-logic nature of Dickens' own analysis
(figure 11). Dickens' argument is significantly refined by John Knesl in an article
called 'The powers of architecture' (1984), and others have demonstrated
the effectiveness of materialist theory in relation to the history of building

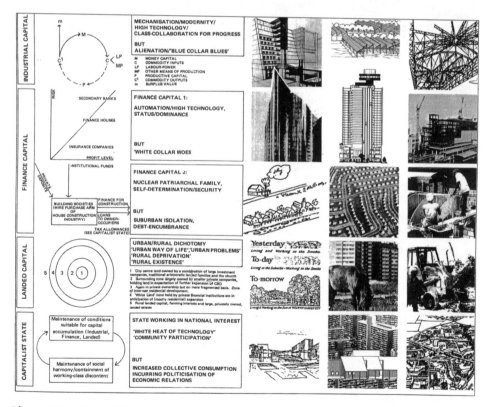

Figure 11   Peter Dickens: huts, machines and organic analogies.
Source: P. Dickens, 'The hut and the machine: towards a social theory of architecture',
Architectural Design, 1:2, 1981.

typologies, for example 'The social production of building form: theory and research' is a classic of its kind (King 1984). While he makes a plea for the eclectic use of theory, his analysis of culture and the place of building form leans heavily on the concept of modes of production, the global relations of production, the reproduction of labour, core–periphery relationships, etc.; in short, the vocabulary of historical materialism and spatial political economy.

Overview

In an overview of the history of urban form and design, there are a huge variety of positions adopted by a significant number of theorists. I have chosen to classify these for the purpose of discussion as chronologies, typologies, utopias, fragments and materialist theory, and I acknowledge that other methods are of course possible. During this review, two key strategies were followed. The first has been to place these various positions into some basic perspective as to their usefulness in explaining the historical evolution of urban form and the design of urban space, and to demonstrate the range of available perspectives. The second is to promote Peter Dickens' proposition that architecture and urban design must reverse their historical relationship with the social sciences, which they have plundered superficially, for too long, and at too great a cost to their own integrity. However, this is not a mandate to rush blindly back to Marx's *Capital* or to adopt wholesale more recent Marxian theory (e.g. Hardt and Negri's masterwork *Empire*, 2000) as the theoretical nexus for studies of urban form and design. While I believe spatial political economy remains the most intellectually coherent and encompassing *episteme* available to us, philosophy has also offered several other significant pathways into the design of cities and this is discussed next in chapter 3.

Chapter Three
Philosophy

Design is the prefiguration of the encounter between ideology and the production process.

Peter Dickens

Introduction: Implications from Philosophy

The shape and form of cities has always been the subject of philosophical discourse, breeding theoretical interventions, utopian visions, symbolic constructs or speculation about the future. Two and a half millennia have now past since Hippodamus, Aristotle, Zeno and Plato raised questions about the ideal size and form of cities as well as their social organisation. After Hellenistic Greece, the practice of philosophy became embedded as an ongoing responsibility of civilised life, more often than not challenging the societies within which it took root. As a discipline, social science has been dominated by the philosophies of Kant, Hegel, Marx, Simmel, Weber, Durkheim and others. Outhwaite (1994) points out that philosophy in the context of social science comes under scrutiny in two respects: first, the idea that social science should be capable of organising its own methodologies without the help of philosophy; the second view takes issue with the proposition that science can be fragmented and so the very idea of a 'social' science should be resisted. This idea was in fact at the centre of the great debate in urban studies from 1970 to 1980, when Manuel Castells raised the problematic that in order to claim status as part of science, urban sociology would have to possess either a real or a theoretical object. If it had neither then it could not claim true status as a science, and would remain as either an ideological construct or an empty empiricism. Outhwaite then goes on to suggest that twentieth-century philosophy of science and social science has three distinct periods. In the first period, seven significant approaches are suggested, three of which have direct relevance for urban studies:

1 the phenomenology of Edmund Husserl and Martin Heidegger;
2 orthodox Marxist approaches and what he terms 'unorthodox' Marxism, namely theorists such as George Lukacs and the critical theory of the Frankfurt School in general;
3 Weberian sociology.

52

The second period was dominated by what was termed *logical empiricism* or *logical positivism*, which arose in Vienna around 1920 and then in the USA twenty years later: 'The standard view in the philosophy of science was a modified logical empiricism, stressing the unity of natural and social science in opposition to more speculative forms of social theory, the importance of empirical testability and the value-freedom of social science. This conception continues to set the agenda for much contemporary philosophy of science' (Outhwaite 1994: 84). The period since that time has been represented in the development of philosophies emerging from stage one, for example neo-Marxism, neo-Kantianism, neo-Nietzscheanism. In addition, three other individuals stand out as having had a major impact on urban design: first, Max Weber whose book *The City* is a classic text, neo-Weberian social theory still having a significant grip in urban studies; second, Ferdinand de Saussure who invented semiotics, sometimes referred to as the science of meaning, and whose students collated his work after his death in 1913 into a text called *Cours de Linguistic Générale*; and third, Walter Benjamin, probably the only figure from the Frankfurt School to have a lasting and direct impact on urban studies. If we accept Charles Jencks' date for the birth of postmodernism as July 1972, some additional refinement is needed. Over that period, the environmental disciplines have been more directly influenced by contemporary philosophy than at any other time, almost all of it originating in France. Dozens of influential philosophers have impacted on architectural, urban and landscape theory, including, but not limited to, Michel Foucault, Emmanuel Levinas, Jacques Lacan, Roland Barthes, Jean-Francois Lyotard, Jean Baudrillard, Gilles Deleuze, Felix Guattari, Pierre Bourdieu, Maurice Merleau-Ponty, Paul Ricoeur, Jacques Derrida, Christian Metz, Ernesto Laclau, Chantal Mouffe and Alain Touraine. Of course none of these came stillborn to the world of philosophy, and represented in their work are 'dominant others', for example Foucault (Marx and Nietzsche), Lyotard (Marx and Kant), Barthes (de Saussure), Lacan (Hegel and Freud). France aside, other philosophers have influenced urban studies, such as Martin Heidegger, Umberto Eco, Julia Kristeva and Frederic Jameson.

From these authors poured an astounding array of concepts and propositions that are still being debated today. The subject matter of their interests is truly Herculean, ranging from the outer fringes of human psychology to the symbolic structuring of language and thought. However, the overall brilliance of this work proposes a precise problematic, the reason for Peter Dickens' admonition that we must move inward from social theory to architecture and urban design. It is too easy for designers in general to plunder this entire body of work for ideas that are then located elsewhere, lacking their original legitimacy and content. Among such a huge array of published work it is difficult to isolate any specific author at the cost of the others, although several do stand out as having singular significance in the areas of architecture and urban design.

Prime among these would probably be Foucault's *The Archaeology of Knowledge* (1977), Umberto Eco's *A Theory of Semiotics* (1976), Lyotard's treatise *The Postmodern Condition* (1985), Frederic Jameson's *Postmodernism, or the*

Cultural Logic of Late Capitalism (1991) and two 'cult' classics, Debord's *Society of the Spectacle* (1967) and Jean Baudrillard's *For a Critique of the Political Economy of the Sign* (1981). From all of this, two observations emerge which will structure the remainder of this chapter. First, that so far we have focused largely on individuals and their philosophical contribution to our area of concern, namely a social theory of urban form and design. However it is also useful to look at collectivities, schools of thought that have locked into particular paradigms having significance for the generation of urban form. Second, that 'dominant paradigms' also emerge from even a brief consideration of the above. Prime among these in assisting us in our understanding of how cities are 'designed' are the long-established developmental traditions of semiotics (de Saussure), phenomenology (Husserl), deconstruction (Foucault) and political economy (Marx), and their influence needs to be systematically located.

Philosophy and Urbanism

While the masters of sociological thought during the nineteenth century were concerned with neither space nor form, the twentieth century generated several significant incursions into the relationship between socio-economic practices, spatial patterns and the built form of cities. There was a similar movement in methods of explanation, from the structuralist functionalism of Marx and Freud to their nemesis within the feminist critique of postmodernism. While the theoretical bridge has been made from social process to spatial patterns, connections to built form, usually seen as arbitrary, have only been given passing consideration. Understanding the environment we live in has preoccupied some of society's greatest minds for centuries. But when we think of philosophy we tend to think of individuals who have somehow turned the course of human understanding. Yet from the beginning of the twentieth century, several schools of thought or pioneering movements investigating urban life arose in several of the worlds' great cities, namely Vienna, Frankfurt, Chicago, Paris and arguably Los Angeles today. Another influential movement, that of the Bauhaus, was not located in a significant urban centre (Weimar and Dessau), yet it effectively set the foundation for the entire modern movement in architecture and other design fields. I use the term 'school' loosely to denote a powerful concentration of intellectual activity where a dominant paradigm, theoretical object or particular cultural world view was set in motion. The 'Paris School' is perhaps an overstatement, but not so in the significance of its impact on urban studies, centring on the work of Henri Lefebvre, Manuel Castells and Alain Touraine. Similarly, I also add the term 'Los Angeles School' as a method of crystallising the immense body of innovative work on urban development that has emerged largely from scholars, particularly geographers, in the Los Angeles region over the last ten years. While only two of these had any direct functional influence on urban design theory (Vienna and the Bauhaus), the remainder have had a significantly greater effect on our ability to understand the meanings secreted in the built environment, and to view its production as part and parcel of social production as a whole. Each of these incursions into urban development has been unique. While they were by no means the only paradigms, they remain influential even today in contemporary thinking about the city, transmuted from established philosophical traditions of the eighteenth, nineteenth and twentieth centuries. In examining each school of thought, I will have as a prime concern their relationship to particular philosophies, before discussing three specific outcomes in the last section.

Paradigms

Vienna

At the *fin de siècle*, on the cusp between the eighteenth and nineteenth centuries, Vienna lay at the epicentre of European culture and civilisation. Vienna had become a vortex of creativity, breaking new ground in the world of art, science and philosophy, with figures such as Arnold Schoenberg, Gustave Klimt, Josef Hoffmann, Richard Strauss, Hugo von Hofmannsthal, Gustave Mahler, Sigmund Freud and a host of other great artists and intellectuals. Congruent with the huge transformations that were taking place in society, the physical fabric of the city was also being torn apart and reconstructed, a symbolic representation of what was happening in music, painting, sculpture, philosophy and other regions of human creativity. The Ringstrasse (the major boulevard encircling the city centre) and everything contained within it was to be rebuilt. The big question was how to do it or, more accurately, in what manner. The battleground was that of physical determinism, which saw no connection between the design of cities and their social organisation. Designing cities was seen to be a technical project inspired by individual genius, focusing on the work of two Viennese architects, Otto Wagner and Camillo Sitte, the latter being the author of arguably the seminal work on urban design, *The Art of Building Cities: City Building According to its Artistic Fundamentals* (Sitte 1889).

It was in Vienna that the actual form of the city and its symbolic content, over and above its component architectural elements, had risen to prominence as a major consideration in the modern world. Sitte advocated a contextual approach to urban form, which was viewed by many as a reification of medieval urbanism and a retreat into historicism. On the other hand, Wagner's utilitarian function-alism, a position which ultimately triumphed, proposed not merely a new vision of urban life but also a new vision of man, a debate which still continues today. Reduced to its essentials, the debate was one of emotion over intellect, or feeling over rationality. At that point a statement was made which asserted that the actual physicality of the built environment mattered, not merely as shelter but as a symbolic manifestation of society's conflicts, histories and aspirations. Clearly this was already understood, for example by dictators such as Napoleon III, who was responsible for Haussmann's great plan for Paris, a project bought at the cost of destroying the medieval city. The difference now was that the form of the city was a subject for debate in a free and egalitarian society.

> Towards the close of the nineteenth century, when the intellectuals of Austria began to develop doubts about the culture of liberalism in which they had been raised, the Ringstrasse became a symbolic focus of their critique... in their contrasting views, Sitte and Wagner brought to thought about the city, the archaistic and modernistic objections to nineteenth century civilization that appeared in other areas of Austrian life. They manifested in their urban theory and spatial design, two salient features of emergent twentieth-century Austrian higher culture – a sensitivity to psychic states, and a concern with the penalties as well as the possibilities of rationality as the guide of life.
>
> (Schorske 1981: 25)

The discussion crystallised around two opposing architectural philosophies that dominated architectural and urban design debates in the twentieth century, namely rationalism and contextualism respectively. Rationalism promotes a functionalist philosophy whereby new urban forms can be invented to suit new social agendas, one where the legacy of history has little bearing. Contextualism argues that no new urban forms can be created, since all of these are already in existence. Instead, we should study historically defined typologies and use these to plan cities, rather than adopting the sterile zoning practices of state-sponsored regulation. Rationalist architecture and urbanism reached its zenith in its coincidence with functionalist social science and the eugenic strategies of fascism, particularly with Hitler and his architect Albert Speer (see figures 12 and 13) and with Mussolini (Marcello Piacentini, Giuseppe Terragni). Thirty years later, another great influential school of thought came into existence in Germany, bridging the second great war of capitalist accumulation.

Frankfurt

The Institute for Social Research (Institut fur Sozialforschung) more commonly known as the Frankfurt School, the birthplace of critical theory, was founded in 1923 and lasted until its demise shortly before 1944 (Slater 1977, Held 1980, Arato and Gebhardt 1982, McCarthy 1982, Kellner 1984). Some of its greatest figures included Theodore Adorno, Max Horkheimer, Wilhelm Reich, Erich Fromm, Herbert Marcuse, Walter Benjamin and Leo Lowenthal. Critical theory was also a key progenitor in the formation of the new left in the 1960s (Held 1980). The diaspora of some of its central figures to the USA prior to the Second World War resulted in a continuation of that tradition outside Germany, by such individuals as Herbert Marcuse (1964, 1968, 1985), Norman O. Brown (1959) and Jurgen Habermas (1976). However, the concept of a school of thought is somewhat misleading since the Frankfurt School could be divided into the Institute of Social Research in Frankfurt and a separate group of scholars centred on the work of Jurgen Habermas. David Held therefore uses the term 'Frankfurt School' in the context of only five scholars: Horkheimer, Adorno, Marcuse,

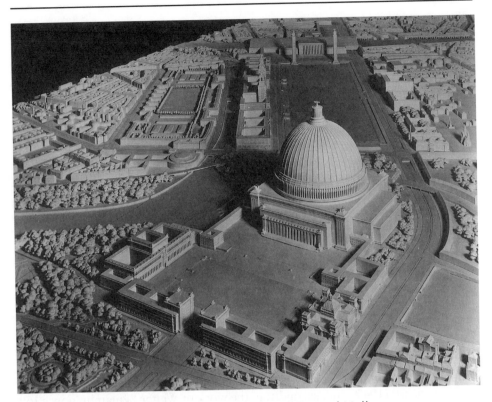

Figure 12   Speer and Hitler's Grand Plaza and Domed Hall.
Source: Landesarchiv Berlin.

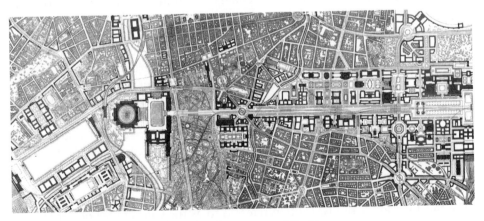

Figure 13   Hitler's grand plan for the centre of Berlin.
Source: Albert Speer, *Albert Speer: Architektur: Arbeiten 1933–1942*. Frankfurt:
Propylaen, 1978, pp. 95–7. Reprinted by permission of Propylaen Verlag.

Lowenthal and Pollock (Held 1980: 15). Nonetheless it is possible to discern an encompassing tradition that held its scholars together: 'The Frankfurt School takes as its starting point what it sees as the obvious divorce between praxis and thought, between political action and philosophy... they do not recognize the existence of any prior historical actors – not even the proletariat or Lukacs version of the party – and therefore inaugurate a total critique of modern society and especially of its culture' (Touraine 1995: 151). They recognised the dangers in what Touraine describes as 'the factory floor' of mass popular culture, viewing it not as a liberating force but one of oppression, a position which Touraine himself refutes. In marrying the philosophical principles of Marxism with Freudian social psychology, the Frankfurt School was centrally concerned with the 'deep structures' driving society and, with the single exception of Walter Benjamin, was wholly unconcerned with either space or form.

While using Marxian political economy as its intellectual base, it also represented the first major attempt to recast Marx's project. For example, it removed culture from the Marxist superstructure and placed it at the centre of the dialectic. In so doing, it stimulated investigation into the psychic development of society; of art, aesthetics and the pursuit of pleasure (Pile 1996).

These apart, two major influences on how we investigate urban life and the form of the city are significant. First, the concept of the 'culture industry' came from Theodore Adorno in an essay entitled 'The culture industry: enlightenment as mass deception' in a book by Horkheimer and Adorno called *The Dialectic of Enlightenment* (1947) and, secondly, in the work of Walter Benjamin, now a folk hero in postmodernist thinking about the city (Benjamin 1968, 1978). So the Frankfurt School has a continuing presence today, reconstructing new interpretations of urban development in economy and culture. Overall, a key contribution to our understanding of urban form emanating from the Frankfurt School was the principle that art and architecture were to be interpreted as 'a code language for processes taking place in society' (Held 1980: 80). This concept was to be echoed half a century later in Paris, giving birth to the discipline of semiotics on the way (Eco 1976). It is also significant that the Frankfurt School contributed to our understanding of urban life in substantially greater depth than anything that emerged from the Bauhaus in Weimar and Dessau over approximately the same period. Nonetheless, while the gulf between physical determinism and social process in Europe remained immense, across the Atlantic seminal studies of the relationship between society and space had begun in Chicago as early as 1916.

Chicago

The third school of thought, often referred to as the Chicago School of Human Ecology, peaked between the great wars, beginning with the work of Robert Park (heavily influenced by Emile Durkheim), Lewis Wirth and Meredith Burgess. Lewis Wirth's paper 'Urbanism as a way of life' (1938) is one of the most famous articles ever published about the city. Wirth's significant alter egos were the philosophers Max Weber and George Simmel (a neo-Kantian). The

Chicago ecologists were driven by a Darwinian concern with biotic processes applied to human communities – competition, colonisation, territoriality, succession, symbiosis, etc. – the prime difference of human communities being perceived as one of mobility, allowing for choice and modification of habitat and therefore enjoyment of a shared culture: 'Once distributed functionally and territorially, however, members of a human population were then in a position to develop new and qualitatively different bonds of cohesion based not on the necessities of the division of labour, but on common goals, sentiments and values' (Saunders 1986: 59). Although the analogy between human and biotic communities was misplaced, the Chicago School did advance many of the concepts upon which the organisation and design of 'human communities' could be established, with studies of population density, movement and differentiation, as well as some speculation over the generic forms of cities and regions in Burgess' concentric zone theory and its derivatives.

While it has been argued that the movement collapsed in the 1950s, the tradition was still alive and well through the 1960s (Gans 1962, Duncan 1964, McKenzie 1967, Hawley 1950, 1956), even into the early work of Ray Pahl (1970, 1975). It also formed an intellectual foundation for Constantinos Doxiadis' ekistic theory of the 1970s and 1980s. Ekistics was one of the more significant attempts at that time to establish a science of human settlements, in an attempt to give urban planning the credibility it has always lacked (Doxiadis 1963, 1968). Doxiadis and his institute spent nearly twenty years involved with what they termed the 'human community', named community class four, in a hierarchy of ten component classes of human organisation that added up to Ecumenopolis, the urban regions of today. This concept of community based on shared values and spatial propinquity lost its currency some thirty years ago as a basis for physical design. As early as 1970, Constance Perrin was proposing that units for analysis should be focused on what she called 'behaviour circuits' rather than any arbitrary spatial unit called 'community'. In the digital information age, ideas of place and locale are now the preferred orientation in urban studies.

In contrast to the great intellectual tradition established in Frankfurt, the philosophy of the Chicago School in aligning itself with human ecology and Darwinism resulted in serious debates as to whether it represented a substantive new paradigm or solely a body of knowledge and a method of urban analysis – a method in search of a theory. In attempting to create a (social) theory of human society that was homologous with a specific (spatial) theory of the city, the Chicago School collapsed due to the sheer impossibility of the project, with the result that 'the relation between ecological theory and urban theory became purely contingent. Now that ecology had found its niche within the functionalist paradigm...it is clear that human ecology is no longer essentially an urban theory and that it cannot provide a conceptual framework within which a specifically social theory can be developed' (Saunders 1986: 82–3). Despite the attempt to generate physical models of urban structure, the Chicago School foundered over the concept of urban political analysis, since there was basically no place within social Darwinism to discuss either economic and political theory or indeed consciousness, arguably the fundamental differences between biotic and human communities. Nonetheless, Manuel Castells (1977: 77) considers that 'the ecological approach was the most serious attempt ever made within sociology to establish a theoretical object (and consequently a domain of research), specific to urban sociology'. While some of the more elementary connections between society and space had been made in Chicago in the 1930s, another major centre, this time in Germany, was simultaneously exploring another facet of structural-functionalism in regard to the material production of the built environment, namely the Bauhaus at Weimar and Dessau.

Weimar and Dessau

> But if design is immersed in fashion, one must not complain, for this is the mark of its triumph. It is the mark of the territorial scope established by the political economy of the sign, whose first rational theorisation was design and the Bauhaus. Everything that today wishes to be marginal, irrational, insurrectionary, 'anti-art', 'anti-design' etc., from pop to psychedelic or to street art – everything obeys the same economy of the sign, whether it wants to or not. All of it is design. Nothing escapes design: that is its fate.
>
> (Baudrillard 1981: 198)

But the Bauhaus had significant roots in England. The author John Ruskin, a socialist, was one of the first to rebel against the conditions of labour established in England during the Industrial Revolution. He viewed technology as anathema to the working class and sought to re-establish medieval methods. One of his students, William Morris, continued this overall philosophy and started a tradition which he hoped would rehumanise alienated labour, increasingly isolated from its own products. By 1880, the movement had become so powerful that it was named the 'Arts and Crafts movement'. The Germans copied the method as a means of re-educating labour in order to compete with Britain as the world's leader in industrial production. By the turn of the century, Germany had not only emulated British methods but had overtaken Britain as the world's leading industrial nation. In the spring of 1919, a German architect by the name of Walter Gropius was named the director of the State Bauhaus in Weimar, Germany. The governing principle was that all forms of art must be craft-based, and therefore the workshop was the appropriate place to learn. In contrast to the British, Germany embraced the idea of mass production and the integration of art and technology. While the craft-based, master–apprentice, workshop philosophy remained, it nonetheless represented an outright rejection of both William Morris' fundamental philosophy and the *Jugendstil* (German art nouveau movement), which were very much in vogue when the Bauhaus was founded. While Morris saw that labour could be rehumanised by reversing the alienation inherent to mass production (especially in the building industry), the Bauhaus, driven as it was by socialist principles for much of its existence, did not envisage that labour within capitalism was about to become a slave to the machine it revered. Apart from its basic political orientation to a socialist philosophy (partly funded by the trade unions), the Bauhaus pioneered structuralist functionalism as its philosophy of design. In this it was assisted by Russian constructivism, a parallel and associated influence that aligned itself with left politics and the integration of art and technology. Both embraced mass production and standardisation as the only methods which would allow workers access to a materially higher quality of life.

The Bauhaus was probably the most influential school of applied art in the twentieth century, whose impact on design remains with us today. Despite the impact of postmodernist thought over the last thirty years, modern architecture and design remains rooted to the philosophy of the Bauhaus, beginning some eighty years ago. From its inception the Bauhaus had a left-wing revolutionary political philosophy, Gropius having been quoted as saying, 'Since we have no culture whatever, merely a civilization, I am convinced that for all its evil concomitants, Bolshevism is probably the only way of creating the preconditions for a new culture in the foreseeable future' (Willett 1978: 48). Unfortunately for Gropius, a right-wing government was elected in 1923 and the Bauhaus was told to close or move. Gropius re-established the Bauhaus in Dessau at the end of 1926, and resigned early in 1928. The architect Hannes Meyer then took over from Gropius and a collectivist philosophy dominated, Meyer being a declared Marxist: 'cooperative ideals were given first priority: cooperation, standardisation, the harmonious balance of individual and society.

Many of these ideas were taken up and politicized by communist students' (Droste 1998: 196). This influence was so great that the Bauhaus became a locus for both communist and Marxist propaganda. Meyers' tacit support as a communist sympathiser resulted in his dismissal, with the appointment of Ludwig Mies van der Rohe to the directorship. Although Mies tried to maintain a neutral political stance, the Nazis nonetheless closed the Dessau Bauhaus on 22 August 1932. Mies was then sent a set of conditions by the Gestapo on which basis the Bauhaus might be reopened, one of which was that Hilberseimer and Kandinsky, being Jews, should no longer be permitted to teach. The staff rejected the conditions and the Bauhaus finally closed. From its inception, the Bauhaus radically affected design across all of the arts, from theatre design to painting, sculpture, textiles, architecture and urbanism, and it is also meaningful that all three directors of the Bauhaus, Gropius, Meyer and Mies van der Rohe, were architects. While Meyer went to work in Russia after his demise as director, both Mies and Gropius went to the USA. While each produced some remarkable buildings that would have a major impact on architecture in the twentieth century, they were primarily concerned with building design, not urbanism. In this respect the Bauhaus' most significant figure was Ludwig Hilberseimer, for whom:

> The metropolis... is a molar machine, involving large scale social, technical and economic systems intercommunicating with architectural elements. The reproducible architectural elements at the molecular level – each identical in size and shape, without a priori determined points of focus or termination – translate and relay information received from the global structure of the city, even as these same elements are, in turn, the prime constitutive elements of that structure.
>
> (Hays 1992: 173)

Hays goes on to argue that in Hilberseimer's urbanism can be detected a movement from humanism to posthumanism. While humanism is often conflated to bourgeois ideology, masking the reality of capitalist class relations, he defines posthumanism as 'the conscious response, whether with applause or regret, to the dissolution of psychological autonomy and individualisation brought by technological modernization; it is a mobilization of aesthetic practices to effect a shift away from the humanist concepts of subjectivity and its presumptions about originality, universality and authority' (Hays 1992: 6). Hilberseimer's ideas on urbanism are distilled in his great utopian concept called *Vorschlag zur Citybeauung* (Project for the Construction of a City; see figure 14). Here he explores how his molar machine would materialise as a metaphor for the city's productive capacity, the urban realm becoming a totalitarian response to the triumph of representation over experience. While Le Corbusier had already presented his Design for a City of Three Million People in 1922 and his Plan Voisin for Paris in 1925, projects that shocked the Garden City movement into the modern world, Hilberseimer's *Vorschlag* took even Corbusier's work to new levels of abstraction and standardisation. The gateways of hope that had been opened up in the Bauhaus of 1919, based on collective labour applied to new technologies within the medium of Bolshevism, socialism and communism, concluded in the despair of totalitarian production and the dissolution of the public realm into the space of circulation. Mass production techniques resisted by the Bauhaus ultimately triumphed, with the concomitant

Figure 14 Ludwig Hilberseimer: Hochhausstadt Project (1924).
Source: Courtesy of The Art Institute of Chicago. Photography © The Art Institute of Chicago.

acceleration of the industrial division of labour, the dehumanisation of the work process, the debasement of craft, and alienation impacted as a way of life through the systematic deskilling of workers.

Paris

While the term 'Paris School' of the late 1960s and early 1970s may overstate the idea of a coherent school of thought, the revolutionary contributions made within the philosophical context of a Marxist retheorisation by Alain Touraine, Henri Lefebvre, Manuel Castells and others to the general field of urban sociology remains profound even today. Originating during a period of extreme social unrest – the explosion of the free speech movement in Berkeley during 1964 and the protest movements of French students in 1968 – the stage was set for both a return to Marxist fundamentalism and later Maoism, as well as a radical critique of the principles upon which social and democratic reform should be based. Central to both protest movements was the influence of a former member of the Frankfurt School, Herbert Marcuse. His 1964 publication, *One Dimensional Man*, launched a withering but misplaced critique of modernist industrial society and technological development (Marcuse 1968, 1985). With this context as a backdrop, two ground-breaking texts emerged, *La Révolution Urbaine* by Henri Lefebvre (1970) and *La Question Urbaine* by Manuel Castells (1972), and the debate on the theory of space finally became central to the development of social science. Lefebvre's critique exposes the homeostatic qualities of capitalist ideology, a system that reproduces itself without any apparent effort. Within this system, Lefebvre viewed space as a material (scientific) object, which therefore gives rise to the possibility of social space being analysed and acted upon according to scientific principles. In *La Révolution Urbaine*, Lefebvre asks, 'What is it that a buyer acquires when he purchases a space? The answer is time . . . Is a system of knowledge – a science – of the use of space, likely to evolve? . . . Perhaps, but it would have to evolve as an analysis of rhythms, and an effective critique of representative and normative spaces' (Lefebvre 1970: 356). Into his critique of ideology Lefebvre (1991: 131) also carries currents of semiotic theory in considering language as space, questions which impact directly on the design of cities, for example:

1   Do the spaces formed by practico-social activity, whether landscapes, monuments or buildings, have meaning?
2   Can the space occupied by a social group or several such groups be treated as a message?
3   Ought we to look upon architectural and urbanistic works as a type of mass medium, albeit an unusual one?
4   May a social space viably be conceived of as a language or discourse, dependent upon a determinate practice (reading/writing)?

While Castells' and Lefebvre's seminal works were written within two years of each other, both sharing a critique of capitalism based on an analysis of ideology, Castells' writing, heavily influenced by Louis Althusser and Nicos Poulantzas, is fundamentally epistemological, rejecting existing theories on the grounds that they worked within, rather than broke with, existing ideological norms. To his credit, Castells, a Catalan who spent his formative years in Paris, shattered the cocoon surrounding traditional aspatial social theory and created a new paradigm called *spatial urban theory*. For the first time, and within this new model, he integrated fundamental relationships between society, space and form and his influence over the entire field has been immense. In *The Urban Question*, Castells also undertakes an original analysis of urban spatial forms as products of basic economic processes – production, consumption, exchange and administration. He also demonstrates as part of this process how ideological structures are contained in symbolic configurations, elements and places. At the same time he breaks with customary Marxian tradition that concentrates on production by focusing on consumption processes as defining the urban. He argues that while industrial production takes place *over* space, social reproduction in the form of collective consumption must take place *within* space, constituting the space of everyday life. This stands out as a singularly insightful attempt to connect the process of designing cities to the overall process of the production of space within capitalism. In another classic *The City and the Grassroots*, from which I have taken my guiding definition of urban design, Castells refines this definition even further by stating that:

> Spatial forms, at least on our planet, will be produced by human action, as are all other objects, and will express and perform the interests of the dominant class according to a given mode of production and to a specific mode of development. They will express and implement the power relationships of the state in a historically defined society. They will be realized and shaped by gender domination and by state-enforced family life. At the same time, spatial forms will also be marked by resistance from exploited classes, oppressed subjects and abused women.
>
> (Castells 1983: 311–12)

Castells' later work advances from this capital-logic position with respect to how such domination will take place in the information age, but many fundamentals remain (Castells 1996, 1997, 1998).

Los Angeles

By the end of the twentieth century, no new schools of thought dealing with the urban realm had come into existence. This is partly due to the fact that most had belonged to some central philosophy, dominant paradigm or code of conduct, sometimes, as in the Bauhaus, to all three. Since the idea of dominant discourses is rejected within postmodern philosophy, this in itself tends to mitigate against any identifiable collective position on the city. Nonetheless, Los Angeles has a powerful group of scholars dedicated to analysing that city as a test bed for urban development and a model for urbanisation into the third millennium. Among the scholars in this group are internationally significant figures, predominantly in the realm of urban geography, such as Allen Scott, Ed Soja, Michael Dear, Jennifer Wolch, Mike Davis and many others. Some of the most significant texts emerging from this source are Allen Scott's *The Urban Land Nexus and the State* (1980), *Metropolis* (1988) and *The Cultural Economy of Cities* (2000a); Ed Soja's *Postmodern Geographies* (1989) and *Postmetropolis* (2000); and Mike Davis' *City of Quartz* (1990) and *Dead Cities* (2002). Had Manuel Castells' appointment been at UCLA rather than Berkeley, it is arguable that Los Angeles would have joined prior influential schools as 'the dominant discourse' at the cusp of the new millennium. The significance of the Los Angeles School has been extensively documented by one of its central figures (Dear 2001).

Philosophy and Urban Design

Apart from the philosophies informing dominant schools of thought about the city that arose from a variety of historical conditions and opportunities, specific modes of intellectual activity have also been instrumental in deepening our understanding of the development and growth of cities. Dominant among these have been the philosophical and practical application of semiotics, phenomenology and Marxian political economy, and a brief overview of each is required to demonstrate their collective importance for urban designers and other individuals involved in giving form to the city. As we shall see, there is a significant interweaving between them and knowledge of any one suffers in isolation.

Semiotics

Going back to Manuel Castells' definition that we call urban design the symbolic attempt to express an accepted urban meaning in certain urban forms, we then have to ask what is constituted in the term 'meaning'. We might then wish to know how meanings are produced, consumed, circulated and exchanged, as well as how they are distorted, disguised, transformed or suppressed, first as a general question and then in relation to the built environment. Although philosophers had argued for millennia over the meaning of life in all its forms, it was a Swiss philosopher called Ferdinand de Saussure who was the first to systematically investigate the chaos of the modern world through a meta-theory called semiotics, the science of signs. I use the term *meta* because of its pan-disciplinary nature, having generated new theoretical insights into a host of disciplines including, but not limited to, history, anthropology, psychology, psychotherapy, sociology, communication theory, literature, painting, cinematography, architecture and urban design. Given that Saussure wrote only one paper during his life on the system of vowels in Indo-European languages and that his doctoral thesis was on the use of the genitive case in Sanskrit, it is astounding that his legacy has endured into the twenty-first century. After his death, it was left to Saussure's students to assemble his notes into *La Cours de Linguistique Générale* (The Course on General Linguistics), a work that was to bring into existence the science of meaning.

Saussurian semiology contends that our cultural environment constitutes an immense system of meanings that is structured around a complex amalgam of codes (Barthes 1964, Eco 1976). These sign systems are composed of messages that become encoded in music, food, gestures, ritual, advertising, buildings, spaces and all other areas of human activity, of which language is arguably the most important. The ideological complex through which society maintains order, socialises its consumers, reproduces its own economic and political power elite, and builds its cities can therefore be considered one vast system of signs. Conversely, sign systems may be decoded, permitting the comprehension, manipulation or modification of human behaviour by such understanding. The method of semiology is first to separate an act (or an object) called the 'signifier' from its meaning, called the 'signified'. The sign may therefore be defined as the union of a form with an idea. The major characteristic of the sign is that it is arbitrary. Words, for example, are simply collective social conventions that can and do change radically over time and which vary from one linguistic group to another. At the same time, intellectual concepts are not universal. Language therefore articulates its own reality as well as its own particular signifying system, so the study of language and the study of semiotics bear a close relation to each other. This is best expressed in the Sapir–Whorf hypothesis that language is not neutral; it is a profound means of shaping a particular culturally defined reality: 'The worlds in which different societies lie are distinct worlds, not merely the same world with different labels attached' (Sapir 1921: 76). Signs therefore constitute units of relations and hence hold the key to the concept of meaning in society, by exposing the existing connections between language, thought and reality.

Semiotics studies all cultural processes as means of communication, and analyses social codes as systems of signification. This has important implications for studies of urban form, since each built environment discipline employs methods of signification that engage particular semiotic opportunities and limitations. Eco creates a general theory of culture from semiotics that in his opinion replaces the discipline of cultural anthropology: 'objects, behaviour and relationships of production and value, function as such socially, precisely because they obey semiotic laws' (Eco 1976: 27). At the same time he is careful to indicate that the radical hypotheses 'culture is only communication' or 'culture is no more than a system of structured significations' are dangerously idealistic. A semiotic analysis is essentially a way of seeing, and its employment can enlighten not only our cultural perspective but also our analyses of other theoretical positions that employ signifying systems. Furthermore, Eco suggests that the three elementary constituent phenomena of any culture may be denied the communicative function; these are (a) the production and employment of objects used for transforming the relationships between man and nature; (b) kinship relations as the primary nucleus of institutionalised social relations; and (c) the economic exchange of goods.

Semiological analysis of urban and architectural form is now an accepted mode of interpretation and an important contributor to design philosophy (*DC* 9). One may cite seminal works in the field by Jencks and Baird (1969), Venturi et al. (1977), Broadbent (1977, 1990), Krampen (1979) and Preziosi (1979), the paper by Broadbent (1977) being an excellent introduction to the subject. The architectonic universe may be defined as a four-dimensional hierarchically organised, codified, cultural and physical system that is articulated by the distribution of mass, space and the properties of materials. Architecture and language are locked together in the human consciousness to the degree that our physical environment has pragmatic, syntactic and semantic features that are represented in both physical and symbolic relationships. Many contemporary architects use a historically derived vocabulary of images and details to generate their own unique form of architectural expression, much of which is ideologically compromised by the nature of their clients, i.e. corporate monopolies, state institutions, private capital, etc. (see for example the work of Michael Graves, Robert Stern, Arturo Isozaki, James Stirling, Charles Moore, Yasafumi Kijima, Mario Botta, Philip Johnson and Ricardo Bofill). In Jencks' own words, 'those who damn Post-Modern Classicism as kitsch and consumer pabulum are pointing to an undoubted half-truth' (Jencks 1977: 75).

Kitsch is also countered by substantial philosophical questions about semiotics that can dominate design, as it has in the case of Italian architects after the First World War who inherited a contemporary history of fascist architecture. Since the representation also borrowed heavily from ancient Rome, the association contaminated their entire urban history. Italian architects therefore had to face one of the most profound philosophical questions of our time: because of their history, their urban symbols could not be reused because of their fascist attachments, of torture, death and the annihilation of peoples. How therefore could they re-semanticise this historical inheritance? How could past symbols be redeployed at another level of signification, as memory from the past, a catharsis in the present and an inspiration for the future? For this reason one could argue that they had only one way out, a process described by Charles Jencks as a 'reduction to archetypes', facilitated by the semiological possibilities of a syntax of empty signs, symbolised by Aldo Rossi in his proposal for Modena Cemetery and the Gallaretese Quarter of Milan.

Semiotics, like all other disciplines, is not above criticism. For example, Preziosi has suggested that the attempt to generate a general semiotics of architecture contains a 'near fatal flaw' in that

> architecture, as an autonomous system of signs, does not really exist except as a lexical label for certain arbitrarily restricted artefactual portions of the built environment, a picture artificially perpetuated by obsolete academic departmentalisation. By hindsight, the attempt to develop a semiotics of building is rather like trying to understand the organisation of language through a study of proper nouns.
>
> (Preziosi 1979: 3)

A semiological approach to urban form has been criticised by both Tafuri (1980) and Scruton (1979). Tafuri attacked semiology on the basis that it is 'behaviourism in disguise'. He remarks that to adopt the semiological function as the main purpose of architecture is to remove it from the world of primary forms, and that such a stance tacitly accepts the peripheral role assigned to it by the present capitalist use of land. Roger Scruton's criticism is based primarily on the limitations of linguistic analogy to explain urban forms, arguing that there seems to be no consensus on the most important features of language to be adopted as a basis for analogue models.

Nonetheless, Henri Lefebvre's proposition that a theory of meta-language should be based upon logical, philosophical and linguistic research reflects the undeniable importance of linguistics as a model for science and scholarship in general. This has been clearly enunciated in Lefebvre (1968), Habermas (1976) and Eco (1984). In *The German Ideology*, Marx and Engels note the important relationship between language and political consciousness. Language codes and socialisation patterns can either extend or hinder the linguistic, social and political competence of the individual, and language may be perceived as an important device in maintaining social equilibrium. Marx himself maintained that all ideologies distort because of their source within the class system. In this respect it would appear that linguistic studies play a significant role in contributing to a Marxist analysis of social class by allowing a more sophisticated interpretation to emerge (Baudrillard 1981). To effectively analyse the overall logic of consumption, Baudrillard suggests the need for four *logics*, a system that could well be applied to the consumption of urban form:

1   a functional logic of use value;
2   an economic logic of exchange value;
3   a logic of symbolic exchange;
4   a logic of sign value.

> The first is a logic of practical operations, the second one of equivalence, the third, ambivalence, the fourth, difference. Or again, a logic of utility, a logic of the market, a logic of the gift, and a logic of status. Organised in accordance with one of the above groupings, the object assumes respectively the status of an *instrument*, a *commodity*, a *symbol*, or a *sign*.
>
> (Baudrillard 1981: 66)

Baudrillard's desire to reject Marxist theory only results in a more sophisticated rendering of Marx's basic project by deepening the signification of culture and ideology through semiotic theory. Umberto Eco has also suggested that the exchange of commodities may be seen as a semiotic event. This observation refers to the process of signification or symbolisation applied to the transformation of use value into exchange value via the cash nexus, a process which also 'stands for' something else (Eco 1976: 25). This is captured in an ineluctable passage from Harvey about the semiotic nature of the built environment and the relationship between labour, capital and the urban landscape, when he says:

Capital represents itself in the form of a physical landscape created in its own image, created as use values to enhance the progressive accumulation of capital. The geographical landscape that results is the crowning glory of past capitalist development. But at the same time it expresses the power of dead labour over living labour, and as such it imprisons and inhibits the accumulation process within a set of physical constraints... Under capitalism there is, then, a perpetual struggle, in which capital builds up a physical landscape appropriate to its own condition at a particular moment in time, only to have to destroy it, usually in the course of a crisis at a subsequent point in time.

(Harvey 1985: 25)

Phenomenology

Phenomenology also features large as a philosophy informing the design of cities, and at its most essential simply means the study of phenomena. Probably its most direct link with sociology is to the Chicago School and its emergent practices (Lewis 2002: 59). Phenomenology is one of the central branches of contemporary philosophy in the twentieth century, while remaining somewhat marginal to social science as a whole. The two great sources of this tradition were the German philosopher Edmund Husserl (who was trained in mathematics) and his student Martin Heidegger (a theologist). The tradition also encompasses the work of Maurice Merleau-Ponty, Peter Berger, Jean Paul Sartre and Alfred Schutz. The key reference points here are Merleau-Ponty's *Phenomenology of Perception* (1962), Martin Heidegger's *Being and Time* (1962) and Sartre's *Being and Nothingness: A Phenomenological Essay on Ontology* (1956). Husserl (1931) argued that in everyday life, the individual's 'natural attitude' merely accepted the world as self-evident. Their reality was accepted but not interrogated. The process of breaking free from this naive understanding of the world required what he called *époche*, the method of suspending belief. All empirical information has to be discarded so that a transcendental state of communication could be achieved. This was almost the complete reversal of the Cartesian *cogito ergo sum* (I think therefore I am), where one's existence had no apparent bearing on one's environment. Husserl's concern was to understand what we do when we try to order or make sense of the world, in other words to comprehend acts of consciousness. The central problem here is that consciousness is always mediated, a process that Husserl wished to bypass so that the real essence of the object could be experienced directly (Fuery and Mansfield 1997). So Husserl was concerned with the nature of *individual* consciousness. As John Lechte (1994: 30) comments, 'for the phenomenologist, there are no ideal, universal certainties at the level of ideas'. Individual consciousness was therefore a condition that required both a knowing subject as well as something that is known: 'the true nature of our knowing a tree, for example, cannot be adduced by examining the tree or by simply assuming that the tree exists. The phenomenology of the tree is embedded in the consciousness of the knower' (Lewis 2002: 60). If we replace the concept 'tree' with the concept 'building' or 'urban space' we can see more clearly how a study of phenomenology has had

significant impact on studies of perception and experience in the built environment. Following from this is the idea that there is no collective perception, all
perception being a function of the lived experience of the individual. As Sartre
has so famously commented, 'Man is condemned to be free', meaning that his
life is truly existential, the moral essence of this condition being the absolute
responsibility of every individual for every action they take from the time of their
birth. Heidegger moved Husserl's work forward: 'the central idea in Heidegger's
work is that understanding is a *mode of being*, rather than a *mode of knowledge*,
an ontological problem rather than an epistemological problem. It is not about
how we establish knowledge; it is about how human beings exist in the world.
Understanding is the basis of being human' (Blaikie 1993: 34).

These ideas, of the knowing subject and of the embedding of consciousness
through lived experience, is symbolised effectively by one of the Frankfurt
School philosophers, Walter Benjamin, in the concept of the *flâneur*. Benjamin's
flâneur is a person who relates to the city solely through the world of the senses,
by direct kinaesthetic and Levantine experience of its places and spaces, wan-
dering from one event to another, spending the time of day soaking up whatever
events occur. However, Griselda Pollock notes that the experience of the
flâneur is wholly masculine and reflects the phenomenology of the male gaze –
consuming, detached, and impassive 'but the *flâneur* is an exclusively masculine
type which functions within the matrix of bourgeois ideology through which the
social spaces of the city were reconstructed by the overlaying doctrine of separate spheres on to the division of public and private, which became as a result of a
gendered division' (Pollock 2000: 162). Whether feminism will ultimately generate a *flâneuse* with her own specified gaze is something yet to be worked
through. The idea of the *flâneur* is also embedded in De Certeau's classic essay
Walking in the City (1993), where he reverses the rational comprehensive
method of traditional planning ideology by a process of designing via direct
experience of urban life (a process which Lawrence Halprin had tried to systematise by analogy with labanotation, the language of dance choreography, over
thirty years ago in 1969).

The most notable phenomenologist in architectural and urban design theory is
Christian Norberg-Schulz and his great trilogy inspired several generations of
architects and urban designers: *Intentions in Architecture* (1964), *Existence,
Space and Architecture* (1971) and *Genius Loci: Towards a Phenomenology of
Architecture* (1979). His important 1976 article, which condensed the essence of
his philosophy, was called 'The phenomenon of place' (*DC* 8). Throughout his
work Norberg-Schulz makes frequent reference not only to Husserl, Heidegger
and Gaston Bachelard (*The Poetics of Space*, 1969) but also to the famous child
psychologist Jean Piaget. Piaget's clear connection to phenomenology was not
through his famous treatise on *Structuralism* (1971) but through a prior and
much more empirical work concentrating on consciousness, called *The Child's
Construction of Reality* (Piaget 1955).

Despite Norberg-Schulz's focus on architecture in the titles of his books, he
designates 'architecture' as having a somewhat encompassing horizon. His

search for 'the elements of existential space' for example, and indeed most of his oeuvre, has as much to do with a theory of space and urban design as it does with a theory of architecture. Indeed, in chapter 2 of *Existence, Space and Architecture*, space is reduced to elementary particles in a series of vectors and diagrams seeking to explain the necessary relation space–existence. Norberg-Schulz, in defining the basic schemata of existential space in terms of a child's perceptions, attempts to construct a spatial vocabulary that is essential and undistorted, reflecting Husserl's concept of *époche*. Norberg-Schulz's typological schemata are therefore much closer to Jungian archetypes than they are to everyday descriptions of place. He talks about levels of existential space (geographic, landscape and urban) within which particular typologies exist, from basic material objects to specific landscape and urban forms. This philosophy is crystallised in his quote from Heidegger when he says, 'Heidegger furthermore points out "when I go towards the exit of a room, I am already there, and would not be able to go there unless I was already there". In other words, *mobility* presupposes a structured image of the environment, an existential space which contains generalized as well as particular orientations' (Norberg-Schulz 1971: 43). Norberg-Schulz also recognises the relation between some of his work and that of Kevin Lynch's attempts to concretise the specificity of urban elements, while criticising his approach for according 'character' and 'meaning' to these. In addition 'he limits himself, however, to discuss the spatial function of these elements, and thus leaves us with a fragmentary understanding of dwelling' (Norberg-Schulz 1979: 124). Curiously, there is no reference to any phenomenologists in Lynch's books (nor even any reference to Norberg-Schulz in Lynch's *opus magnum* of 1981, *A Theory of Good City Form*).

The basic tenets of phenomenology feed into urban design in a variety of ways, the closest direct link being through environmental psychology and, by extension, into behaviourism. These disciplines deal with the mediation of the politically incorrect man–environment relations (Proshansky et al. 1970, Downs and Stea 1978, Hollahan 1982). One of the most debatable outcomes of this overall process resulted in Oscar Newman's ideas on defensible space (1971, 1973, 1976, 1980), much criticised in a withering analysis by Bill Hillier ('In defense of space', 1973), on the dominance of the symbolic over the material aspects of urban space. In recent years environmental psychology has run out of steam, probably due to an inadequate articulation with any substantial theory, phenomenology in particular. Phenomenology has had a diffuse application across a variety of concerns, primarily in architecture and urban design, for example in interpretations of history and theory (Norberg-Schulz 1964, 1971, 1979), in the workings of power (Dovey 1999), in perceptions of space (Kallus 2001), in regard to placemaking and authenticity (Salah Ouf 2001, Aravot 2002, Jiven and Larkham 2003), in the restatement of the idea of 'community' (Schusterman 1999, Hillier and Hanson 1984) and in the actual physical design of urban space (Relph 1976). Most of the important applications of phenomenology have been in the context of creating 'place' and its associated concepts of placemaking, placelessness, identity, and so on. In a recent work, Aravot (2002) argues for going back to phenomenological placemaking, despite much recent criticism of the position based upon its essentialism, claims to universals, its humanistic leanings, the deconstruction of its basic tenets by Derrida and Lyotard, and the association of one of phenomenology's leading figures, Martin Heidegger, with the Nazis. Despite these criticisms, Aravot defends phenomenological placemaking as central to urban design:

> There is little dispute about the multidimensionality of sense of place; it is cultural, physical, spiritual and social. Therefore phenomenological placemaking is more a guiding principle than a model. It may be compared to Harvey's account of the concepts of justice and rationality, which are expressed in very different forms, in different forms in different places, times and cultures, but nevertheless retain their abstract functions as ideals.
>
> (Aravot 2002: 209)

Phenomenological criticism extends beyond the actual experience and design of urban space into architectural form, a movement spearheaded by Alberto Perez-Gomez, Dalibor Vesely and others at the University of Essex in the UK. Perez-Gomez's main text, *Architecture and the Crisis of Modern Science* (1983), argued against the abstract mechanistic rationalism of modernist architecture in favour of an architecture whose foundation was based in direct experience of the world. He argues that architects have been sorely limited on the basis that:

> A simplistic view of human experience derived from the projection of human scientific models on to human reality, exemplified by certain aspects of behaviourism and positivistic psychology, has hampered our understanding of the essential continuity between thought and action, between mind and body. Because architectural theory is assumed to imply absolute rationality, it has been considered capable of standing on its own, free of all relations to fundamental philosophical questions.
>
> (Perez-Gomez 2000: 469)

Marxian political economy

> Marx is the first great post-modern intellectual because he is an antihumanist and because he defines progress as the liberation of nature, and not as the realization of a conception of man. The important thing about Marxist thought is that it replaces a rebellion waged in the name of the human subject with an analysis of the contradictions of capitalism.
>
> (Touraine 1995: 104)

Tom Bottomore notes that Marx began his life as a philosopher, a discipline that he was later to reject as potentially harmful to understanding since it was so far removed from the material reality of everyday life: 'of all types of theory, it is science that is closest to reality and most capable of depicting it, whereas philosophy is a form of theory that subjects even its most penetrating insights to systematic distortion' (Bottomore 1983: 370). Despite suggesting the end of philosophy and its supercession by science, Marxism had profound relationships with the Hegelian tradition, French socialism and British political economy, not to mention Aristotle and Darwin. From these origins, Marx synthesised his own unique philosophy, which has itself undergone various interrogations and transformations by other great thinkers such as George Lukacs, Louis Althusser, Antonio Gramsci, Jurgen Habermas, Klaus Offe, Alain Touraine, Manuel Castells, David Harvey, Antonio Negri and many others. Of these, probably Althusser was the most significant critic of Marx's original philosophy. Althusser resisted the Hegelian influence in Marx with its humanist tendencies, maintaining that Marxist philosophy was in fact a philosophy of science, despite its political and ideological focus. The power of the Marxian tradition remains with us and has affected many theorists across a whole range of disciplines. It also endures as a significantly contested region of intellectual investigation, even among those who remain its most ardent supporters, for several main reasons. First, not only is it a philosophy, it is simultaneously a theory of history, sociology, a science, a theory of economics, an ideology and an epistemology. Second, while one could argue for redundancy in every avenue of Marxian thinking, this would be a serious mistake as well as a major misunderstanding of his work by ignoring the transformative nature of his ideas. Indeed, the more people rail against Marxism (in any of its reincarnations), the longer its relevance survives and the more enduring it becomes. Third, there are few disciplines within the social sciences that remain untouched by his method. Fourth, it remains the best critique of capitalism ever written.

Fundamental to Marxian philosophy is the principle of dialectical materialism, which maintains that our reality is composed of contradictions that drive historical development. 'Matter' and 'mind' are conceived of as opposing dimensions of a reality where the material element is primary. Marxian theory suggests that some rather fundamental laws govern the processes of human evolution, and that such laws relate directly to the historical thresholds of the various forms of capital development. All human requirements in this continuum are seen to be contingent upon both social and economic structures which change dynamically over historical time. As human beings come together to manufacture the material necessities of life, the productive process becomes transformed into a social event.

As society reproduces itself, a set of social and property relations are also established and reproduced over time, based upon the private ownership of, or control over, land, property and the means of production. This cleaves society into two divisions: those who possess capital in its various forms, and who are therefore in a position to purchase labour power, and those who are forced to sell their labour in order to survive (Marx sometimes referred to three classes, labour, landowners and capitalists). The real foundation of society is therefore its economic structure (base), upon which superstructural forms are then built (legal, political, institutional, ideological, etc.). Because of the fantastic divergence in privilege, power and the material necessities of life which exist between these two classes, as well as their overwhelming difference in membership, superstructural forms may be interpreted either as necessary social controls or as forms of domination that are required to reinforce the social hierarchy. The state is called into existence to manage the affairs of capital so it can get on with doing what it does best, generating interest, rent, profit and surplus value from labour.

A historical materialist conception of ideology therefore links ideological forms (organised religion, the law, education) to their historical degrees of salience, to their articulation with other ideologies, and in their relation to different social classes and class relations where the controlling ideology remains that of the dominant class. As David Harvey observes, 'What Marx depicts therefore, are social processes at work under capitalism conducive to individualism, alienation, fragmentation, ephemerality, innovation, creative destruction, speculative development, unpredictable shifts in methods of production and consumption (wants and needs), a shifting experience of space and time, as well as a crisis-ridden dynamic of social change' (Harvey 1989: 111). In Frank Stillwell's recent book *Political Economy*, he denotes nine important themes emerging from Marxian philosophy that remain important today, from concepts of the nature of social change and social class, the expansionary nature of capitalism, uneven development, monopoly power and the role of the state, to its effects in the realm of commodification, exploitation and alienation (Stillwell 2002: 98).

Post-Marxist theory has developed not only from inconsistencies and faulty deduction in the original exposition but also from the inability of orthodox interpretations to explain the dynamic complexity of contemporary capitalist development. This reformulation is due in part to the empirical evidence that was available to Marx during his lifetime and to the actual historical evolution of society over the last 150 years that has contradicted many of his original assumptions. Marx's concentration on productive forces does not for example reflect the dominant importance of service economies within advanced capitalist societies and the functions of management and information as major economic activities, nor indeed the changes involved in the move from mode of production to mode of information (Castells 1989, 1996, Poster 1990, Sassen 1991, Smith, N. 2001). Nor did he ever anticipate the extent to which the exploited mass of labour, and its reserve army that acted as a safety valve for the exigencies of capitalist production, would be transformed. The conditions of organised labour necessarily improved in line with the ever-improving means of capital reproduction, in the provision of housing, education, health, welfare and other facilities. In addition, the political power of labour to generate change had a revolutionary effect on its own material life conditions via trade unions, urban social movements and other forms of resistance (see Smart 1983, chapter 1, 'The limits and limitations of Marxism'). Others, however, would argue that the overall trajectory of capitalism is lumbering forward on roughly the same principles, although with a vastly different dynamic and strategic focus (Harvey 2003). Globalisation can be seen as another triumph for capital, extending its boundaries beyond those of the nation state, opening up new markets and exploitive possibilities at a global scale. Imperialism is alive and well, driven by geopolitical strategies such as the recent 'wars' in Saudi Arabia, Afghanistan and Iraq. The condition of labour is now sufficiently improved so that the state can reduce in size and focus its attention away from social reproduction, to assist in new forms of capital accumulation through public–private partnerships. Problems of ideological dominance, alienation and commodity fetishism also remain, despite an increasingly articulate manipulation of difference – gender, ethnicity and religion for example, in the culture/capital relationship.

The direct consequence of all this to the study of urban form or to any emergent theory of urban design is that the forms of the built environment cannot be disconnected from the totality of the mode of production, to how space is allocated, owned, exchanged, transformed and institutionalised, to how it symbolises the relations of the society from which it emerges. This focuses attention on the actual reproduction of space, on the spatial forms of consumption processes and on the design and reproduction of the physical environment. As labour productivity increases, the reproduction of the social relations of production become increasingly important, and hence a change of emphasis is required within the economy from production to consumption and hence to social conflict related to the reproduction of labour power. Relevant here are problems related to urban development, the deployment of the consumption fund, to the increasing complexity of social structure and the competing interests which exist between classes and 'fractions' of classes, of problems related to the functioning of the state and its ability to subvert market laws, of urban planning and urban social movements, and to conflict related to the political allocation of urban space.

The central agency in this process is the state and the overall role of urban planning is critical, since it sets the environment for urban design. Here we get into somewhat deep water in the sense that the role of the state within capitalism is riddled with controversy. Serious questions exist about its structure, its relation to capital and the relative autonomy or otherwise of its various components. There are various ideological positions (conservative/liberal, classical Marxist, neo-Marxist, state derivationist, corporatist/managerialist, neocorporatist, etc.) as well as at least six possible classifications within a historical materialist position alone (Jessop 1977: 354–7). Added to this, Boris Frankel in his classic *Beyond the State* published over twenty years ago rejected the idea of 'civil society' and the division of all social relations neatly between the state, civil society and the economy (Frankel 1983). Frankel also maintains that there are at least four dominant misconceptions of the state: as a thing, an ideal type, a subject or a derivative part of capital. We can compound these difficulties even further by considering the vastly differing views of Marx and Foucault on power (Louis Althusser being one of Foucault's former teachers). We can parody this relationship by saying that within Marxism, domination is always implicit, whereas for Foucault, since power is not located in subjects, resistance is not confrontational since power is not conceptualized as a possession or a privilege; rather it is considered to be exercised through 'dispositions, manoeuvres, tactics, techniques, functionings'. Power relations are not localized in confrontations between social classes or between citizens and the state; rather they are conceptualized as existing at the most elemental level of the social domain and might be said to constitute it.

(Smart 1983: 87)

Isolating out the Marxian perspective, the relationship between urban planning, the state and space has been widely discussed in Preteceille (1982), Scott and Roweis (1977), Kiernan (1983), Harvey (1985), Dear (1986, updated in Dear 2000) and Merrifield (2000).

Undeniable, however, is that urban planning, unlike its associated 'environmental' disciplines (architecture, landscape architecture, urban design, environmental design) is the only discipline wholly dependent on its embeddedness within the state apparatus. In other words, it comes into existence solely on the basis of its juridical (ideological) function, and is defined by it:

The planner requires something else as well as a basic understanding of how the system works from a purely technical standpoint. In resorting to tools of repression, cooptation, and integration, the planner requires justification and legitimation, a set of powerful arguments with which to confront warring factional interests and class antagonisms. In striving to affect reconciliation, the planner must perforce resort to the idea of the potentiality for harmonious balance in society. And it is on this fundamental notion of social harmony that the ideology of planning is built.

(Harvey 1985: 176)

All of these considerations impact heavily on urban design. Just as the practices that constitute urban planning discourse are a subset of the legal code, the practice of urban design is multivalent in that its power does not originate from a single source. Urban design practice is located across all state planning departments, dependent agencies, private sector firms in all environmental disciplines, and across many academic programmes within tertiary education. Urban design in this context has at least four levels of functioning, where the interpenetration of one level with another is complex and not reducible to a single formula without extensive qualification.

1   Urban design reinforces those processes of production that underwrite the reproduction of the financial/informational mode of capitalism, specifically related to land development, for example in conceptualising the most efficient use of space for the maintenance of property values, and in perpetuating and extending the incessant reproduction of capital from land via development and redevelopment. At the centre of this process is the exploitation of land as a commodity and its appropriate packaging for sale, furthering the interests of property capital and its relationship to the establishment of land policies that enhance the extraction of ground rent, profit from floor space and surplus value from construction. Urban design assists in correlat-

ing patterns of land ownership and tenure, reinforcing state policies related to land development, and in lubricating the workings of the juridical system in legitimising the whole operation. In addition, urban design also has a role in conflict resolution between the various capitals interested in land development – property, industrial and finance capital in particular. Overall, since fixed capital in the built environment is constantly degrading, continued opportunities for recycling profits must be maintained: 'Having devoured the resources of urbanization, capital complains of diseconomies, urban anarchy and pathology' (Preteceille 1977: 23).

2 Urban design is the central process for implementing state planning policies with regard to spatial requirements for individual, collective and luxury consumption, and to the overall spatial needs of urban administration. This involves impacting institutional and class locations and boundaries through socially appropriate technologies and bureaucratic procedures (codes, statutes, policies, plans) through to administering 'planning' policy (development and design controls in particular). The central focus here is the public realm, the space where social reproduction connects with the market and where civil society spends its leisure time. The role of urban design is indispensable since policy planning is incapable of conceptualising appropriate spatial forms and relationships. Urban design also has a key role in mitigating outcomes – social conflict which may arise from the inadequate provisions of the consumption fund, resulting in demands (qualitative and quantitative) at individual and collective levels.

3 Urban design is also involved in facilitating commodity circulation, in the physical design and organisation of infrastructure at all levels, and in the provision of facilities for transport functions. Of significance here is the increasing role of urban design in the production of spectacles as intra-urban competition grows and cities become locked into a Darwinian struggle for survival. Spectacular production in the form of Olympic Games, trade and world fairs, grand prix, international conventions, political summits, art festivals and other events may represent the difference between financial success and failure. Or, as in Bilbao, the right building at the right moment can rejuvenate an entire city.

4 Finally, urban design assists the ideological, symbolic and semiotic requirements of the various capitals and the state in relation to an appropriate codification of their ideological needs. Symbolic representation is present even in negation, and ownership of the image, branding and corporate symbolism increasingly configure urban design with a continually changing urban semiotic of space and form.

In other words the design process is embedded at every level in the social hierarchy. It also impacts vertically through the overall system of urban practices, and thus reflects the contingent ideologies of the various capitals as they percolate down through the operational mechanisms of the state to reappear on the other side of the process as urban form. This situation above all others appears to deny the possibility of any coherent theory of urban design ever emerging, except as it directly relates to these encompassing processes.

These four levels of analysis address both urban (production) and non-urban (consumption) functions, as well as those of circulation and exchange. A strict definition of 'urban' design in Castells' terms would therefore limit itself to the manner in which the spatial aspect of consumption processes was physically organised and appears in building form. It would correspond to the configuration and locational pattern of everyday life, dissociated from the processes of production, storage, individual consumption, etc. There would appear, from the above analysis, to be sufficient evidence to propose at least one axiom which of itself contradicts most urban design theory, that all urban space is designed. The assumption that chance and probability operate in some areas and not in others is to be avoided. Urban design is a process which applies to the totality of the built environment, not simply to those examples of professionalised urban space that accommodate the most concrete if transient and expedient manifestations of capital development.

Chapter Four
Politics

Politics is war without the guns.
                    Mao Tse-tung

Introduction: Politics and Ideology

Discourses are loci of power, they must be read from the
vantage point not of the author or the intended audience,
but from the perspective of how they constitute a power
relation.
                            Poster (1984: 131)

Space has been shaped and moulded from historical
and natural elements, but this has been a political
process. Space is political and ideological. It is a
product literally filled with ideology.
                            Henri Lefebvre

The above quotation by Henri Lefebvre suggests how crucial it is for urban designers to study the political dimension of urban life and to comprehend the significance
of ideology to this process. Politics is represented at the intersection of the economic
with the social, mediated through ideology. Urban design is an instrument of class
politics as well as an important method of social control and liberation. It constitutes the space where political ideologies are played out in concrete form. While the
role of economic systems in creating spatial structures is well understood, exactly
how ideological systems do the same thing remains open terrain. Not only does
urban space provide the theatre for social struggle, as many great urban spaces will
attest, it is also the ultimate symbolic representation of the conflicts, aspirations and
values of past generations. The complex matrix of buildings and spaces in all great
cities embraces us with the stories, philosophies, consciousness, religions, wars,
heroes and heroines, of the failures, victories and dreams of our ancestors, all
immortalised within the public realm (Madanipour 1999).

   Urban designers are charged with the custodianship of a complex archaeology
that contains the memories, reflections and dreams of their culture, materialising

as the architecture of public realm. Their mandate is to contribute meaningfully and consciously to this process. On the surface, urban designers may be involved in the somewhat mundane process of fulfilling a client brief, implementing a local area environmental plan, or assembling development controls for some nebulous planning authority. These processes are however contingent upon much deeper and enduring undercurrents. At a fundamental level, and as a matter of their own legitimation, urban designers should remain conscious of their involvement in the historically generated ideological process of reproducing urban space. This awareness will allow them to realise how they fit into the overall trajectory of social development, how the culture and civilisation they have been privileged to serve should be recorded in stone and mortar for future generations, for their children, and for their children's children. This is one of the most important tasks in society, for philosophies and ideologies do not represent themselves abstractly in our environment but in and through its architecture and urban spaces.

Modern political ideologies come in many forms (Dunleavy 1980, Vincent 1992, Leach 1993). Within contemporary western democracies, where there is a separation of powers between the political process, the judiciary and organised religion, traditional political forms begin with the left (anarchism, communism and democratic socialism), through liberalism in the centre, extending to conservatism and fascism on the right. In addition, contemporary politics have generated other important ideologies that Leach (1993) refers to as 'cross spectrum ideologies' such as imperialism and racism, arguably pan-political strategies, and others such as feminism, the Green movement and the Rainbow Coalition that are centred round issues of equality between the sexes, the environment, gender issues, etc. This picture is made even more complex by the idea of supra-national ideologies such as neocorporatism, the ideological strategy of business in a world where national boundaries (and hence national ideologies) become eroded in the interests of the global marketplace. There are of course at least another two worlds where these ideologies do not wholly comply: firstly, within totalitarian state socialism in China and, secondly, in Islamic states where feudal social relations maintain a homology between politics, religion, the judiciary and the military, yet operate within the capitalist world economy. Political ideologies are fundamentally unstable. They have shifting relationships with other ideological systems as well as being subject to internal conflict and competition between subgroups. Great wars have been fought between capitalist states, which have the same ideology, and between groups with the same religion, for example between Iran and Iraq.

It should be quite clear to urban designers, even at a very simplistic level, how specific ideologies have had huge impacts on urban space and form. Socialist cities in China had, until recently, an almost uniform density and height from one side of the city to the other, resulting from the prevalence of use values and the abolition of private property and private business: there was no 'central business' to conduct and therefore no central business districts that characterised the capitalist cities of the West. Cities in the Islamic world (there are no 'Islamic cities') have evolved unique forms of architecture and urban space based upon religious beliefs and, in extreme cases, almost total segregation of the sexes and the incarceration of women. The semiotics of urban space is similarly affected: what is expressed, what is hidden and what is stored in memory has infinite variation, reflecting historically contingent, dominating and dependent ideologies. It is clear that urban designers are bombarded, covertly or otherwise, with a whole series of ideological constructs, from the overall progress of global capitalism to their own education and beliefs. Yet while ideological intervention at the urban level is a complex intangible process, it materialises and is articulated within state institutions, dominated by the legal system, and in the expression of private sector influence across the entire economic spectrum. The specific ideology most directly affecting urban designers is therefore that of urban planning and its statutes which legitimise state ideology in regard to the reproduction of land for development. However, before we look at the actual material effects of ideological production on urban form, we must briefly look at how ideologies are to be understood, how they are constructed and configured, and how they contour and support various forms of power.

To consider ideology in any depth is a lifetime's work, and large tracts of library stacks are devoted to its study (Gramsci 1971, Althusser 1984, Laclau and Mouffe 1985, Habermas 1987, Castoriadis 1987, Balaben 1995). The problem can be made simple if we say that ideology can be defined as any system of belief along with the institutions that support it. Whenever we move from this position, the world becomes infinitely more complex:

> Ideologies are bodies of concepts, values, and symbols which incorporate conceptions of human nature and thus indicate what is possible or impossible for humans to achieve; critical reflections on the nature of human interaction; the values which humans ought either to reject or to aspire to; and the correct technical arrangements for social, economic and political life which will meet the needs and interests of human beings.
>
> (Vincent 1992: 16)

Problems of ideology therefore begin to access almost every dimension of intellectual investigation, in its relationship to history, science, politics, ethics, culture, philosophy and religion. In this context, any coherent picture of what ideology *is* becomes almost impossible, and a retreat to Marx's simple definition that ideology is merely false consciousness is enticing in its elegance. Marx also suggested that ideology was an inverted version of the truth, comparing it in *The German Ideology* to a camera obscura where the real image (truth) becomes inverted. Vincent goes on to suggest that the fundamental difference between ideology and philosophy is the active role played by ideology within society. In other words, ideologies are the militant aspect of philosophy. To live they need to be practised. Ideologies cannot sit on the shelf waiting for things to happen, but exist as systems of practices or *discourses* and are open to massive shifts in their own internal logic and objectives; witness Marxism over the last 150 years. Power is the medium through which ideologies function, and how power is formed, captured, owned, traded and distorted is central to an understanding of ideology (Lukes 1986).

Power: Rights and Laws

The concept of control lies at the heart of any social system. Indeed the terms 'society', 'control' and 'repression' are to a large extent synonymous. Societies differ in regard to the nature and form of control exercised over the physical and mental bodies of individuals via childhood socialisation processes, education, religion, language, urban politics and other important elements. So the argument is not one of more or less control, but of the historical relation between social control and individual rights. As history progresses, it appears that the nature of such control diversifies as the technological, bureaucratic and customary rule systems through which social life is conducted rapidly multiply. At the same time the underlying quality of these controls has shifted in both form and content over the last century, from the physical to the psychological, from the body to the mind, from coercion to persuasion, from domination to negotiation, from active consumption to passive compliance, from social space to what Foucault terms the 'heterotopic' spaces that exist outside the communion of the social body, and from the lumbering progress of industrial capitalism to a new world order (*DC* 26).

While Marx's concept of power is inseparable from capital, diametrically opposing views also exist. For example, Foucault's concept of power cannot be detached from its foundation in knowledge (Gordon 1980, Smart 1983). Foucault rejects the idea that power can only be deduced from the economy, where it is defined purely in terms of control over the means of production. He maintains that power cannot be held in the manner of property. It cannot be owned like capital, it is not located in subjects and it cannot be traded like a commodity. Therefore domination in the Marxist sense cannot exist. Rather power reflects how society is structured within historically constituted and evolving grids of practices (discourses), which necessarily hold *all* classes captive.

Foucault maintains that power is not a monopoly to be wielded by any single individual, organisation or state institution. In order to make this distinction clear, he used the terms 'power/knowledge' together in order to remove power from any concept of sovereignty, and the term 'disciplinary power' to distinguish his modernist concept of power from the old prohibitive and repressive forms of the Enlightenment. In the Marxist model where the concept of repression is alive and well, domination is implicit but so is resistance. To Foucault, however, the concept of resistance is irrelevant. There can be no counter-domination since power is not located in subjects. If resistance exists, it does not function politically in the Foucauldian model. Rather it is seen to act through the individual's opposition to the disciplinary power exerted upon, and at the level of, the human body. In this sense the exercise of power is not monolithic but multivalent. It affects the individual's power to move and to think and to feel, to imagine and to dream, in short to be human.

Foucault's dialogue with Marxism (he is quoted as saying, 'for me, Marxism does not exist') is also exemplified in his resistance to definitions of power originating from either a juridical–liberal or a Marxian materialism. While varying in their basic assumptions, both are reducible to the determinism of economic forces. In the former, power is commodified and possessed as a right. That is, it becomes a material object within capitalism, and fits within the prevailing system of values. In the latter, power is conceived as maintaining and extending the forces and relations of production. In both, power serves the economy as a whole. Rather than creating an inseparable link between politics and economics, Foucault maintains that in removing that relation one also removes bias from the process of analysis (Smart 1983: 81). This does not mean that Foucault refuses to accept the concept that economic exploitation conditions power relations, but he rejects outright the idea of homogeneity of power relations based upon this principle. Similarly, he rejects the assumption that ideology or the Marxist 'false consciousness' are vehicles for power relations (Gordon 1980: 118–19). His position is that power does not emanate from a particular institution, organisation or social class, but is dispersed and intermingled within the social fabric. In order to understand power from a Foucauldian perspective, we must begin with the assumption that it is not part of any subject. The most important tasks in analysing power relations are therefore to reveal how discourses act as 'a system of formal statements about the world' and 'to analyse their articulation with, and regulation by, non-discursive practices (social and institutional practices)' (Smart 1983: 96). As with all ideologies, it is futile to try to establish the primacy of one form of interpretation over another. Each may have benefits depending on social context, history, mode of investigation and other factors. I have found it useful to temper Marxian interpretations with those from other sources, for example Foucault, Habermas, Bhabha and Said. Overall, the most important ideological concept of urban designers, from whatever orientation, is the concept of *right*, and of the law in relation to urban planning as a set of discursive ideological practices (Castells 1983, Clark and Dear 1984, Sandercock 1990, Yiftachel and Alexander 1995).

Central to urban design knowledge is the concept of the right to the city, on which basis the concept of the public realm is established, and how the custodianship of this realm is legitimated. At its root, the principle of right is an analytically treacherous concept. Rights are not universal and unchanging but are defined within social systems and are dependent on society and environment for their meaning (Hobsbawm 1986). The concept of right is also tied into a complex value system that necessarily addresses concepts of democracy, justice, civil society, equality and social control; the *liberté, égalité, fraternité* sought by the French Revolution. In order to have discrete properties these must be connected to a system of government within which a particular pattern of social relations has been established. Even at the most general level, the principle of human rights and therefore of a Bill of Rights is alien to most modern societies (Rawls 1999, Harvey 2000 chapter 5). Such rights would include for example the right to life, to work, to have children, to share a public realm with other citizens. These rights should be inalienable and beyond the manipulation of the state or the private sector. In practice things are different. These basic human rights intersect with civil and political rights, the first involving the right to a particular way of life, the second the right to be involved in the organisation and administration of the state. In practice, human civil and political rights are conferred through the state, which administers the allocation of space and is responsible for its surveillance (Dandeneker 1990, Bogard 1996, Parker 2000). State power in this sense means the ability to control subject populations through a multiplicity of means, first as an ideological mechanism implementing the dominant prevailing ideologies, second in its command over repressive state institutions, and finally over the production of information and disinformation. As vehicles for state policy, the environmental professions assist this process, usually unwittingly, by creating, packaging, manipulating and designing spaces to suit. In this regard the question of the right to the city has become increasingly important to the conscience of urban planning, which actively negotiates the boundary between social relations and spatial structures on behalf of, or as proxy for, the state. As I have already suggested, state neocorporatism then places in serious doubt the idea that the state can retain any impartiality in a process thoroughly permeated by the ideology of private capital.

Here the central concern of urban designers is with the concept of the *public realm* and how this is constituted in practice. It is the space where use-values predominate and people lead their daily lives. Capital views the so-called public realm as a barrier to capital accumulation, a space for social purposes that might better be used for development. We have all seen manifestations of this as urban open space is constantly under siege. In cities where the most rapacious form of capitalism exists, such as Hong Kong, open space has been wholly expunged from urban areas. Offer the most beautiful and revered public space in any city to private developers to turn into any form of commercial development and the offer is unlikely to be refused. So at a fundamental level the concept of the public realm can be viewed as a space of conflict, one where civil society struggles to retain a significant urban presence and in the process erects barriers to further accumulation from land development. This is due to the fact that, in theory, the public realm is not commodified and therefore is not circulated as part of the urban land market. In practice, commodity circulation as part of the expansion of capital frequently needs more space for this activity. One of the first land uses to come under pressure is therefore the public realm, and there are countless examples of the erosion of public space for transport and other functions. The concept of the public realm and the right to the city is also being eroded by two other processes that I have documented elsewhere in two articles, 'The right to the city' (Cuthbert 1995b) and 'Ambiguous space, ambiguous rights?' (Cuthbert and McKinnel 1997). Here, two central questions are discussed in relation to Hong Kong that also hold general relevance for other world cities, namely the increasing neocorporate encroachment into the public realm and, in concert with this, deepening social control through surveillance activities. As a general principle, and in order to reduce the costs to the state of servicing, managing and policing public space, such spaces are increasingly being controlled and manipulated by private sector interests. This results not only in an escalation of both active (policing) and passive surveillance systems (telecommunications, environmental design), it erodes the concept of the right to the city through the increasing ambiguity of spaces and places, where one's right to possess the space as a citizen is by no means clear. These events are supported and propagated by urban planning and the environmental professions in general, a process which compounds social control by the state, and both physical control and electronic surveillance by private capital (Lyon 2002, Taylor 2002).

Law as Ideology

The manner in which the politico-juridical system impacts on spatial structures, whereby space is crafted, bounded, annexed, delineated and institutionalised to serve specific economic and political intentions, has been widely acknowledged. In addition, in so far as a large part of the social wage is explicitly organised via spatial units, the state derives functional benefits from the jurisdictional fragmentation of space (Kirby 1983: 228). Hence the continuing importance of political boundaries at the national, regional and local level, as well as the juridical fragmentation of space within individual plots is evident. Kirby empha- sises the bounding of space for political purposes, the function of the judicial system in organising the social wage via spatial units, and in the establishment of exclusionary practices which codify class interests in relation to spatial struc- tures: 'one implication of these analyses is that the location of boundaries is as important as what goes on within them' (Kirby 1983: 230).

Castells uses the term 'institutionalised space' to refer to the social processes which, on the basis of the juridico-political apparatus, structure space. He also denotes the ensemble of processes within which the institutional organisation of space is determined as those of integration, repression, domination and regula- tion (Castells 1977: 209). In contemporary capitalist societies Dear (1986: 379) has suggested that planning practice 'has devolved into a ritualised choreog- raphy of routines <and> will survive purely as a subordinate technocracy'. Preteceille denotes the juridical code as the embodiment of state intervention in the relations of production and circulation. He notes the important function which the state plays in operating 'a juridical definition of the conditions under which the different social agents can appropriate urban space, by defining land regulations and thus the type of possible use on a piece of land' (Preteceille 1977: 141). In addition, he reflects that this intervention in space also codifies social relations, in the present and in the future, by anticipating the controlled output of use-values.

In the literature on socio-spatial structures, two texts stand out in their effort to confront the ideological nature of planning law. First, a major work by McAuslan (1980) entitled *The Ideologies of Planning Law* is of singular import- ance in understanding the ideological foundations upon which legal practice sits in regard to socio-spatial problems. He says that 'the law is coming to be seen much more clearly for what it is: *a partisan participator in the struggle for control over power and resources*' (McAuslan 1980: 270; my italics), and identifies the three main ideologies traditionally associated with planning, stating that the law exists and should be used:

1   to protect private property;
2   to advance the public interest;
3   to advance the case of public participation.

Second, in *State Apparatus: Structures and Language of Legitimacy*, Clark and Dear (1984) set out to investigate the relationship between the state apparatus and the socio-spatial organisation of capitalist society. In this context, the nature of political language is emphasised as a vehicle in the social structuration of class relationships within capitalism. In the context of the legal system the authors make a preliminary attempt to analyse the state in linguistic terms, 'on the basis that all other articulations of the state to be examined in the book may properly be regarded as aspects of political language' (Clark and Dear 1984: 102). The most important contribution of this book is in its landmark attempt to connect language, law and space within the structure of political action.

Politics and Urban Planning

Theories of urban planning may be divided into two main perspectives: those that originate from an a priori theorisation about the organisation of society and the production of planning and planning knowledge from within that society, and those that do not. The latter (which incorporate most planning theory) see planning as a product of specific epistemological directives, unitary modes of thought or of development processes. While these frequently provide insightful and accurate accounts of how planning functions, they fail in the last analysis to generate a truthful synoptic explanation of how planning operates as part of the historical reproduction and development of society as a whole.

In the absence of this context, the function of planning (like law) within society is mystified by the inference that it is an autonomous and neutral agent, motivated by abstract ideas of the common good, with the object of improving the welfare of the entire population. While this has indeed happened within the developed economies, it was not because planning was permeated by altruistic motives. For example, the improved condition of the working class in the core imperialist economies was to a large degree predicated upon the deprivation and exploitation of labour power in the developing world as a result of colonial development (Warren 1980, Hoogveldt 1982). Arguably this situation has deepened, albeit in new forms, into the third millennium.

Accounts of planning theory that emerge from a claimed neutrality, while frequently offering coherent accounts of physical, economic and social processes, fail to explain their own ideological role. Therefore almost all theorisations of planning from within its own boundaries, however sophisticated they might be, are with rare exceptions either descriptions of capitalist urbanisation or ideological (false) accounts of the functioning of the capitalist system in regard to the built environment (Kiernan 1983). The superficial political neutrality of neoclassical economic theory is an example of one such philosophy, which has had a direct impact on urban planning. It was reinforced by the emergence of systems theory that drew from a range of disciplines as diverse as ecology and operations research. In fact the production of the first major critique of planning theory edited by Andreas Faludi in 1973 also marked a general reaction to the widespread deployment of systems theory within urban planning practice over the previous decade, whose attempts to depoliticise the planning process remain with us.

Materialist theory, on the other hand, views planning as an intervention in the overall process of production and circulation of commodities by the state, which is also called upon to manage conflicts emerging from the unequal distribution of the surplus product. Whereas a concept of equality exists within the law, as far as the formation of urban spatial structure is concerned, control over the procedures whereby space is appropriated remain private and are only limited by the order imposed through state regulation. Essential conflicts are then generated between the conditions required by the processes of capital accumulation with respect to space and the creation of use-values for the reproduction of labour power. The privatisation of urban land on the basis of individual legal control leads to a situation where the urban land nexus becomes somewhat anarchic and the most important role assigned to planning within it is to manage the extended reproduction of labour through the provision of items for collective consumption, such as housing, schools, health facilities, recreation (Castells 1977). Therefore urban planning practice and the mainstream planning theories which inform it

> can only be elucidated if seen as serving the ideological and apologetic functions that must inevitably arise in a society whose social and property relations are such that:
>
> 1   they call for ever escalating planning intervention on the one hand, while resisting and obstructing such intervention on the other; and,
> 2   they result in a form of state intervention that by its very nature produces massive systematic biases of various kinds in the distribution (and redistribution) of material rewards and penalties.   (Scott and Roweis 1977: 1114)

So planning is required to address problems which it is incapable of solving (the inherent contradictions of the capitalist state) and to mediate in problems that planning itself impacts (deriving from the unequal distribution of the socially designated surplus product). Furthermore, planning is also viewed with suspicion by the various capitals that sanction its efforts in providing controls that mediate between their various interests. Planning is therefore caught in the proverbial Gordian knot from which an intellectual or strategic exit is an unlikely possibility. Because of this situation, combined with the undeniable relationship between big capital and the planning function, Castells rejected orthodox planning practice as a process that could ever fairly represent the interests of labour. He relies instead on the idea of urban social movements as the most appropriate and truthful mechanism for the consolidation of urban problems. Interests are represented directly and immediately in relation to a commonly perceived problem, frequently bypassing the narrow sectarian interests of social class, gender, ethnicity, etc. Examples of this might be the alignment of freeways through urban areas, airport noise and the siting of runways, the relocation of nuclear reactors and nuclear waste, and the destruction of first-growth forests.

What then does this mean for our understanding of urban design? If we return to the idea that urban design is the symbolic attempt to create a certain urban meaning in certain urban forms, how do ideology, politics as ideology and planning as ideology, promote or stifle the production of symbolic arrangements, mediated through urban form? Here we can denote at least ten levels of structuration, each containing several key implications for urban design. These in turn will be elaborated in the examples that occur in the remainder of this chapter. Urban design knowledge is affected at every level and political ideologies impact on our knowledge/practice. At least a dozen important manifestations of this can be identified.

1   Through particular economic forms, for example capitalism, which commodifies land as a basic factor of production, packages it for sale and incorporates it into the realm of exchange (Scott 1980, Harvey 1985). Until recently, socialist states had provided entirely different ideological assumptions for urban development and design, and even within capitalism huge ideological differences exist from nation to nation.
2   In the West, this has had the historical effect of parcelling land in particular locations, dimensions, configurations and densities on the basis of specific social and property relations.
3   More germane, this process has involved the partition of space into public and private in accordance with a social and gendered division of labour, frequently supporting the spatial segregation of social classes.
4   In specific attitudes to nature, epitomised by the Judeo-Christian ethic where nature has always been placed in opposition to man, over which dominion had to be established. Western ideologies as a matter of principle tend to operate round binary oppositions of this kind (Harvey 1996).
5   In portraying nature in its entirety as a phenomenon to be subjugated through commodification and technology, and by transforming natural processes into ideologically contrived forms for manipulation, entertainment and ridicule, such as parks, botanic and zoological gardens, reserve areas, boulevards, sports grounds and other functions.

6   The state, within its shifting mandate and guided by dominant ideologies, expropriates land via the planning apparatus for certain necessary features of social reproduction (education, welfare, recreation), for the circulation of commodities, and for its own ideological presence. As a broad generalisation, this constitutes the public realm. Where necessary, it also expropriates space in support of big capital in its various forms (commercial, industrial, informational, etc.).

7   Through the representation and broadcasting of ideological formations, specifically the state apparatus in the form of law, the military, education, its ability to stage spectacles (for military authority, hero worship, state funerals, etc.); through the power of capital and its institutions; through religious ideologies, etc., all expressed in architectural and urban form, through complex semiotic codes, and usually allowing spatial dominance in their location. Ideological formations are frequently used as structuring devices in cities.

8   In portraying the mythic and symbolic dimension of history through physical markers that denote, celebrate or condemn specific events, concepts, individuals and places. Taken together, these markers form a semiotic web that may bear little connection to any 'truth', since their primary function is to create social cohesion, reinforce dominant values and transmit an acceptable history that supports the general trajectory of capitalist development. This is usually done through the medium of monumental architecture and urban spaces.

9   In the formation of the public realm through the shape and form of its associated spaces, its scale in relation to functions associated with it, and the signifying presence of the adjacent urban envelope.

10 In signifying class, ethnic, religious or gendered spaces in terms of their possession, use, imagery or control (see chapter 6).

11 In reinforcing all of the above in the configurations of architectural form and its semiotic possibilities, through the association of forms, materials and spatial relationships, sculptural elements, historical referents and other ideological devices.

12 Overall, urban design is involved in the generation, transmission and storage of what Christine Boyer has called 'collective memory' in her book *The City of Collective Memory*, an idea that has significant intersections with what the great psychologist C.G. Jung referred to as the 'collective unconscious'.

The Public Realm

Analysis of the public realm in relation to its political and ideological function is uncommon in the literature on urban design, although a whole range of scholars has made excellent contributions from other disciplines (Harvey 1979a, Rubin

1979, Kiernan 1983, Knesl 1984, Jencks and Valentine 1987, Marcuse 1998, Cartier 1999, Dovey 2001). More directly, the significance of the public realm has also been addressed in Webb (1990), Boyer (1993) and Madanipour (DC 10). In essence the public realm asserts a fundamental principle of democracy that has existed since ancient Greece – the right to freedom of assembly, the space they called the agora or *res publica*, which lay at the physical and ideological core of Greek *demokratia*. Agora means 'a gathering place' or, as Hannah Arendt (1959: 176) has preferred to call it, 'the space of appearances'.

The agora was the location of monumental architecture in the form of public buildings and state institutions, as well as stoas, colonnades used as a shading device where goods and conversation about politics, philosophy and the arts could be traded. The agora usually had spatial propinquity with the acropolis, the religious centre, and a huge typology of building types for indoor and outdoor assembly, worship, sport and other functions was highly developed. Even at that time, the political and ideological function of urban space was apparent in a multitude of ways, for example in symbolically expressing a democracy that was only available to free male citizens, that the democracy was based in slavery and that the senate was usually dominated by a few powerful families. The actual location, appearance, positioning and detailing of civic buildings were all highly significant. For example, Jencks and Valentine (1987) analyse the ideological functions of architecture of democracy and comment that the symbolic location of primary seats of power were deliberately understated in relation to the agora. This conveyed two messages: first, that the reality of government was suppressed and, as a corollary, that the primacy of the people and civil society was promoted. Number 10 Downing Street, the residence of the British Prime Minister and the symbolic centre of government in the UK, apparently no more than a domestic residence, conveys a similar message. The Roman Forum or *fora Romana* developed the idea of containing the institutions of the First Republic, symbolising the imperialism of Rome over its colonies (as indeed other forms of imperialism would later do). Ideologies were not only expressed at the civic level of triumphal arches, temples and palaces, but even at fine levels of detail in the columns of buildings, types of sculpture and other forms of decoration. Even the ideological presence of a single creature, the eagle, has had enduring monumental significance: 'The eagle on Trajan's column, symbol of imperial power, can be seen on almost every democratic government building of the nineteenth and twentieth centuries. It is also found on Nazi and Soviet buildings. Yet the eagle is presumed by each culture to represent not just power, but patriotism to one's particular form of government' (Jencks and Valentine 1987: 16) (see figures 15 and 16). The authors go on to demonstrate the political referents of the piazza and palace during the Middle Ages, and to the institutions of mass democracy in the present. They conclude with an exhaustive analysis of the political and ideological nature of L'Enfant's plan for Washington (as well as that of Leon Krier's bicentennial master plan of 1985) with the observation that 'An architecture of democracy that is uniform is as absurd as a democracy of identical citizens. Conversely, an architecture where

Figure 15 Example of the symbolic use of the eagle in fascist architecture.
Source: Courtesy of akg-images.

every building is in a different style is as privatised as a megalopolis of consumers. Thus a democratic style, if we generalise from these extremes, is at
once shared, abstract, individualised and disharmonious' (Jencks and Valentine
1987: 25).

Given this historical context, it is clear that the design of cities is a process
replete with meaning, of memories, reflections and dreams, a battleground
where ideologies are challenged and the content of history is brought to trial.
Nowhere has this constellation of qualities been better expressed than in the
brilliant debate between two sociologists over the monumental rebuilding of the
centre of Berlin, including the new centre of German government and specifically over the erection of a monument to the Holocaust victims of the Second
World War (Marcuse on *DC* 11, Campbell 1999). The conflict, despite its

Figure 16 Symbolic use of the eagle in spectacles by the Third Reich.
Source: Courtesy of akg-images/Ullstein Bild.

galactic dimensions, gets down to the use of a single word describing the monument, the chosen term being *Mahnmal*, a warning monument, rather than *Denkmal*, a memorial. While the chosen site is located between two major squares, Potsdamerplatz and Pariserplatz by the Brandenberg Gate, one site was actually proposed within the government complex itself. At root, Marcuse's concerns lay fundamentally with the potential rebirth of the German political landscape of the Third Reich, the reification of the German state within the context of a unifying European market in a new multibillion dollar architectural complex, and its relationship to the *Mahnmal* for Holocaust victims (figure 17). In contexts such as this, urban design clearly possesses a monumental capacity for the expression of symbolic meaning in specific urban forms.

Marcuse enunciates the meaning behind every single signifying architectural element in the new proposals in great detail, joining a significant number of other prominent intellectuals and politicians in 'speaking out against a massive Holocaust memorial proposed for the centre of Berlin, expressing the impossibility of representing and explaining a monstrous historical period through an abstract design of sculpture and landscape architecture' (Campbell 1999: 173). Marcuse argues that the project in its entirety unduly emphasises German

Figure 17   Monument to the Holocaust victims (*Mahnmal*), Berlin.
Source: By permission of Susan Thompson.

history before 1914 'where the meaning of each building, each style, each façade, the construction materials, the location and its significance in various historical periods – the Empire, the First World War, the Weimar Republic, fascism, post Second World War, the divided and re-united city are elaborated, with the prevailing philosophy of critical reconstruction' (Marcuse 1998: 154). Marcuse's critique is withering in its perception, to the point where no designer could possibly lay a single stone without serious self-analysis. He debates the issue discussed by Korn in the newspaper *Frankfurter Allgemeine Zeitung* as to whether art after Auschwitz is possible, and refocuses the conflict from a problem of aesthetic packaging to one of moral and political consciousness, 'what Germans today want to say about Germany and the Holocaust' (Marcuse 1998: 336). Marcuse's concern also reflects an important property of built form: it can lie very easily or, in Habermasian terms, is capable of significantly distorted communication. So he questions the capacity of urban design to tell the truth, about its capacity for concealment and deceit: 'the issues are power and its uses, wealth and its uses: framing the debate as one about form trivialises the issues, trivialises the history, serves to distract attention (perhaps deliberately?) from the underlying decisions' (Campbell 1999: 174). While this is true, it nonetheless does not solve the problem of what to do, that a single stone in the right (or wrong) spot can form a monumental statement about national identity. For example, the Scottish Stone of Scone, a symbol of Scottish independence, was removed to Westminster Abbey in London in 1296 and was only recently returned to Scotland after the creation of the Scottish Parliament in 1999. However, Marcuse's own answer to the problem, an anti-memorial of a barren site and a simple sign indicating that nothing can be built until the motivation behind German atrocities is fully understood, is unlikely to be realised. The social vortex surrounding the new government centre and the construction of the *Mahnmal* come within the category referred to by Christine Boyer as the 'politics of representational form'. She suggests that:

Because every economic formation or structure engenders a cultural form or an aesthetic convention, it can be expected that the representational forms of the city as a work of Art, Panorama or Spectacle reflect different stages of capitalism... historicism reigned for the plundering of old styles such as the Gothic, Baroque, or Classical <which> could all be used to cover changes wrought by political revolutions, industrialization, urbanization, even the rise of the bourgeoisie with their materialistic aspirations and blatant pretensions. The battle of styles and the city as a work of art were consequently nothing other than a backward binding gesture: trying to secure the turbulent present by tying it to the great artistic inheritance of the past, and mirroring through stylistic references the security and traditional order of pre-revolutionary times.

(Boyer 1994: 59)

While this is no doubt true, the statement actually short-changes the sheer scale of representational possibilities with a capital-logic argument, ignoring as it does the archaeology of human experience and imagination embedded in the stones of the city. Several of these are acknowledged by Boyer herself elsewhere in the book, for example what she calls the 'solipsistic aesthetic' of the global electronic media and its recursive serial mentality, or the embodiment of collective memory in fragments throughout the urban landscape. The idea of urban landscape is itself both an ideology and typology of form, critically assessed by Dennis Cosgrove in *Social Formation and Symbolic Landscape* (1984), where he gives an insightful account (among many) of the underlying ideological formations in one of the most important urban spaces on the planet, namely the Piazza San Marco in Venice. Likewise, Dolores Hayden, author of *The Power of Place: Urban Landscapes as Public History* (1995), has written widely on the idea that urban political ideologies run as undercurrents across a range of issues. One theme running through the book is that while dominant interests and ideologies are represented, the symbolic dialogue with the past can also be uplifting and empowering to the human spirit, since history has provided ordinary people with significant victories as well as defeats. She points to one important notion, that many practitioners in the fields of public history, architectural preservation, public art and other fields 'are dissatisfied with the narrative of city building as *conquest*. There is a broad interest in ethnic history and women's history as part of interpretive projects of all kinds, and a growing sympathy for cultural landscapes in preference to isolated monuments' (Hayden 1995: 47).

Nonetheless, the idea of conquest and domination is present even in the concept of physical scale, where monarchic, political and religious leaders have frequently resorted to inhuman scale to impress their power and ideological supremacy on subject populations. One of the most obvious devices urban design has inherited from the past is contained in the idea of the monumental, both in architecture and engineering works, as well as in public art in the form of sculpture, murals, triumphal arches, columns, obelisks and other devices (Harvey 1979b, Cosgrove 1984, Agnew 1989, Wagner et al. 1991, Johnson 1995). Taking only one simple device, the triumphal arch, we can see how the same symbolic and architectural construct has been transported over space and time.

The triumphal arch of ancient Rome has gone through many transformations. Hadrian's Arch from Imperial Rome has been physically reproduced around the world, with corresponding shifts in meaning and signification (figure 18). The arch as symbol has also been physically transformed in a multitude of representations, probably the most outstanding being Eero Saarinen's Gateway Arch in St Louis, Missouri (figure 19) or La Grande Arche at La Défense in Paris (figure 20).

In 'Cast in stone: monuments, geography and nationalism', Nuala Johnson (1995) exposes the function of monuments to national identity, specifically the

Figure 18   Sebastiano Serlio: the triumphal arch of Castel Vecchio in Verona.
Source: S. Serlio, *Five Books on Architecture.* New York: Dover, 1982, p. 61. Reprinted by permission of Dover Publications.

Figure 19   The Gateway Arch, St Louis, Missouri, designed by Eero Saarinen.
Source: © CORBIS.

Figure 20   La Grande Arche at La Défense.
Source: Courtesy of akg-images/Stefan Drechsel.

Irish case. She underscores the contestation of 'the other' within the British context, noting that the popular imagination is not completely ubiquitous and becomes territorialised at a variety of geographic scales. In this context there are a series of ideological battles being fought, for example between the need to symbolise a single national identity, and of identifiable local identities and, within each, of the requirements of social elitism against the will of the people, between male domination and gender equality. Johnson notes the significance of war and gender in portraying memory, noting 'how the imaginary unfolds in the discursive practices of identity formation' and 'the manner in which divided identities are structured and maintained in the geographies of everyday life through the analyses of public art, popular parade and ritual' (Johnson 1995: 58, 63).

The overall contestation of political ideologies by urban design, public art and aesthetics probably has no better example than the astounding circumstances surrounding the installation of a single piece of sculpture in New York's Federal Plaza, Lower Manhattan, in 1981. In contrast to the location of the *Mahnmal*, where events of mythic dimensions were being debated, the furore over Richard Serra's sculpture *Tilted Arc* resulted from the coincidence of an empty public space with Serra's imagination. Nonetheless, the outcome also resulted in questions of national significance, of constitutional and moral rights, of meanings attached to the terms 'public' and 'use', of the relationship between art and society, of aesthetic ideologies turned to political purposes, and the eventual removal of *Tilted Arc* eight years after it was built (Deutsche DC 11, Beardsley 1996, Cooper-Marcus 1996, Finkelpearl 2000). Due to the site-specific nature of the work, removal constituted destruction, since it was conceived in relation to its surroundings. Superficially, the removal of the sculpture was intended to improve public use of the space and to re-establish its coherence, since Serra's work was quite monumental, being some 35 metres long and 4 metres high (figure 21). However, as Rosalyn Deutsche contends, the subtext was not about the correct use of the public realm, since 'proponents of a political site specificity are skeptical about spatial coherence, viewing it not as an *a priori* condition subsequently disturbed by conflicts *in* space, but as a fiction masking the conflicts that *produce* space'. As Deutsche also notes, language served a huge ideological function in the overall process since *Tilted Arc's* most powerful opposition insulated themselves against criticism with recourse to universal absolutes such as 'common sense', 'reality' and 'the people's interest'. In the official hearing, the political use of language, the subversion of democratic rights, and state ideological intervention all prevailed, and

> a rhetoric of democracy pervaded the debate, demonstrating the degree to which public art discourse had become a site of struggle over the meaning of democracy. Government officials disparaged critical art under the banner of 'anti-elitism', a stance consistent with a general tendency in neo-conservative discourse to accuse art of arrogance or inaccessibility in order to champion privatization, and justify state censorship in the name of the rights of 'the people'.
>
> (Deutsche 1996: 265)

Figure 21 *Tilted Arc*: sculpture by Richard Serra for Federal Plaza, New York.
Source: Copyright © 2005 by ARS, NY and DACS, London.

After the removal of *Tilted Arc*, another landscape architect, Martha Schwartz, was hired to redesign the plaza (renamed Jacob Javit's Plaza) and to replace what was described as Serra's obstruction of the site with more user-friendly functions, the single prescribed use being to cater for weekday lunchtimes of adjacent office workers (Miller 2001) (see figures 22 and 23).

The form of cities is a symbolic representation of the historical contiguity between social relations and spatial structures. In the geography of uneven capitalist development, the built environment is a form of accumulation that represents not only the materialisation of capital in what Harvey calls 'the second circuit of capital' but also the powerful conflicts implicit to that regime (Harvey 1985: 9). Cities inherently represent this conflict because invested capital takes on fixed and immobile qualities that form barriers to further accumulation as well as limiting the basic processes of production, circulation and exchange. As Harvey (1985: 25) says, 'the geographical landscape that results is the crowning glory of past capitalist development. But at the same time it expresses the power of dead labour over living labour, and as such it imprisons and inhibits the accumulation process within a specific set of physical constraints'. But the materialisation of the city reveals much more than a single

Figure 22 Landscape project by Martha Schwartz to replace the sculpture by Richard Serra: plan view.
Source: T. Richardson (ed.), *The Vanguard Landscapes and Gardens of Martha Schwartz.* London: Thames and Hudson, 2004, p. 171.

Figure 23 Landscape project by Martha Schwartz to replace the sculpture by Richard Serra: perspective view.
Source: T. Richardson (ed.), *The Vanguard Landscapes and Gardens of Martha Schwartz.* London: Thames and Hudson, 2004, p. 171.

level in the archaeology of human history, the logic of capital being only one dimension in the production of space. As Marx pointed out, the material basis of life also affects consciousness. The operations of capital are not value free and are directed by powerful political ideologies that manipulate and craft space, from the morphology of the city to the form and content of the public realm and the nature of individual architectural expression. Consciousness, memory and human aspiration are the tools of urban designers as much as the choreography of bureaucratic regulation. The expression of these qualities in symbolic form results in dialogues, narratives, mythologies and histories, some lying, some telling the truth, but all forming the matrix of human experience and its expression that we call culture, and the culture of cities is what we now turn to.

Chapter Five
Culture

Another problem, our problem, is to discover the place and the laws of articulation of this context, that is to say, of the spatial forms, in the social structure as a whole. For if it is true that, in order to identify them, new phenomena have been named according to their place of origin, the fact remains that 'urban culture' as it is presented, is neither a concept nor a theory. It is, strictly speaking, a myth, since it recounts, ideologically, the history of the human species.

Manuel Castells (1977)

Introduction: Culture and Urban Design

Today, culture can be viewed as yet another battleground round which the central questions of social development evolve (Agger 1992, Blau 1998, DC 13). This fact was well represented in a recent article in the *Sydney Morning Herald* about how the National Museum portrayed Australia's history (Morgan 2003). Not only was the museum reviewed as to its political correctness and found to be squeaky clean on the basis of 140 expert submissions, but also the $A220,000 spent in the process simply reinforced the same opinion reached in a prior review three years earlier. While the review again exonerated the museum's position, other issues came to the surface: 'rather than a truce in the culture wars, the review has opened a new front in the way the nation sees itself' (Morgan 2003: 30). The debate raised issues of national identity, settlement, migration, native title, corporate involvement, feminism, as well as those of method (chronological progression, narratives, foundation myths, theming, heroic figures, etc.) and had to consider ideological criticism of the museum's 'Marxist rubbish'. All of this was over the exhibits in a single building. Clearly, culture is a continuing arena of debate with a greater significance for many people than the political process itself.

Similarly, anyone involved in designing cities is bombarded with a plethora of cultural referents to distil into some comprehensible framework. We hear of commodity culture, postmodern culture, global and local culture, the cultural economy, the culture industry, multiculturalism, cultural capital, cultural regeneration, cultural planning, cultural policy and cultural heritage, to mention but a few. How do we make sense of all these terms and why is culture so important to us? If society and culture are not homologous, how should we draw distinctions between them? How does culture intersect with urban politics and urban design? Should culture in fact be the central focus of urban designers, i.e. to translate cultural practices through processes of representation into appropriate urban forms?

Without doubt, culture is central to urban design knowledge, despite the fact that Castells (see epigraph) accords it mythological status and Mitchel (1995) suggests that it does not exist at all. Up until relatively recently, however, culture has seldom taken central stage in urban design to the degree that it could be incorporated into the fabric of a definition as suggested above. Overall, urban designers have had a largely functional relationship to culture in two predominant areas, environmental conservation and environmental psychology, regions where pseudo-science abounds. While the former has concerned itself with the preservation and conservation of the built environment, in so far as its buildings and spaces are concerned, the latter has focused on the relationship between people and space, often referred to as environment and behaviour studies, whose dominant organisation has been the Environmental Design Research Association (EDRA). Today, the terms 'environmental design', 'sustainable development', 'environmental conservation' and 'cultural conservation' segue into each other in singular complexity, and there are major differences of interest in how these terms are deployed between nations, as well as within the government, the private sector and the academy (Bassett 1993, Griffiths 1993; see also chapter 7). In order to gain some perspective on the complexity of this situation, we need to return briefly to some of the more important markers over the last sixty years so that the complex interactions between urban design and urban culture may be understood.

For Louis Mumford, the culture of cities was of seminal significance to our understanding of the relationship between culture and the design of urban form (Mumford 1938). The same was true of E.T. Hall's three texts, *The Silent Language* (1959), *The Hidden Dimension* (1969) and *Beyond Culture* (1976), particularly the first, where he defines culture simply as communication. He maintained that ten primary message systems constituted a generic and universal 'map of culture'. These also offered designers, probably for the first time, an actual organisational template upon which their designs could be based and different cultural practices compared (see chapter 10). But if we scrutinise the 40 classic texts I outlined in table 1, we can see that culture, like other major aspects of the social structure (economics, politics, etc.), suffers virtual exclusion from the mainstream urban design literature. When it is addressed, it is couched in the functionalist and behaviourist theories popular through the 1960s, 1970s and 1980s with a significant carry-over into the present. Examples of this are represented in Rudofsky (1969), Sommer (1969), Proshansky et al. (1970), Rapoport (1977), Alexander (1977) and Gehl and Gemzoe (1996). Much of the research undertaken was concerned with a central feature of urbanisation usually allocated to culture, namely that of density, and density and crowding studies, their effects and implications, embodied a large part of this effort (Cuthbert 1985).

In the article 'Major changes in environmental form required by social and psychological demands', Christopher Alexander argues that 'we must face squarely, just what the task of city planning is: it is nothing less than the design of culture. A culture is a system of standard situations. Each of these situations specifies certain roles, certain allowed limits of behaviour for the persons in these roles, and the requisite spatial setting for this behaviour' (Alexander 1969: 79). As his intellectual justification for his proposals, Alexander leans heavily on the work of Bronislaw Malinowski and three behavioural psychologists, Abraham Maslow, Alexander Leighton and Erik Erikson. Alexander uses the codified version of each theorist's work to determine how each element of urban structure should emerge from Malinowski's seven basic needs, Maslow's hierarchy of evolutionary requirements, Leighton's ten basic striving sentiments and Erikson's eight stages of crisis. Here, as a basis for cultural planning, Alexander adapts certain perceived fundamentals of human existence derived from behavioural psychology to a series of spatial patterns, a process which would be more fully realised in his *A Pattern Language* of 1977.

Another significant debate over a more sinister aspect of culture, namely surveillance and policing, which originated around the same period, had its epicentre in two publications by Oscar Newman, namely *Crime Prevention Through Architectural Design* (1971) and *Defensible Space* (1972). The story continued in *Design Guidelines for Creating Defensible Space* (1976) and *Community of Interest* (1980) and was still being presented as a new planning technology twenty years later in 'Defensible space: a new physical planning tool for urban revitalization' (1995). However, Bill Hillier's initial reprise of 1973 was devastating. He argued that Newman's behavioural functionalism (and, by default, much of the work listed above), based in physically deterministic solutions to social problems and with its attendant dependence on territoriality, ignores the fact that human occupation of space is heavily symbolic: 'human territoriality is largely discredited, and simply fails to explain the historical and ethnographic evidence that has been amassed in the last half century...to try to derive <a> complex understanding from an accumulation of territorial behaviour is as ridiculous as it is uninteresting' (Hillier 1973: 540). He goes on to dismiss behaviourism, which originated in the 1920s and was largely based on animal ethology (much of which permeated design theory). It was promoted by major figures such as Konrad Lorenz (1963, 1981), a supporter of the Nazi eugenics programmes of the 1940s. Even some of Newman's elementary statistics appear to be gross misinterpretations of his own research. Hillier concludes thus:

> Newman is not saying anything new, of course, and it is important that he is not. He is merely proposing a refinement of an old theme, the creation of social order by

architecture. Yet it was precisely this kind of thinking – again based, as we have discovered, on a total ignorance of the nature of relationships between space and human behaviour. What we are being offered is not the antidote but another dose of the poison in a redesigned bottle.

(Hillier 1973: 544)

While firmly rooted to the politically incorrect man–environment studies, and to a certain extent the behaviourism dismissed by Hillier, yet another opportunity had been ignored to inform the next generation of designers with a grounding in how culture was embedded in spatial practices. By 1980, the realisation had fully dawned that something was missing, and the something was the inclusion of symbolism within any consideration of culture and design. Signs of this realisation emerged in Amos Rapoport's *House, Form and Culture* (1969), a book which represented a watershed in the development of environmental design, since it moved beyond functional criteria into the realm of symbolism in its final chapter. Donald Appleyard affirmed the importance of symbolic content in 'The environment as a social symbol' (1979), reinforced three years later by Ross Woodward's 'Urban symbolism' (1982) and Rapoport's *The Meaning of the Built Environment* (1982).

Over the last twenty years we can also see that key urban design texts have largely eluded any serious influence from cultural studies. Since Kevin Lynch wrote *A Theory of Good City Form* in 1981, little progress has been made overall. Lynch concluded his book with a review of what he called 'functional' theory, having failed to rise much above it himself. Despite this, much of his critique remains valid, since key texts since then have dealt with urban morphologies and typologies (Hillier and Hanson 1984, Trancik 1986, Gehl and Gemzoe 1996, Hillier 1996), case studies (Barnett 1982, Broadbent 1990, Lang 1994), historicism (Gosling and Gosling 2003) and design theory (Alexander 1987, Katz 1994, Madanipour 1996b). A few authors, such as Boyer, Ellin, and Dovey, stand out in their approach to urban design as part and parcel of urban social theory. But in order to contextualise this general problematic, we must examine how culture has been defined, why it has become so important and how the political economy of culture can assist in revealing just why culture, particularly its symbolic aspect, is so important for urban designers (Stevenson 1992, Bassett 1993, Griffiths 1993, Frow 1997, Kincheloe and Steinberg 1997, Throsby 1997).

The Culture of Modernism

As I indicated in my introduction, the twentieth century began with the question of culture when Camillo Sitte and Otto Wagner sought to embody the spirit of their time into the urban fabric of Vienna, a conflict which symbolised the birth of the urban culture of modernism. In *Fin-de-Siècle Vienna*, Schorske appropriates Marx's definition of ideology as culture when he says that 'I shall first consider the Ringstrasse itself as a visual expression of the values of a social class', with the rider that 'It is important to remember, however, that there was more to municipal development than the projection of values into space and stone' (Schorske 1981: 24). So modernism, defined as post *fin de siècle*, and postmodernism were both massively predicated upon the exigencies of economic development over Giovanni Arrighi's 'long twentieth century'. One of the first distinctions that has been made about culture (to be refuted later) is that it is fundamentally a superstructural form, a servo-mechanism of capital that reflects dominant discourses, interests and politics. While Marx had virtually nothing to say about culture per se, he did point out that paradigm shifts in superstructural forms such as ideology and culture did not take place independent to the massive economic and political changes occurring in society as a whole.

Marx's view of consciousness in general, and culture in particular, was that they were wholly determined by the means of production. The superstructure that emerged constituted both institutions and the forms of awareness generated by them. Marx considered that the division of labour arising from industrial capitalism, and the alienation of workers both from each other and from the objects of their labour, made any coherent working class culture impossible. Engels, on the other hand, was prepared to accord some primacy and self-determination to the superstructure and its capacity to affect the economic base, particularly through resistance to various forms of oppression. This position is still alive and well in more contemporary Marxian literature, exemplified for example in David Harvey's *The Condition of Postmodernity* (1989) and Frederic Jameson's *Postmodernism, or The Cultural Logic of Late Capitalism* (1991). David Harvey insists on preserving traditional Marxist categories by retaining a clear distinction between culture (as aesthetic production) and the economic (as material production). In other words, it is useful to retain the words 'modern' and 'postmodern' in relation to culture, and 'industrialism' and 'postindustrialism' in relation to the development of capital, a point which Jameson clearly reinforces in reference to postmodernism:

> the fundamental ideological task of the new concept, however, must remain that of coordinating new forms of practice and social and mental habits... with the new forms of economic production and organization thrown up by the modification of capitalism – the new global division of labour – in recent years... it should be added that *culture* in the sense of what cleaves almost too close to the skin of the economic to be stripped off and inspected in *its own right*. [my italics]
> (Jameson 1991: xiv–xv)

Jameson also points out that his own use of the term 'late capitalism' derives from the Frankfurt School of Social Science, who used the term in a somewhat Leninist fashion, corresponding to Lenin's ideas on monopoly capitalism, which denoted imperialism as 'the highest stage of capitalism'. However, Jamieson uses the term in contradistinction to prior concepts of imperialism, and in relation to new forms of internationalisation that have gone far beyond old-style conflicts between colonial powers. This link to the Frankfurt School also underscores the fact that it was probably the most consistent interrogator of the idea of culture in the twentieth century, from the mid-1920s to mid-1930s, generating a tradition that remains with us today. This is reflected in such contemporary journals as *Telos, Theory and Society* and others (Held 1980, Arato and Gebhardt 1982, Kellner 1984, Fuery and Mansfield 1997). The Frankfurt School was founded on two philosophical bases: first, on the traditions established from Kantian critical philosophy; and second, by Marxian attitudes to ideology (the subplots behind historical events), restated by George Lukacs, whose enduring influence prevailed over the institute. Andrew Arato notes the ambiguity in the Frankfurt School's interest in culture when he says:

> More often than not, 'culture' is represented as the sum total of the activities that possess the aura of intellectuality or spirituality, that is the arts and the sciences. But there is also an important usage, especially, but not only, that defines culture as the ensemble of those intersubjective traditions, meanings, values, institutions, rituals, customs and typical activities characteristic in space and time of a given social formation.
>
> (Arato and Gebhardt 1982: 185)

While this duality was noted by the Frankfurt School theorists in general, they were predominantly focused on culture in the former sense, and it was up to three theorists in particular to probe the specificity of culture within a Marxian framework, namely Max Horkheimer, Theodore Adorno and Walter Benjamin. Together, Horkheimer and Adorno wrote a chapter called 'The culture industry' in their book *The Dialectic of Enlightenment* (1944). Adorno later published another essay called 'The culture industry reconsidered', not to mention one called 'How to look at television' (1991a,b). *The Dialectic of Enlightenment* is probably one of the most famous essays in social science, given its historical context – ten years earlier, fascism had hijacked Germany's entire historical culture in favour of totalitarianism, and the finale to the Second World War had not yet taken place. In opposition to the 'high art' of painting, sculpture, music and literature, Adorno's primary interest was in the relationship between the proletariat and the mass media of the culture industry. Of central concern was the ability of a rationalised capitalism to deepen capitalist social relations through the socially contrived opiate of the mass media, thus impacting systems of domination while at the same time generating even greater profits by controlling and manufacturing popular culture: 'The omnipresent laughter of mass culture is dismissed by Adorno and Horkheimer as "the instrument of fraud practiced on happiness", and represents the narcotic dulling of that critical self-consciousness necessary to open up the claustrophobic self-identity of the modern world to alternative ideas and experiences' (Connor 1996: 349). Walter Benjamin, a somewhat marginal member of the Frankfurt School, did not share Adorno's pessimism that all new technologies were evil. His position was that the mechanical reproduction of art demanded that the concept of authenticity had to be rethought, along with the authority allocated to 'original' works, heralding Roland Barthes' later pronouncement of 'the death of the author' (Benjamin 1978). In many ways, this idea of authenticity lies at the heart of many urban design problems and will be revisited below.

In the immediate postwar period, Raymond Williams published his classic text *Culture and Society* (1958), followed by *The Long Revolution* (1965) and *Culture* (1981), marking Williams as one of the two key figures in British cultural studies along with E.P. Thompson (*The Making of the English Working Class*, 1963) and, later, Stuart Hall and his colleagues at the Birmingham Centre for Contemporary Cultural Studies. All these thinkers were, to a large degree, locked into a concept of ideology that had strong connections to a Marxian class analysis. This was strongly reflected in the work of Williams, Thompson and Hoggart (1958), who reified the idea of an autonomous working class culture, each individual being heavily influenced by prior Marxist thinkers, for example Williams by Antonio Gramsci and Hall by Louis Althusser. Here, concepts of culture were again refined and tensions revealed between Marx's original disinterest in culture and the incapacity of revisionist theories to deal with the explosion in informational technology and its effects from around 1970 onwards: 'For Hall, the theoretical interests of Marxism and cultural studies were never perfectly matched, most particularly because Marxism fails directly to address the key concerns of cultural studies: culture, ideology, language and the symbolic' (Lewis 2002: 133). To this one could also add ethnicity, gender, age, sexuality, the disabled and other key social issues.

Overall, the idea of resistance to domination had been too narrowly confined to class issues, with insufficient attention being paid, for example, to the fact that women could be freed from class distinctions but remain dominated on the basis of their gender, or that domination had a multitude of forms, many of which evaded a capitalist class analysis. Similarly, the mechanisms through which ideologies are implemented had been relegated to the background, particularly in relation to communication, language and commodity fetishism. Understandably, there had to be a significant reaction from culture as ideology, into culture as systems of difference and otherness. This did not mean that capitalism was no longer a system of domination. What it did mean was that each system of difference was perhaps addressing domination in a different form, to the point that authors like Foucault called into question the whole idea of domination as a conspiratorial social construct. There was an increasing awareness of the idea that many aspects of culture were not merely a reflection of the economic base. That the mental was indeed as important as the material was asserted in the birth of postindustrialism and a new postmodern attitude to culture at the beginning of the 1970s.

Postmodern Culture

While modernist analyses of culture had significant origins from the left in Germany and Britain, profoundly influenced by Gramsci and Althusser, there is no doubt that French philosophers and social theorists have dominated postmodern thinking, beginning with such writers as Michel Foucault, Jean-François Lyotard, Paul Ricoeur and Jean Baudrillard (see chapter 3). It must also be said here that distinctions between modernism and postmodernism are fraught with angst. Indeed the very term 'postmodern' is a clear signifier that postmodernity remains embedded in modernity, in the same manner that poststructuralism refers to something that comes after structuralism, both terms incorporating their antecedent without a clear terminological break from the past. Given the diaphanous nature of much postmodern theory, this is probably just as well. Barry Smart for example says that 'Ambiguity follows from the fact that the notion of the postmodern may be read as implying sequentiality, something which comes after the modern, and that indeed is how some analysts have employed the term'.

But postmodern does not necessarily signify that we have taken leave of the modern; on the contrary, the term may be employed to refer to a critical relationship with the modern and as such it appears closely, if not intextricably, articulated with the modern in response to the question 'What is the postmodern?' Lyotard has answered that 'it is undoubtedly part of the modern' (Smart 1996: 397). In other words, modernist and postmodernist aspects of cultural development segue together in ways not yet fully understood (Mitchel 1995). In addition, postmodern culture is also defined negatively in relation to the dying gasps of modernism and, in fact, to the end of social theory as we know it, for example in Baudrillard's 'the end of the social', Fukuyama's 'the end of history', Debord's observations on 'the end of cultural history', Barthes' 'the death of the author', Rifkin's 'the end of work', Gibson Graham's 'the end of capitalism', Nigel Harris' 'the end of the third world', and so on. What is implied by these statements is not that the world has come to an end, but that a wholly new meaning of the social is emerging, one based upon such concepts as simulacra (Baudrillard), hyperreality (Eco), heterotopia (Foucault), mediascapes (Appadurai) and other emerging terminologies (Lewis 2002).

Nonetheless, it is possible to identify certain features in the cultural transformation of Western societies. In the *The Condition of Postmodernity*, David Harvey has assembled some of the schematic differences between the old capitalism and the new, between modernism and postmodernism (after Hassan, Halal, Lash and Urry, and Swygendow and others, Harvey 1989: 42, 174–9). While these tables are complex and difficult to understand, what seems to characterise the move from Fordism into flexible accumulation and postmodern culture is the overall ephemerality of its qualities, e.g. from design to chance, from hierarchy to anarchy, from presence to absence, from centring to dispersal, from signified to signifier, from narrative/*grand histoire* to anti-narrative/*petit histoire*. Even these qualities are misleading, for once again they reflect a dyadic approach to history. In other words, postmodernism is seen as qualitatively opposed to modernism, which, as I have indicated above, is not a particularly revealing method.

Nor is it constructive to see the emergence of new cultural forms purely in oppositional terms, although the dyad class–capital, resistance–domination remains significant. Given the semantic shift from discussion of culture to that of cultures, any idea of resistance to capital in the form of an organic working class culture has to be consigned to the trashcan. The fragmentation of working class interests into the politics of difference paradoxically generates greater apparent equality at the cost of any coherent resistance to capital. Indeed, the greater the number of separate associations, the less coherence any resistance could possibly have. The only unifying element then becomes the commodified relations of the market, the perfectly unified cultural expression of a totally fragmented populace. Indeed a politically contrived multiculturalism such as exists in Australia is the perfect tool to match commodified social relations with divisionary political agendas (Jayasuriya 1990, Clark et al. 1993). Harvey raises this issue, the revolutionary potential of postmodernist culture in relation to the shaping of space, noting that it is precisely during periods of paradigm shift, as in modernism to postmodernism, that the greatest spatial changes occur.

> If space is indeed to be thought of as a system of 'containers' of social power (to use the imagery of Foucault), then it follows that the accumulation of capital is perpetually deconstructing that social power by re-shaping its geographical bases. Put the other way round, any struggle to reconstitute power relations is a struggle to re-organise their spatial bases. It is in this light that we can better understand 'why capitalism is continually reterritorialising with one hand what it was deterritorialising with the other' (Deleuze and Guattari 1984).
>
> (Harvey 1989: 238)

Here an important question is the extent to which difference fragments working class culture or homogeneous other cultures into microterritories and sectoral cultural identities, while at the same time reinforcing a nascent global commodity culture as in that of Hardt and Negri's *Empire* (Murphy and Watson 1997).

While the reorganisation of space on the basis of new social relations is undisputed, such action is itself predicated on the process at the core of capitalism, namely that of commodity production in general and the idea of commodity fetishism in particular. What we have to remember here is that the commodity is not merely a thing but a fundamental representation of capitalist exchange, a social relation, symbolic of the power difference between owners holding capital and those whose labour is marketed. This idea was central to one of the most radical diatribes written about the specificity of the commodity in the realm of culture, namely Guy Debord's short monograph *La Société du Spectacle*, first published in 1967. Debord argues that with the deepening of capitalist relations of production, relations between people, and therefore 'culture', become defined wholly and completely as commodity relations: 'In societies where modern conditions of production prevail, all of life presents itself as an immense accumulation of spectacles. Everything that was directly lived has moved away into a representation' (Debord 1967: 1; see also Ley and Olds 1988, Cosgrove 1997). Here we move from Gramsci's concept of culture as a lived system of values into a new context where use-values have been transformed: 'what matters now is not the "reality" of labour and production, but the autonomous regulating force of the languages and codes which govern the production and circulation of values' (Connor 1996: 357).

Connor goes on to comment on Baudrillard's idea that modern developed capitalist economies have satisfied basic needs and therefore commodity production must now focus on desires. In order for capitalist production to expand and counteract the falling rate of profit from the provision of goods necessary to sustain life, capital must generate artificial requirements for wholly unnecessary products via the mass media. The aestheticising of desires so created then generates a symbolic world of signs, whereby individuals become absorbed into a system of spectacular production of their own volition. While needs can be easily fulfilled, desires can be endlessly renewed, and so the deepening of commodity relations becomes complete on the basis of an apparently limitless horizon to commodity production. As Connor remarks, 'The important thing is not that gratification is delivered to the consumer, but that the consumer is delivered to the dynamic needs and need-production, that is at once an economic system, a culture, and a technology of political control and integration' (Connor 1996: 358). Which cultural forms will ultimately persist and which mutations of culture will develop, as commodity fetishism envelops social relations, is anybody's guess. What is certain is that culture will remain 'the battleground of the modern world system' for some time to come (Wallerstein 2000: 31).

Commodity fetishism was the term that Marx used to describe the reduction of social relations to commodity relations within capitalism, later traced to its overall social implications in Debord (1967). In principle, the relationship between human beings first becomes mediated, then defined through their relationship to objects. In the production process, different quantities of labour time are incarcerated within commodities. Since labour cannot be directly exchanged in the marketplace, this takes place within the sphere of commodity circulation as a symbolic exchange of value. 'Once these relationships between things are established they become coercive. Individuals cannot avoid submitting to the social process which is the consequence of the mass of individual transactions between producers' (Urry 1981: 48). Fetishism is involved when people fail to recognise in commodities the abstraction of human values which has taken place, and identify with the objects themselves. Fetishism involves symbolism, abstraction and association, and opens up the possibility of a theory of ideology and culture built around manipulation of the commodity relation to maintain or direct social change.

Globalisation, Culture, Economy

The idea of a globalisation has been widely researched by a multitude of scholars, primarily from an economic and political perspective. But the concept of 'global culture' has not undergone quite the same scrutiny (Featherstone 1990, 1991, Urry 1990, 1995, Lash and Urry 1994, Appadurai 1996). In his introduction to *Global Culture* (1990), Mike Featherstone asks, 'Is there a global culture?' His answer is that if we conceive of global culture in the same way as national culture, then the answer is no. Any integrated global culture would similarly require a global state, an unlikely possibility for some time into the future. However, it is quite clear that the American domination of world markets in terms of its corporate monopolies, combined with the power of its media industries, has already saturated many other nation states not only with the necessary ideological *emballage* but also with cultural products: movies, junk food, sportswear, music, cosmetics and other items. To the extent that people relate to the resultant spectacle of luxury consumption that ensues, there is clearly a matrix of desires already in place that transcends socially necessary consumption and shared cultural interests based on professional, ethnic, gender and other associations. Smith (1990) indicates the importance of a common language as the basis of culture, pointing to the qualities of English, French, Spanish, Arabic and other languages that are transnational in their use. On the other hand, the capacity of universalised electronic media to bypass linguistic and local cultural differences threatens to relegate spoken languages to second place in the culture war.

This point is not new of course, and we can return at least to Marshall McLuhan's *Understanding Media* (1964) to discover forty years ago that 'the medium is the message'. More recently, Manuel Castells has reversed this idea, stating that 'the message is the medium' on the basis that the mass media will tailor programmes to any message people want to hear. The interconnection of the global media via satellite communications has also encouraged Castells to suggest that 'we are not living in a global village, but in customized cottages globally produced and locally distributed' (Castells 1996: 341). He also makes the interesting point that even at the level of the culture of real vitality, the interests of professional and managerial classes prevail, since they, more than the mass of population, 'are living symbolically in a global frame of reference' (Castells 1996: 364). In the virtual world of images, class interests maintain dominance over essential territories. This reflects Castells' fundamental views on any attempt to implement the idea of 'urban culture' since spatial forms are predicated by the historical specificity of social relations (DC 1). Nonetheless, the coincidence of globalisation with commodity fetishism generates the framing of new horizons in capital accumulation, through the absorption of culture as a factor of production rather than a consequence. In the process, the conscious colonisation of popular culture represents a new form of imperialism over image, representation and language, mediated through the web of an all-encompassing culture industry.

As a backdrop to this process, global economic restructuring is already fulfilling the expectation that the third millennium will generate circumstances wholly unanticipated in history. For the first time, economic forces evade political control, as international financial markets transcend the ability of any single political organisation to govern their operations. A key feature of this global economy is its tendency to break down production processes hierarchically, not only as an inherent technological necessity but also as a geographic or sociospatial feature that permits the necessary exploitation of labour markets in the second, third and fourth world orders. Within nation states, the culture industry is concerned with two fundamental events. First, there is the manufacture of specific *culturally generated commodities* in the realm of production (Scott 1997, 2000b). Architecture and urban design are of course an integral part of this process and many countries are waking up to the fact that the 'international style' which was an inherent part of modern architecture has been wholly destructive to national unity and a regional heritage that reinforces local cultures, identity and history. The second is the creation of specifically *cultural experiences* (in the realm of consumption). Tourism is the largest single activity combining both of these into a single economic process. Here, the migration of populations from the wealthier countries in search of so-called 'authentic' experiences must be contrasted with the migrations of people from poorer countries in search of work, from persecution or from material deprivation, where it is estimated that over 40 million persons are displaced on a continuing and increasing basis (Britton 1991, Featherstone 1991, 1993, Chambers 1997, Rojek and Urry 1997).

One striking characteristic of the culture industry, which tends to counteract the tendency towards an all-consuming globalisation, is that significant cultural production must, by definition, emphasise culture. Traditionally, this has been a feature of nation states, i.e. authentic, national culture. In fact, one could argue that the greater the tendency for any cultural product to 'go global' would be self-defeating. Its market advantage is due precisely to the fact that it is not reproducible elsewhere. It is clear, however, that even within commodity production it may be impossible to localise completely, for example fashion houses and perfumeries in France may still have to import materials from other countries. Nonetheless, other features of the process dominate sufficiently for a cultural hegemony to prevail (Molotch 1996). While there is no doubt that global production and marketing is generating a culture of its own – with an overwhelming desire to have everyone running in the same Nike shoes, wearing the same Ray-Ban sunglasses, listening to the same rock groups and watching the same movies – paradoxically it is the conservation of difference that underwrites the success of the culture industry.

Here, a major question driving current research into the culture industry concerns the extent to which the spatial organisation of the material production of cultural products differs from traditional manufacturing processes, and the extent to which the consumption of these same products differs in terms of markets. In parallel with this process of production, tourism, in so far as it represents the market, constitutes an ever-shifting matrix in the demand and supply of experiences, one in fact that authenticity can never satisfy. An important difference between the cultural products and the cultural experiences that combine to form the culture industry is that while commodities tend to be produced in one place and consumed in another, the tourist experience by definition must be consumed where it is produced.

The design of the built environment is central to this overall process, providing venues for an unimaginable range of activities. The production of architectural and urban forms exists at the material level of function, providing airports, cultural centres, museums, galleries, hotels, convention centres, theme parks, restaurants and the plethora of uses required to accommodate a myriad of activities. But urban design also represents symbolic capital in equal complexity: state and private sector interests, national identity, civil society, popular and high culture, the commodity culture of the market, personal and corporate power, as well as collective history, memory and aspirations (Breen 1994).

Authenticity and Symbolic Representation

One of the central cultural principles debated from the 1960s to the 1980s, with a trickle-down effect into the present, was the concept of 'community' (Doxiadis 1968, Perrin 1970, see chapter 9). Endless research was carried out into every possible aspect of existing communities in terms of their functional character-istics of size, shape, form, demographics, economic base, social structure, etc., as the basis for giving designers some social dimensions upon which design de-cisions should be made. Beyond establishing the most elementary foundation for social provision (schools, shops, welfare facilities, etc.), the idea of 'designing' communities remains elusive. Instead there has been a shift to the idea of place and placemaking, which skirts the problem of dimensions and focuses instead on the idea of identity (Carter et al. 1993, Massey 1994, Liggett and Perry 1995). Here, two of the most significant concepts for urban designers working today are the related ideas of authenticity and symbolic representation, closely linked to the New Ruralism/Urbanism to be discussed below.

The idea of the authentic is bound to all aspects of culture and therefore to all aspects of urban design. It is linked at the philosophical level to concepts of truth and reality; to experience, for instance in relation to travel and tourism; and to the actual representation of the physical world of architecture, urban space and landscape. It is also closely related to post-colonial cultures and the re-establish-ment of their own 'authentic' practices and environment, as well as to developed countries, which are seeking to retain their own national identity in the face of globalisation (Said 1978, 1994, Bhabha 1994). For post-colonial cultures the problem is immense, although the dilemma posed by the demand for authenti-city is immediately apparent. Colonialism has had the most profound effects on many cultures, frequently lasting hundreds of years. How therefore can such experience be considered inauthentic, i.e. fake or artificial? On the other hand, how are the useful aspects of colonisation, such as infrastructure, architecture, legal and administrative systems and language, to be rationalised within the framework of national sovereignty and identity? 'The problem with such claims to cultural authenticity is that they often become entangled in an essentialist cultural position in which fixed practices become hybridized or contaminated. This has as its corollary, the danger of ignoring the possibility that cultures may develop and change as their conditions change' (Ashcroft et al. 1998: 21). Essentialism is therefore something of a Gordian knot. In order to break free from the bonds of imperialism, essentialism becomes a legitimate strategy since it consolidates a unique and shared set of values. The corollary is that if it continues beyond liberation, then it either represents a false reality since it may not incorporate the colonial experience, or it becomes a stereotype where the dynamic nature of culture becomes suppressed. Oppression from the outside is then replaced by oppression from within. All of this raises serious questions for urban designers in the design and development of towns and cities across the globe, even setting to one side the training that many designers receive in countries other than their own.

On the modern cultural stage, one region where problems of authenticity abound is in its relation to tourism and its impact on culture. Here, the progress of tourism may be characterised in five stages. The first phase could be characterised by the search for the authentic, up until about 1950. Genuinely authentic experiences could still be obtained by visiting other cultures prior to the development of mass tourism ten years or so after the Second World War. The second phase could be characterised by inauthenticity or what is called 'staged authenticity' (MacCannell 1989). Arguably, all modern tourism comes into this category, where tourists are prepared to accept a staged version of the authentic dictated by their own mass presence. Tourists then gaze on artificially constructed sites, events and artefacts that bear no relation to the original, but which are nonetheless an acceptable compromise in the context of bucket-shop airfares, air-conditioned rooms and aerosol mosquito repellant. The term 'post-tourist', someone who actually welcomes the inauthentic and for whom the reality of indigenous life would be anathema, marks the third phase. As John Urry (1995: 140) remarks,

> the post tourist delights in the multitude of games that can be played, and knows that there is no authentic tourist experience. They know that the apparently authentic fishing village could not exist without the income from tourism or that the glossy tourist brochure is a piece of pop culture. It is merely another game to be played at, another pastiched surface of postmodern experience.

It is but a short jump from post-tourism to phase four, where the construction of physical sites or 'theme parks' on a wholly unprecedented scale bypasses any concept of authenticity (see also chapter 8). Some of these are already in existence, for example new designs for cruise ships expressed as floating towns which move around, but whose passengers never disembark; massive shopping malls such as the Winnipeg Mall that herald qualitatively different consumption experiences; and the idea that airports could become 'themeports', destinations rather than points of transfer. Plans are in progress at the moment to build a shopping mall in Dubai costing $US7 billion in order to attract international tourism, dimensions that will dwarf even the spectacle at Winnipeg. The complex will have theme parks, hotels and a Formula 1 racetrack, will cover some 600 million square metres and will take six years to complete. It is planned to accommodate 15 million tourists a year, where the only thing otherwise on offer is millions of square kilometres of sand (*Asian Financial Review*, 27 October

2003). Stage five in the tourist experience is the actual construction of alternative realities in cyberspace, where the expense, inconvenience and hazards of tourism are removed entirely, to be replaced by increasingly sophisticated computer imaging and equipment (Bogard 1996). By that time, concepts of authenticity will have taken on entirely new meanings.

The second important concept, one inseparably tied to authenticity, is that of symbolic representation. Authenticity and experience are directly connected through material and symbolic constructs, which represent or signify 'otherness' in a multitude of dimensions. The built environment is arguably the most significant of these, incorporating archaeologies of meaning signified in most of the chapters of this text. For urban designers, authenticity and symbolic representation are therefore central to the idea that urban design is the symbolic attempt to express an accepted urban meaning in certain urban forms. Manifestations of authentic experience are inexorably tied to place, and placemaking is one of the key outcomes in the overall process of representation accommodated in the design of cities. As we have seen, it is bound to the level of global tourism and also to the space of everyday life. As Harvey (1993: 12) remarks, 'Place is becoming more important to the degree that the authenticity of dwelling is being undermined by political–economic processes of spatial transformation and place construction'. Harvey is referring here to the search for, or association with, authentic community, something that was perhaps only possible before capitalism had fully fractured labour, leisure and domestic life (Berman 1982). In this regard symbolic representation is not necessarily a conscious process, and may in fact be so much a part of people's lives that it occurs naturally.

On the one hand, we can see from the organisation and design of tribal and agrarian cultures that symbolic representation is homologous with daily life and is not a contrived art form. This process is well described in one of the first books that tried to bring the realm of symbolic representation into the design process, *Shelter, Sign and Symbol* (Oliver 1977). Here the phenomenal richness and integration between the culture of daily life and the symbolic structuring of reality and space are manifest. At an altogether different level of development, since the built environment professions in developed countries operate within the encompassing tentacles of capitalism, political and economic assumptions are automatically built into the process of constructing the built environment, the most obvious of these being social class, the power of capital and the authority of the state. Tables 7 and 8 demonstrate how this process operates with regard to public housing in Hong Kong (Cuthbert 1987: 146–7). Symbolic representation at both of these levels of engagement has serious implications for urban form, neither of which represents conscious design processes.

On the other hand, urban designers are frequently faced with problems of cultural representation, which are tantamount to insoluble with the tools available. In the Masters of Urban Development and Design course at the University of New South Wales in which I have played a key role over the last ten years, we have devoted one-third of the programme to projects in Southeast Asia and beyond. Over this period two projects have been conducted annually, with a

Table 7 State control (housing authority) over the reproduction of labour and private sector development. Functional and signifying properties of urban space.

	Functional expression	**Signification**
Aspatial		
Political	Instrumental nature of public housing	Reproduction of labour power
Ideological	Provision of social welfare	Legitimation of the system
Economic	Low rents	Subsidy to private sector wages
Administrative	Collection of administered prices	Exclusion from the property market
Legal	Tenant's 'rights'	Absence of purchasing power
Physical	Mass housing estates	Class structure/captive markets
Spatial		
Location	Marginality, lowest land values	Poverty
Organisation	Modular, highly structured	Functional economics
Density	High-rise, high-density	Repression
Appearance	Architecture of 'cages'	Crowding
	Externalisation of domestic processes	'Cultural innovation'
Construction	Labour intensive	Surplus value extraction
Amenity	Institutionalised and elementary	Technically demanded by daylight standards
Dynamic	Static	Absence of choice
Form	Monumental	Identity unimportant

Source: A. R. Cuthbert, 'Hong Kong 1997: the transition to socialism–ideology discourse and urban spatial structure'. *Environment and Planning D: Society and Space,* 5, 1987, p. 147. Reprinted by permission of Pion Ltd, London.

total of some twenty projects in fifteen different countries. In every case we have been involved with real situations, working with international agencies, federal, state and local governments, private sector institutions and academic institutions, sometimes simultaneously (Cuthbert 2001). Two projects that manifested the relationship between authenticity and symbolic representation were those conducted in Bali and Beirut in 1997 and 1998 respectively.

The Bali project was located in Karangasem province, one of nine ancient kingdoms on the island. The general area had as a major tourist feature several beautiful water palaces built during Dutch imperial rule, of which Tenangan was the most famous; 1500 hectares of adjacent land had been targeted to create what can only be described as a Balinese version of Disneyland. Our objective was to reorient this perceived need into a more appropriate strategy, whereby the dynamic of local cultural traditions could be encouraged and enhanced through balanced eco-tourism. This implied sustainable strategies for the local environment, with new facilities, training programmes and employment opportunities for local people. Here, questions of authenticity and symbolic representation were profound, since Bali still maintains one of the most distinctive and

Table 8 State control (town planning authority) over the reproduction of labour and private sector development. Functional and signifying properties of non-urban space.

	Functional expression	Signification
Aspatial		
Political	Minimal control over free market systems	Ad hoc control via individual agreements
Ideological	To promote the health, safety and general welfare of the community	Mystification of the political process
Economic	Superprofits from land development	Finance and development capital tied to planning
Administrative	Constant change of apparatus	Internal power politics
		Continual realignment to market conditions
Legal	Minimal code	Maintenance of elastic productive conditions for capital accumulation
	Exclusion of public involvement	
Physical	Rapid physical change	Money more important than memory
	Absence of conservation	
Spatial		
Location	Central access to transportation modes	Economic power
Organisation	Zoning policy	Commodification of land and building
	Emphasis on land 'parcel'	
Density	Non-statutory control over intensity of use	Increased adaptability of system to private sector needs
Appearance	Architecture of façades	Extreme land prices and rents
	Private sector institutional domination over 'symbolic'	
Construction	Labour intensive	Surplus value extraction
Amenity	Degenerate 'urban design' quality and environmental monitoring	Absorption of 'social space' into the sphere of the market
Dynamic	High velocity of construction and deconstruction	Few restrictions to speculation
Form	Unique physical qualities of many buildings	Extreme intensity of use

Source: A. R. Cuthbert, 'Hong Kong 1997: the transition to socialism–ideology discourse and urban spatial structure'. *Environment and Planning D: Society and Space,* 5, 1987, p. 146. Reprinted by permission of Pion Ltd, London.

integrated cultural traditions worldwide, for example in the discourses of *Tri Angga*, the philosophy of spatial orientation, and the Nawa Sanga or Sanga Mandala, both derived from the Hindu religion (Suartika 2005).

While these two concepts applied at every level of cultural engagement, problems surrounding the redevelopment of the water palace at Ujung and the form of tourist villages indicate the kind of dilemma faced in many similar projects across the globe. The water palace at Ujung had, in an earlier time, been almost destroyed by a severe earthquake. The Dutch government had decided to fund the rebuilding of the palace, and there were at least four possible design solutions. First, the palace could be viewed as a sign of imperialist rule and eliminated as inauthentically Balinese. Second, the site could be preserved as it was, a true representation of the course of history, of the wrath of the gods and as a physical reminder of imperialism, whose memory had faded with the fading of the crumbling monument. Third, the site could have been redeveloped for any other uses deemed appropriate. The fourth alternative represented the chosen option, namely to leave the site intact as a true incorporation of the memory of the people, but to include a small museum that displayed collective memory using a variety of media, including the original drawings of the palace which remain in existence. It was also hoped that a perfect replica of the original could be built with the funds from the Dutch government as a central feature of the community, but with the use transformed into collective social use. In the second problem, that of the formal representation of community, the preferred option was to use the most traditional and 'authentic' form of Balinese settlement as a prototype, namely the Bali Aga, from which several transformations were evolved (Cuthbert 2001) (see figure 24).

The second example of the ineluctable problems surrounding authenticity and representation comes from an urban design project which we carried out in Beirut, the capital of Lebanon, under the auspices of Solidere, the company charged with the responsibility of creating a new central business district for the city. Much of the urban area and most of the central business district were destroyed during the civil war, which continued intermittently from 1975 until 1990. The famous Green Line, which separated Christians from Muslims, ran east to west and divided the city into two, along the axis of what used to be the old city centre. It also cut through the old entertainment and commercial heart of the city that previously contained the old souks, a place called Martyr's Square, now derelict and virtually eradicated. The project was to redesign the square and the surrounding district (see figure 25).

Martyr's Square, even in a state of total annihilation, represented a site of collective memory such that any building or monument placed in any location would immediately be challenged, so the problems involved in rebuilding were profound if not impossible. To begin with, how was history to be represented? And whose history should it be? What, for example, constituted authentic Lebanese culture, given that it had been split asunder by two major world religions, Islam and Christianity? In addition, Lebanon has been colonised at various times by so many imperial powers as to redefine the concept of a

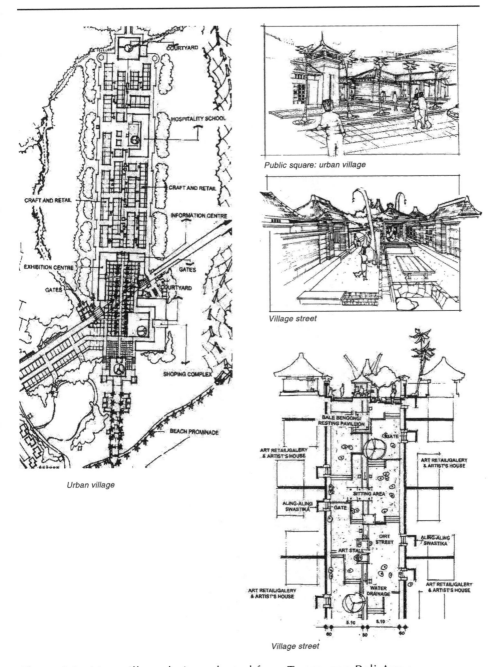

Urban village

Public square: urban village

Village street

Village street

Figure 24 New village design adapted from Tengangan Bali Aga.
Source: A. R. Cuthbert, *MUDD Yearbook 1997–1998.* Sydney: Faculty of the Built Environment, the University of New South Wales, 1998, p. 36. Reprinted by permission of the Faculty of the Built Environment.

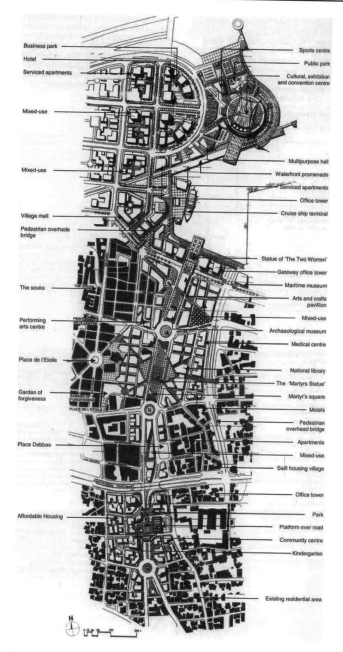

Figure 25   Beirut: Martyr's Square Corridor Project. Master of Urban
Development and Design Programme, University of New South Wales.
Source: A. R. Cuthbert, *MUDD Yearbook 1997–1998.* Sydney: Faculty of the Built
Environment, the University of New South Wales, 1997, p. 48. Drawn by Siew Leng
Leung. Reprinted by permission of the Faculty of the Built Environment.

'post-colonial society'. In the Beirut central business district alone there are at least ten archaeologies of settlement, going back to the Iron Age, six of which are currently visible. At the turn of the century, Lebanon was referred to as the Levant, giving its name to the word 'Levantine' as a respected symbol of tolerance, sophistication, intellectual discourse and humane living.

This came to an abrupt end when the Ottomans murdered thirty Lebanese nationals of various religious denominations during the Turkish occupation, naming Martyr's Square as the site of their execution. Here we now have a major paradox. Since that time, the square has symbolised national unity, resistance and sacrifice. Paradoxically, it also represented, on the basis of the civil war, a symbol of national division, war and self-immolation. Layered into these tragedies were images of erotic and other desires, since the square had been the locus of the red light district, entertainment and other material pleasures. Martyr's Square in other words represents the historic and collective memory of an entire nation, one that will not easily be resolved in bricks and mortar (see figures 26 and 27). The departure of Syria in April 2005 opens up the possibility for history to repeat itself or for Lebanon to become once again the acme of sophistication in the Middle East.

Figure 26   Beirut: Martyr's Square (formerly La Place des Canons).
Source: Fouad Debbas, *Beyrouth, Notre Mémoire.* Paris: Éditions Henri Berger, 1994, p. 71.

Figure 27   Beirut: dynamiting of the Rivoli Cinema, opening up the Martyr's Square axis to the sea.
Source: A. Gavin and R. Maluf, *Beirut Reborn: The Restoration and Development of the Central District.* London: Academy Editions, 1996, p. 58.

The New Ruralism/Urbanism

In concert with material commodity production and the production of commodified experience qua tourism, we have in parallel the shifting geographies of production and consumption in both regions. But any analogy between the geography of production vis-à-vis cultural commodities and the geography of consumption on the basis of mass tourism can only go so far. In the material production of commodities, the experience of production is not being sold, it is the manufactured object. In tourism, the objects of tourism (airlines, hotels, theme parks, beaches, marinas, architectural sites, etc.) are not being sold, it is the experience. In each case not only the resultant geography but also the ultimate effect on and concern for the built environment is completely different. The organisation of material commodity production consists primarily of spatial relationships and patterns with little concern for the physical world so created beyond market efficiencies, as in the association and clustering of production activities. In contrast, in the manufacture of experiences, the actual physical organisation of the world, i.e. its 'architecture' in the most general sense, is of paramount importance: 'In this perspective, postmodernism could be considered the architecture of the space of flows' (Castells 1996: 420).

Within postmodernism, architectural and urban design paradigms have several loosely related components. First, there is an international 'postmodern ideology', which itself embraces an eclectic range of styles into a recognisable pastiche of dissociated images. Second, in line with and consequent upon the ascendancy of Southeast Asia as an economic power, there is the idea of 'critical regionalism', the suggestion that architectural and design outcomes should reflect culture and place, not merely a faceless internationalism. It rejects Western hegemony over architectural aesthetics, Eurocentrism in design, and the abstract faceless values of functionalist aesthetics (Squire 1994). Third, there is the concept of the New Urbanism as the emergent design philosophy referred to in my introduction (Audirac and Shermyen 1994, Katz 1994). This movement is a reaction to the urban–suburban dichotomy, reflecting a perceived need to reinforce three primary qualities within cities: a sense of community, a sense of place and a respect for the natural environment. Its contemporary origins are primarily from North America and Europe, although Asia and other parts of the world are fast becoming attracted to the basic ideology (see figures 28 and 29). To a certain extent the movement is reactionary in both its philosophy and objectives, assuming that communities can design themselves out of economic, security and other problems on the basis of plundering accepted historical forms, and it remains to be seen what the enduring effects of this movement will be.

Less explored is the effect of global tourism on cultural production and built form in rural areas, particularly where first-world travellers descend on the tribal or feudal societies of the developing world and the rural areas of their own. In order to describe this phenomenon, I coined an obvious phrase to describe the economic and cultural environment of our study – the New Ruralism (Cuthbert 1997). This New Ruralism exists on the fault line between international global tourism and its search for 'difference' and the need of local cultures (e.g. in India, Malaysia, Indonesia, Australia and elsewhere) to survive. As a trend it is significantly affected by the cultural/informational economy and is now creating new rural spaces, not merely in abstract geometric patterning of activities, but in its physical and symbolic expression. In this coincidence between postmodern cultural production and exotic tourist sites or, more accurately, the pursuit of the exotic wherever it occurs, there is a tendency to 'Disney-fy' the latter and to reinforce the former as spectators of emergent cultural disaster zones. In order to move forward, the New Urbanism and the New Ruralism must be seen as aspects of the same problem rather than separate events in the cultural economy of the planet.

While the New Urbanism and the New Ruralism can both be viewed as products of globalisation, the analogy ends at that point. The New Urbanism is clearly a class-based reaction to perceived problems of postmodern life in cities; in other words it is ideological. The New Ruralism is the manifestation of a tectonic shift in postmodern production. Apart from the ability of the World

Figure 28 The town of Kentlands.
Source: P. Katz, *The New Urbanism*. New York: McGraw-Hill, 1994, p. 43.

Wide Web to shift industrial (informational) activity anywhere it chooses, and hence reorganise physical space, the New Ruralism shares on an international basis the need to generate economic development in the form of cultural production, and to enhance the revenues of both via the global tourist gaze. Six important implications for built form in the New Ruralism are as follows.

1 The integration and reinforcement of commodity space in a web-based rural–urban continuum via the culture industry.
2 The orientation of commodity production including architectural and urban forms to enhance the sale of cultural emblems and representations.
3 The use of informational strategies in minimising urban/rural differences.
4 The conscious exploitation of the cultural uniqueness of place as a revenue-raising activity (landscape, traditions, architecture, flora and fauna, etc.).
5 The nostalgic use of traditional and symbolic forms as an architectural and 'urban' design vocabulary.
6 The expansion of the term 'heritage' to cover entire local environments and their lifestyle.

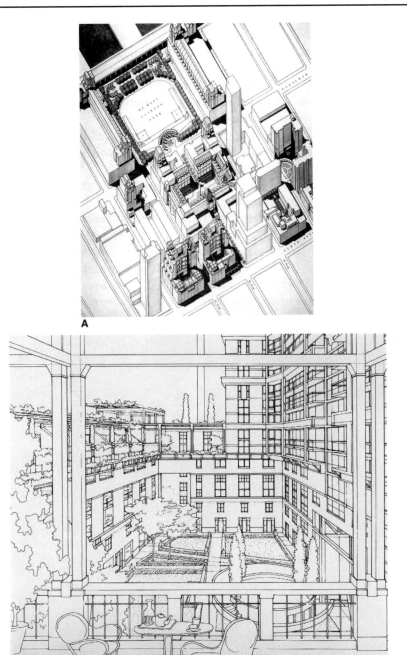

Figure 29 Clinton Community Masterplan.
Source: P. Katz, *The New Urbanism.* New York: McGraw-Hill, 1994, p. 208.

The physical expression of the New Ruralism also contains a kernel of resistance, as local cultures, particularly in the developing world, struggle to retain feudal identities, traditions and practices, which are being eroded by post-tourism and the culture industry. The critical regionalism of developing nations seeking a reinforced or new identity after colonisation, seminally expressed by Kenneth Frampton twenty years ago, is today gathering momentum (Frampton 1983, 1988). Frampton used the term 'critical regionalism' to denote a situation where 'a local culture of architecture is consciously evolved in express opposition to hegemonic power'. In developing countries such as Malaysia, Indonesia and Vietnam, architecture and urban form are important signifiers in eroding the impact of colonial ideologies and in the reconstruction of identity and collective meaning. The same is true of attitudes to landscape, as recounted in the work of Cosgrove and Daniels (1988) and Hester et al. (1999). Whereas the New Urbanism surfaces as a conservative and reactionary movement based on self-interest and isolationism, the New Ruralism has revolutionary potential since it is geared to escaping from the bounds of imperialist expansionism. Whether this reconstructed semiotics of space will be capable of expressing resistance to new forms of domination remains to be seen.

Chapter Six
Gender

The worker is the slave of capitalist society, the female worker is the slave of that slave.

James Connolly

Introduction: Gender, the Missing Component

Until relatively recently, the relation between gender and urban space has been isolated to the periphery of investigation into the social relations of capitalism, and urban life in general. But in the field of urban design, the concept has virtual exclusion in university programmes, and in the foremost publication in the field, *Journal of Urban Design*, only two articles have dealt with this issue in the last six years: 'Introducing gender to the critique of privatized public space' (Day 1999a) and 'From abstract to concrete' (Kallus 2001). The journal *Built Environment* has had two special issues on feminism (Bowlby 1984, 1990) but has been silent on women's issues since that time. While each of these deal in detail with the subjective experience of women in the city, none is fully situated within the huge literature in urban sociology, human geography and cultural studies that has become progressively available over the last twenty years. This general field is encompassed by the ideas expressed in articles called 'Sexuality and the spatial dynamics of capitalism' (Knopp 1992) and 'Feminist empiricism and the geography of social relations' (McDowell 1993). More importantly, *none* of the 40 texts listed in table 1 as representing mainstream urban design deal with this problematic, even peripherally. If we separate architectural from urban design, architecture has a somewhat better record in addressing questions of sexuality and gender in building design. Dolores Hayden's *The Grand Domestic Revolution* (1981) was a symbolic marker of the beginning of a new consciousness in this regard, and a handful of more recent publications, such as *Sexuality and Space* (Colomina 1992), *The Sex of Architecture* (Agrest et al. 1996) and *Gender, Space and Architecture* (Rendell et al. 2000), have illuminated the problems associated with gendered space and design. Nonetheless, in regard to the form of the city, urban design remains resistant to issues of gender and sexuality. It is also quite clear from the wealth of recent research in other areas that urban designers are missing out on an important region of knowledge,

127

which despite prevailing attitudes is undoubtedly central to the discipline. In order to bring this issue to the forefront of urban design (where it should be), we first have to consider some of the fundamental relationships between gender, patriarchy, capitalism, urbanism and the production of space, before looking at their collective effect upon the form of the city and the implications for design.

Gender and Society

While sexuality has been biologically determined since time immemorial, that is we are allocated a particular sex at conception, gender is a social construct that confers concepts of masculinity and femininity in the process of socialising individuals. Given current developments in genetic engineering, not only can our sex be artificially determined but it can potentially be constructed or even cloned in accordance with the needs of our parents. What the future holds is anybody's guess, but some indication can be gleaned from *Sex/Machine* (Hopkins 1998), which probes the relationships between culture, gender and technology. While it might appear that the biological determinism of sex and sexuality renders the topic relatively distinct, biology generates anomalies such as hermaphrodites, where even sexuality becomes problematic. Also, two sexes do not easily translate into two gender divisions either, since certain pre-feudal cultures such as the Nahane and the Mohave have four gender divisions, where both men and women can cross over. The Navaho have three gender divisions, where promotion to womanhood for someone of male gender represented elevation within the culture, since women had a higher social status than men (Kimmel 2000: 59). In modern society there are also examples of gender roles being temporarily negotiated, such as in prisons for example, and in certain other male-dominated institutions.

Within the capitalist system, relations are gendered and sexually coded, and their interaction is both volatile and complex. While it is tempting to consider gender, sexuality and social class as somehow independent phenomena, this position is now in question, since the alternative view 'that it is possible to classify certain aspects of our interactions neatly as "sexual relations", "gender relations", or "class relations", and that some might be logically or empirically prior to others – has been shown increasingly to be untenable' (Knopp 1992: 652; see also *DC 15*). In other words, we are not primarily formed by any of these qualities as singularities, so much as by the relations between them, despite essentialist arguments about biological determinism. Knopp goes on to argue that while sex and gender are intimately constituted, the social dimension is also powerfully woven into the equation. Other elements such as race, class and ethnicity are equally important in the formation of complete human beings. Since these relations require to be configured in space, the spatial dimension in its totality is a vast signifier of gendered relations (Little et al 1988, Bondi 1990, Knopp 1995, Longhurst 2002). So while each society presents its members with gender models, our gender is in fact negotiated against the many variants within the masculine/feminine model as part of our own life process.

Since the concept of gender is also contested terrain, there are significant differences among feminist scholars over which theoretical position offers the most powerful insights, where the three significant dimensions are the socio-sexual division of labour, gender symbolism and the processes of constructing an individual gendered identity (McDowell 1993: 162). While a significant number of male writers are concerned with gender studies, the area is colonised by women writers for obvious reasons. Within feminism, four central theoretical positions can be determined, namely radical feminism, Marxist feminism, liberalism and dual systems theory (Walby 1990). Others such as Lovell (1996) question the nature of feminist theory and suggest that a qualifier must always be added (Marxist, postmodernist, poststructuralist, Foucauldian, psychoanalytic, liberal, etc.), rendering any simple summation of 'feminism' seriously problematic. While being forced into embracing and confronting Marxism over issues of class, modes of production, etc., feminism is also antagonistic to Marx – at another level he is the ultimate patriarch. Radical feminism focuses on gender inequality and the institution of male domination and supremacy through patriarchy. This involves everything from the domination of personal behaviour and interpersonal communication, sexuality, domestic life and the forms of violence involved in all of these, to the political economy of labour relations, including women's subordinate roles in the workplace, differential remuneration and work conditions. 'The main problems critics have raised about radical feminism are a tendency to essentialism, to an implicit or explicit biological reductionism, and to a false universalism which cannot understand historical change or take sufficient account of divisions between men and women based on ethnicity and class' (Walby 1990: 3).

Radical feminism also tends to reject the qualifiers noted above, in particular Marxist feminist theory, gendered as 'malestream' theory, and its tendency to ignore relations of reproduction that occur within the domestic sphere and outside the mandate of the capitalist state: 'Marxist feminist theory has been the family household, where biological reproduction, childcare and the primary socialisation of children, and the rest and replenishment of the worker to restore "used up" labour power typically occur' (Lovell 1996: 310). Marxist feminism views capitalist social relations as an encompassing totality, where gender relations are established as an inherent part of class structures, and where patriarchy is embedded within capitalist class relations and does not constitute a separate and independent system. The tendency here, as with other Marxian projects (e.g. the environment, see chapter 7), is to reduce all social relations to political and economic forms, ignoring both the ideological and psychological dimensions and rendering interpretations of gender in historical periods problematic, both within and outside industrial capitalism. Until recently, Marxism has also had the enduring problem of dealing with reproduction as well as production. Liberalist attitudes towards gender are no different to liberalist attitudes towards any other aspect of society. In portraying development as essentially a benign process deprived of any inherent exploitation, domination or hegemony, liberalism is incapable of adequately addressing the inequalities involved in gender differentiation 'but rather conceives this as the summation of numerous small-scale deprivations' (Walby 1990: 4). Dual systems theory is a combination of Marxism and radical feminism, where capitalism and patriarchy are viewed as interdependent structures, and where gender relations are determined by the ongoing dialectic between them.

Once problems surrounding gender are placed at the centre of our concern rather than the periphery, many of our assumptions about society are irrevocably altered. Nothing looks quite the same. For issues of gender are enmeshed with all others, from capitalism and patriarchy to poststructuralist theorising, the nature of power, hegemony, sexuality, culture and experience. More specifically, gender forces us into reconsidering space and territory, from the global to the domestic arenas. In considering gender and the existential place of women as 'other' within patriarchy, we are also compelled to consider both direct and subtle forms of oppression and violence, not only against women but also other oppressed groups such as ethnic and religious minorities, children and those with physical or mental disabilities, as well as non-human forms of life (see chapter 7). Problematic also is the fact that feminism does not view women as a single monolithic group but a form of belonging that has a myriad facets. As we have seen, there is no single accepted orthodoxy in forms of interpretation from within the female gender, and feminism has frequently divergent intellectual positions, theoretical interpretations and political agendas. Because of this, feminist studies of gender now cover a huge terrain, for example in relation to social science (Momsen and Townsend 1987, Maynard 1990, Kimmel 2000), the developing world (Brydon and Chant 1989, Ostergaard 1992), history (Scott 1988), space and place (McDowell 1983, 1989b, 1993, England 1991, Massey 1994, Ainley 1998, Day 1999a,b), social class (Huxley 1988, Bagguley 1990, Regulska 1991), oppression (Hearn 1987, Valentine 1990, Pain 1991, Namaste 1996), public space (Gardner 1995, Ruddick 1996), zoning and planning theory (Sandercock and Forsyth 1992, Rizdoff 1994), architecture (Boys 1984, Colomina 1992, Rendell et al. 2000), urban design (Hayden 1981, Boys 1990, 1998, Roberts 1998) and the urban landscape (*DC* 16).

Gender and Patriarchy

Patriarchy refers to male dominance in all societies and across all historical periods, and therefore constitutes a virtually universal phenomenon. While industrial and postindustrial societies offer greater opportunities to women, men still dominate all important spheres of influence, in government, the military, business, education and other regions of social development. The reason most frequently given for this is women's biological constitution, their child-bearing capacity and a dependency on men for providing the material basis for

the family. While sociologists are somewhat dismissive of biological determinism, they are frequently operating with a Victorian concept of biology rather
than what biology represents today (Lovell 1996). In pre-industrial societies and
in societies whose social relations still demand that women's role is limited to the
domestic sphere, as for example in many developing countries and those with
fundamentalist religious practices, patriarchy remains entrenched. Since patriarchy preceded capitalism and also exists within socialist and communist states,
the one cannot be directly conflated to the other. Hence the actual forms of
patriarchy within particular modes of production become significant, along with
the specificity of gendered roles and the oppression of women. In addition, the
spatial organisation of gender roles is frequently extreme, as for instance in
certain Islamic societies where segregation between men and women (and also
between children) verges on the absolute. In the developed countries of the West,
women now represent a significant portion of the labour force, which remains
structured on the basis of gender. While the figure varies from place to place,
roughly twice as many men are employed as women. Despite this apparent
liberation, women occupy a disproportionate number of low-status and low-
prestige positions, such as secretaries, nurses and waitresses, as well as in
assembly line operations, sweat shops such as the garment industry, and other
menial tasks. Along with this comes lower remuneration, benefits and opportunities for promotion, and the poverty trap that many women find themselves
in. Walby recognises that patriarchy as a system of social relations needs to be
theorised on a series of levels, not just as organised labour. In recognising the
limitations of any classification and the false reality it indicates, and that patriarchy and capitalism are not homologous with each other, nonetheless 'patriarchy is composed of six structures: the patriarchal mode of production,
patriarchal relations in paid work, patriarchal relations in the state, male violence, patriarchal relations in sexuality, and patriarchal relations in cultural
institutions' Walby (1990: 21).

As we can see, only the first three categories respond to an orthodox Marxist
analysis, the remainder being a product of superstructural phenomena dealing
with ideology and socialisation. Overall Marx paid little attention to patriarchy
as an institution and, as Marxist feminism has noted, not at all in the domestic
sphere, a situation somewhat corrected by his benefactor Friedrich Engels in *The
Origin of the Family, Private Property and the State*. Since that time, patriarchy
has been subject to many definitions and forms of interpretation. It has been
argued that any analysis of patriarchy must combine the gendered division of
labour with control of fertility and biological reproduction. Another dimension
of this same problematic seeks to incorporate patriarchal control over women's
sexuality *and* their access to work (Fraad et al. 1994). Hearn maintains that both
of these approaches are essentialist in the sense that they place economic class in
a binary relation to fertility and sexuality, rather than building 'an understanding
of women's oppression by and *social relation* to men, and men's oppression of
and *social relation* to women, that is total yet neither reductionist nor imprecise'
(Hearn 1987: 42). This has been partially accomplished within dual systems

theory where the concept of a mode of production has been transferred to the domestic realm, although feminist theorists tend to emphasise the concept of patriarchy and gender domination.

But even this combination of Marxist and radical feminism is also open to criticism despite the fact that it combines the concentration on labour, ideology and class of the former with an essentialist view of women's position and the specificity of other forms of oppression. Some of this is at least partly due to Giddens' concept of structure/agency, with a move to the latter in understanding domination (Giddens 1979, Bryant and Jary 1991): 'so it is not patriarchy, "the system" which oppresses women. Rather it is men who are the unambiguous agents of women's subordination. This emphasises the everyday and non-mediated experience of oppression. It stresses the existence of active agents who "do" the oppressing' (Maynard 1990: 274). Even this idea is denied if we consider women's relation to patriarchy through a Foucauldian lens. An important dimension of Foucault's conception of power is that 'although power is described as having an objective or aim, it is not the product of intentionality on the part of a subject. Second, the very existence of power relations presuppose forms of resistance, not as an external effect or consequence of the exercise of power, but as an inherent feature of it' (Smart 1983: 90). So the idea that people 'do' the oppressing may be to deny the essence of the power relation, which Foucault considers is contained within the anatomo-politics of the human body, and the bio-politics of the population. Much feminist theorising depends heavily on a simplistic concept of power on the part of some oppressor – father, husband, boss, priest, state, etc. What Foucault suggests is that we must completely transform the concept of domination/resistance based on sourced oppression to a much more ambivalent, subtle and pervasive reality centring on the idea of discourse/practice. Here, everyone is simultaneously oppressor and victim, a situation perfectly expressed by Franz Fanon in relation to French Algeria, where he comments, 'The new relations are not the result of one barbarism replacing another barbarism, of one crushing of man replacing another crushing of man. What we want to discover is the man behind the coloniser; this man *who is both the organiser and the victim* of a system that has choked him and reduced him to silence' (Fanon 1986: 63; my italics). What Foucault opens up is the vast dimension of human subjectivity within patriarchy and its incorporation into the overall equation: the place of psychoanalysis and the psyche, how submission is psychologically constituted, the coding of sex drives and the constitution of sexuality, as exemplified in the work of Deleuze and Guattari, Jacques Lacan, Julia Kristeva and others.

Gender and Capital

The importance of gender to the development of social theory cannot be overestimated, since it was probably the single major issue that derailed structuralist thinking about capitalism. Prior totalising theoretical constructs in economics and social science were incapable of incorporating the critical aspects of power, subjectivity and difference that constituted contemporary society. At the same time, the idea that the 'social relations' of capitalism were also formed as sexually coded, gendered relations was nowhere mentioned. Marx's concentration on modes of production, the division of labour and class conflict wholly excluded the dimensions of gender and sexuality from the analysis of society, despite the fact that it was largely men who were exploited by capital and men who exploited women through patriarchy. In addition, the immense economic contribution made by women's domestic labour was also unaccounted for in the Marxian concept of surplus value. For all practical purposes, women's labour had no economic dimension. Exploitation in the classic Marxist sense refers to the production of a surplus by one section of society that is controlled by another. Hence women's position is usually referred to as one of superexploitation. Men's labour was exploited, but women's unpaid domestic labour was subsumed to men's labour and therefore represented an added bonus within the capitalist class system. Women were therefore not only subordinate to men within a system of patriarchy, but were doubly exploited within the economy as a whole. On top of this, women have been historically constituted as a non-class, involved almost exclusively in social reproduction and non-paid labour. Even a woman's social class was established in relation to her husband. While retaining elements of a traditional class analysis as significant, Marxian feminists have transformed the concept of mode of production into the 'domestic mode of production' to account for women's labour, and others have gone even further to locate it within a system of non-capitalist production, thus creating a parallel reality to traditional patriarchal economic theorising.

Classical political economy has therefore been severely criticised for these omissions and the consequences that flow from them. In *The End of Capitalism (As We Knew It)* (Gibson-Graham 1996), the authors provide a withering critique of political economy and, in the process, challenge most of its presumptions about how society is organised (despite being self-confessed Marxists). A major point in their attack is a rejection of the concrete encompassing qualities, assumed in a materialist analysis of capitalism, which accord the capitalist system with fixed and enduring properties, i.e. everything takes place within capitalism. In adopting the idea that capitalism is all-encompassing, we deny other forms of development and the realities they embody; after all, existing capitalism lives alongside pre-capitalist and feudal social relations in many parts of the world. In an effort to clarify the nature of this rigidity, they point to a dimension that they term 'non-capitalism'. This includes such disparate elements as self-employment, peripheral economic development that is not fully capitalist, and the place of women in the domestic mode of production. Within materialist analyses, domestic life is de-noted as the space of commodity consumption or social reproduction, not as the space of non-capitalist production and consumption: 'In the hierarchical relation of capitalism to noncapitalism lies (entrapped) the possibility of theorising economic difference, of supplanting the discourse of capitalist hegemony with a plurality and heterogeneity of economic forms' (Gibson-Graham 1996: 11).

The most significant of these recent 'economic forms' is the phenomenon of globalisation, which adds even greater complexity to the relationship between gender and capitalism, where much of the theorising is carried out within the confines of the nation state, or at least within the developed countries of the West. Here, in the new international division of labour, traditional categories of domination and exploitation take on new dimensions. Surplus value is now extracted at a global scale, and the relationship between capitalism in the developed world and gender in the developing world remains problematic (Momsen and Townsend 1987, Brydon and Chant 1989, Willis and Yeoh 2000). Given globalised communications, gender orthodoxy within traditional communities has been severely challenged. Mass media such as film, television and the Internet have exposed individuals to a multitude of other possible gender roles. These new codings have the potential to destabilise entire cultures, and so the political economy of feminism is fraught with conflict over how fast social change should take place in relation to the gendered division of labour and to cultural practices. All traditional institutions, including marriage, family structure, child-rearing, forms of inheritance, etc., become seriously challenged. Significantly, women are placed in conflict with other women over the status quo, between those who seek change and those who wish to maintain the traditional roles of nurturing and domestic life. The same is true of men. So the binary opposition implied in masculine/feminine is a crude if not impossibly oversimplified terminology. Also, because gender roles are defined in relation to a social totality, changes in the role of one gender will automatically have effects and implications for the other.

The global migration of female workers creates new racialised geographies of indentured labour from enforced prostitution to near slavery, much of which involves the global criminal economy (Castells 1998, Pritchard and Morgan 2000). Unlike men, who are merely exploited for their labour, women are once again superexploited and trafficked, both for their labour and their sexuality. This arises most significantly in the relationship between global tourism and global prostitution, one which also involves a parallel and integrated relationship to the exploitation of children. Not only are children exploited for cheap industrial and domestic labour, but also as part of sex tourism, sometimes simultaneously: 'These domestic workers work as much as 10–15 hours a day, and studies report what ILO describes as "alarming evidence" of physical, mental and sexual abuse of adolescents and young women working as domestics' (Castells 1998: 151). On this basis entire markets are established, such as sex tourism to places like the Philippines, Thailand, Cambodia and Vietnam, and domestic labour in Hong Kong, Singapore, Saudi Arabia, the USA, and other countries. Domestic labour hence becomes a sphere of exchange, where educated middle-class women in the developed world are released into the workforce on the basis of exploiting working-class women in the developing world. Here, traditional assumptions about 'domestic life' become challenged in both regions. Many women are the only breadwinner for families in the developing world and gender roles become reversed. The same can occur in the trade-off, since this transfer of women's labour can also result in women earning more than their husbands in both locations. Hence the authors of *The End of Capitalism* suggest that the objectification of women, rather than improving, is actually extended within globalisation. They maintain that from a women's perspective globalisation is merely another form of rape, and even the gendered language of development denotes violent sexual connotations (domination, invasion, penetration, virgin territory, etc.), and that 'Consistent with the often expressed view that the one thing worse than being exploited by capital is not being exploited at all, there is a sense that not being penetrated by capitalism is worse than coming within its colonizing embrace' (Gibson-Graham 1996: 121).

The domestic mode of production must therefore be accounted for in relation to the dominant system of capitalism, if for no other reason than the world would grind to a halt without it. Despite the above 'non-capitalist, non-class' descriptors, it is clear that the domestic sphere cannot be adequately theorised as a separate and distinct system due to the myriad connections between the spheres of domestic reproduction, wage labour and capital. As Christine Delphy remarks:

> Like all modes of production, the domestic mode of production is also a mode of circulation and consumption of goods. While it is difficult, at first sight, to identify in the capitalist mode of production the form of consumption that distinguishes the dominant from the dominated, since consumption is mediated by wage, things are very different in the domestic mode. Here consumption is of primary importance, and has this power to serve as the basis for making discriminations, for one of the essential differences between the two modes of production is that domestic production is not paid but rather maintained. In this mode, therefore, consumption is not separated from production, and the unequal sharing of goods is not mediated by money.
>
> (Delphy 1988: 261)

Delphy is also conscious of the fact that the economic subordination of women can only be partially explained by the domestic mode of production, and that it is difficult to contest 'difference' when the concepts and terminology remain unchanged. Her main contribution to our understanding of the domestic sphere is to reverse our traditional framing of the gender/capital relation. In this context it is normal to situate the constraints on women's capacity to work within the domestic sphere where patriarchy determines how a woman may or may not think, act, reason or believe, and on this basis what role she may play, if any, within the economy. Delphy considers that the reverse is true. In actually existing capitalism, labour markets, through systematic discrimination and exploitation, in fact condition women's trajectory into domesticity. Social reproduction, wholly necessary to capital, then becomes an unpaid form of labour. While the oppression of women remains undeniable, and the movement towards equality glacial in character, the fact remains that women in the developed world are advancing towards a greater share in the non-domestic economy. While women in the first world can at least contemplate working outside, and therefore entertain the idea of an escape from domesticity as desirable, racism and colour add an altogether different dimension (Brydon and Chant 1989). Where black nations were oppressed under capitalism, and black women further exploited under their own systems of patriarchy, levels of oppression are such that traditional feminist attitudes to the domestic sphere as one of oppression can be reversed for black families living in white societies: 'Yet for black women, the family can be a refuge in a heartless world of racism, somewhere secure to return to, and develop a resistance to, the external world of racism outside' (Maynard 1990: 280). Taken to extremes, we can see from the example of the Bedouin in Israel, a nomadic tribe with no fixed settlements, how space, when stripped down to absolute essentials, is even more strictly gendered than it is within developed urban society (Fenster 1999). Space for Bedouin women is divided into 'forbidden' and 'permitted', distinctions which seriously limit their mobility according to patriarchal principles, analogous to our distinctions between private and public space. Even the boundaries of permitted spaces are determined on the basis of the type of clothing a woman wears. The embodiment on cultural meanings attributed to space 'include codes of "honour", "modesty", "shame", "disgrace", "manhood", "women as property", and "men as women's owners". These codes determine the spatial boundaries of the individual' (Fenster 1999: 228). When settled, women are limited to home and neighbourhood and are prohibited from going to other areas in any town. Fenster points out that the concept of the 'tent' is also symbolic and that when a stranger enters the house, the space s/he occupies immediately becomes public and the woman has to vacate the space. Settlement for the Bedouin therefore denotes a serious entrenchment of cultural codes surrounding a woman's modesty. As we shall see below, this general condition of fear is, for women, universal.

Gender and Space

At the most elementary level, the gendered division of space reflects the historical relationship between production and reproduction, between the economic and domestic spheres. The geography of gender also cuts across 'rural' and 'urban' distinctions. Manuel Castells, in concentrating on the sphere of reproduction, brought the problem of gender into high relief when he defined the urban as the sphere of collective consumption, which some might argue finally branded women's own collective sphere (see chapter 9). In regard to women's unpaid domestic labour, Castells comments that 'If these women who "do nothing" ever stopped to do "only that", the whole urban structure as we know it would become completely incapable of maintaining its functions' (Castells 1978: 177–8). Despite this contribution, Castells has been criticised for ignoring domestic labour: 'His focus on collective rather than privatized consumption, or more generally on the social relations of the reproduction of labour power means that the city itself tends to be seen as the agent of reproduction. Consequently the role of the family and patriarchy is neglected' (McDowell 1983: 60). Castells apart, other highly influential (male) theorists, for example David Harvey and

Ed Soja, have come in for withering criticism from feminist urban theorists in articles such as 'Boy's town' (Deutsche 1991) and 'Flexible sexism' (Massey 1991). This can be easily seen as a reflection of an entire field, since urban geography has predominantly concerned itself with the public sphere: 'Thus in common with the other social sciences, geography takes for granted the Enlightenment distinction between the public and the private, and implicitly, the gendered association of these spheres' (McDowell 1993: 165).

While it is tempting to argue that women's position within the 'economic' mode of production has altered radically and that women are now significantly more emancipated than they were within prior feudal or pre-capitalist modes of production, it is probably more correct to say that the difference is primarily technical rather than social. Women simply have better technology to undertake similar roles. They drive children to school rather than walking or carrying them. They use washing machines, driers and vacuum cleaners rather than performing such work by hand. Women's behaviour and mobility, and therefore their occupation of space, remains constrained, from the type of clothing they are expected to wear to their continuing role as low-paid workers and domestic servants, otherwise known, in more politically correct terms, as 'carers'. While employment clearly plays a major role in the spatial structuring of gender roles, other factors such as patterns of inheritance, gentrification and the differential distribution of childcare facilities and schools all have significant influence. Added to these, the material dimension must also be balanced by ideological and symbolic qualities, and the meaning of home, as well as the entire realm of women's perceptions and preferences, must be accounted for.

Gender and space interact in highly complex ways within the overall process of reproducing the social and property relations of the capitalist system. But these phenomena do not exist in an existential despatialised vacuum. They stretch across historical time, sedimenting physical and symbolic archaeologies in space, constructing environments, and building cities that mirror the inherent architecture of our societies. This is also echoed in their planning. Here three different types of planning theory emphasise practice, political economy and meta-theory, each requiring that differing gender issues should be addressed. '<While> a distinctive feminist epistemology would be controversial, feminist insights, however, would expand the planner's perspective beyond scientific and technical knowledge to other ways of knowing' (Sandercock and Forsyth 1992: 52). Entire city structures have been generated on the basis of patriarchal capitalism: land-use zoning patterns, including the form, location and type of residential areas, transportation networks, public open space, and the relationship between work and home result from male-dominated expectations and values. But people do not occupy space according to the same conventions and constraints. As the environment we have constructed mirrors social class, so it also reflects the gender of its occupants, and the geography of these relationships is now a major field of study (McDowell 1989, 1993, England 1991, Massey 1994, Duncan 1996, Roberts 1998, Longhurst 2002). Any aerial photograph clearly illustrates class distinctions and the difference between upper-class areas, with large houses, swimming pools, two-car garages, proximity to parks and services, etc., and the poorer sections of the population, with smaller cramped accommodation, poor maintenance, lack of open space, proximity to major roads and sources of pollution. On the other hand, gender distinctions are not so readily apparent, at least to men, simply because patriarchy is part of our psychological make-up and is not constrained to a single social class.

A man looking at the same cadastral map would probably be conscious of the class nature of physical space ('his' house being larger or smaller than someone else's). But a woman would also read the gender implications. For example, suburbs in their entirety remain a potent symbol of women's non-capitalist, gendered, domestic realm (Saegert 1980, Watson 1986, Fraad et al. 1994). The sexual division of labour is expressed not only in the location of housing in relation to work but also in the physical layout of dwellings and how space is occupied within them (Hayden 1981, Hanson and Johnson 1985, Rizdoff 1994, Ainley 1998). In addition, women would look at all sporting venues as spaces of male domination (think cricket, football, rugby match). Similarly, open spaces, parks, gardens and so on, while representing opportunities for physical exercise and leisure, also offer opportunities for sexual and physical violation of women in a multitude of forms, and public urban space in general is frequently prob-lematic (Lofland 1984, Boys 1985, 1990, Gardner 1989, 1995, Valentine 1990, Pain 1991, Ruddick 1996, Drucker and Gumbert 1997). McDowell (1993: 169) has noted that 'studies have shown how women feel that their freedom to use urban spaces varies over the day, as well as how men's differential control over private and public space affects women's behaviour'. The physical world is therefore read and experienced differently by men and women (Ardener 1981, Bowlby 1990, Walker 1998).

Public and private spheres became increasingly polarised within capitalism due to the increasing separation between consumption/reproduction and pro-duction, which corresponded partially to the removal of production from the domestic sphere in developed countries. Along with this came the generation of particular forms of space for both activities, connected by what is referred to as the public realm. Particular gendered spatial forms for extended reproduction then became part of the spatial typology of modernism – new towns, suburbs, high-rise apartments, walk-up flats, duplexes, single family homes – all of which contoured gender relations in highly specific ways, in particular the idea of the nuclear family and its attendant ideologies. England gives the example of Roosevelt's Greenbelt Towns programme under what was called the New Deal, where 'The preferred tenants were the "traditional" nuclear family with a commuting husband and home-maker wife; indeed, two earner couples were often prohibited, as the wives of employed husbands were not permitted to have paid jobs' (England 1991: 138). However, it became apparent with the rise of feminism in the 1960s that suburban life spatially disadvantaged women. The low densities of most suburbs meant that many women were detached from any significant social network, as well as the facilities of the central city, particularly transportation. While women are mutually isolated and simultaneously deprived of economic opportunity in the suburbs, the corollary is that dense urban spaces have a liberating and empowering potential for women. Where extensive commuting by car for men was the rule, women can also spend a disproportionate amount of time on simple domestic duties. This quickly leads to the situation where 'married women are less positive and less satisfied today about living in the suburbs than their husbands...men also enjoy being able to retreat from their hectic city jobs to a relaxed life which offers many outdoor activities' (England 1991: 140). The spatial design of homes not only reinforced the whole notion of gendered space but also reinforced the idea that these spaces would be heterosexual spaces for families, leaving out single people as well as lesbian and gay domestic arrangements (Lauria and Knopp 1985, Knopp 1990, Adler and Brenner 1992, Duncan 1996). Valentine (1995) shows that the preferences of gay and lesbian communities have had a profound effect on the socio-political geography of American cities in terms of neighbourhood development, gentrification and commercial facilities. Importantly, she demonstrates the significance of transcending the materiality of social space 'to examine how lesbian spaces are also produced or claimed through collective imaginings, and sometimes fantasies focused upon social networks, individual celebrities and specific sites' (Valentine 1995: 97).

Gender and Urban Design

Probably the best the design professions can do in promoting gender equality is to appreciate in significant detail exactly how they have been complicit in the gendering of our existing environments, consciously or otherwise, by the processes explored above. This takes a multitude of forms, from the blatant phallic symbolism in the competition between cities to build the tallest building; to the gendered layout of towns into central business districts and suburbs; to the nature and expression of our architecture, monuments and symbolic spaces; to the internal layout and external landscaping of buildings and spaces; and to the gendered content of retail outlets. It should be clear from the preceding commentary that a non-sexist city requires nothing less than a Copernican revolution in how we think about the world and each other (Burnett 1973, Weisman 1992, Valentine 1993, Borden 1995, Eichler 1995, Roberts 1998, DC 10). This would necessarily start with the socialisation of children and proceed through all aspects of the economy into the actual physical configuration of space by design. The question then arises as to whether there may be aspects of gender difference that are wholly constructive, that individuals of whatever gender might agree should be maintained. Also transparent is the fact that the patriarchal nature of capitalist development, with the concomitant burden of care placed on women, will not be radically altered overnight. While design strategies for a non-sexist city are yet to be determined, nonetheless it is important that designers become involved in three associated areas of knowledge, namely the historical record, socialised domestic work and implications for the public realm.

The historical record

While the idea of gendered environments might seem a new concept to introduce into design, it has a long history. It was also a concept that had to arise from within a socialist consciousness since it remained the only political perspective that embodied real equality between men and women as fundamental values. Hence the utopian socialism of the early nineteenth century saw figures such as Robert Owen in Scotland, Charles Fourier in France and John Humphrey Noyes in the USA propose changes to the social and moral order of the day, combined with radical adaptations to settlement organisation and the design of buildings. Both came as a reaction to the decay of the Industrial Revolution, with the object not merely of changing the condition of the working class, but to accomplish the task on the basis of gender equality. In order to do this, the non-capitalist, non-economic domestic sphere of women had to be reconstructed. Men had to participate equally in this sphere, and in order for this to happen spatial relationships had to undergo radical transformation, and the kitchenless house became a potent symbol of women's liberation. In 1800, Robert Owen, a Welshman, was among the first visionaries to put socialist principles into practice in an experimental town in Scotland called New Lanark. At its peak, the community he organised had a population of 2,500 persons. His unrealised ideal, a community called the Institute for the Formation of Character, was one where women were fully liberated to work equally with men on the basis of collective childcare, food supply, laundry work, etc., and where both sexes had a commitment to domestic duties.

Owen's ideas transferred to the USA in 1824 and generated a spate of similar projects. Charles Fourier's approach was even more radical, his communities being referred to as Phalansteries, although the fullest expression of his philosophy was realised by his student, Jean Baptiste André, who built what he called Familistère at Godin in France in 1859. The largest expression of utopian socialist ideals in the Fourierist tradition was a new town called Topolobampo in Mexico, designed by Marie Howland and Albert Kimsey Owen (figure 30). For the first time, the physical design of these communities obviated the concept of the single family house, not merely because it was difficult to have collective facilities on the basis of privatised accommodation, but also to encourage a new moral order implicit in collective social life: 'In contrast to the private household which all these reformers denounced as isolated, wasteful, and oppressive, the communitarians hoped to build communal or cooperative facilities for domestic tasks, tangible architectural demonstrations of the workings of a more egalitarian society' (Hayden 1981: 37). In many socialist designs from this period, the symbol of women's enslavement, the kitchen, was ritually planned out of many domestic arrangements (see figure 31). These basic principles continued as a major theme throughout the nineteenth century and into the twentieth, where they were revisited by Ebeneezer Howard and his associates Barry Parker and

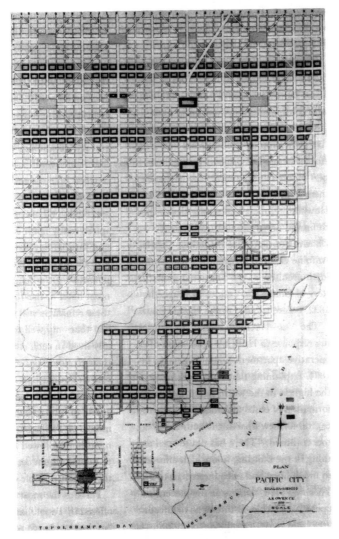

Figure 30 Master plan for Topolobampo.
Source: D. Hayden, *The Grand Domestic Revolution: A History of Feminist Designs for American Homes, Neighbourhoods and Cities.* Cambridge, MA: MIT Press, 1981, p. 107.

Raymond Unwin. Cooperative housekeeping was incorporated into one of the first new towns they designed at Letchworth in 1909.

The domestic sphere

While socialised domestic work remained a feminist strategy until 1920, suburban expansion enabled by corporate capitalism radically inhibited the collective ideal, which was based on increasing rather than reducing urban densities. The

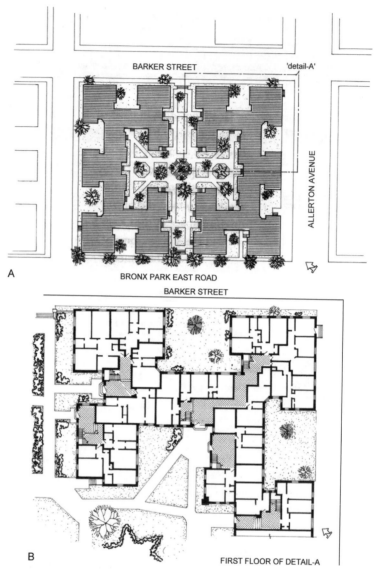

Figure 31 Herman Jessor: workers' cooperative colony of 750 units of housing with collective services, New York (1926): (a) site plan; (b) detail.
Source: D. Hayden, *The Grand Domestic Revolution: A History of Feminist Designs for American Homes, Neighbourhoods and Cities.* Cambridge, MA: MIT Press, 1981, p. 256.

rise in private motor vehicle ownership was also a significant contributor in two major dimensions. First, it accelerated the complete separation of workplace from home life, thus impacting the role of women in the domestic sphere of the suburbs (Davis 1990). Second, ownership of only a single car led to the acute isolation of women from each other and from all forms of service. Given that diminished densities also implied diminished public transport, mobility became seriously problematic. Combined with inclement weather, young children and the absence of an extended family, many women did not view garden suburbs with the same enthusiasm as their male advocates. Whatever the configuration of suburban space, the existential place of women remained unaltered. The combined effect of labour-saving devices, fast food and television actually increased women's labour rather than reducing the time she spent working.

> Capitalism had socialized only those aspects of household work that could be replaced by profitable commodities or services, and left the cooking, cleaning and nurturing for the housewife...Although the dense urban environments of industrial capitalism ultimately gave way to an artificial privatism in the United States, and workers' suburban habitations proved that Fourier and Olmsted, Marx and Engels, Bellamy and Gilman had misjudged the pace at which the urban concentration caused by industrial capitalism was hastening socialism and women's liberation, the debates they began have not yet finished.
>
> (Hayden 19981: 26)

Dolores Hayden had also expressed many of these ideas in two prior publications: first, *Seven American Utopias* (1976), which illustrates clearly the differing aspirations of men and women with regard to housing and urban design; and second, 'What would a non-sexist city be like?' (1980), in which Hayden suggests that while most women are not interested in pursuing a communal lifestyle, they are interested in the provision of community services that support the household. She suggests a basic organisation called 'Homes' (Homemaker's Organisation for a More Egalitarian Society) and proposes six basic properties that are required if housing, housework and residential neighbourhoods are to be transformed (Hayden 1980: 272).

1 Involve both men and women in the unpaid labour associated with childcare on an equal basis.
2 Involve both men and women in the paid labour force on an equal basis.
3 Eliminate residential segregation by class, race and age.
4 Eliminate all federal, state and local programmes and laws that offer implicit or explicit reinforcement of the unpaid role of the female homemaker.
5 Minimise unpaid domestic labour and wasteful energy consumption.
6 Maximise real choices for households concerning recreation and sociability.

Paradoxically, in the twenty-five years since that article was written, informational capitalism has differentially affected most of these relationships, with the potential for many people to work wholly or partially from home via a combination of the Internet, faxes, broadband and other innovations, making access to the family car less problematic and caring for children potentially more equitable. In addition, the continuing oil crisis, combined with gentrification, has encouraged increased residential provision in central cities. Given the high cost of such developments, in the last ten years there has also been a proliferation in the variety and configuration of housing types, including experiments in 'co-housing' which combine privately owned personal space with collectively owned domestic facilities and living spaces. This idea has also been developed in Sweden, and fifteen such projects are assembled and reviewed in *Femton Kollektivhus* (fifteen collective houses) (Lundahl and Sangregorio 1992).

The public realm

Due to the erosion of the public realm by state corporatism, the cohesion of any 'public realm' has been rendered analytically indistinct (see also chapter 4). Firstly, the concept of the public realm is by no means guaranteed, that is, it exists to the extent that it is enshrined in law and is part of the make-up of civil society. In many societies the public realm has no legal existence, which makes the concept somewhat tenuous. So 'public space' has at least two fundamental conditions, legal and permitted, borrowing a term from Fenster (1999). In the private realm, urban designers also have to distinguish between private space and privatised public space. Similarly, privatised public space also has two faces. First, there is space that is privately owned to which the public has necessary access in order to support personal and luxury consumption and the sale of commodities, for example shopping centres, malls, large stores, entertainment and sporting venues (Kayden 2000). Second, there is also space leased or other-wise managed by the private sector on behalf of local government. I have referred elsewhere to this as ambiguous space, since it is unclear as to what rights individuals actually retain in space which is public but otherwise managed by private sector interests (Cuthbert 1995b, 1997, Mitchell 1996). Public or private, gendered space is the norm in whatever form it arises, and it is germane that even the *flâneur* of French urban life who freely wanders the city in search of new experiences has male gender. The *flâneuse* is nowhere to be seen. This is clearly due to men's domination of space and the forms of behaviour that reinforce it. As a result, women's conception of permitted space is intimately connected to their vulnerability and the fear that this engenders, and it is essential that any male involved in designing urban space addresses women's spatial psychology and deals with it accordingly. It is also telling how much of the literature on women's relation to public space begins and ends in fear (Boys 1984, Valentine 1990, Pain 1991, Bowman 1993, Gardner 1995, Namaste 1996, Day 1997).

For example, Day (1999b) exposes in significant detail the complexities of class and race in women's fear of public places, from white middle-class women to poor Hispanic and black American women. Despite women's emancipation, fear is legion, and improvements in women's status simply swap one matrix of fear for another. Race, social class and gender interlock in complex ways to structure fear in a multitude of differing dimensions, and at various physical scales. She states that in the 'new segregation, women constructed race borders round some such cities, ascribing racial identities to many of them. ...Public spaces were selected or avoided such that most places in some cities (especially "white" cities) were seen as safe from crime, and most public spaces in other cities (especially "Hispanic" or "Asian" cities) in Orange County were seen as dangerous' (Day 1999b: 312). According to her research it was cities that were feared, not individuals. She classifies public space into four generic categories of fear, embassies, neutral zones, carnivals and outposts, which she defines as follows (Day 1999b: 316–19).

1   Embassy public spaces are those which offer white women experiences of foreign or exotic cultures without crossing city race borders.
2   Neutral zones are public spaces that in contrast with embassies do not target particular racial or ethnic groups.
3   Carnival public spaces are those where middle-class women encounter racialised others, also outside perceived race borders.
4   Outpost spaces are those where white women experience racialised others by crossing borders into outpost spaces where white people are minorities.

While these categories are framed in terms of white women, both black and Hispanic women have their own sense of fear based on racial discrimination, and this too has a class dimension. While Day's research was limited to the American experience, there is good reason to assume that women in other Western societies share certain generic qualities. Overall, it seems that women's mental maps of their environment are composed of entirely different propositions to those of men, and the behaviour of men that makes these feelings possible has been well documented (Ardener 1981, Mackenzie 1988, 1989, Gardner 1995, Duncan 1996, Walker 1998). However, it is not merely the trilogy of race, class and gender that is significant. The actual contouring of space itself into physically designed environments is also deterministic of psychological content as to which spaces are perceived as 'safe', 'dangerous', 'welcoming', 'threatening', 'tranquil' or other qualities. Hence the design of all buildings, spaces and landscaping that make up the built environment has a massive influence on the personal security and well-being of women (Keller 1981). While much of this has been discussed in the context of Oscar Newman's concept of defensible space (see chapter 5), the idea has yet to be extended to cover the entire public realm, not merely that of housing typology and layout, although this by itself is extremely important.

In 'Beyond maps and metaphors', Boys (1998) indicates how the land and building development markets, along with their attendant regulatory regimes, provide an infrastructure for the public realm that assumes specific design outcomes based on a masculinist rationality. This results in what Valentine terms the 'heterosexing' of space as a product of congealed assumptions inherent to public life. Important also is how this 'public' life becomes privatised. Reinforcing this position, Day (1999a) offers an in-depth analysis of gendered, privatised, public spaces such as shopping malls, festival marketplaces and themed historical destinations in southern California. She points to the prototype of accessible urban space, the Greek agora, noting that it was a space confined to men and the wealthy. She also observes that the major role trad-itionally consigned to public space by men, that of information exchange, is closed to women 'since women of colour and white women often access different information in different spaces' (Day 1999a: 161). Also important is the fact that in privatised public space, women frequently need to combine pleasure and domestic life into semi-leisure space which combines caring functions with leisure activity, for example jogging while pushing a pram; thus 'Women's work in privatized recreational space is often invisible. At the same time, privatized spaces traditionally associated with work may provide leisure oppor-tunities for women' (Day 1999a: 162). What is happening in effect is that women are carving out their own 'public space' which is configured from the resources they use on a daily basis – libraries, supermarkets, parks, grocery stores, restaurants, school playgrounds, shopping malls, and other places – as a parallel gendered universe to that of men. The inferences of this for design are both revolutionary and profound.

Finally, apart from the spatial division of the built environment into two major divisions for production and consumption, there are the other two significant dimensions of architectural space and symbolic representation in monuments. While I do not wish to discuss the gendered space of architectural interiors, this too has had significant coverage over the last twenty years in edited collections by writers such as Rendell et al. in *Gender, Space and Architecture* (2000). Much of this literature also feeds into the conceptual framework of urban design, for the simple reason that the concept of gender covers all forms of space and is not limited to any single sphere. Similarly, it is frequently difficult to isolate the interior space of buildings from the exterior space of the public realm. As we have seen above, these concepts overlap and interact in singular complexity.

Of greater concern to gendered urban design is the rich symbolic matrix sedimented in towns and cities in the form of sculpture, obelisks, statues, fountains, follies, towers and other monumental and symbolic constructs – the typologies of the urban landscape, a topic which I broached in chapter 4. Monumental architecture provides focal points, permits orientation, reinforces identities, celebrates events and expresses the aspirations and expectations of generations, and it is frequently impossible to separate the concept of monu-mentality from spatial, architectural and other sculptural constructs. Monu-ments condense history into accessible symbolic forms and situate a wealth of cultural capital for citizens. They contextualise and articulate places for public life – celebration, remembrance, worship and nationhood – and frequently overwhelm local architecture as signifiers in a multitude of realms. Of inter-national repute are monuments such as the Eiffel Tower, the Statue of Liberty, the Monument to Vittorio Emmanuel II in Rome (figure 32) and the Brandenberg Gate in Berlin. Individual buildings also stand as monuments apart from their functional use as churches, opera houses, offices or whatever. Some of the most famous of these are buildings such as Sacré Coeur in Paris, St Peter's Basilica in

Figure 32   Rome: Monument to Vittorio Emmanuel II.
Source: Courtesy of Hulton Archives/Getty Images.

Rome, the Pentagon and the Sydney Opera House. As in other dimensions of urban life, gender differentiation is not constrained to domestic and public space; it pervades every aspect of human creativity, and monumental architecture and sculpture are no exceptions to this rule. Here we find male domination endlessly expressed in wars, heroes, philosophers, dictators, kings and artists, all in a continuing symphony to patriarchal capitalism, imperialism and the symbolic adulation of the male gender.

Where women are represented, they tend to be representations of men's idealised 'other', from the caryatids on the Acropolis in Athens to the *Venus de Milo* and the Statue of Liberty in New York, rather than the recognition of women's material achievements: 'The body is still the map on which we mark our meanings; it is the chief among metaphors...men often appear as themselves, as individuals, but women attest the identity and value of something else' (Warner in Johnson 1995: 57). Hence women tend to be used in an allegorical fashion, where history is fundamentally promoted and interpreted by men. The public realm is therefore the space where gendered meanings are imposed or negotiated. The monument to Anna Livia Plurabelle, erected in Dublin in 1987 in the form of a fountain, is a prime example (figure 33). Anna was a character in the Joycean epic *Finnegan's Wake*, and is a symbolic representation of the city of Dublin and the river Liffey that flows through the town. Shortly after its

Figure 33 Dublin: statue of Anna Livia Plurabelle, 'the Floozie in the Jacuzzi'.
Source: © Rose Hartman/CORBIS.

construction, it went through a series of renamings, from 'the Floozie in the Jacuzzi' to 'the whore in the sewer', an undisguised attempt by men to recapture the dominant gendered position by debasing the female image. Johnson goes on to articulate the deep psychological structure of patriarchy expressed within the binary opposition of acceptable (domestic) and unacceptable, (public sphere):

> The female figure . . . invokes gender-coded stereotypes of women in public space as whore, temptress, pollutant, and scaled to virtual anorexic proportions as she bathes in the waters of the city. Although allegorical figures of women as 'mother-land' and protector of the private sphere of home and family enjoy acceptance in

nationalist discourse, in the city, woman's role is confined to that of prostitute or seductress strolling streets normally occupied by men.

(Johnson 1995: 57–8)

This type of imagery is prototypical across urban space in all Western cities. Clearly there is much work remaining to be completed, both in our minds and in our environments, before the fact of a truly democratic and non-sexist city can be realised.

Chapter Seven
Environment

I heard the ruin of all space, shattered glass and
toppling masonry, and time one livid final flame.

James Joyce

Introduction: Nature and the City

The use of the term 'environment' is fraught with consequence. While it embodied the hopes of an entire generation, it is a word which now has little or no
substance. When it was first brought into currency by Rachel Carson in *Silent
Spring* (1962), it was pregnant with meaning. This was arguably the seminal
work that directly focused attention on the harm that was being wrought on our
environment through the use of pesticides. From that time until today, an entire
vocabulary has come into being to denote both personal and political preferences towards the problems of urbanisation and environmental degradation in
all its forms. Since then, the 'environmental movement' of the 1960s has given
way to a plethora of descriptors and competing discourses: environmentalism
(O'Riordan 1976), ecology (Odum 1971), Marxist ecology (Grundmann 1991,
Benton 1996, Burkett 1999, Foster 2000), deep ecology (Zimmerman 1987),
transpersonal ecology (Fox 1995), ecological socialism (Dordoy and Mellor
2000), ecological economics (Costanza 1991), political ecology (Clark 2001),
green politics (Irvine and Ponton 1988, Reolofs 2000), environmental discourse
(Young 1990, Hajer 1995), liberation ecologies (Peet and Watts 1996), eco-
feminism (Mies and Shiva, 1993, Mellor 1999), trans-species ecology (Wolch
1996, DC 20), ecosophy (Naess 1989) and many others. There is also a varying
degree of overlap, from almost total separation to a complete homology among
and between each of these positions. Across this semantic minefield, those
concerned with the form of cities usually resort to the term 'sustainable development' for clearly the form of cities and their design has an immense impact on
how resources, both human and natural, are deployed.

As we shall see, the term 'sustainable development' is paradoxical, referring in
current practice to how much abuse nature can withstand rather than to how
much it should be respected. For the term 'sustainable', applied either to nature
or to urbanisation, remains wedded to the underlying assumptions of capital and

its ideologies, which contain inherent and irresolvable conflicts. True sustainable development relies at its core upon the supercession of the capitalist system as it is currently constructed. So the contemporary use of the term remains a contested ideology that contains inherent and serious flaws. As a subset of this system, the idea of sustainable urban design is built on sand, and can only be promoted as a concept if it bypasses significant theory: 'most in the eco-city movement ignore critical left traditions, class structure, militarism and imperialism' (Reolofs 2000: 139). Hence the tendency of most writing on sustainable urban design is to jump immediately into 'practical' solutions to the problems of urban growth and change, with a heavy dependency on three central ideas.

First, that physical determinism, and the assumption that questions surrounding concepts of density, growth forms, architectural configuration, land use, etc., contain the key to more efficient cities, without any required shift in the underlying system of morality, ideology or economy (Hough 1984, McLoughlin 1991, Breheny 1992, Newman 1994, Troy 1996, Frey 1999, Williams et al. 2000). Second, that improvements in technology can be relied upon to reduce vehicle emissions, create more efficient forms of transport, improve waste disposal, reduce pollution from industry and generate other forms of renewable energy through wind, water and solar power (Newman and Kenworthy 1999, Stone and Rogers 2001). The third concept involves that of urban governance: cities will become more sustainable if they are managed more efficiently via the mechanism of urban planning (Haughton and Hunter 1994, Gilbert et al. 1996), and I have already outlined the planning–capital relation in previous chapters.

Overall, the basic assumptions are that answers to sustainability lie in formal solutions supported by appropriate technologies and better management of available resources. In the absence of a supporting political agenda, these assumptions seem highly questionable. While urban growth may indeed be improved through many such devices, within the usual economic and political constraints, another three facts stand out. In the case of physical determinism, it is transparent that architects, urban designers and urban planners (who are responsible for manipulating density, land use, etc.) implement, but do not direct, urban development, which is predominantly determined by urban politics in conjunction with the market and market speculation. Those most directly involved in advocating so-called 'solutions' to sustainable cities have their noses stuck securely to the grindstone of capitalist production. In the second case, improved technological production is part and parcel of resource depletion and, as we shall see, at a global level also carries serious implications for third world debt and domination. As to urban governance, this is massively affected by neocorporate planning strategies whereby capital and the state in the form of urban planning are seen to have congruent interests, or at least none so conflicting that the 'stakeholders' will not ultimately agree on outcomes. The solutions implied in physical determinism, 'the technological fix' and better urban management support the prevailing ideology of sustainability in the fractured political economy of globalisation. As we now live in a borderless planet of electronic communication, so do we live in an environment where the growth of cities and the destruction of nature discriminately affect everyone. In order to give meaning to the process of designing cities, and to escape from the unwitting alliance the term 'sustainable' imparts, we must return to a point forty years ago in order to cast light on the present and to place our knowledge of urban design in a viable context.

Origins and Development

Once again, the great critical tradition initiated by Marx, which continues today in a multiplicity of new forms, was the first to document and theorise the ravages of capitalist development during the Industrial Revolution in Britain in the middle of the nineteenth century, and has the longest history of addressing environmental issues (Castro 2004). Likewise, his friend and benefactor Friedrich Engels, in his masterpiece *The Condition of the Working Class in England*, one of the most measured texts ever written in the face of such oppression, documented the environmental degradation that ensued from the unlicensed greed of capitalism (we can forgive him for including the populations of Glasgow and Edinburgh as part of the English working class). His lesser-known text, *The Dialectics of Nature*, published in 1925, situated his previous work within more general 'environmental' concerns. In volume 1 of *Capital*, Marx refers with supreme irony to the destruction of first-growth European forests and their new growth as 'the primordial forest rate of interest', a scathing commentary on the destruction of wilderness as early as 1860, and a battle still being fought today (Marx 1959: 363). It was Marx himself who argued that capitalism was environmentally unsustainable in a quote from *Capital* that encapsulates the basis of environmental Marxism:

> But the way that the cultivation of particular crops depends on fluctuations in market prices and the constant changes in cultivation with these price fluctuations – the entire spirit of capitalist production, which is oriented towards the most immediate monetary profit – stands in contradiction to agriculture, which has to concern itself with the whole gamut of permanent conditions of life required by the chain of human generation.

> (Marx 1981: 754)

At the beginning of the twentieth century a new generation of thinkers continued the struggle against the ills of environmental degradation, such as Patrick Geddes, Ebeneezer Howard, Louis Mumford and others. However, it was during the period after the Second World War that the environmental revolution gathered real momentum. This was due to many factors: the aftermath of two world wars, burgeoning population growth, the accelerated use of fossil fuels, mass production of motor vehicles and increasing prosperity. But it was the need for improved agricultural production that generated the first diatribe against the diabolical misuse of nature that was taking place. Although the United States Government had passed laws against the use of pesticides as early as 1910, the widespread development of pesticides after the Second World War quickly resulted in two further acts being passed by Congress in 1947 and 1952 (Marco et al. 1987). Ten years later, Rachel Carson wrote *Silent Spring*, a book that was revolutionary in its consequences, since it challenged the entire foundation for pesticide use and its effects on all living creatures. Indirectly, it also questioned the monopolistic practices of multinational companies and the role of state regulation in support of big capital.

Carson was one of the first to question the use of DDT, now banned in many developing countries, and the synergistic effects of chemical pesticides on the environment. While standards for each might be within 'safe limits', the combined ingestion of many could result in the disruption of key metabolic pathways and the production of tumours and leukaemias in animals and humans alike. The use of pesticides, while destroying the natural capacity of the earth, also polluted groundwater, with devastating effects on plant and animal communities worldwide. Others quickly followed Carson's book, albeit with different trajectories. One with similar impact, which was adopted by several generations of designers, was Ian McHarg's *Design with Nature* (1969), still unsurpassed in the clarity of its message 'that natural process, unitary in character, must be considered so in the planning process: that changes to parts of the system affect the entire system, that natural processes do represent values, and that these values should be incorporated into a single accounting system' (McHarg 1969: 65). On this basis, McHarg proposed a complex sieve method for urban development based upon ecological principles, as well as one for mapping human pathology.

While Carson and McHarg were concerned with the toxic effects of development and ecology respectively, Schumacher's *Small is Beautiful* (1973) was among the first to look at economic questions, challenging most of the tenets of economic orthodoxy. What he did not recognise was that underdevelopment is a product of capitalist imperialism, not merely a stage in the overall process of capital accumulation. He proposed what he called 'intermediate technology' as a method whereby developing countries might become sustainable without becoming dependent on the technology and surplus capital of the first world. While the texts of Carson, McHarg and Schumacher were extremely influential, each in its own way was a polemic against injustice, exhibiting missionary properties and flavoured with anarchism. Schumacher's chapter on Buddhist economics for example was unlikely to go very far in the West. McHarg's book was displaced from substantial theory, and Carson had no support when others were invited to undertake her project (Marco et al. 1987: 4). In addition, each was largely divorced from any significant social movement or key paradigm that would allow the work to be embedded in a larger body of social theory.

These three classics were closely followed by Dennis Meadows' research for the Club of Rome (1972) called *The Limits to Growth*. This latter study was both challenging and influential. It was also primarily neo-Malthusian in approach, questioning the natural resource base of the planet to support a burgeoning population (Ehrlich and Ehrlich 1990, 1992). Importantly, Castro (2004) notes that the sustainability movement appeared as a reaction to the

Limits to Growth literature, which proposed a massive reduction in the consumption of natural resources, both in developed and developing countries. This was given official license by the United Nations, which enshrined the concept of sustainable development in two reports: the report of the World Commission on Environment and Development (1987) followed by Agenda 21, the outcome of the Earth Summit in Rio de Janeiro (1992). These were immediately followed by the launch of the European Sustainable Cities Programme in 1993 (see table 9). From this brief account of a few key moments in the development of the environmental movement, two things become obvious. First, the stimulus given by visionaries such as Carson, Schumacher and McHarg has now developed into significant movements that have prodigious political and social influence. These may yet change the course of capitalist development for the better. A review of critical theory demonstrates both a rapid acceleration of interest in the environment combined with a splintering or valorisation of such interest since 1980, and an even greater surge since the Earth Summit in 1992. Second, sustainability is a politically charged concept. It has been swallowed by big capital and promoted as a benevolent and sensible method of dealing with urban growth and change. Good people from all sectors of society have been deceived into supporting the very strategies and tactics that in the long term will undermine the very foundation of their lives. In order to see more clearly why sustainable development is fundamentally unsustainable, we must link together certain key concepts, beginning with the relation people–nature.

People–Nature

For thousands of years the Judeo-Christian ethic has survived on the fundamental principle of antagonism against nature, where the basic strategy has been to 'multiply and subdue the earth'. The evolution of early animism and pantheism into monotheistic institutionalised religion corresponded to the separation of man from nature and the placing of nature as 'other' in the new pantheon of religious practices. Not only was nature 'other', it was also to be feared, tamed and subjugated. From the beginning, the philosophy was written into the bedrock of Western civilisation:

> On the subject of man–nature, however, the Biblical creation story of the first chapter of Genesis, the source of the most generally accepted description of man's role and powers, not only fails to correspond to reality as we observe it, but in its insistence upon domination and subjugation of nature, encourages the most exploitive and destructive instincts in man, rather than those that are deferential and creative.
>
> (McHarg 1969: 26)

Once again there are vast numbers of texts written on Western attitudes to nature, some of the more insightful being those of Smith (1984), Merchant (1989), Grundmann (1991), Fox (1995), Soule and Lease (1995), Eder (1996),

Table 9 Major international and European-level policies and initiatives on sustainable urban development.

Events and initiatives	Year	Link to sustainable city agenda
United Nations Conference on the Human Environment (UNCHE)	1972	Recommendation I: Planning and Management of Human Settlements for Environmental Quality
Habitat 1 (Vancouver)	1976	Establishment of international programme designed to slow down the growth of urban areas
Establishment of United Nations Centre for Human Settlement (UNCHS)	1978	Specific remit to deliver more sustainable patterns of living in urban and rural areas
World Commission on Environment and Development Report	1987	Chapter 9, 'The Urban Challenge', describes the need to create more sustainable urban communities in both the developed and developing worlds
United Nations Sustainable Cities Programme	1990	Integration of the sustainable development remits of the UNCHS and the United Nations Environment Programme (UNEP)
European Commission's Green Paper on the Urban Environment	1990	Response by the European Commission and leading European cities to the perceived neglect of urban environmental issues relative to those of rural areas
European Commission's Expert Group on the Urban Environment	1991	Independent group composed of national representatives and experts with a remit to consider how future town and land-use planning could develop the urban environmental facets of the European Community's Environmental Programme
United Nations Conference on Environment and Development	1992	Agenda 21, Chapter 2, 'Promoting Sustainable Human Settlement Development'
European Sustainable Cities Programme	1993	Launched by the European Commission's Expert Panel on the Urban Environment
European Sustainable Cities Campaign	1994	Coalition of 80 urban and regional authorities implementing sustainable urban policies
Habitat 11 'The City Summit'	1996	Focus on the implementation of Local Agenda 21 in urban areas

Source: M. Whitehead, 'Re-analyzing the sustainable city: nature, urbanization and the regulation of socio-environmental relations in the UK'. *Urban Studies* 7, 2003, p. 1185. Reprinted by permission of Taylor & Francis Ltd.

Harvey (1996) and Castree and Braun (1998). Asian traditions not addressed here are outlined in Calicott and Ames (1989).

In his classic text, *The Social Construction of Nature*, Klaus Eder suggests that this fundamental process can be viewed either as the natural constitution of society or as a social construction of nature. These in turn result in either naturalist or culturalist positions, embodied at different periods of their intellectual output by both Marx and Durkheim. In the naturalist position, domination is the governing mandate, conducted through technical and managerial processes, with problems that are readily discernible to all. On the other hand, the naturalistic position also has problems, because 'There is no natural economy. The idea of nature as an exchange value is likewise a fiction; Nature does not yield to the rules of the market without problems. Instead, the normative content of nature slips beneath the laws of the market... there is no economy beyond a moral economy' (Eder 1996: 26). Eder does not try to replace these theories, but to reinterpret them in the light of a cultural sociology of nature, whereby social evolution is conceived of as part of a human history of nature rather than an antagonism. In order to do this he proposes three 'framing devices' in order to construct a new moral economy. First, there is the moral framing device of man's responsibility towards nature. Second, the adoption of empirical objectivity leads to a mechanistic conception of nature. Third, there is the concept of nature as a subject of aesthetic judgement. Taken together, Eder claims that they represent a symbolic packaging, which enables the construction of a 'protest frame' within which three types of environmentalists (conservationist, ecological and fundamentalist) can constitute themselves as protest actors:

> The conservationist package is *separating* nature and society, reserving for each a part of the world. The political ecology package, contrary to the first, is *integrating* nature and society. The fundamentalist package is *fusing* nature and society: nature becomes a fellow creature. These different ways of linking nature and society are *frames* of collective action, which give both meaning and purpose to it. These frames then are the material with which public discourses on nature are constructed.
>
> (Eder 1996: 177)

Another attempt to grapple with the complexity of positions in man's relationship to nature is given by Warwick Fox in *A Transpersonal Ecology*. Fox argues that most philosophers who are engaged with this dilemma are interested in developing a theory of value in relation to the non-human world, both of which leave out what he considers to be the most significant departure from this tradition, namely Arne Naess's 'deep ecology'. The two positions referred to are *instrumental value* and *intrinsic value* theory. Instrumental value theory has three heuristic configurations, all of which are rejected on the basis that nature must be accepted for its intrinsic value, not merely as use-values for human exploitation in one form or another. First, there is unrestrained exploitation and expansionism, which is characterised by the transformation of the physical world without measuring the consequences. This approach is anthropocentric, and follows the basic dictum that growth is equal to progress. Blind faith in technology is usually seen as the antidote to ignorance and stupidity. Second, resource conservation and development accepts that material resources are finite and therefore they should be exploited efficiently. This position is merely a longer-term approach than the first. It contains the same underlying anthropocentrism, and a concentration on the extraction of the highest sustainable yields that can be generated. Fox points out that transnational capital can distort the supposed rationality of this principle in accordance with its own geographic compass, by acting unsustainably in some countries, then moving the base of its operations to others. The third approach, resource preservation, is merely a difference of emphasis, since the instrumental value of the natural world is still the operational principle driving development. He points to Godfrey-Smith's four basic categorisations of the arguments normally used for preserving the non-human world: the silo, the laboratory, the gymnasium and the cathedral (Fox 1995: 155):

1   as a stockpile of genetic diversity for agricultural, medical and other purposes (the silo);
2   for scientific study (the laboratory);
3   for recreation (the gymnasium);
4   for aesthetic pleasure/spiritual inspiration (the cathedral).

Fox suggests that the latter category should be split into two, since aesthetics and religion might be seen as separate events, hence 'art gallery' may be added for a tally of five positions. To these, four more can be added to make up for some clear deficiencies in this list:

1   free goods and services (the life support system argument);
2   as a thermostat for (1) (the early warning argument);
3   as a symbolic referent (the monument argument);
4   as therapy and bonding (the psychogenetic argument).

The argument in the first case states that because nature provides us with free goods and services, we should respect it since it constitutes our livelihood. In the second, the instrumental value of nature is held due to its ability to warn us of impending crises in the life support system. The monument argument is a catch-all for any position that views the non-human world as a symbolic referent for human existence, or which views its essential function as instructional, providing lessons that we should live by. The psychogenetic argument is based on the idea that we are more than physical bodies and that the physical environment also provides us with the opportunity to develop a healthy psychological existence as well.

   Each of the 8 instrumental approaches to nature collapse round one simple idea, that nature is not granted its own intrinsic value and subjectivity as a living organism. It is always viewed as 'other', however deferential or sympathetic the position might appear. The central problem in environmental ethics in recent years has therefore been how to construct a theory of nature whereby its intrinsic value is recognised in relation to human action (Regan 1983, Naess 1986, Nash 1989, Harvey 1996). Fox discusses these in the context of various ethical approaches (ethical sentientism, autopoetics ethics, ecosystem ethics and cosmic purpose ethics, Fox 1995; see also Hargrove 1989). Overall, the most powerful approaches to intrinsic value theory are those of ecology, particularly deep ecology, and post-Marxist theory, particularly materialist eco-feminism. The extension of one ideology into another is obvious. Ecology extends into deep ecology but also into eco-feminism. This crosses into post-Marxist theory through materialist approaches to ecology, for example eco-socialism and materialist eco-feminism (Castro 2004). The nature of the debates that surround these ideologies is so intense that it is easy to forget that for all practical purposes the same outcomes are sought. Basically these are, first, to accept that we are an integral part of the natural world; second, that preservation of biodiversity in all its forms is fundamental; and third, that a Copernican revolution in human values is required, with a resulting change in social organisation, development and aspirations. It is the question of how to achieve these objectives that are contentious. The madness, as it were, is in the methods, and the frequently conflicting philosophies, values and objectives that accompany them.

The difference between the ecological approach and that of deep ecology is a case in point. Charles Odum was arguably the founder of the ecology movement, and his text *The Fundamentals of Ecology* remains a classic. Since then the word has come into common currency, and the term has become all-encompassing (Bateson 1972, Bookchin 1980, 1982, Grundmann 1991, Sachs 1993, Mellor 1999, Foster 2000). Ecology retains the values of science, and 'stands in relation to ecological politics as physics does to machine engineering... But the problem is that ecological politics or ecological landscape planning, or urban planning, whenever they want to prove they are participating in saving the world with their limited designs, only very rarely understand "ecology" in the technical sense' (Trepl 1996: 86). Ecology has also been criticised as 'anti-urban' with conservative tendencies and a class bias as well (Trepl 1996). Overall the traditional ecological approach does not engage with the reality of politics or social life, and views the natural world as an object for scientific enquiry. In this equation, urban ecology reduces nature to symbolic concepts of landscape and aesthetic preferences, with orientations such as ecological urban design ensuring that nature remains unattainable in the context of urbanisation. Professionals adopting an ecological approach therefore tend to isolate issues such as air, noise and water pollution and look for technical fixes for these problems. Ian McHarg's sieve-mapping process is a case in point, where he uses the rational scientific method to compensate for the ravages of urbanisation without addressing the underlying problems. Deep ecology, founded by Arne Naess the Norwegian philosopher, tries to compensate for the limitations of the ecological approach (Naess 1986, 1989, Luke 1988, Rothenberg 1993). He also draws attention to the fact that deep ecology is not an excuse for either extremism or radicalism. Its power is in 'asking us to articulate why we believe what we do about the singular importance of nature, and helping us to determine what basic changes in society are most worth fighting for to realise the goal of a sustainable world, where humanity thinks of more than its own welfare' (Rothenberg 1993: 127). The fundamental principle here is that man is subsumed to the intrinsic value of nature and is not separate from it. Bookchin (1980, 1982) attacks this position on the basis that it tends, in the process, to ignore the political reality of social life and its inherent responsibilities, and proposes instead what he calls social ecology, an attempt to fuse deep ecology with urban political economy. So far we have only looked at nature and how our perceptions of nature structure attitudes and ideologies. Layered on top of this, however, is the problem of urbanisation and capitalist development in the context of 'sustainable' development.

Sustainability and Development

Sustainable development is without doubt one of the most closely contested ideas within modern society. It is also a concept almost as nebulous as 'the environment', given that it can mean anything from having chickens in your backyard to international agreements about the biosphere. The World Commission on Environment and Development (1987) otherwise known as *The Brundtland Report*, had arguably the greatest significance for sustainability, where sustainable development is defined as development that 'meets the needs of the present without compromising the ability of future generations to meet theirs' (in Castro 2004: 197). We could speculate that compromising the future is exactly what we must do in order to survive. Overall there are two main approaches to how sustainable development is constituted, namely mainstream and critical perspectives (Eichler 1995, Benton 1996, Castro 2004). The mainstream position accepts the capitalist system as a fact of life. Progress is defined largely in terms of gross domestic product. Faith in the market mechanism generates the belief that adopting this system and waiting for it to deliver its bounty will solve problems of underdevelopment. Aid from more developed countries will act as an interim measure until economies mature and lose their dependency. Any problems of capitalist development in the core economies will also be solved through the principle of supply and demand. When overproduction occurs, the reserve army of labour will increase through unemployment, labour costs will decrease and capital will be switched to investment in other sectors. Since the market seeks equilibrium, it is only a matter of time until the system self-corrects. Mainstream approaches are fundamentally liberal, technocratic, economistic (so-called environmental economics) and have blinkers to the political realities of capitalism.

At present, half the world's population lives in urban areas, around 3.25 billion people, with this figure set to double over the next thirty years. Mainstream approaches view this as primarily an economic problem, with solutions relying heavily on the market mechanism and increased productivity. In regard to developing countries, Castro places the whole mainstream position squarely on the establishment, from the United Nations to the World Bank, supported by a raft of neoliberal agendas. Rather than benefiting the third world, Amin (1997: 24) asserts that the World Bank has acted 'as an agent whose task is to support capital's penetration of the third world through transnationals' and points to 'an endless round of strategies targeted on the dependent integration of third world economies', a process which results in massive debt, the destruction of subsistence economies, the annihilation of the peasant world, the exploitation of first-growth forests and the erosion of communal land. After promoting such destruction, the United Nations remains convinced that 'poverty' is the prime cause of environmental degradation, not the fact that the developed world consumes a vastly disproportionate quantum of available resources per capita. So the underlying assumption of liberalist sustainable development is that the problem of third world poverty can only be solved when the developing world approaches the wealth of developed countries. It also ignores the reality that globalisation is fundamentally about the deepening not the amelioration of capitalist social relations, through the erosion of national boundaries, the reproduction of political and economic instability as a basis for such exploitation, the commodification of culture, and the plundering of the third world for labour and natural resources, whom as Amin (1997: 125) asserts, 'experience actually existing capitalism as nothing short of savagery'.

The paradox here is self-evident. Despite liberalist claims to improved prosperity for all through more of the same treatment, an increasingly international division of labour results in a geographic structure of exploitation and poverty at a global scale that parallels the class division within nations. Chossudofsky's blistering attack on the operation of the IMF and the World Bank is a case in point (*The Globalisation of Poverty*, 1998). He demonstrates that the world is governed by a handful of international banks and global monopolies, and that regulation of world markets, which depends on the supply of money, is in the hands of private creditors. Certain of these monopolies now parallel the market capitalisation of nation states. He notes that central banks in developing and developed countries alike have an illusory independence, and largely operate on the guidance of the state's creditors, i.e. the private sector. More 'open' markets supposedly designed to bring about an overall improvement in the world system massively favour wealthy nations over the poor (Escobar 1995). Supposedly 'free' markets are a euphemism for manipulation and financial genocide of the economies of smaller nations: 'The power of the Wall Street–Treasury–IMF Complex is both symbiotic with and parasitic upon a coercively imposed financial system built around the so-called Washington consensus and later elaborated through the construction of a new financial architecture' (Harvey 2003: 73). The necessary improvement of living standards on the periphery also demand that their economic growth be based upon a monopoly of intellectual capital and technology in core economies that the third world will have to purchase through the vehicle of loans or aid in lieu, and through the exploitation of their natural resources. Hence their dependency is maintained at the same time that they are plundered for their raw materials, and their governments undermined by first-world markets, politics, monopolies, subterfuge and outright aggression as we have seen in the case of Iraq: 'This ideology, without the environmental aspect, existed before the environmental crisis, and in spite of having failed so far to develop the periphery, it still remains the fundamental approach to poverty and environmental degradation . . . On this basis *sustainable development* suspiciously sounds like plain old development' (Castro 2004: 198).

Hence the entire economic appropriation of world surpluses in all of their forms by private capital, through the manipulation of 'free market' mechanisms and the ritual exploitation of nature, must have a limited future even for its perpetrators. On the basis of the above processes, it can easily be argued that the term 'sustainable development' has been hijacked and presented as the benevolent face of capitalism (Hawken et al. 1999). It disguises the fact that not only the fundamental exploitation of nature (including human and non-human species and their habitats) is still taking place, but also that these processes are being further consolidated, deepened and extended through globalisation. There is no better exposé of the central flaw inherent in the concept of sustainable development than James O'Connor's classic essay 'The second contradiction of capitalism' (O'Connor 1996; see also Toledo 1996, Panayotakis 2003, Castro 2004). O'Connor starts with Polanyi's masterpiece *The Great Transformation*, which describes how the capitalist system set about destroying its own conditions of production that it depends on for survival.

The first contradiction O'Connor refers to is that between the forces and relations of production and the actual conditions of production, between production and the realisation of value and surplus value (profit from labour). Since capitalist development is geared to profit not to equality, periodic crises ensue due to the overproduction of commodities, which in turn are rooted to the unnecessary exploitation and ultimate exhaustion of nature. Paradoxically, these crises are based upon overproduction founded in scarcity, a condition that is socially manufactured within capitalism. O'Connor's first crisis exposes the perverse nature of capitalist production, which manages to create crises from excess, to manufacture poverty from plenty, and to threaten its own existence from the overconcentration of the surplus in the hands of the few. The second contradiction refers to the production of natural scarcity from the exploitation of resources, hence 'After turning scarcity into a purely social phenomenon that could be overcome through a social reorganization that would use technological development to satisfy human needs and enrich people's lives, capitalism threatens to close the window of opportunity for a freer society that it had itself unwittingly opened' (Panayotakis 2003: 97).

In contrast to mainstream liberal theories of sustainability, traditional materialist theory has been criticised in its attitude to nature as being no different from religious orthodoxy. While religious believers were urged to multiply and subdue the earth, Marxist theory, based in the labour theory of value, could be seen as no different. Nature was merely an object of labour to be transformed by the means of production into exchange values. Subduing the earth through technology was an intrinsic part of this process. However, this reading of Marx is somewhat narrow and out of context. It ignores both Marx's own development, as well as the development of materialist theory over the last century and a half. Others argue that humanity's essential rootedness with nature was Marxism's starting point:

> It sees humanity as both embedded in the ecosystem and embodied within its own physicality. In this it shares elements of deep ecological thought based in ecological wholism. The importance of the materialist eco-feminist analysis is that it sees the externalization of women and nature as central to the material basis of male-dominated socio-economic systems. This analysis makes a theoretical distinction between social and deep materialism. Social materialism describes the structures of economic exploitation within socio-economic systems based on sex, class, race, colonialism and so on. Deep materialism refers to the structures of exploitation based on work that needs to be done to make human life possible on a daily basis.
>
> (Dordoy and Mellor 2000: 42)

In other words, the connectedness of woman and nature is not essentialistic, it is socially reproduced by the mediating role women play in society, and the fact that women create surplus labour time for men, by caring for children, the elderly and the sick. Eco-socialism focuses on ending both the exploitation of nature and the mass of the world's population for the benefit of a tiny fraction of the world's rich, and the disproportionate allocation of benefits that results from such exploitation. Eco-feminism adds the gendered division of labour into this equation, where the concept of alienated labour must be extended to include other forms of social discrimination. Here we can see that one of the fundamental differences between the mainstream and critical approaches turns round the idea of emancipation and alienation of racial and gendered subjects.

It is therefore easy to see why critical theory denied the approach to development and sustainability promoted by liberal thought, since it propagated the very model that refuted any prospect of meaningful sustainable development and social change. The accumulation of capital at a global scale and the values that go with it are so fraught with conflict and crisis that it is difficult to align economic growth and sustainable development as viable partners. This is even more evident when developing countries are expected to repress economic growth on the basis of global warming. The only real alternative for sustainability in this context is for the first world to downgrade economic production, due to the fact that a more equitable distribution of wealth would compensate for O'Connor's first law of capitalism. All third-world debt should also be cancelled and non-polluting technologies provided free of charge. Developing countries could then gradually eliminate poverty and a sustainable level of global equity might then be achievable. Attitudes to nature and critical theories of development also come together in relation to urbanisation, and to the concept of the sustainable eco-city.

Sustainable Cities

Following the above argument from nature and development to urbanisation, it is clear that cities must also be considered unsustainable as part and parcel of the whole process of capital accumulation. Rural–urban migration is based on the fact that in certain countries, agricultural production has improved to the point where the current level of urbanisation can be serviced. This remains true as long as we externalise the environmental costs of erosion, pollution, genetic modification of plants and effects on other biosystems such as animal and marine life, not to mention the social cost of unemployment. On this basis it may be claimed that cities are not environmentally sustainable a priori: 'by definition, their territory is too densely populated with humans to be self-supporting. A world where urbanization is increasing fast, and moreover, where urbanization is characterized by urban sprawl, is thereby a more unsustainable world. Indicators of unsustainability are also indicators of social conflicts at different scales' (Martinez Alier 2003: 49). Sustainable cities have three major dimensions corresponding to different levels of analysis, although each has significant correlations with the other two. Only the last is commonly referred to in the 'sustainable' urban design and urban planning vocabulary. First, we must consider the position occupied by the built environment in relation to capital accumulation, and how capital formation affects the very nature and foundation of sustainable cities. Second, we must assess whether the outcomes of this process are sustainable in terms of social justice and democracy – social and political inequalities, such as class struggle, access to resources, levels of violence and crime (DC 7). Third, there are the material problems of physical sustainability, predicated on the geographic distribution and allocation of space, commodity circulation, transport and energy transfer, pollution, etc. This last category I will deal with under the heading of sustainable urban design.

In the first case, it goes without saying that Western cities within capitalism are a reflection of the value systems they embody, and we have to begin by making the simple observation that none of these cities has ever been constructed, even remotely, on the idea of sustainable development in any form. So how could they possibly become 'sustainable' on the basis of technical progress alone? The concentration of capital as an economic reality has a corresponding geographic concentration within and between cities. Characterised by central business districts and their satellites, the concentric growth of Western cities mirrored the parasitic nature of their economic systems, where in order to expand, each ring in the concentric pattern was forced to devour the one adjacent to it. To a certain extent, the same was true *within* each ring as powerful institutions expanded at the cost of their neighbours.

Overall, Western cities have been structured largely on the basis of market principles, the symbolic needs of dominant hierarchies, and shifting ideologies through which the reproduction of systems of domination remained covert. Competition between institutions for symbolic and cultural capital, combined with ever-increasing land values, sponsored taller and taller structures, and there is as yet no end in sight to this insanity. In contrast, in socialist cities such as Hanoi, one is usually impressed by the fact that they have no such uneven urban development and a uniform density prevails across the entire city. The same has also been true of China for example, up until recent market reforms. Since socialism has no private enterprise, no private ownership of land and promotes use-values, the concentric growth of cities on the basis of central business districts did not exist – there was no central business to conduct, no conflict over symbolic capital and no land market. Hence an even distribution of land-use functions became possible at near uniform densities across urban areas, with corresponding efficiencies in associated land-use functions. Forces behind this phenomenon as well as an idealised territorial socialist formation have been discussed by Enzo Mingione (1981) and Ivan Szelenyi (1983).

In David Harvey's classic text, *Social Justice and the City* (1979b), he discusses the relationships between social processes and spatial form, the redistribution of real income, concepts of social justice, urban land use and the spatial circulation of surplus value. Later, in *The Urbanisation of Capital* (1985) he lays bare exactly how these processes overwhelm ideas about the city that choose to view it as a mere cluster of inefficient technologies. Harvey begins from the same point as O'Connor (see earlier), and the dilemma that capitalist strategies in aggregation run against their own long-term interests and survival. This is based on certain inescapable properties of the capitalist system: the overproduction of commodities leading to crisis, falling rates of profit, an oversupply of capital and labour and switching crises between various sectors of the economy. Harvey characterises this process as three circuits of capital (figure 34).

The primary circuit of capital occurs when investment concentrates on primary production and the manufacture of commodities. When overproduction occurs, capital is switched into the secondary circuit of capital, which Harvey refers to as the built environment for consumption. By consumption he does not mean the consumption of products, but the infrastructure that makes such consumption possible. He also points out that transportation systems for example can act for both production and consumption, depending on their use. The built environment represents a form of capital unlike others, since it is fixed in space and therefore constitutes a long-term and immobile investment. Over-investment or crisis in this sector is then switched into the tertiary circuit of capital, where investment is directed into two main areas: first, into science and technology, and second into the extended reproduction of labour (hospitals, schools, welfare services, recreational facilities, etc.). Harvey goes on to explain in detail both the instability and tendency to crisis in this system as a permanent feature. In an essay entitled 'Urbanism and the city' he notes that under capitalist conditions of production, cities reproduce three transmuted forms of surplus value in the form of monopoly and differential rent (on floor space), interest (on loans) and profit (on capital investment) (Harvey 1973: 239). These do not even have sustainable economics in mind, let alone other forms of sustainable development.

None of this implies that cities do not grow and change, just that they cannot grow and change in a sustainable manner, simply because the entire system they represent is not driven by sustainability but by profit and class exploitation. Hawken et al. (1999) try to argue that these values can coexist. They maintain that in the next industrial revolution, what they call 'natural capitalism' will prevail, a new society where everyone comes out winning. Words missing from

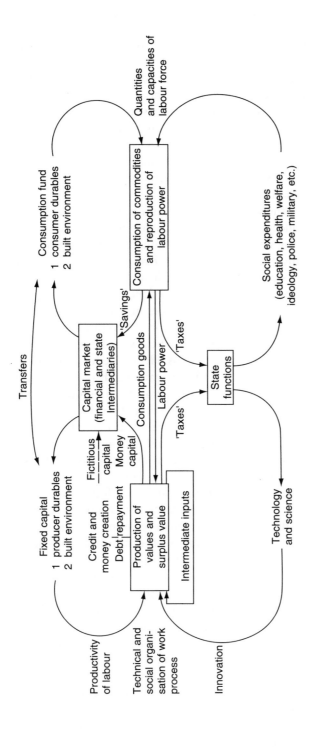

Figure 34 David Harvey's primary, secondary and tertiary circuits of capital.
Source: D. Harvey, *The Urbanization of Capital*. Oxford: Blackwell, 1985, p. 9. Reprinted by permission of Blackwell Publishing.

the index to the book include the following: urban, exploitation, politics, equality, inequality, militarism, development, debt, justice, and so on. The book describes a global environment where the third world for all practical purposes does not exist, and the few references in the index to developing nations are almost completely absent in the text. It relies almost exclusively on a virtual alchemical process of turning lead into gold by means of technological progress, without questioning the global political environment that dictates resource distribution. How nature will be able to sustain the required level of technological progress in the USA alone, let alone bring the rest of the world into the frame, remains unexplained.

In the second case, the nature of social and political inequalities also has a profound effect on concepts of sustainability. For in discussing sustainability, we are not merely mapping properties of a sustainable environment that efficiently stores, circulates, transforms and disposes of resources, but one which offers a sustainable life to its occupants, one which includes human and non-human living organisms. Indeed in *Social Conflict and the City*, Enzo Mingione (1981) is critical of Harvey's position, relying as it does on past accumulation and insufficiently on the complexity of the renewal process and future accumulation in the broad sense. Either way, they both agree that class confrontation, that is between capital and labour, is central to this process. Hence the fundamental problems of sustainable cities are not those of efficient garbage disposal and pollution-free transport, but of increasing social disintegration consequent upon issues of segregation on the basis of class and race, ethnicity, urban land use, marginalisation of the young and old, women's rights, gendered spaces, as well as deprivation in terms of education, health and access to affordable transportation, unemployment, poverty and freedom from fear, among others.

Since it can be argued that under state neocorporatism urban planning increasingly comes under the control of capital, any foundation for meaningful social change is usually promoted by urban social movements (Castells 1983). In this context, both the function of state urban planning and the legal system that supports it fall increasingly under private sector influence, and the privatisation of urban land use increasingly tends to anarchy: 'precisely because urban land development is privately controlled, the final aggregate outcomes of this process are necessarily and paradoxically out of control' (Scott 1980: 130). Apart from this fundamental unsustainability, Scott also points to the control of monopolies over basic goods and services (water, power, electricity, transport, communications, etc.). Since it is in the very nature of monopolies to capitalise on their control over markets, discriminatory pricing results, and the smooth operation of civil society can be seriously disrupted: 'Urban planning is then left with an after the fact search for feasible remedies to the negative outcomes of this contradictory process of land development' (Scott and Roweis 1977: 1109). Overall, it is clear that tackling energy or sustainable questions without dealing with the instability of the economic system and its social consequences will not result in environmentally sustainable cities. Furthermore, the process of capital accumulation via the urban land nexus has also resulted in a very different kind of unsustainability, one where the natural world of plants and animals has been ritually eliminated except for certain hybrid environments such as apiaries and zoos, landscaped gardens, theme parks and other institutions.

Our relation to animals as non-human results largely in attitudes that they are good to eat, good to lock up in zoos, good to provide us with their skins for shoes, good to genetically modify and provide spare body parts, and good to kill for entertainment. Relatively recently the ontological separation between animals and humans and the entire realm of animal welfare and animal rights has been raised as a serious ethical, moral and social issue generally, and also in the realm of sustainable development, urban environmental planning in particular (Soule 1991, Platt et al. 1994, Wolch DC 20, 1996, Davis 1998, Hester at al. 1999). The debate is sparked by many difficult questions. Do animals feel pain? Do animals possess consciousness? Do they have a sense of species being? The basic issue is over the subjectivity of animals as sentient beings, and as such to command jurisdiction over their right to life. Wolch in her landmark paper 'Zoopolis' points to the fact that this disregard for non-human life is not encompassed in any urban theory at all, mainstream, neoclassical, post-Marxist or feminist. She suggests that in order to make up for this deficiency, a trans-species urban theory is necessary to progress an eco-socialist, feminist, anti-racist urban practice: 'Today the logic of capitalist urbanization still proceeds without regard to non-human life, except as cash-on-the-hoof headed for slaughter on the "disassembly line" or commodities used to further the cycle of accumulation' (Wolch 1996: 22). She argues that granting animals subjectivity is a necessary first step in a process of recognition, and that this is not for their material benefit but as a necessary part in developing our own humanity. Wolch calls for a renaturalisation of cities by accepting a bioregional paradigm whereby both human and non-human creatures are provided with appropriate habitats in the context of urbanisation (figure 35). Part of a trans-species urban practice therefore depends on:

> the utility of reconceptualising cities as ecological disturbance regimes rather than ecological sacrifice zones... This in turn could inform decisions concerning prospective land use changes (such as suburban densification, or down-zoning, landscaping schemes, and transportation corridor design), and indicate how they might influence individual animals and faunal assemblages in terms of stress levels, morbidity and morality, mobility and access to multiple sources of food and shelter, reproductive success, and exposure to predation.
>
> (Wolch 1996: 39)

Clearly any development of the concept of sustainability in cities must be prepared to accept the embeddedness not only of the city in nature but also of nature in the city. Given the dynamics of urban land markets, it is unlikely that large tracts of land will be bought up and devoted to wilderness corridors. But if we do not engage fully with these ideas in designing cities, then the idea of sustainable development will be even further alienated from its own implicit meaning and sense of purpose.

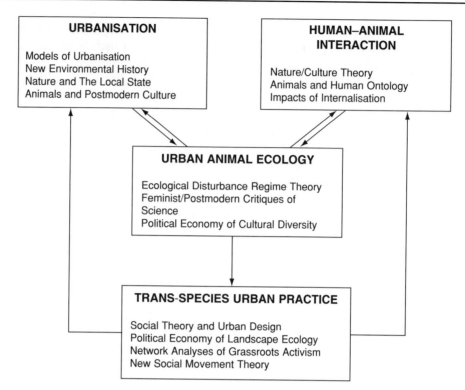

Figure 35   Ways of thinking animals in the city.
Source: J. R. Wolch, 'Zoopolis', *Capital, Nature, Socialism: A Journal of Socialist Ecology*, 7:2, 1996, p. 31.

Sustainable Urban Design

Sustainable urban form and design is now a recognisable subfield of the discipline, although it only started to coalesce relatively recently, with a significant number of texts on the subject over the last ten years (Breheny 1992, Haughton and Hunter 1994, Eichler 1995, Gilbert et al. 1996, Jenks et al. 1996, Moughtin 1996, Frey 1999, Newman and Kenworthy 1999, Jenks and Burgess 2000, Randall 2002, Whitehead 2003). Collectively they all adopt a mainstream approach to urban theory, where the city is viewed as a passive container of fixed and mobile objects, which generate air, water and soil pollution, consume resources inefficiently, manufacture energy that is not utilised, and which need to be more efficiently organised through more enlightened government. Each of these issues are specifically covered in significant depth on a variety of fronts, for example global warming (Samuels and Prasad 1994), the greenhouse effect (Newman and Kenworthy 1999), the green dimension (Moughtin 1996), urban systems (Ravetz 2000), thermal efficiency and the heat island effect (Stone and Rogers 2001) and automobile dependency (Wachs and Crawford 1992). In addition, conservation of the built environment and urban regeneration is viewed as part and parcel of these necessary efficiencies (Bassett 1993, Griffiths 1993, Gaffkind and Morrissey 1999, Wansborough and Magean 2000, Ashworth *DC* 19). Overall, *Compact Cities* is a good example of the mainstream approach that characterises the literature overall. It is simultaneously an interesting and useful book and at the same time one that symbolises the lack of critique that permeates the idea of sustainable urban development. It also addresses the single idea of urban density, around which debates have raged for many years without any resolution. While I have already discussed above the type of critical and qualitative thinking that urban designers should be aware of, the idea of density and urban consolidation represents the major interface between urban politics and urban efficiency, and needs a brief consideration to conclude this chapter.

In the literature on sustainability and urban form, the terms 'sustainability' and 'consolidation' have a corresponding resonance. Consolidation often doubles as 'densification', 'urban containment' or 'urban intensification'. These terms are used as binary opposites to 'urban sprawl' and 'suburbanisation'. The debate over consolidation or 'suburbification' continues, one that has raged for many years, and Australia represents a classic example of the issues involved (Bunker 1983, McLoughlin 1991, 1992, Troy 1996, Newman and Kenworthy 1999). Newman and Kenworthy's analysis is totally pitched at the problem of automobile dependency, and provides an exhaustive analysis of all aspects of the problem. The conclusions are too extensive to state here but are summarised in *DC* 18. Nonetheless, two of these are singularly important and directly connected: first, that automobile dependency can no longer form the basis for urban planning, and second, that the collapse of the public realm as an outcome of this process must be restored. This view is by no means generally accepted, and Gordon and Richardson (1990), on a pro-automobile ticket, have savaged their earlier conclusions on this subject on the basis that the process of decentralisation and non-work-based trips were discounted. Troy (1996) has a radically opposite view from Newman and Kenworthy as well, a position made clear in his book *The Perils of Urban Consolidation*. Troy (1996: vi) argues that 'infrastructure costs and environmental stresses can and should be reduced. But it points out that these objectives can be achieved without changing the traditional form of our cities'. In Australia, this amounts to a reification of suburban living. He also argues from a polar opposite position, that increasing housing density decreases our capacity to deal with domestic waste and recycling, harvest rainwater, produce food and deal with air pollution, and decreases wildlife habitats, etc. McLoughlin (1991, 1992) argues Troy's position somewhat differently when he suggests the real fallacy is that 'increased residential densities save land; clearly they save quite insignificant amounts, even under the most favourable assumptions, and they do so at what may be considerable social, economic and environmental costs' (McLoughlin 1991: 155). The differences expressed here by extremely erudite scholars are not simply minor, they are mutually exclusive. What then is the problem? And how are we to understand this debate over the ideal sustainable urban form?

To answer this we have to go back to the seminal paper by Scott and Roweis 'Urban planning in theory and practice: a reappraisal' to get below the statistical blitzkrieg of these debates (above). In deriving a theory of urban planning, they 'reject right at the outset any attempt to derive such a theory out of abstract, normative principles as to what urban planning *ought* in ideal circumstances to be. Our concern is uniquely with what planning *is*' (Scott and Roweis 1977: 14). From the perspective of political economy, all the above debates ignore the reality of urban planning, pointing instead to a hypothetically ideal situation. While one might agree completely with the positions of Newman and Kenworthy, or Troy and McLoughlin, they collectively ignore the internal dissonances of the accumulation process, and the shifting relationship between capital, the state, urban planning and the morphology of cities. What is nowhere considered are the inherent contradictions of capital accumulation in Harvey's second circuit, between the free operation of the market and the state regulation of urban land. Added to this, 'capitalist urbanization processes simultaneously require and resist planning; that is, the social and property relations of capitalist society create an urban process which repels that on which its continued existence ultimately depends; collective action in the form of urban planning' (Scott and Roweis 1977: 24). Since urban planning is a product of, and is embedded within, the operation of the capitalist urban land market, it necessarily reflects the inherent contradictions of the overall system. These contradictions are that in order to have maximum room for exploitation, a free market ideology must operate. On the other hand, it is also clear that some regulation must take place otherwise anarchy will ensue. Because the urban land nexus is fundamentally out of control, such a balance is seldom achievable.

To assume, on this basis, that somehow the answers to sustainable urban development lie within the planning apparatus is to deny its confusion when faced with the realities of the capitalist land nexus. The same logic also suggests that a rational choice can be made between consolidation or continued expansion, when the very foundation for such rationality is largely absent. Over the last twenty years, the privatisation of planning has been consequent upon the deconstruction of the welfare state, the rise of the neocorporatist state, and its relationship to the built environment professions as a whole (see chapter 10). In functional terms this simply means that an increasing number of government operations are commodified and packaged for sale to the private sector, a process that further integrates state–capital interests. State planning products are then marketed to the private sector like any other good. As Mike Dear succinctly states in *The Postmodern Urban Condition*, 'privatisation portends a fundamental, even irrevocable change in the way in which planning is conducted ... e.g. the growth of planning personnel in private sector positions, the packaging and marketing of planning services for sale, and the prominent trend in planning education towards a development oriented curriculum' (Dear 2000: 125). Hence as McLoughlin succinctly concludes, 'policies for density increase are not a very effective part of an urban consolidation strategy' (McLoughlin 1991: 150). What he did not say was that a continuing strategy of pursuing the status quo is not very effective either.

Chapter Eight
Aesthetics

The allotted function of art is not, as is often assumed, to put across ideas, to propagate thoughts, to serve as example. The aim of art is to prepare a person for death, to plough and harrow his soul, rendering it capable of turning to good.

Andrey Tarkovsky (1994)

Introduction: Aesthetics – Objects and Experiences

Why did Marx insist so vigorously in his early work on explaining the aesthetic, on searching out its sources and defining its nature? ... He was looking for man, or more precisely, social, concrete man, man who, in the historical and economic conditions of capitalist society, destroys, mutilates, or denies himself. This mutilation or loss of humanity takes place in work, in material production – that is, in the sphere which has made possible aesthetic creation and in which man should affirm his humanity. In his search for the human, for our lost humanity, Marx found in the aesthetic a stronghold, as well as an essential sphere, of human existence. If man is creative he cannot keep from aestheticising the world – that is assimilating it artistically, without renouncing his human condition.

Adolfo Sanchez Vasquez (1973: 47)

Of all the qualities of cities, arguably the one that concerns us most is the nature of the aesthetic experience. Why are some cities more beautiful than others? What makes a city beautiful? Why do cities with a long history invariably possess greater beauty than those of more recent times? Then there are the more academic questions surrounding the idea of aesthetics. Are aesthetics and beauty necessarily related? Is the aesthetic experience purely personal, or are there generic qualities shared by all under given conditions? How is the aesthetic experience embodied in cities? What is the relationship between form and content? When I began writing this text, I assumed that this chapter would be the easiest to write, since the connection between design and aesthetics would seem most apparent. Yet it has turned out to be the most difficult. The central problem is that few antecedents exist that directly address the question of aesthetics in urban design. Most of those that do, conflate the problem to one of architectural design rather than urban design, although clearly there is a significant intersection between them. Aesthetic theory is of course legion, since it is the central focus of all the arts and represents a central object of philosophy, witness Wittgenstein's concern for colour in his famous *Philosophical Grammar.*

> What is the distinction between blue and red? We feel like answering: the one is blue and the other red. But of course that means nothing and in reality what we're thinking of is the distinction between the surfaces or places that have these colours. For otherwise the question makes no sense at all.
>
> Wittgenstein (1974: 208)

More recently, Roger Scruton confronted the question of the aesthetic experience in *Art and Imagination* (1974), later taking his argument into *The Aesthetics of Architecture* (1979). Scruton introduces the former book with the statement:

> There is a tradition in aesthetic philosophy, which perhaps derives from Kant's *Critique of Judgment,* that seeks to define concepts of aesthetic judgment and appreciation in terms of the 'uniqueness of the aesthetic object'...I see the object as an isolated, unique occurrence, and to the extent that I appreciate it aesthetically, I neither bring it under concepts, nor relate it to any practical end.
>
> (Scruton 1974: 15)

Scruton then goes on to explain at length the fundamental difference in two seminal attitudes to aesthetics, namely the relationship between aesthetic activity and scientific activity. He says, correctly, that when we examine something scientifically, we are comparing one object to another and in the process we are searching for general rules on which to base universal laws. In contrast, he maintains that under the aesthetic experience we are not interested in such comparisons, paraphrasing Kant, 'in aesthetic judgment, the object is not brought under concepts at all' (Scruton 1974: 15). What he is saying is that we cannot explain the aesthetic experience in terms of the properties of any object under our gaze, that our experience of a painting, a piece of music or an urban landscape is independent to whatever qualities these objects actually possess. He deepens the equation by pushing the idea even further: 'Moreover, once we abandon the theory of aesthetic perception, the notion of an aesthetic feature, as whatever is referred to by an aesthetic description, becomes extremely problematic' (Scruton 1974: 44). Scruton concludes by aligning aesthetics with moral judgement rather than with properties allocated to objects. He then applies his philosophical aesthetics to architecture, and in so doing elaborates the relationship between architecture and aesthetic judgement. A central chord in his argument concerns the idea that architecture is a language, and in rejecting this idea he works through concepts of meaning derived from Marx, Freud and Saussure: 'The Freudian and Marxist approaches to "meaning" fail partly because they provide no meaning to the architectural experience that is not external to it – that does not consist in some value, feeling or state of consciousness related to the building, not intrinsically, but as cause or effect' (Scruton 1979: 158).

One factor is therefore beyond doubt, that across the entire spectrum of the arts one would find little agreement on exactly how 'the aesthetic' should be defined, let alone its constituent parts, often stated in regard to architecture as firmness, commodity and delight. In this regard, aesthetics is usually bounded within the contours of a particular form, to music, painting, sculpture, dance, architecture and a host of other art forms. The question then surfaces as to how these forms are to be defined in the first place. In other words we must answer the question 'What is music?' before we can deal with the aesthetics of music. No doubt countless answers would result, and herein lies the essential problem. Perhaps, like Marx, it is easier overall to arrive at a definition of humanity and society, and progress from there, than to try to isolate a single aspect of the aesthetic development of the social. Indeed, I will later adopt this position in regard to urban design as I have done in other chapters, namely that urban design must be theorised in all its component parts with some fundamental connections to society and economy, instead of arbitrary and detached opinion, however persuasive it might be. I will begin therefore with traditional approaches to the aesthetics of urban form, prior to pursuing this position.

The Aesthetics of Urban Form

While the *New Oxford Dictionary* defines aesthetics simply as 'a set of principles concerned with the nature and appreciation of beauty', the term 'aesthetic' and its Greek root are singularly more revealing: 'origin late 18th century (in the sense "relating to the perception of the senses") from the Greek *aisthetikos*, from *aistheta* meaning "perceptible things" from *aesthesthai* "perceive"'. However, when we access the meaning of beauty it takes us on a circular path back to aesthetics: 'a combination of qualities, such as shape, colour, or form, that pleases the aesthetic senses, especially the sight'. Another definition of beauty under the same category is more revealing: 'a combination of qualities that pleases the intellect or the moral sense'. This indicates that aesthetics is not merely concerned with personal pleasure but also with qualities of the mind. It must consider both social conscience and morality, reflecting Scruton's concern with moral judgement. This opens up the general question as to whether aesthetics necessarily deals with pleasure/beauty or whether it exists in an entirely other dimension.

In *Designing Cities*, I selected three articles because they illustrate generic concerns about aesthetics in the context of urban design (*DC* 21, 22 and 23). The first of these by Jon Lang, 'Aesthetic theory', denotes two broad approaches to the study of aesthetics: 'the first involves the study of the processes of perception, cognition, and attitude-formation, while the second involves the study of aesthetic philosophies and the creative processes' (Lang *DC* 21: 275). Lang then moves from his two basic divisions of speculative aesthetics and empirical aesthetics, prior to formulating an approach to environmental aesthetics as a whole. In the first category he includes hermeneutic, phenomenological, existential and political approaches. Empirical aesthetics includes another four basic approaches, namely information theory, semantic, semiotic and psychobiological. Following Santayana, he suggests that an environment is aesthetically pleasing if it provides three basic ingredients: pleasurable sensory experiences, a pleasing perceptual structure and pleasurable symbolic associations.

Second, Aldo Rossi's article 'The urban artifact as a work of art' implies an objectification of aesthetics: 'our task consists principally in defining an urban artifact from the standpoint of its manufacture' (Rossi *DC* 22: 285). While Lang's concerns are primarily with individual experience, Rossi's are with the properties of the architectural object, noting that collective memory is the central feature of urban artefacts. Third, Barbara Rubin adds another dimension to this debate in 'Aesthetic ideology and urban design' (*DC* 23). She disagrees with both prior approaches in principle when she says that

> This dichotomy between urban function and urban 'culture' reflects a deeper polarization in Western civilization wherein sensitivity to art, music, poetry, and other 'exalted manifestations of the human spirit' are appreciated essentially and ostensibly for their own intrinsic formal qualities. By placing a primary value upon aesthetic behaviours associated with transcendental aspirations, students of culture have been unable to come to terms with the city – the modern city – as a symbolic manifestation of values mediated by forms.
>
> (*DC* 23: 291)

To these we could add a fourth dimension from the theoretical section in *Designing Cities*, that of Paul Clarke's article on 'The economic currency of architectural aesthetics' (*DC* 2). Here, the relationship between economy and aesthetics is located in the interaction between aesthetic production and commodity production. In this process, the aesthetic experience becomes closely linked to the production of symbolic capital and the reification of commodities in support of flexible accumulation. Traditional ideas of aesthetics as experience or object become linked prima facie to the processes of production in advanced capitalism: 'Late capitalism or the multinational world system . . . penetrates and colonises the unconscious . . . with consumerism, with the enormous colonization of the apparatus of the media, mass culture and the various other techniques of the commodification of the mind' (Jameson 1991).

The above positions are not hermetically sealed from each other, and to a certain extent reflect the process of history and the refinement of ideas over historical time. In order to place each in historical perspective, we must take a look at how the aesthetics of urban form have been viewed over the centuries. Four major considerations dominate. The first is with abstract ideas of beauty tied into the discoveries of the ancient Greeks in mathematics, physics, philosophy and medicine, symbolised in the work of Pythagoras, Euclid and Hippocratus. The second consideration is with urban morphology, where certain morphological arrangements are seen to possess greater or lesser aesthetic appeal, a project that came to fruition at the end of the nineteenth century with Camillo Sitte and Otto Wagner. This conflict concretised into two seminal movements in architectural and urban design, namely the contextualist and rationalist schools of thought discussed in chapter 3 (Sharpe 1978). The third concern is referred to as the 'picturesque', an aesthetic position governed more by landscape painting than by any derived from urban form and structure (De Botton 2002). While this movement has no figures comparable to Pythagoras, urban designers have reified the work of Gordon Cullen in this respect, as well as others who have advanced his elementary ideas on serial vision (Smith 1974, 1976). From this point we will investigate how particular contemporary approaches to aesthetics either advance or refute our adopted definition, that urban design is the symbolic attempt to express an accepted urban meaning in certain urban forms, pursuing the idea of symbolic capital derived from Pierre Bourdieu.

Mathematics and the Divine Order

In his book *Zero: The Biography of a Dangerous Idea*, Charles Seife notes, 'To the Pythagoreans, ratios and proportions controlled musical beauty, physical beauty, and mathematical beauty. Understanding nature was as simple as understanding the mathematics of proportion' (Seife 2000: 31). The concept of zero, and by extension the 'void', were antithetical to both the Greek universe and the Christian. For this reason, the refusal of the Greeks to incorporate zero into their system of logic constrained mathematics and science for nearly 2000 years. The mystical symbol of the Pythagoreans was the pentagram, a five-sided figure, and Pythagoras' invention of the musical scale, with its reliance on mathematical ratios, led to the idea that aesthetics in all things had a mathematical essence. Within the boundaries of the pentagram was embedded the 'golden ratio', often referred to as the 'golden section', the key to the most beautiful proportion ever conceived. Not only does the golden ratio exist in mathematics, it is found everywhere in nature, from the shape of galaxies to the archetypal nautilus shell or the pattern on the sunflower and the pine cone. While the problem with zero was that it had neither shape nor size, and defied nature when used to multiply or divide, the golden section was also irrational, since at its core lay the ratio of the square root of 2, a number of infinite length (1.414213562...). These irrational numbers threatened the Greek cosmos, and Pythagoreans were sworn to secrecy, never to reveal the key that could destroy their world: 'Even today, artists and architects intuitively know that objects that have this ratio of length to width are the most aesthetically pleasing, and the ratio governs the proportions of many works of art and architecture...The supernatural link between aesthetics, ratios, and the universe, became one of the central and long lasting tenets of western civilisation' (Seife 2000: 32–4).

As all architects are aware, the most famous building of ancient Greece incorporates the golden section throughout its construction, namely the Parthenon, the central showpiece of the Athenian Acropolis. But mathematics was not the only principle governing architectural aesthetics in ancient Greece. Science and medicine also played a huge role in refining the appearance of buildings. The work of Hippocrates and knowledge of medical optics further revealed the imperfect nature of the human eye, which perceived straight lines as curved due to changes in perspective. Euclid was also fascinated by optics. On this basis the Greeks built a slight curvature into most long straight surfaces, called entasis, in order to correct an inherent deficiency of the human eye and in the interests of mathematically perfect architecture. Temple columns were given a slight outward curve along their length, the outside columns were off vertical and leaning inward, and temple bases were curved upwards in order to compensate for normal vision. All of this convinces many architects even today that Greek architecture was the finest ever built, at least in terms of its attention to detail. Until relatively recently, it was thought that these refinements were limited to the architectural object, and that the design of urban space remained ad hoc, depending very much on the layout of the site, functional relationships between buildings and other such considerations.

However, a relatively unknown text of Constantinos Doxiadis called *Architectural Space in Ancient Greece*, based on his doctoral thesis for the University of Berlin, demonstrated that the golden section was applied not only to urban space but also as a fundamental tool in site planning, along with what Doxiadis calls 'the system of polar coordinates'. These principles were followed throughout ancient Greece in the planning of monuments and marketplaces. As Doxiadis states, 'Just as we can consider a temple as representative of Greek architecture, so we may consider the layout of an entire sacred precinct as typical of all Greek spatial complexes. The layout of the agoras at Miletus, Magnesia, and Pergamon for example, appear to have been governed by the same laws as the sacred precincts' (Doxiadis 1972: 24). Doxiadis states that site planning in both the Hellenistic period and the Archaic and Classic periods that preceded it were precisely calculated. He notes that despite their interest in geometry, and despite their use of the grid system for military settlements in Asia Minor, the ancient Greek builders did not use a rectilinear system of coordinates (Wicherley 1967). The unique properties of each site were first explored, and polar coordinates established on the basis of the human viewpoint, usually a vantage point that encompassed the entire site. From that point radii were placed so that a three-quarter view could be obtained of each important building, and a complex system of angles, distances from the viewpoint, principles of accentuation of the landscape and other factors were all considered in accordance with specified rules. While the use of the golden section did not appear to play a major role in Greek site planning, mathematics still dominated, for example multiples of a thirty-degree angle (30, 60, 90, 120, etc.) were also held to possess divine properties, as well as figures such as the equilateral triangle, which was associated with the goddess Athena. Mathematical systems and forms were therefore accorded divine status within the Greek cosmos, where it was considered that the central questions of existence could be reduced to mathematics.

The golden section, or 'golden mean', discovered by the Greeks was lost for centuries until it was rediscovered by Leonardo Pisano. Born in Pisa in 1175 at the beginning of the so-called First Renaissance, Pisano (often referred to as Fibonacci), an Italian merchant and mathematician, evolved a series of numbers that accorded closely to the Pythagorean's golden section. The mathematical sequence called the Fibonacci series was first named by a French mathematician, Edouard Lucas. It consists of the sequence 0, 1, 2, 3, 5, 8, 13, 21, 34, 55, 89, 144, 233, 377, etc. The higher the numbers go, the more closely they correlate with the golden section. Fibonacci numbers represent the mathematical basis for Pythagorean rectangles, and therefore hold the secret to the golden section and its extensions, a process which has absorbed mathematicians for centuries. Today, the sequence has immense application, from predicting stock market patterns to complex applications in mathematics, and the journal *Fibonacci* continues to explore the implications of Pisano's original idea.

It was not until two centuries later, around 1400, that the Italian Renaissance began to flower, and painters who were also mathematicians first applied Fibonacci's discoveries. His series was then used as the basis of linear perspective and structural harmony in proportional systems applied to painting, sculpture and architecture alike, linking the arts to nature on the one hand and to science on the other, the harmonia mundi or harmony of the world. The foremost Renaissance architect, Leon Battista Alberti, was completely aware of the significance of mathematics to architecture, and deployed classical systems of proportion in his buildings. The great artist Leonardo da Vinci also recognised the power of the golden ratio, and collaborated with a Minorite friar called Luca Paciole, who published a book called *Divina Proportione* in 1503, with illustrations by Leonardo. The golden section and the closely related symbol ϕ approximated the 8:5 ratio which Leonardo noted was the proportion of the human body when divided at the navel, as illustrated in his drawing of universal man. So the divine nature of the golden section continued to be recognised throughout the Renaissance because the proportional systems it implied were seen to permeate the universe and therefore reflected the work of God.

By the end of the sixteenth century, many fundamental properties governing the aesthetics of urban design had been formulated: the organising frameworks of the grid and polar coordinates, laws governing harmony and proportion in architecture and site design, incorporation of the laws of optics, the nature of perspective, and principles bearing on questions of proportion, scale, dimension and form (Stephenson 1992, Padovan 1999). For 2000 years since the time of the ancient Greeks, mathematics was the supreme principle governing the art of city design, one that extended right into the twentieth century and which has influenced many architects working today. The person responsible for continuing the work of Pythagoras and Fibonacci was the French architect Le Corbusier, arguably the most important figure in twentieth-century architecture. Corbusier wrote two extended texts incorporating principles derived from Fibonacci, called Modulor 1 and Modulor 2 (2000, original 1955). Le Corbusier also believed that the human figure contained perfect proportions (as indeed did Leonardo) and that buildings should embody these perfect proportions, which incorporated the geometry of the golden section. Le Corbusier's basic unit was a man 6 feet (1.8 metres) tall, the foundation of the Fibonacci series used in many of his buildings. In addition, he claimed that this system resolved discrepancies between metric and imperial units. Le Corbusier derived two scales from Fibonacci. The first scale, called the red series, followed Leonardo's lead, and is the ratio between the total height of his universal man and the height at his navel. The second scale was based on the ratio between the total height of a man

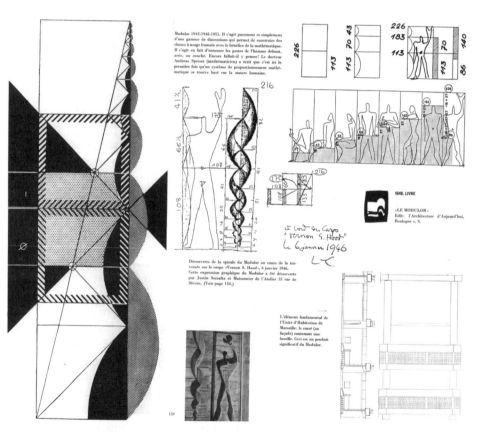

Figure 36   Le Corbusier: use of Fibonacci series as a proportional system for architecture.
Source: Reprinted by permission of Le Corbusier Foundation and the Design and Artists Copyright Society. Copyright © 2005 by FLC/ADAGP, Paris and DACS, London.

with his hand upstretched and the height at his navel (figure 36). The two series were then related to basic human postures as well as to spatial organisation and proportional systems. From the classical Greek period to the Italian Renaissance and into modern times, the power of mathematics as a fundamental tool in structuring architectural and urban space is unquestioned. At the end of the nineteenth century, however, an entirely different dimension was being explored in the search for a true aesthetic for urban design, that of urban morphology, symbolised in the writings of the Viennese architect Camillo Sitte.

Contextualism

Sitte's collection of essays, *Der Stadtebau nach Seinen Kuntslerischen Grundsatzen* (original 1889), is accepted by most urban designers as the book that gave birth to the profession of urban design. Until this time, architecture had been influenced by many great texts, prime among them being Vitruvius' *Ten Books on Architecture* (1775), Leone Battista Alberti's *De Re Aedificatoria* (1485), Andrea Palladio's *The Four Books of Architecture* (1570), Sebastiano Serlio's *Five Books on Architecture* (1611) and Quatremère de Quincy's *Historical Dictionary* (1832). More recently, there have been several massive tomes dedicated to architecture history and theory (Kruft 1994, Hays 1998, Bierman 2003), all of which have progressed well beyond Sir Bannister Fletcher's seminal *History of Architecture* (1961). While the subject matter in all these texts was primarily focused on the design of plans and the entire vocabulary of architectural detailing, some consideration was given to the layout of towns and cities, particularly in the work of Alberti during the Italian Renaissance. It was, however, left to Sitte to open up an entirely new horizon by extending the aesthetics of architecture into the aesthetics of urban form, by first investigating in great detail the physical qualities of European towns and cities that had survived relatively intact over the centuries (Collins and Collins 1986). While Sitte is known in English for *The Art of Building Cities*, this is largely due to the fact that it is his only work to be translated into English, and many more remain in the original German.

The school of thought that Sitte brought into being is referred to as *contextualism*, which focuses fundamentally on space rather than building, although clearly they cannot be separated.

> The continuity of space, in which buildings were mere instances or provided a transitory framework, and the continuity of time, which caused a permanent revolution of the urban fabric, were for Sitte, the fundamental aspects of older towns. In the apparently chaotic jumble of the unplanned, he searched for an inner structure, a hidden pattern, that allowed for unending change in response to the demands of time.
>
> (Collins and Collins 1986: 14)

Sitte's position reflected the philosophy of Charles Darwin, whom he admired equally with Beethoven and Wagner. Sitte supported the inner laws of organic

growth and evolution, against the unnatural and meaningless geometries of
many urban plans. The mathematics of the Pythagoreans and the Renaissance
were anathema to Sitte, who denied any inherent virtue in Euclidean geometry
applied indiscriminately to city design, an implicit rejection of the Greek's sense
of order based in numbers. For Sitte, aesthetics were inherent to the timeless
traditions established by the great faceless builders of the ancient, medieval and
Renaissance periods. He was not concerned with aesthetics as an abstraction,
but sought to derive laws from what already existed, from the pre-existing
actuality of urban growth. Hence his concentration on elementary units was of
utmost concern, particularly in the interconnections and relationships between
streets, squares, monuments and private spaces such as courts and crescents
(Webb 1990, see also chapter 9). Sitte's ideas on contextualism, extensively
illustrated 150 years earlier in Giovani Battista Nolli's plan for Rome of 1748,
have frequently been interpreted as reactionary, a retreat into history, and a
denial of development (figures 37 and 38). Clearly this was not Sitte's position,
given that evolution is a dynamic process. Mimesis was not his advocated
position, which very much reflected the abandonment of style and its replacement by principles that could grow and change in accordance with the laws of
natural selection, the survival of the fittest. Despite Sitte's overt concern with
what he calls 'the laws of beauty', he never clearly articulated what these were,
although a concern for high art, a system of polar coordinates and the rejection
of symmetry – 'the notion of symmetry is propagating itself today like an
epidemic' (Sitte 1945: 32–3) – all dominate his vision.

Figure 37   Nolli's plan for Rome, sector 5, amended by Paolo Portoghese.

Figure 38 Examples of contextual urban space as promoted by Camillo Sitte:
(A) Rome; (B) London; (C) Copenhagen; (D) Kyoto.
Source: P. Bosselman, *Representation of Places: Reality and Realism in City Design.*
Berkeley, CA: University of California Press, 1998, p. 48.

However, Sitte's aesthetic was wholly Eurocentric, reflecting pre-existing historic conditions in cities such as Salzburg, Munster, Kiel, Copenhagen, Perugia, Mantua, Vicenza, Autun, Budapest and other major centres. Despite the fact that the modern movement personified the rationalist approach after 1910, contextualism was still in full flight at CIAM 8, the Congress International d'Architecture Moderne in 1945. Jose Luis Sert and Siegfried Giedion lectured the audience (including Le Corbusier) on the aesthetics of contextualism as *the* method of designing the centres of towns and cities. However, the observation that 'since then, modern architects have erased from their memory, a language for discussing the urban context' (Shane 1976: 24) could easily be supported today, as the social is subsumed to the technical in architectural discourse at the end of the millennium. Shane outlines the methodology behind the contextualist aesthetic as follows:

> The contextualist is concerned with the figure–ground interface. This is a double pre-occupation that can be confusing, for both figures and grounds have a life of their own, which can be classified as *regular* or *irregular, formal* or *informal, types* and *variants*. Each figure (or its ground) can be considered as a *field* (zone), a precise area that has a sharp pattern. Such an area has its *center* or centers, a supporting *infill* or *tissue*, and a clearly defined *boundary edge*. A well-defined relationship between figure and field is termed a *set-piece*, with all its parts and relationships known and fixed. Set pieces should occur between fields or at the point of overlap of fields, as a resolution of an implicit geometric conflict.
>
> (Shane 1976: 25)

The question as to whether Sitte's ideas are relevant in today's metropolis must be met with a resounding 'Yes!' The propagation of Sitte's basic philosophy is legion. Almost a century after the publication of Sitte's *Der Stadtebau*, Rob Krier published *Urban Space* (1979b). Krier's analysis is a superb extension of Sitte's basic thesis on urban typology and aesthetics, which he has built into his own urban design projects across Europe (Berke 1982). Rowe and Koetter's influential *Collage City*, discussed at length in chapter 1, also owes its existence to Sitte's philosophy, as does the even more recent *City of Bits* (Mitchel 1995). But we have to return to the late 1950s to detect the origins of another dimension in the aesthetics of urban design, namely the Townscape movement. A brief glance at *Der Stadtebau* is sufficient to demonstrate that Sitte was predominantly concerned with the figure–ground relationship or what is called the 'gestalt', which the French refer to as the 'psychology of form'. His text is infused with countless examples of urban spaces in Europe, while perspectives, sketches or photographs are limited to around half a dozen examples. While Sitte was clearly aware of the effects of perspective, he did not articulate the idea of 'serial vision' that drove the Townscape movement in Britain. This new approach was in fact initiated not by any particular text but by a journal called *The Architectural Review*, which published two special issues in 1956 called 'Outrage' and 'Counter-attack'. Collectively, these issues laid bare the disastrous environmental inheritance of the Industrial Revolution and the Second World War. Gordon Cullen's *Townscape* (1961) was the first organised response to the situation exposed by *The Architectural Review*.

While it is somewhat of an oversimplification, we may argue that while Sitte's aesthetics were concerned with the position of an observer *within* space and how space was enclosed and bounded, Cullen raised the idea of the position of the observer *through* or *across* space. To this degree Cullen's vision was dynamic, dealing with kinaesthetics (sometimes called the sixth sense, that of movement) as a fundamental quality of the aesthetic experience of cities. To Cullen the experience of movement was all important. In describing one English village for example, Cullen says 'The following sequence in Blandford Forum covers in a few hundred linear yards no less than six different effects of closure, all gained through the medium of the main road' (Cullen 1961: 107). Reflecting the Greek experience, Cullen denotes three items in his aesthetic that are paramount. First, optics, by which he means the sequence through which urban space reveals itself and generates emotion through the medium of serial vision (see also Thiel 1961). Second, there is a concern with place and the body: 'At this level of consciousness we are dealing with a range of experience stemming from the major impacts of exposure and enclosure' (Cullen 1961: 10). Third, concerning content, Cullen defines this as the fabric of the town, which involves 'colour, texture, scale, style, character, personality, and uniqueness' (Cullen 1961: 11). From a single book, Gordon Cullen had an immense impact on the theory and practice of urban design, the tradition being continued through texts and articles such as Worskett's *The Character of Towns* (1969), Peter Smith's *Syntax of Cities* (1976) and *The Dynamics of Urbanism* (1974), Olsen's *The City as a Work of Art* (1986) and Nigel Taylor's 'The elements of townscape and the art of urban design' (1999).

Cullen's *Townscape*, which was based largely on the aesthetic qualities of English towns and villages, also brought into high profile the entire idea of the vernacular, and a renewed interest in Italian hill towns, Greek Cycladic villages and other seminal urban forms that have been described as 'architecture without architects' (Rudofsky 1969). Neither could this perspective be detached from the English landscape and landscape architecture, which had significant origins in painting and what is termed the 'picturesque', particularly such painters as Constable, Gainsborough and Turner (Watkin 1982, Andrews 1989, De Botton 2002). Nor was this limited to England, and the relationship between painting, landscape design and architecture has parallels across the world, from China, Japan, Persia and India to France, Italy, England and the USA. The word 'picturesque' is derived from the Italian *pittoresco*. While one might expect it to refer to the actual properties of landscape, it originates in the word *pittore*, meaning 'painter', and the even earlier Latin word for a painter, *pictor*. Hunt (1992) demonstrates the powerful effect that painting had on landscape design and the idea of the garden as a metaphor for culture.

In this regard, landscape architecture can be viewed as an embodiment of cultural ideas, which relate man to nature, and has for millennia symbolised our place in the cosmos (Cosgrove 1984, Relph 1987, Swaffield 2002). Landscape paintings and landscape gardens therefore constitute complex textual referents that can be deconstructed for meanings sequestered within their structure and organisation (Bourassa 1991, Edquist and Bird 1994, Birkstead 2000). The aesthetic, semantic and functional connections between landscape architecture, landscape planning and the urban landscape cover a long and complex history and have had a significant impact on the aesthetics of urban design (Lovejoy

1979, Adams 1991, Hunt 1992, Turner 1996). Hunt points to the fact that the Roman poet Cicero inferred a primal unmediated nature prior to human origins, which might be referred to as 'wilderness'. He also made reference to a second nature, *alteram naturam*, or the cultural landscape produced by human action and evolution, a functional definition of culture. On top of this, there is a third nature, first noted by Jacopo Bonfadio in the sixteenth century:

> The implication of this third nature, as indeed of Cicero's second, was its augmentation of an existing state of affairs. Gardens went beyond the cultural landscape, and therefore those humanists drawing upon Cicero, invented new terminology. Gardens were worlds where the pursuit of pleasure probably outweighed the need for utility, and accordingly where the utmost resources of human intelligence and technological skill were invoked to fabricate an environment where nature and art collaborated.

(Hunt 1992: 4)

Landscape painting and architecture therefore had a huge effect on aesthetic sensibilities in urban design, not only in the context of the picturesque townscape tradition. What is now referred to as the urban landscape is a metaphorical extension of the concept of landscape into the urban realm. The sheer scale of many landscape projects, and their close integration with the architectural design of the buildings that they incorporated, meant that the design of cities and the design of nature went hand in hand. This effect continues even today in the idea of 'environment and sustainability', discussed in the previous chapter, where a new aesthetic is demanded in urban design based upon the principle of conservation, and in all areas of human action.

Rationalism

Whichever aspect of contextualism we look at, from Cicero to Sitte to Krier, we are dealing fundamentally with feeling, intuition, emotion, experience and the world of the senses, aesthetics qua experience. *Rationalism* is motivated by reason, calculation and concept, aesthetics qua logic. Going back to the *fin de siècle* and Sitte's attempts to restore the place of history in the contemporary development of his time, another movement that affected the aesthetics of urban design is represented by his nemesis, the architect Otto Wagner. Wagner personified everything that Sitte was against, primarily his need to symbolically reinvent the wheel, where a powerful new idea rather than the idiosyncrasies of history drives motivation and action. He was fundamentally a rationalist. The twentieth century in its entirety constituted a theatre for conflict between two positions, between the contextualist/empiricists on the one hand and the rationalist/functionalists on the other (Sharpe 1978).

Otto Wagner's plan for Vienna came four years after Sitte's *Der Stadtebau*, and for all practical purposes it might as well not have been written. Wagner's plan for the city (as opposed to his prior plan for the Ringstrasse) anticipated the functionalism of infrastructure-led modern town planning, and was based upon a circumferential series of four road and rail systems, communications, sanitation and land use. Any attempt at aesthetics in this plan was all but abandoned in favour of functionalist pursuits. Schorske (1981) explains in great detail how Wagner's original renaissance style gradually gave way to his use of art nouveau to decorate the engineering works that he had to execute. Wagner's functionalism derived from his involvement with architectural engineering, carried over into his rationalist aesthetic in urban form, where his acceptance of all things modern stamped him as one of the key strategists in the functionalist tradition. Wagner embraced functionalist economics, functional planning and functional aesthetics. Nowhere was this more evident than in his plan for a modular city district of 1911 (figure 39). This philosophy implied the acceptance of unlimited urban expansion, commercialism, the subjugation of nature (no green belts) and capitalist economics as form giving, with uniformity, hierarchic structures, monumentality and consumerism as the basis of his aesthetic. Schorske sums up the difference between the two great architects of the period, which in reducing differences to their simplest components is represented in the typologies of street and square:

> Camillo Sitte and Otto Wagner, the romantic archaist and the rational functionalist, divided between them the unreconciled components of the Ringstrasse legacy.

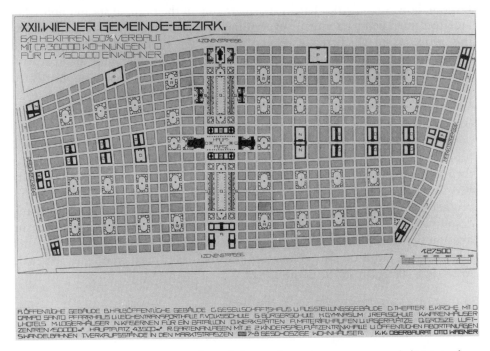

Figure 39 Otto Wagner: site plan of the projected twenty-second district of Vienna.
Source: Copyright © by Direktion der Museen der Stadt Wien.

Sitte, out of the artesan tradition, embraced Ringstrasse historicism to further his project of restoring a communitarian city, with the enclosed square as his model for the future. Wagner, out of a bourgeois affirmation of modern technology, embraced as essence what Sitte most abhorred in the Ringstrasse, the primary dynamic of the street.

(Schorske 1981: 100)

Even through the postmodern movement, the rationalist approach affected architectural and urban design with equal force. Fundamentally, rationalism is a philosophy that architecture has borrowed to substantiate and explain a particular theoretical approach. Beginning with Plato, and continuing through Descartes and Kant, rationalism in architecture, despite its superficially logical position, was fundamentally rooted to intuition and the 'eureka principle' as the basis for design, exemplified in the work of Louis Kahn, James Stirling, Mies van der Rohe, Le Corbusier and others. Empirical research, evidence and proof of their ideas were all cast to the wind. Intuition ruled as much for the rationalists as it did for the contextualists. While the rationalists were prepared to adapt prior historical typologies and to invent new typologies appropriate to the time, the functionalist branch of rationalism sought to discard the ancient city in its entirety: 'Their view was that such types and forms are dead without modern meaning, and that they could be collaged together, as Piranesi collaged Roman monuments, without reference to their past or past rules' (Shane 1976: 26). Overall, however, Charles Jencks is disparaging of the rationalists and notes, 'an architect must be able to justify everything he does, Laugier averred, and it was this proposition which really proved fatal to the rationalists. Their assumed truths, like the primitive hut or the grid used for all planning, have always seemed embarrassingly absurd. How could one possibly base a sophisticated urban architecture on such simple notions?' (Jencks 1977: 68). Jencks also notes an unfortunate tendency of rationalism to go hand in hand with totalitarianism (i.e. fascism) 'because they both emphasise order, certainty and clarity, and they both tend to look to a classical past for inspiration... this poses a great semantic problem for architects such as Aldo Rossi, because try as they might to dissociate themselves from the fascist architecture of the 1930s, their style is historically tied to it' (Jencks 1977: 74). Interestingly, Jencks classifies Rob Krier and his brother Leon as rationalists (although somewhat less irrational than others), despite the fact that they clearly follow Sitte's example. So it is clear that the division between contextualism and rationalism remains a contested space, and that there are limits on the explanatory possibilities of such typologies (Perez de Arce 1978, Petersen 1979, Berke 1982).

Symbolic Capital

As we have seen, the aesthetics of urban design derive from diverse sources: philosophy, mathematics and painting to name but a few. It is also apparent that while each would seem to be unrelated to any of the others, there are powerful interconnections, which have been suggested above. Another central and potentially dominating theme is that of capital. While Marx would seem to be an unlikely source for any aesthetic, let alone urban design, Sanchez observes 'If, as Marx said in *The Economic and Philosophical Manuscripts*, man is human to the extent that he is able to raise himself above nature to become a *human natural being*, then art is that activity through which he elevates this specific capacity to humanize everything he touches' (Vazquez 1973: 105). Marx clearly recognised the importance of art and aesthetics as a fundamental quality of being human. He also held the opinion that capitalism was basically hostile to art since capital valued production for the sake of production, i.e. in its own interest, and not because it contained any inherent capacity to humanise society. Within capitalism, art is commodified: it becomes a part of the exchange values of capitalism, an investment for the sake of material gain, and part of the general system of capital accumulation. Specific paintings by Van Gogh, Gauguin and Picasso for example, which the artists could not sell when they were alive, are now worth in excess of $US50 million each, and the art 'industry' has been recognised for decades as a major form of speculation and profit.

There is no better example of the production of art as concrete labour than in the medieval and Renaissance cities discussed by Camillo Sitte, where the reliance on crafts humanised and perfected every aspect of building. Here the urban aesthetic was underwritten by each part of the labour process incorporating its own artistry through the efforts of each individual to master and improve their craft. Labour had not yet become alienated from production as it would later through Fordist and Taylorist production strategies applied to the building industries. In reality, when we admire the beauty of medieval towns and cities such as Florence, Sienna or Bruges, we are first and foremost respecting a form of production and consciousness that has passed into history, namely that of merchant capitalism. The urban landscape so produced was a direct product of the material relations of the time, wonderfully portrayed by Dennis Cosgrove in chapter 1 of *Social Formation and Symbolic Landscape*. I have also demonstrated the paradigmatic role of modernism and industrial capitalism in the emergence of a rationalist approach to urban form in Vienna. In today's world, however, we are faced not with one but with a multiplicity of different capitals – industrial, commercial, informational, cultural and symbolic. But it is to the latter form that we must now turn in order to investigate the dominant forms of aesthetic production in the built environment of the twenty-first century.

Within the overall context of culture within capitalism, Pierre Bourdieu was arguably the foremost philosopher dealing with the concept of symbolic capital, exchange and taste (Schusterman 1999, Bourdieu 2000). Post-Marxist theory dispenses with the rigid distinctions between the economic base and the ideological superstructure (culture), and recognises the difficulties involved in any attempt to separate these theoretically. Ideologies, meaning systems, identity and image are intimately tied to consumption, rendering any isolation of 'the economy' from culture as seriously problematic. In this context, Bourdieu argued that this transition to symbolic capital was brought about through the accumulation of surplus value in developed economies, where elementary material (survival) needs had been met. Hence economies are now aligned to the production and consumption of symbolic values, and luxuries not demanded by the materiality of everyday life. Since labour is now almost wholly alienated from any unity with aesthetic production, i.e. where culture and work coincide, the formation of culture moves from production to consumption, a process that then permits the establishment of commodity culture and commodity aesthetics as a central pillar of informational capitalism. In this process, needs (now satisfied) become overtaken by desires, a process with unlimited potential for manipulation and control (Haug 1986, 1987). Each commodity constitutes a text that can be constructed in accordance with images, aspirations, meanings and identities, designed and targeted to consumption territories within society on the basis of age, ethnicity, religion, sexual orientation, gender or other association or affiliation. The mass media plays a key role in the continuing reproduction of referents with which individuals may associate. As with other forms of capital, symbolic capital can also be accumulated in the process of consumption. In a society where art and aesthetics have been commodified, there is clearly a correlation between 'taste', the type and value of commodities purchased, and the accumulation of symbolic capital which results. The entire panoply of relations so generated is what Debord referred to as 'the society of the spectacle', a process which not only applies to art and commodity production but also to architecture and urban design, where symbolic capital in many cases transcends the use-value of built form (figure 40). Pierre Bourdieu delineates his ideas on symbolic capital as a scientific theory of social meaning in *Outline of a Theory of Practice* (1977), and across many of his other works. *Pascallian Meditations* concludes, for example, with a section on the significance of symbolic capital:

> Every type of capital, (economic, cultural, social) tends, to different degrees, to function as symbolic capital, (so that it might be better to speak, in rigorous terms of the *symbolic effects of capital*), when it obtains an explicit or practical recognition, that of a *habitus* structured according to the very structures of space in which it has been engendered... produced by the transfiguration of a power relation into a sense relation, symbolic capital rescues agents from insignificance, the absence of importance and of meaning.
>
> (Bourdieu 2000: 242)

The terms 'cultural capital', 'habitus' and 'symbolic capital' are central concepts in Bourdieu's work (the French *œuvre* is a better term, literally translated as 'work', but in this context infers Bourdieu's entire philosophy and writing). The term 'habitus' is similarly complex. Literally meaning field (of study, influence, concentration), habitus is used by Bourdieu to mean one's entire life-world, from the gestures one makes, to the places one inhabits, to the people one associates with: 'Although sometimes mistaken for specific routines of everyday life, or as a synonym for socialization, habitus is in fact part of Bourdieu's theory of practice as the disposition of articulations in social space... Habitus is a kind

Figure 40   Cover from Debord's *Society of the Spectacle.*
Source: G. Debord, *Society of the Spectacle.* Detroit, MI: Black and Red, 1983.

of grammar of actions which serves to differentiate one class (e.g. the dominant) from another (e.g. the dominated) in the social field' (Lechte 1994: 48). Or otherwise, 'The Habitus acts through its bodily incorporation of social relationships and meanings (i.e. those involving reference to others) but without needing to articulate them in terms of explicit rules or practice' (Schusterman 2000: 5). Symbolic capital is not merely another form of accelerated accumulation in the form of surplus value, profit, land rent or whatever. Symbolic capital represents the added value over the material value/cost of any product, process or situation. Hence, for example, the symbolic value of Norman Foster's Hong Kong Shanghai Bank, the most expensive building in the world at the time of its construction, is only partly represented in its cost. The image it generates, which attests to the good taste, alpha-corporate image of its builders, is arguably worth more in the marketplace than the cost of building it. Ownership of the image and its aesthetic properties, the creation of difference, the unique qualities of the architecture, its command over urban form and its ability to dominate its immediate environment and like images across the planet have generated a wealth of symbolic capital on top of any accrued material value. This value is also extended in varying degrees, and by association, to its occupants, users and even those whose gaze falls upon it as tourists (Rojek and Urry 1997). 'On this basis "symbolic capital" should not be thought' of as a kind of capital, but as a way of emphasizing certain relational features of capital in general' (Earle 1999: 182).

There is no doubt, however, that symbolic capital also feeds back into added value for real investment and production (Zukin 1991). The aesthetics of urban form is therefore intimately connected, on the one hand, to the production of culture through the culture industry and its associated commodities and, on the other, to the accumulation of symbolic capital. Allen Scott points out the essence of this process in the conclusion to his seminal work *The Cultural Economy of Cities*, where he sums up his study of cultural production with the observation that there remain many puzzling issues related to spatial organisation: 'not the least of these is the tendency for the emerging global cultural network to condense out in the landscape in the form of a scattered patchwork of urban and regional production systems, constituting the basic nerve centers of contemporary aesthetic and semiotic production' (Scott 2000a: 216).

The production of symbolic capital is also closely related to the production of cultural capital and the cultural economy as a whole. In the urban design process this usually means the ability to capture some aspect of historical or cultural development, and the desire to package this for sale as some kind of new experience that retranslates or transcends the old. This process is most obviously manifested in the attempt to capture the tourist dollar, while at the same time blurring the boundary between tourist and local consumption in order to capture an extended market. Countless examples of this abound, from the famous Edinburgh Tattoo, to the operas staged in the ancient Greek theatres in Athens, to the repackaging of old Gold Rush towns in Australia and the USA as cultural attractions. These sights integrate history with contemporary spectacle in order to establish economic, cultural and symbolic capital, a process that now underwrites much of the design of cities and their aesthetic assumptions:

> Underpinning much discussion of new urban spaces is Pierre Bourdieu's notion of symbolic capital. The reinvention of city centre spaces since the 1980s has largely involved a pursuit of external sources of investment – jobs, companies, tourists and wealthy residents for example. For this to be successful, cities have to accumulate reserves of symbolic capital, for example, blue chip architecture, loft living spaces, public art, aesthetisised heritage litter, and other gilded spaces, to help create the appropriate 'aura' of distinction with which the providers of these sources of investment wish to associate themselves.
>
> (Miles and Hall 2000: 99)

At another level, symbolic capital also represents the insatiable nature of human consumption, whereby several forms of entertainment/experience need to be combined to satisfy the desire for difference. Airports for example are gradually turning into themeports, providing the international traveller with shopping centres, theatres, galleries, restaurants and a plethora of services such that a surrogate tourist experience is being created: the airport becomes a point of transit for international 'tourists' and a destination for local people to visit and be entertained. This blurring of differences between tourist and local is as much a consequence of economic necessity, avoiding the need to double up on facilities, as it is in providing for difference. In a very real sense, we are all tourists, since the search for authenticity in the tourist domain becomes nullified by the standardisation of commodity markets, hotels, restaurants and the entire production of surrogate tourist experiences, as well as the homogenisation of products manufactured for the tourist industry. To a certain extent this trend to entropy through standardisation is offset by the culture industry, a process that seeks 'to go beyond, though not to abandon entirely, the notion of the cultural economy of cities as either (a) the commercialization of historical heritage, or (b) large-scale public investment in artifacts of collective consumption in the interests of public renovation' (Scott 2000a: 5) The forms of cultural capital produced by the culture industry adopt four main forms (Craik 1996: 470):

1   built environments (amusement and theme parks, cultural centres, casinos, shopping centres);
2   spectacles (events and festivals);
3   property markets (internationalisation of real estate speculation and development);
4   festival markets (dock redevelopments, tourist-oriented malls and entertainment centres).

Craik also points out the influence that these forms of development have on labour markets and trends in infrastructure development, and notes the increasing coincidence between patterns of behaviour shared by tourists and those of local people: 'Thus the continued growth of the tourism industry must be placed in the context of new forms of consumer development, and in particular, the convergence between patterns of consumption, leisure and tourism' (Craik 1997: 125). The overall fundamental shift in the aesthetics of urban design as a consequence of these forces is therefore profound, and some of the major considerations driving the evolution of aesthetic production have already been indicated above (see also DC 2, 14 and 26; Harvey 1989, Soja 1989). We can however summarise the most significant of these influences as follows.

1   The deliberate formation of cultural economies across the globe based in harnessing cultural capital as a form of monopoly aesthetic. This involves everything from the manufacture of clothes to the commodification of history represented in architectural and urban form.
2   The demands for symbolic capital by the neocorporate state, resulting in an aesthetic of neocorporate power and symbolism, which is slowly replacing that of traditional state power and authority. While this is ubiquitous, it predominates in the central city and its satellites or edge cities (Garreau 1992).
3   New urban design philosophies, such as postmodernism, critical regionalism or the New Urbanism, which have a profound ideological impact on

practitioners (and sometimes both of these in combination). The aesthetic of the New Urbanism for example is having an international impact, although it appears to contain significant reactionary elements.

4   The provision of venues for spectacles and spectacular production as part and parcel of competition between cities at all levels in the hierarchy: convention centres, sites for expositions, Olympic and other forms of sporting venues, theme parks, hotel and tourist facilities, signature and 'blue chip' architecture, etc.

5   The process of branding and advertising in both visual and electronic forms. Media-generated environments, particularly at night, have the capacity to totally dominate built form by the use of light, image and sign. Physical architecture then becomes a prop to the electronic.

6   Post-Taylorist forms of production permit off-site manufacture of building components, leading to entirely new possibilities in the appearance of individual architectural elements.

7   New building technologies, which arise out of the informational economy, and the manufacture of new materials and products by industry (this results in altogether new methods of building, new perspectives in shaping and forming of materials, as well as their increased durability and strength).

8   The increased potential of computer graphic languages to construct complex geometries, and to portray three- and four-dimensional images. Ward (1996) also points to the consolidation of cultural capital in the design process by large corporate firms, due to the major capital investments required by new technologies and software copyright fees.

On this basis, there is no use trying to determine some kind of single universal aesthetic that is gradually overwhelming the design of cities. Rather the above forces will create an immense variety of environments when combined with specific geographies, populations and urban administrations. Each will have its own particular political economy of space and aesthetics. So it is more significant to establish the forms of aesthetic production of urban design than it is to predict specific forms of appearance in particular locations. Here we can identify two central processes. First, regulation of the built environment by the state in the form of densification, design control and conservation, all of which overlap in complex ways. Second, there is the idea of theming, a process both voluntarily and deliberately set in place by private sector interests in order to establish a unified aesthetic which promotes the sale of commodified products and experiences, Disneyland being the classic example.

Regulation

A fundamental property in the aesthetic production of urban form is that of density of development and its human impact in terms of crowding (Cuthbert 1985). While the history of the twentieth century has corresponded to the decreasing density of cities as a whole, through expansion of the periphery, this trend has also incorporated increasing densification of particular sites such as central business districts and 'edge cities' (see also Dovey 1992, Cartier 1999). Increasing competition between regions and nations, combined with the ever-increasing demand for symbolic capital by multinational corporations, has resulted in central business districts being forced to accommodate a never-ending spiral of high-rise development, and the associated need to build the world's, region's or nation's tallest structures (Abel 2004). It remains to be seen what effect the destruction of the World Trade Center's two towers in New York on 11 September 2001 will have on high-rise development in general. But since the proposed replacement project by Skidmore/Liebeskind contains two 1665-foot towers with a spire to 1776 feet, they are significantly taller than those they are replacing. So it seems that the race is still on. Paradoxically, developing countries such as India, Malaysia and China seem to have learned nothing from the obsession of Western economies, particularly the USA, with high rise. As a symbol of national achievement and corporate power, skyscraper architecture, the most inefficient form of building, will remain part of the dominant aesthetic of urban form for many years into the future, if cities like Shanghai become a symbol for developing nations.

A second feature of aesthetic production is that of design control. As opportunities to increase the complexity of urban form and structure expand through the eight properties described above, so national and local governments are forced to deal with the problem of the regulation of the built environment as a whole, and aesthetic production as a specific subset (Carmona 1996). The entire apparatus of urban planning has regulation as its primary obsession, in an attempt to control development and design in accordance with economic and aesthetic imperatives. While urban design is wholly controlled by this system, the predominant mechanism in many developed countries is 'design guidelines'. These form a loosely coordinated set of principles that attempt to govern the dominant features of any development project, such as building envelope, access and egress, setbacks from roads, the use of materials and other factors. Some countries have several levels of design guidelines, and a system whereby each specific development site will have its own system of design controls attached to planning consent. The main problem with design guidelines is that they attempt to govern urban design outcomes by regulating the appearance of individual architectural elements, conflating the aesthetics of urban design with the aesthetics of architecture. These are entirely different problems, and an appropriate system of regulation for urban design remains to be developed.

Moving on to the third case, while I have already discussed conservation in the previous chapter, I did not comment on aesthetics. This subject could occupy an entire volume and I will only give a few examples of this process in the production of cultural and symbolic capital. Setting aside questions relating to the political battleground constituted in conservation (for what reason, in whose interest and for what purpose), it is clear that history plays a major role in the aesthetic properties of any city. Historical elements in the city maintain difference, contrast, memory and culture, and significant traces of historical morphologies remain in the alignment of roads and other infrastructure, the location of significant buildings, and landscape elements. Nonetheless, the quotation from Miles and Hall above and the scathing reference to 'aestheticised heritage litter' contains a certain element of truth. In many developed countries the frantic search for symbolic capital has resulted in a situation where 'conservation' means anything from facadism to holes in the ground, and the idea of 'authenticity' has undergone a Copernican shift in meaning. In Sydney for example, the majority of buildings downtown suffer from this phenomenon, where only the facades of the original buildings remain, and 'original' buildings may only be 300 millimetres deep. Other examples are not so easy to judge. I was recently on a design jury, also in Sydney, where a prize for conservation was awarded to a project which celebrated the *absence* of the original building except for the front portico, the rest of the building in its entirety having been demolished and the site left empty (figure 41). In Hong Kong, during my ten-year sojourn, the last bastion of colonialism, the Repulse Bay Hotel, was totally demolished and all its historic artefacts auctioned off to make way for a new high-rise development. Due to a property slump, a large hole in the ground remained for some three years. When the project was finally built, the developers decided they had made an error and rebuilt the Repulse Bay Hotel on exactly the same spot using the original drawings stored in government archives. The restoration was hailed as a masterpiece of conservation (figure 42). Also in Hong Kong, an important historic government building, the Murray Building, had to make way for new high-rise accommodation to house the government bureaucracy. The building was taken apart piece by piece and stored in a warehouse for fifteen years, before it was reconstructed on a new site in Stanley on the other side of the island, now housing a variety of Thai, Chinese and other restaurants and memorabilia for tourists (figures 43 and 44). In each case 'conservation' was deliberately used as a descriptor for the manufacture of symbolic capital, first in the absence of the original building, second in the building's total replacement and third in totally removing it from its original site. Even from these limited examples, it is transparent that 'conservation' as a concept has moved so far from its original meaning as to be unrecognisable, and that the aesthetics of conservation is a wholly negotiable proposition in the production of symbolic capital.

Theming

Closely related to the question of symbolic capital and the aesthetics of urban design today is the concept of theming. Themed environments have been around for millennia in one form or another (Calvino 1986, Jencks 1993, Gregory 1994, Gottdiener 1997, DC 9) but theming has only been actively incorporated into the system of accumulation over the last century, when world's fairs such as the Chicago Exposition of 1893, the St Louis Exposition of 1904 or the Pan Pacific

Figure 41 Former baths at Coogee Beach, Sydney: conservation of doorway and original site.

Exposition in San Francisco of 1915 set the standard of reference for appropriate aesthetics for urban design of the time (figure 45). Over the same period that a whole new aesthetic realm was being imposed in Vienna for the rest of Europe to emulate, Rubin (1979) demonstrates that in the USA the wealthy aristocracy whose fortunes had been based in agriculture ran into direct conflict with bourgeois urban entrepreneurs who had not yet adopted the mantle of social responsibility and philanthropy that their wealth entailed. In moving to the city,

Figure 42   The copy of the original Repulse Bay Hotel in Hong Kong.

the old agrarian elite still dominated in the realm of good taste, and expected the city to provide them with symbolic capital in the form of an elegant urban environment, which reflected the sophistication of their country estates. Rubin demonstrates that 'the tyranny of high culture aesthetics' had been set in place over the last half of the nineteenth century, where 'the good taste industry' was relatively new. Legislated aesthetics did not take place in the USA until the middle of the twentieth century, when the Federal Housing Act of 1949 used the concept of blight to achieve specific aesthetic objectives (Rubin 1979: 294). The propagation of themed environments in the form of expositions were therefore adopted by commercial capital as the central medium for promoting 'good' over 'bad' taste, almost exclusively in the form of classical, Renaissance or baroque environments and architecture: 'The Columbian Exposition at Chicago, or "White City" (1893), as it was popularly called, had a phenomenal impact. Its courts, palaces, arches, colonnades, domes, towers, curving walkways, wooded island, ponds, and botanical displays elicited ecstatic responses from visitors, to whom the "White City" was little short of a fairyland' (Rubin 1979: 294).

The concept of themed environments has gone through a myriad of transformations since that time, from closed commercial environments such as

Figure 43 The original Murray Building in Hong Kong.
Source: S. Lee, *Hong Kong Past and Present*. Hong Kong: Form Asia, 2005.

Figure 44 The Murray Building rebuilt and moved to Stanley Village.

Figure 45   The Court of Honour, World's Fair, Chicago (1893), planned by Daniel Burnham.
Source: Copyright © Bettmann/CORBIS.

Disneyland, to entire cities such as Las Vegas in Nevada or to new urban projects such as Babylon Court at the Hollywood and Highland site in Los Angeles (*DC* 26; see figures 46 and 47). These examples are, however, early prototypes of the concept. From world's fairs to Disneyland, the realisation of theming was geographically bounded, and had not as yet morphed into an entirely different dimension as it has with heterotopias. Old-style theme parks are still mutating across the planet in the form of major tourist developments, international expositions, shopping centres and multi-media environments, and even 'authentic' versions of a copy of the original – Disneyland (Anaheim) into Disneyland (Orlando) into Euro-Disneyland, dubbed by the French 'a cultural Chernobyl' (Scott 2000a: 213). More recently, theming has adopted a plethora of new forms as a method of aestheticising the built environment in the interests of symbolic capital. These extend from theoretical concepts in architecture such as the New Urbanism, which represents a contemporary worldwide movement to good taste based on both reactionary aesthetics and politics (Al-Hindi and Staddon 1997),

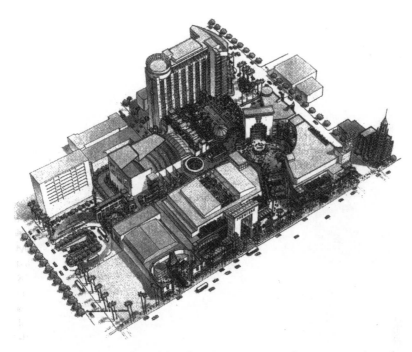

Figure 46 Hollywood and Highland Project, Los Angeles: perspective of project.
Source: Courtesy of Ehrenkratz Eckstut and Kuhn Architects. Reprinted by permission
of Blackwell Publishing.

to the hyperreality of the virtual urban stage, exemplified in the avatar-populated 'metaverse' in Neal Stevenson's novel *Snow Crash* (Stevenson 1992).

The concept of hyperreality goes back at least until 1972 when Italo Calvino's essays *Travels in Hyper-reality* were first published in Italian. Calvino points out that hyperreality does not just apply to themed environments as a whole, but to the entire edifice of unreality that people choose to live with on a daily basis, much of which deals with how the past is represented. Calvino denotes various types of institution in America: 'Fortresses of Solitude', including art galleries and museums, particularly wax museums ('Satan's Crèches'); libraries, mausoleums for the dead, Lyndon Johnson's mausoleum in Austin being a paramount example; 'Enchanted Castles' such as William Randolph Hearst's castle at San Simeon in California and the Ca d'Zan in Sarasota, Florida; and 'Monasteries of Salvation', including cemeteries and places like the Getty Museum, which he compares to 'the crocodile tears of the Roman Patrician who reproduced the grandeurs of the very Greece that his country had humiliated and reduced to a colony' (Calvino 1986: 39), or as Jean Baudrillard notes in *America*, 'The Getty museum where old paintings look new, bleached and gleaming, cleansed of all patina and *craquelure*, with an artificial luster that echoes the fake Pompeian decor all around them' (Baudrillard 1986: 33). Calvino elucidates an entire taxonomy of urban forms that are real, unreal or partially real in his search

Figure 47   Babylon Court, Hollywood, and Highland Project, Los Angeles.
Source: Courtesy of Ehrenkratz Eckstut and Kuhn Architects. Reprinted by permission
of Blackwell Publishing.

for the absolutely fake city, with Disneyland and Disneyworld coming out on top
of the list, and as a headache for conservationists, says:

> The United States is filled with cities that imitate a city, just as the wax museums
> imitate painting, and the Venetian Palazzos or Pompeian villas imitate architecture.
> In particular there are the 'ghost towns', the Western Cities of a century and more
> ago. Some are reasonably authentic, and the restoration or preservation has been
> carried out on an extant, 'archaeological' urban complex; but more interesting are
> those born from nothing, out of pure imitative determination. They are 'the real
> thing'.

(Calvino 1986: 41)

The issues Calvino raises indirectly are legion, particularly that our environments are entirely saturated and themed, not only with images from the past, but
with the reconstruction and transformation of the past as an ongoing process. In
turn this raises questions not only of the real and the unreal, the authentic and
the inauthentic, the true and the false, it scrambles our value systems as to right
and wrong, good and bad, morally justifiable or criminally negligent, when
faced with aesthetic questions in urban design, none of which have easy or
formulaic answers.

Chapter Nine
Typologies

In the work of the new rationalists, the city and its typology are reasserted as the only possible bases for the restoration of a critical role to public architecture otherwise assassinated by the apparently endless cycle of production and consumption.

Anthony Vidler (1978)

Introduction: Taxonomy, Typology, Morphology, System

The concept of typologies is one that has permeated urban design in regard to structure, function and form, in its recent history. The word itself does not belong to urban design. It reflects a fundamental need in many disciplines to classify the component parts of any problem or situation being investigated. Whereas taxonomy is the science of classification and is used across many disciplines, for example in archaeology and biology, typologies usually go beyond classification. Within the concept is nested the idea of the whole system and hence it is strongly related to the idea of hierarchic structures (Wiener 1948, Bertalanffy 1968, Simon 1969, McLoughlin 1970). Typologies are part of the workbench of urban designers. They can be used as tools in problem-solving. On the other hand, tools are usually made to perform a single task, and typologies are usually adaptable and extendible to fit a variety of contexts. In urban design the concept of morphology is also significant since it deals with spatial structure and form. In Herbert Simon's book *The Sciences of the Artificial* he discusses the idea of artificial systems. By artificial he does not imply any falsity, reflecting that the word 'artifice' from which 'artificial' is derived simply means 'man-made'. In relation to systems, he suggests that the perfect typology is obtained when all the elements of a system are stated in such a way that nothing can be added (redundancy) or nothing removed (depriving the system of some essential element). Typologies in general attempt to do the same thing, that is, to state the irreducible components of a particular problematic. In taxonomies, things are classified but do not necessarily relate. In typologies the relational aspect is critical. The ten elements that structure this book consist in a typology for urban design at a particular level of the problem, and the relationship between the elements and the degree of overlap which joins them is critical. While it is possible to read the book in any order, something major would be missed if

201

indeed all chapters were not read. At this level it is important to note four major systemic aspects of knowledge, which we can apply to urban design.

1 Metaphysics: the philosophical foundation for an adequate theory of urban design knowledge.
2 Epistemology: the development of a specific urban design method or methods.
3 Logic: the canons of valid reasoning in urban design theory.
4 Ethics: the basic rules of conduct for participants in the process of urban design.

Associated with the problem of typologies is the closely related concept of modelling. Model building is an essential part of learning, and our earliest memories are invariably connected to processes of representing the world we live in. The essential question here is whether typologies are also models of processes or structures of some kind. The best way to answer the question is that taxonomies, typologies and models are three steps towards some representation of reality. While taxonomies classify and typologies outline and relate elements, models claim to represent actual living and non-living systems with varying degrees of accuracy. To structuralist theorists such as Troubetzkoy, Piaget and Lévi-Strauss, the concept of model building was intrinsic to their investigations. Since the use of models and modelling is part of every creative art, the question is not 'Should models be used?' but 'Does the model in question best represent the phenomena under investigation?' It is also wise to bear in mind that the question of modelling cities has been severely criticised on two basic fronts. First, models tend to leave out those elements that disturb their assumed logic. Second, what is left out are invariably qualitative and subjective considerations that by definition do not lend themselves to quantification, e.g. urban politics (Sayer 1976). The subjective dimension of life is eliminated in the process. Closely associated is the question of structure. Lévi-Strauss, the great structuralist anthropologist, clarifies both of these ideas. In *Totemism* he is explicit as to the structural method and its operations.

1 Define the phenomena under study as a relation between two or more terms, real or supposed.
2 Construct a table of possible permutations between these terms.
3 Take this table as the general object of analysis which, at this level only, can yield necessary connections, the empirical phenomenon considered at the beginning being only one possible combination among others, the complete system of which must be constructed beforehand.   (Lévi-Strauss 1962: 28)

He then continues in *Structural Anthropology* to give his own definition of structure. This consists of a model meeting certain specific requirements which correspond to its structural value, and points out that the question is not essentially anthropological but belongs to the methodology of science in general.

1   First, the structure exhibits the characteristics of a system. It is made up of several elements, none of which can undergo change without affecting changes in all other elements.
2   Second, for any given model, there should be a possibility of ordering a series of transformations resulting in a group of models of the same type.
3   Third, the above properties make it possible to predict how the model will react if one or more of its elements are submitted to certain modifications.
4   Finally the model should be constituted so as to make immediately intelligible all of the observed facts.   (Lévi-Strauss 1978: 279–80)

One might assume from this that structuralism is a method rather than doctrine, and to a certain extent this is true, a trait enduringly exposed by postmodernism. However, a major problem in uncritically adopting postmodernist thinking is that the question of structure cannot simply be disposed of as a useless concept. This tends to be the case with much postmodernist theorising, and the term 'poststructuralism' is in many ways a better concept, one that accommodates structuralism and tries to take care of its deficiencies. A consideration of the idea of structure leads to two common aspects of structuralism. Firstly, we have the principle that structures are self-sufficient. In order to comprehend them it is unnecessary to consider all ancillary relationships. Secondly, structures in general seem to exhibit certain common properties in spite of their fundamental diversity. Piaget defines the concept of structure and its central properties as follows:

> At first approximation we may say that a structure is a system of transformations. Inasmuch as it is a system and not a mere collection of elements and their properties, these transformations involve laws, which never yield results external to the system nor employ elements that are external to it. In short, the notion of structure is comprised of three ideas: the idea of wholeness, the idea of transformation, and the idea of self-regulation.
>
> (Piaget 1971: 5)

Many of these ideas are implicit to typologies, in that the concepts of structure and system, as well as Piaget's ideas of wholeness, transformation and self-regulation, usually apply in varying degrees. Apart from exhibiting these features, typologies can be viewed as either programmes or meta-programmes, although in general the latter is usually the case. The difference between them concerns the question of representation at various levels of the problem, by creating a distinction between the surface structure of any programme or ordering system and the meta-programme, which underlies, reinforces or defines it. Meta-programmes are also useful in learning how to learn, since they operate at the level of language, symbol and metaphor. While Christopher Alexander and others have exposed the problems of hierarchic thinking that plays a significant part in most typologies, Herbert Simon has also noted that the mind works hierarchically.

While this is inescapable, it nonetheless allows us to recognise this limitation and to compensate accordingly. Alexander's famous article of 1973, 'A city is not

a tree', does precisely that. Architects such as Peter Eisenman have used over-
lapping grids to create randomness in architectural and urban designs in order to
obviate our inherent tendency to hierarchy, noted above (figures 48 and 49).
Despite this, Herbert Simon claims that if there are important systems in the
world, which are complex without being hierarchic, they may to a considerable
extent lie outwith our observation and understanding. By definition, such systems would also lie outside our ability to conceive them. This is in the nature of
our limitations and of the distinctions we must make. While this might lead one
to think that Simon would be generally supportive of the idea of a general theory
of systems – one which abstracts out the properties of various types of system,
the features they hold in common – he is suspicious of the idea when he says that
'systems of such diverse kinds could hardly be expected to have any nontrivial
properties in common. Metaphor and analogy can be helpful, or they can be

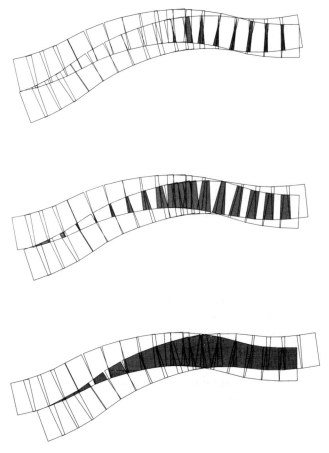

Figure 48   Peter Eisenman: Aronoff Centre, conceptual grid.
Copyright © Eisenman Architects.

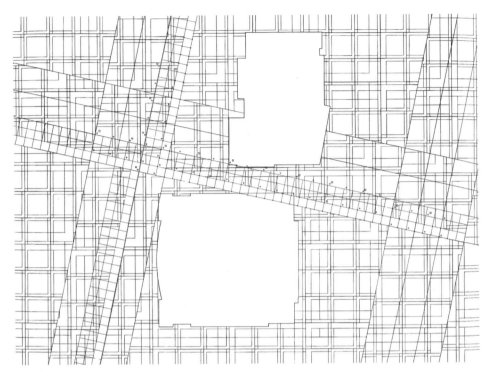

Figure 49 Peter Eisenman: Wexner Centre, conceptual grid.
Source: Copyright © Eisenman Architects.

misleading. All depends on whether the similarities that are captured are significant or superficial' (Simon 1969: 84).

The basic meta-programmes deployed in human thought patterns are facilitated through the use of hierarchically organised list structures, which function via symbolic codes of some kind in their basic manner of operation. We think using the medium of these codes, which we call languages, structures that are a necessary prerequisite for any advanced intellectual activity. In addition there are three main types of code according to whether the sign stands in a logical relation of exclusion, inclusion or intersection with the phenomena being represented. These list structures can be classified as *diacritical* (distinctive), *taxonomic* (classificatory) and *semantic* (signifying) respectively. Pierre Guiraud (1973) has given examples of each kind of set. A phonological system is by its very nature purely diacritical. In human speech, tone and articulation are independent to each other. The signs themselves have no absolute meaning, and derive their significance purely from their relationship. A taxonomic system integrates signs into a system of relations which are necessary, unidirectional and inclusive: ' "mammal" necessarily implies vertebrate' (Guiraud 1973: 12). The latter adds no information to the former. The semantic or lexical system includes both meaning and information, and the signs have a necessary degree of overlap. Leaves are generally green. The idea of the colour 'green' is normally constituent of the object 'leaf'. But leaves occasionally change colour and it is not true to say that all green things are leaves. Guiraud makes the point that the more meaningful a code is, the more it is constrained, structured and socialised. These principles apply across a wide range of disciplines, and they help us to understand typologies in general and the discipline of urban design in particular. In the examples I have chosen as illustrations, I will concentrate on those where the semantic function is maximised.

Within urban design, it is clearly impossible to discuss all the typologies that have been deployed in order to understand urban design in theory and practice: almost every author who writes about the subject has developed a typology in some shape or form. Christopher Alexander is probably the best example of this, offering a typology of 253 interacting patterns for designing urban space, all the way from the regional level to the design of windows, seats, dormer windows and other architectural details (Alexander 1977). Krier has written two entire books on the subject of typologies, in terms of the elements of architectural composition and the organisation of urban space (Krier 1979b, 1988). In addition, I have already considered or outlined several different typologies in previous chapters. While it would be possible to return to ancient Greece for inspiration starting with Plato, due to the immense range of possibilities I can only illustrate the idea with recourse to some of the more notable examples. I will also limit this choice to typologies that bear on urban design knowledge over the last fifty years, with the single exception of Patrick Geddes (originating in 1915). There are also many ways this could be done, for example by function, structure or chronology, but I will adopt the following three categories for the remainder of the chapter, i.e. typologies derived from associated disciplines, traditional urban design perspectives, and spatial political economy.

Typologies Derived from Associated Disciplines

Patrick Geddes

The archetypal typology for many urban planners, designers and environmentalists was initiated by the Scottish philosopher, sociologist, botanist, naturalist and planner, Patrick Geddes (Delfries 1924, Kitchen 1975, Boardman 1978, Meller 1994). Geddes was born in Ballater in Scotland in 1854. Generations of students in a whole series of disciplines have been influenced by his work, as well as major theorists in urban history (Lewis Mumford), natural ecology (Ian McHarg) and even in contemporary design movements (the transect of the New Urbanism). While Ebeneezer Howard was the originator of the Garden City movement, which preceded the formation of the Town Planning Institute, Geddes provided a much-needed philosophical and intellectual foundation for urban planning in the UK, and is credited with the birth of modern town and regional planning, principles of economic regeneration, environmental management and sustainable development. While Howard was influenced by the Russian geographer Peter Kropotkin (who was responsible for developing the theory of anarchist communism), the sources of Geddes' inspiration were the

French philosophers Frederick le Play and Auguste Compte, as well as his mentor, the great natural scientist T. H. Huxley.

Geddes was a student in Paris and was able to study the interaction between the three coordinates of Le Play's social theory, *lieu, travail et famille*, which Geddes translated as 'place, work and folk', or geography, economics and social science. During a period of temporary blindness resulting from a severe illness, Geddes played with three-dimensional thinking machines, which later resulted in his 'wheel' or typology of life (Geddes 1915; figure 50). This was arguably the first serious attempt to relate the activity of urban and regional planning to economics, sociology, geography, psychology and space. The diagram generates a complex system of relationships from his original 'place, work and folk'. It should also be expressed three-dimensionally, due to the fact that there are several levels of complexity in each section. In each quadrant there are three major activities on the diagonal, whose effects are plotted in the other six boxes. In each of the four quadrants the three elements with their six derivatives are addressed at qualitatively different levels of functioning, active or passive, objective or subjective. The critical contribution made by Geddes in this

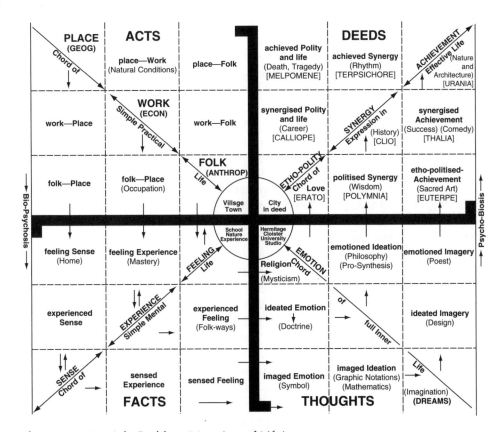

Figure 50 Patrick Geddes: 'Notation of Life'.
Source: A. Delfries, *The Interpreter Geddes.* London: Routledge, 1927.

typology was a reflection of three basic principles that he used in teaching: sympathy for people and the environment, the synthesis of all significant factors, and the synergy of energies that fuel the process. Geddes' vision of planning was of a multidimensional systemic process that respected nature and was capable of critical self-reflection as his wheel of life dictates. This typology was not only formative of contemporary urban planning, but today might also act as its conscience. Unlike many planners who came after him, Geddes did not professionalise his views on the urban environment, and always insisted on the synergy of elementary ecological, economic, social and psychological structures as a foundation for appropriate planning action.

Constantinos Doxiadis

The Greek Constantinos Doxiadis was one of the most famous architect/planners in the latter part of the twentieth century, particularly during the period from 1960 to 1980. He is best known for his attempt to generate a science of human settlements, which he called ekistics after the Greek work *oikizo* meaning to 'make a settlement'. *Ekistics*, the journal he founded, is still operational today. Doxiadis was born in Greece in 1913, and was awarded his doctorate from Charlotteberg University in Berlin. Despite his academic qualifications, Doxiadis was first and foremost a businessman who had a rather chequered career, emigrating to Australia early in his working life where he made a fortune growing tomatoes. Returning to Athens, he then started, in quick succession, Doxiadis Associates, an international architectural and planning firm; a tourist business; Athens Institute of Technology; and Athens Centre of Ekistics, the latter being a research centre to promote the concept of ekistics, one heavily supported by the Ford Foundation. Doxiadis Associates carried out many large-scale projects in the Middle East, Africa and the USA, his most notable project being Islamabad, the capital city of West Pakistan, as well as the University of the Punjab in Lahore. He was also involved in designing master plans in Ghana, Iran, Nigeria, Saudi Arabia, Rio de Janeiro and Detroit to name but a few. The one place where he was systematically ignored was in his own country. While he carried out intensive research on the city of Athens, he was never awarded any major projects in Greece during his lifetime.

Doxiadis had four major research projects, which occupied him for much of his life. One of these dealt with ancient Greek cities; the other three formed a closely interlinked typology, which was simultaneously survey, analysis and synthesis. They probably constituted the most exhaustive studies of their kind ever conducted. The first was called 'The City of the Future,' which Doxiadis named Ecumenopolis. The second was 'The Capital of Greece', a study that used his concept of the dynamic city or Dynapolis. The third was called 'The Human Community', community class four in his hierarchy of communities. Doxiadis' ideas drew from a multiplicity of sources.

Doxiadis' conceptual framework was straightforward and never altered during his lifetime. He held that the Megalopolis made famous by Jean Gottman

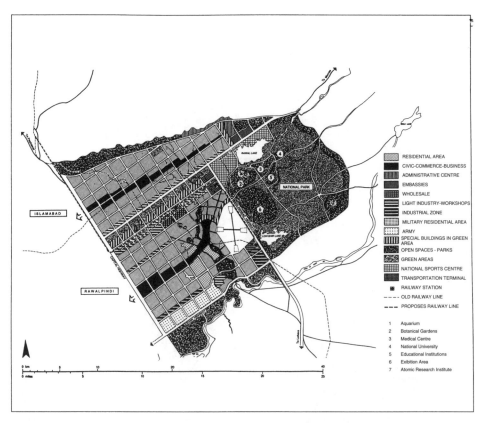

Figure 51   Constantinos Doxiadis: plan of Islamabad (1960).
Source: Ekistics, 62: 373. Reprinted by permission of The Athens Center of Ekistics.

would have to develop into Ecumenopolis if the world was not to sink into a situation of total urban decay. Ecumenopolis was his sane version of the future. The structure of Ecumenopolis was organised on the basis of directional growth between regions and major centres. Because the concentric growth of cities was seen to be the major cause of their decay (each ring in the pattern successively devouring the one next to it) and because linear cities could not work in practice (a centre would always develop on the point of maximum accessibility of the line), Doxiadis proposed the idea of Dynapolis, a dynamic city centre whose growth would be directed towards the next major regional attraction, and whose centre travelled along a corridor that expanded as it grew. He maintained that there was also a basic building block to cities, which he called 'community class four', roughly the same as what most planners would understand by the term 'neighbourhood'. Furthermore, this basic building block was nested within a hierarchic structure of units, each defined by the quality of their central functions, all the way from community class one to community class ten. He applied these ideas in his own designs (see figures 51 and 52). Much of this has been

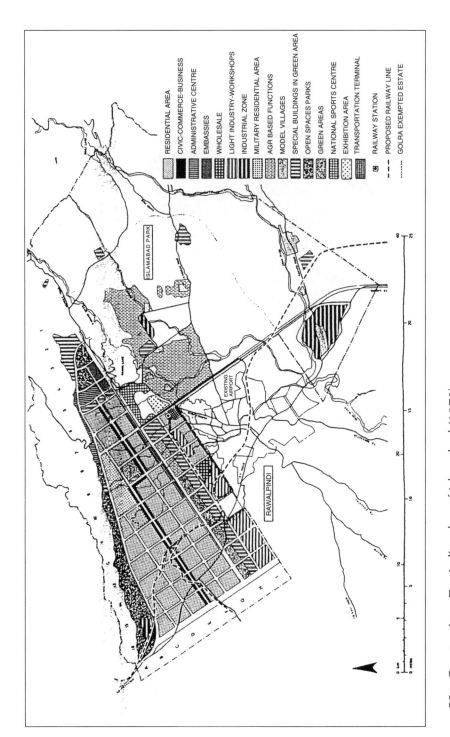

Figure 52 Constantinos Doxiadis: plan of Islamabad (1978).
Source: Ekistics, 62: 374. Reprinted by permission of The Athens Center of Ekistics.

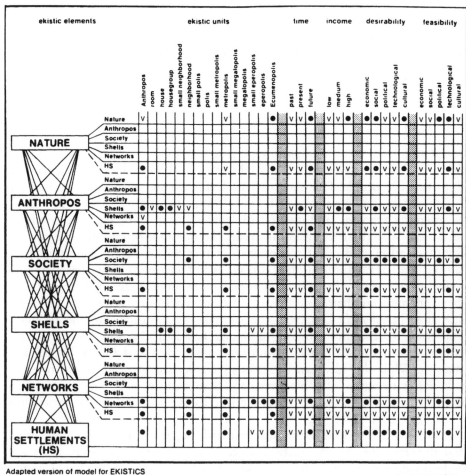

Figure 53 Constantinos Doxiadis: ekistic grid.
Source: Ekistics, 62: 375. Reprinted by permission of The Athens Center of Ekistics.

written up in *Ekistics* as well as in several personal publications (Doxiadis 1963, 1968, 1974, 1975, Doxiadis and Papaoanniou 1974).

Over the course of a lifetime's work, Doxiadis resorted to the use of grids to explain relationships between his ideas, and his three basic concepts, Ecumenopolis, Dynapolis and The Human Community, were supported by a basic conceptual framework (typology) which he called the ekistic grid (figure 53). Here, Geddes' basic 'place, work and folk' was expanded into five elements – nature, man, society, networks and shells – corresponding to ecology, anthropology, sociology, transportation and architecture. These five basic interacting elements of his typology were then expanded into a complete series, and presented as his ekistic grid. This is an extremely useful tool for urban designers to use in executing urban projects. The basic use of the grid is a simple and effective method of relating the complexity of factors normally encountered in urban analysis.

E.T. Hall

Social anthropology is another discipline that has impacted on urban design in the general area of *proxemics*, a discipline that deals with the proximal relationships between people. One theorist who has had a significant impact on urban design was the anthropologist E. T. Hall (1959, 1969, 1976), specifically because he offered a typology and method for analysis that simultaneously combined social and spatial structures. Hall treats the question of culture as a form of communication, and offers a contextual rather than a verbal definition in his famous matrix of culture (table 10). He maintains that culture has biological roots in the ways through which people experience the world and how they communicate their ideas. Three different types of consciousness or awareness may be identified, namely the formal, the informal and the technical. This triad incorporates a theory of change based on the principle that people progress from formal belief, to informal adaptation and finally to technical analysis. While this idea can be seriously challenged by more recent research, it is easier to agree with his statement that 'culture hides much more than it reveals, and what it hides, it hides most effectively from its own participants' (Hall 1959: 39).

  Hall also believed that culture was primarily dependent upon communication, and therefore the communication process and its typologies were central to understanding how any culture worked. His Map of Culture is based upon a typology of ten separate types of human activity, which collectively incorporate the most important features of human interaction. The first, primary message systems (PMS), involves language. The others are all non-linguistic forms of communication. The existence of such a model offers a singular matrix to urban designers who wish to analyse how space interacts with other dominant aspects of culture, such as learning or play, and as a means whereby they can base their designs in the context of a particular culture or cultures, and also as a cross-cultural comparative method. PMS uses the following elementary taxonomy:

1 interaction,
2 association,
3 subsistence,
4 bisexuality,
5 territoriality,
6 temporality,
7 learning,

8   play,
9   defence,
10 exploitation.

Hall stresses three principal considerations when using this method: firstly, that each PMS must be accepted at a biological level first and foremost; secondly, that each PMS may be examined by itself, but will ultimately be measured by its systemic contribution; and thirdly, that the ultimate object is to expose the general network of the cultural matrix as a framework for social and spatial organisation.

Constance Perrin

Another person who was centrally concerned with introducing a social dimension to urban design was Constance Perrin (1970), a time when environmental psychology and human studies into the inception process in environmental design were just evolving. This movement was in part a reaction to the master architect's assumption that somehow his designs could accommodate every human need, provided the design was sufficiently brilliant. The general reaction to this situation is well stated in the following quotation: ' "If anyone will tell us architects what people need, we'll tell them how to build it. We can only reflect what civilization and what culture we have" said Mies van der Rohe, to whom no one seems ever to have said what they need; so he maintained his prerogative to build for himself' (Perrin 1970: 113). That prerogative expressed a view of power over environment that is passing: the unified plan, the single idea carried out to perfection – whether it is a Mies van der Rohe building or cities like Washington or St Petersburg – is always a manifestation of unshared power. In order to compensate for the wholly unreliable intuition of architect-designers when it comes to human needs and behaviour, Perrin made reference to the motivational theories of people such as Abraham Maslow, Karen Horney, Erich Fromm, Hans Selye and others, as a conceptual bridge between environmental design and the human sciences. She focuses on the work of psychiatrist Alexander Leighton in his book *My Name is Legion: Foundations for a Theory of Man in Relation to Culture*, where he fully explains his typology of 'ten essential striving sentiments'. This typology represents a grouping of schemata (behavioural data) that should be incorporated into any basic design process along with the usual demographic statistics, and requires a response from the environment to fulfill ten specific basic needs:

1   physical security;
2   sexual satisfaction;
3   expression of hostility;
4   expression of love;
5   securing of love;
6   securing of recognition;

Table 10 E.T. Hall's matrix of culture.

Primary message system	Interactional 0	Organisational 1	Economic 2	Sexual 3	Territorial 4	Temporal 5	Instructional 6	Recreational 7	Protective 8	Exploitational 9
Interaction 0	Communication Vocal qualifiers Kinesics Language 00	Status and role 01	Exchange 02	How the sexes interact 03	Place of interaction 04	Times of interaction 05	Teaching and learning 06	Participation in the arts and sports (active and passive) 07	Protecting and being protected 08	Use of telephones, signals, writing, etc. 09
Association 1	Community 10	Society Class Caste Government 11	Economic roles 12	Sexual roles 13	Local group roles 14	Age group roles 15	Teachers and learners 16	Entertainers and athletes 17	Protectors (doctors, clergy, soldiers, police, etc.) 18	Use of group property 19
Subsistence 2	Ecological community 20	Occupational groupings 21	Work Formal work Maintenance Occupations 22	Sexual division of labour 23	Where the individual eats, cooks, etc. 24	When the individual eats, cooks, etc. 25	Learning from working 26	Pleasure from working 27	Care of health, protection of livelihood 28	Use of foods, resources and equipment 29
Bisexuality 3	Sex community (clans, sibs) 30	Marriage groupings 31	Family 32	The sexes Masculine vs. feminine Sex (biological) Sex (technical) 33	Areas assigned to individuals by virtue of sex 34	Periods assigned to individuals by virtue of sex 35	Teaching and learning sex roles 36	Participation in recreation by sex 37	Protection of sex and fertility 38	Use of sex differentiating decoration and adornment 39
Territoriality 4	Community territory 40	Group territory 41	Economic areas 42	Men's and women's territories 43	Space Formal space Informal space Boundaries 44	Scheduling of space 45	Teaching and learning individual space assignments 46	Fun, playing games, etc. in terms of space 47	Privacy 48	Use of fences and markers 49

Continues

Table 10 *Continued*

Primary message system	Interactional 0	Organisational 1	Economic 2	Sexual 3	Territorial 4	Temporal 5	Instructional 6	Recreational 7	Protective 8	Exploitational 9
Temporality 5	Community cycles 50	Group cycles 51	Economic cycles 52	Men's and women's cyclical activities 53	Territoriality determined cycles 54	Times of sequence cycles Calendar 55	When the individual learns 56	When the individual plays 57	Rest, vacations, holidays 58	Use of time-telling devices, etc. 59
Learning 6	Community lore: what gets taught and learned 60	Learning groups 61	Reward for teaching and learning 62	What the sexes are taught 63	Places for learning 64	Scheduling of learning (group) 65	Enculturation Rearing Informal learning Education 66	Making learning fun 67	Learning self-defence and to stay healthy 68	Use of training aids 69
Play 7	Community play: the arts and sport 70	Play groups: teams and troupes 71	Professional sports and entertainment 72	Men's and women's play, fun and games 73	Recreational areas 74	Play seasons 75	Instructional play 76	Recreation 77	Exercise 78	Use of recreational materials (playthings) 79
Defence 8	Community defence: structured defence 80	Defence groups: armies, police, public health, organised religion 81	Economic patterns of defence 82	What the sexes defend (home, honour, etc.) 83	What places are defended 84	The when of defence 85	Scientific, religious and military training 86	Mass exercises and military games 87	Protection 88	Use of material for protection 89
Exploitation 9	Communication networks 90	Organisational networks (cities, building groups, etc.) 91	Food, resources and industrial equipment 92	What men and women are concerned with and own 93	Property that is enclosed, counted and measured 94	What periods are measured and recorded 95	School buildings, training aids, etc. 96	Amusement and sporting goods and their industries 97	Fortifications, armaments, medical equipment, safety devices 98	Material systems 99

Source: E. T. Hall, *The Silent Language.* New York: Doubleday, 1959.

7   expression of spontaneity;
8   orientation in terms of one's social position;
9   securing of membership in a definite human group;
10   a sense of belonging to a moral order.

These essential striving sentiments represent 'a clustering of human tendencies, basic urges, affects, drives and instincts' which individuals require in order to fulfill their sense of competence and self-esteem (Perrin 1970: 123). Reflecting the work of Roger Barker, Perrin then goes on to develop a method of analysis based on what she calls behavioural expectations, circuits and events, in an attempt to facilitate the design of flexible, liberating and supportive environments over those which are highly structured and authoritarian. In her appendix to *With Man in Mind*, Perrin elaborates Leighton's typology into an extensive set of attributes that should *not* be present in order for a neighbourhood to have amenity. While this typology is too extensive to reproduce here, urban and environmental designers should refer to this process as a foundation for design studies that have low adaptive costs for inhabitants, rather than relying on past experience, client briefs or some arbitrary overarching design concept.

Typologies Derived from Traditional Urban Design Perspectives

Anthony Vidler

Typologies derived from traditional perspectives on urban form are legion. Probably the most famous essay that deals directly with the subject is Anthony Vidler's 'The third typology' (*DC* 24, see also Vidler 1978). Vidler begins by arguing that traditional architectural production has been legitimated by two specific typologies. The first of these reflects back to the natural origins of architecture, the idea of the primitive hut (after Laugier 1755). The second emerged as a consequence of the Industrial Revolution, where architecture surfaced as a logical outcome of machine production, exemplified in Jeremy Bentham's *Panopticon*. To these two, Vidler suggests that a third typology needs to be added:

> We might characterize the fundamental attribute of this third typology as an espousal, not of an abstract nature, not of a technological utopia, but rather of the traditional city as the locus of its concern. The city, that is, provides the material for classification and the forms of its artifacts over time provide the basis for its recomposition. This third typology, like the first two, is clearly based on reason, classification and a sense of the public in architecture; unlike the first two, however, it proposes no panacea, no ultimate apotheosis of man in architecture, no positive eschatology.
>
> (*DC* 24: 317)

Vidler notes that Laugier's metaphor for the city was the forest, where the basic Judeo-Christian philosophy of 'multiply and subdue the earth' was paramount.

The rational model of the city was therefore the garden qua tamed forest. In this relation to the natural world, Vidler argues that the transfer of the term 'species' to architecture then became a logical progression; hence 'the external effect of the building was to announce clearly its general species, and its sub-species. Later this analogy was transformed by the functional and constitutional classification of the early nineteenth century (Cuvier)' (*DC* 24: 318). In the second typology, the nature of artifice dominated by way of machine-generated mass-production processes and the social technologies that accompanied them, such as Fordism, Taylorism and in-time production today. Robotics introduced the possibility of machine reproduction paralleling that of humans: 'the pyramid of production from the smallest tool to the most complex machine was now seen as analogous to the link between the column, the house and the city' (*DC* 24: 319). This general *Weltanschauung* was reified in Le Corbusier's dictum that 'a house is a machine for living in', and echoed in such texts as Reyner Banham's *Theory and Design in the First Machine Age* (1960). While the first two typologies seek to legitimate architecture as a natural process, in the third the nature of architecture becomes self-contained. Vidler comments that the third typology, as exemplified by the new rationalists, empties the city of any social content or analogies with nature, allowing theorists to deal with urban form as a purely academic exercise. This is perhaps more concisely described as the ideological neutralisation of the city (Goode 1992). Overall, the former is a paradigm of urban design that I have tried to disavow throughout this text, one which basically ignores the idea of the production of architectural and urban form as a consequence of its social history, thus allowing an approach to urban form that could best be described as 'content free'.

> The city is considered as a whole, its past and present revealed in its physical structure. It is in itself and of itself a new typology... No longer is architecture a realm that has to relate to a hypothesized 'society' in order to be conceived and understood; no longer does 'architecture write history' in the sense of particularising a specific social condition in a specific time or place. The need to speak of nature of function, of social mores – of anything, that is, beyond the nature of architectural form itself – is removed.
>
> (*DC* 24: 320)

An interesting extension of Vidler's critique in 'The third typology' (1978) is Terrance Goode's 'Typological theory in the United States: the consumption of architectural authenticity' (1992). Goode traces forward the history of typological theory from Quatremère de Quincy, Laugier and Nicholais Durand to Le Corbusier, Rob Krier and Aldo Rossi. Goode explores typological theory in the context of authenticity, a concept I have enunciated at length in chapter 5. He traces the central problem in the USA to the relationship between type and authenticity, to the ownership of image and the commodification of social space, in a manner that its European counterpart would not permit with the same facility. Interestingly, Goode points to the idea expressed in the quotation from Vidler (above), rejecting the typological project of modernism, and noting that 'the failure of the typological project as a strategy of resistance, reflects its failure to effectively resist absorption within the political economy of contemporary architecture, an economy that operates within the marketplace of architectural discourse as well as within the realm of broader consumer culture' (Goode 1992: 12). The project of the new rationalists also conforms to the first of another three typologies given in Hillier (1989: 6) as fundamental laws necessary for understanding the city:

> Type 1: Laws for the generation of the urban object, i.e. laws governing the ways in which buildings can be aggregated to form towns or urban areas: these we might call the *laws of the object itself*.
>
> Type 2: Laws of how society uses and adapts the laws of the object to give spatial form to different types of social relation: these we might call the *laws from society to urban form*.
>
> Type 3: Laws of how urban form then has effects back on society, i.e. the old issue of architectural determinism: the *laws from urban form to society*.

Oren Yiftachel/Chris Abel

Moving from Vidler's large-scale historical perspective, Oren Yiftachel and Chris Abel offer typologies of theory and form respectively. Yiftachel's paper of 1989 is self-explanatory, 'Towards a new typology of urban planning theories', in which he attempts to systematise the academic discourses surrounding urban planning for theoreticians and practitioners alike, although it now needs to be brought up to date given the sixteen years of development since it was written. Nonetheless there are few papers since that time that have attempted to explain the overall development of planning typologies with such clarity. As a foundation for his typology, he divides planning theory into three streams of thought, where each one addresses a fundamental aspect of the planning process. Each of these represents a self-contained debate about the analytical, formal and procedural aspects of urban planning. Yiftachel also comments on the functions of typologies: 'A typology is a tool with three basic functions: it corrects misconceptions and confusion by systematically classifying related concepts, it effectively organizes knowledge by clearly defining the parameters of a given subject, and it facilitates theorising by delineating major subparts of distinct properties and foci for further research' (Yiftachel 1989: 24).

Since 1982, Faludi had dominated planning theory by dividing it into two typologies, namely procedural and substantive theory. Yiftachel points to the work of another major planning theorist, Philip Cooke, who rejected Faludi's distinction as a false dichotomy, on the basis that substantive and procedural theory were not two separate theories but necessary aspects of the same theory (Cooke 1983). Cooke elaborates three types of theories of planning and spatial relations: theories of the development process, theories of the planning process and theories of the state. As a basis for establishing the spatial dimension of planning, Cooke also offers an extensive typology of spatially discontinuous labour markets, using theories of class structure and class relations as a basis for planning decisions (Cooke 1983: 223, also 265). In summary, Yiftachel notes the importance of state theory in determining how planning functions, since planning theory, whether substantive or procedural, explanatory or prescriptive, is enveloped by, and embedded in, the political economy of the state. Yiftachel then organises his typology of planning theories round the types of debate indicated above: the analytical debate ('What is urban planning?'); the urban form debate ('What is a good urban plan?'); and the procedural debate ('What is a good planning process?') (see figure 54).

On the other hand, Chris Abel has, as a central concern, Yiftachel's second debate – what is a good urban plan? Abel has been at the centre of mainstream architectural theory and criticism since 1969, when his landmark article 'Ditching the dinosaur sanctuary' was published in *Architectural Design* (see also Abel 1988, 2000, 2004). In 'Analogical models in architecture and urban design' (1988), he outlines a general typology of the models that have traditionally been used as paradigms in designing cities. He argues that a mature architect will design in accordance with some overarching theoretical model of architecture: 'This theoretical model constitutes an *a priori* system of integrating ideas or interpretive framework which largely predetermines all the relations between the different factors the architect must consider, and the values he attaches to any of them' (Abel 1988: 163). Abel then enunciates fifteen analogical models that have had a dominant influence on the design of cities. These he divides into two groups. The first group of eleven models are sources of formal imagery, and involve the use of metaphors in their construction. The second analogical group are also powerful metaphors, but refer to processes of some kind, rather than formal imagery.

Formal analogies
   Spiritual model
   Classical model
   Military model
   Utopian model
   Organic model
   Mechanical model
   Artistic model
   Linguistic model
   Commercial model
   Identity model
   Self-build model
Process analogies
   Scientific model
   Systems model
   Semiotic model
   Legal model

While this typology attempts to reduce the complexity of analogical models to a manageable set, Abel notes that the generation of theoretical models is part of

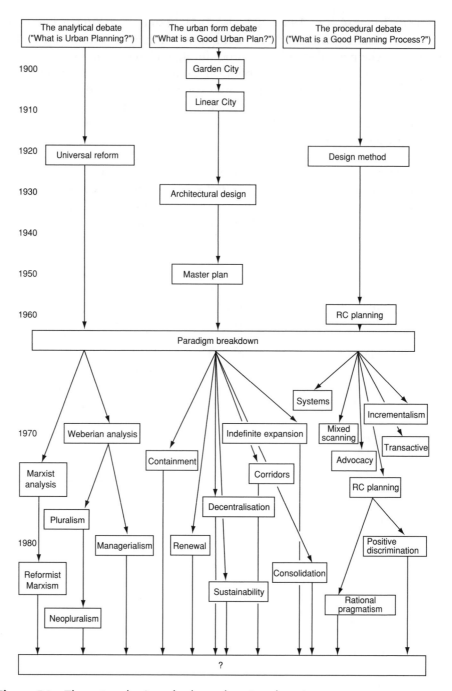

Figure 54   Three typologies of urban planning theories.
Source: O. Yiftachel, 'Towards a New Typology of Urban Planning Theories',
Environment and Planning B: Planning and Design 16, 1989, 23–39, p. 24. Reprinted
by permission of Pion Ltd, London.

the process of design innovation which cannot be separated from the design process as a whole, since 'Even when a dominant model is established, the analogical processes involved provide opportunity for seemingly endless variety in interpretation of the central metaphor' (Abel 1988: 179).

Rob Krier

While Yiftachel is concerned with urban design as a central chord in the planning process and the production of plans, and Abel is concerned with the actual models that are used in design, Krier adds yet another level to the idea of typologies in his focus on the actual discernible units of space that are available to the designer (*DC* 25). Krier's book *Urban Space* is subtitled *Typological and Morphological Elements of the Concept of Urban Space* and the book in its entirety is dedicated to revealing the inherent geometry of urban form. While Rob Krier has sketched out the framework for a typology of urban spaces, it is useful to note that urban design has spatial and building typologies as core elements in both theory and practice. Squares for example have been exhaustively researched (Zucker 1959, White 1980, Vance 1981, Webb 1990), and the same with streets (Rudofsky 1969, Brienes 1974, Anderson 1978, Appleyard 1981, Moughtin 1992, Jacobs 1993, Celik et al. 1994). Related to streets is the idea of arcades, and Geist's *Arcades: The History of a Building Type* (1985) is exemplary. Fascinating also are the typologies of housing revealed in Burnett's *A Social History of Housing* (1986), one of the few that locates housing typologies in their economic and social context. In addition to these, Spiro Kostoff looks at the totality of elements of urban form throughout history in his books *The City Shaped* (1991) and *The City Assembled* (1992).

In contrast to other theorists who have chosen to remove urban form from the realms of ideology and politics, Krier's work is deeply engaged with significant theory. It is also difficult to separate his work from that of his brother Leon, and a reading of both immediately reveals major common interests. For example, in Leon Krier's book *The Reconstruction of the City* (1975) his critique of the modernist project and the Charter of Athens is devastating: 'One can say that in the post-war years, the European cities have been more destroyed both physically and socially than in any other period of their history, including the two world wars. Our generation is both witness and victim of a cultural tragedy to which there is no precedent in history'. He allocates the blame fairly and squarely on the radical commercialisation of the city, facilitated by manifestos of the modern movement such as the Charter of Athens, assisted by 'the architects as servile executioners of grand speculation' (Krier 1975: 38). The Krier's philosophy is well summed up by the following statement from the same source:

> The problem of rational architecture cannot therefore be one of choreography. It cannot find its motivations in a 'state of mind', in the fictions of artistic or technical progress, but in the reflection of the city and its history, on its social use and content. The revolutionary element of this new architecture does not lie in its form

but in the model of its social use, in its coherency, in the reconstruction of the public realm.

(Krier 1975: 39)

The Kriers, apart from a somewhat fundamentalist Marxian analysis, also share the idea of architecture as a history of types, of settlements, spaces, buildings, forms and elements of construction. In many ways this might be called an anti-aesthetic since the primary focus is to delineate forms of urban space outside of any aesthetic criteria or assumptions. Also shared is the rejection of the bourgeois attachment to monumentality, typified by L.N. Durand's Typology of Institutional Monuments in favour of the actual production of the 'ordinary fabric of the city' resulting from building traditions. Implicit to this position is the recognition of alienated labour as a result of modern methods of production, and the responsibility of architects to recognise this in their designs. The use of historically based typologies of urban space are therefore viewed as part of a complex process of restoring the public realm, reconstructing the social life of the city, reversing the process of alienated labour, reconnecting the city to its historical origins, and providing architects with a meaningful social theory of architecture (see Leon Krier's plan for Luxembourg, figure 55). While these intentions remain laudable, the continued erosion of the public realm, increasingly commodified labour and a neocorporate state definitely restrain these ideas.

Rob Krier's position in 1979 echoed that of his brother, and was centrally focused on the need to systematically reveal the typologies of urban space, which underlay the aesthetic character of cities. He maintains that this is doubly

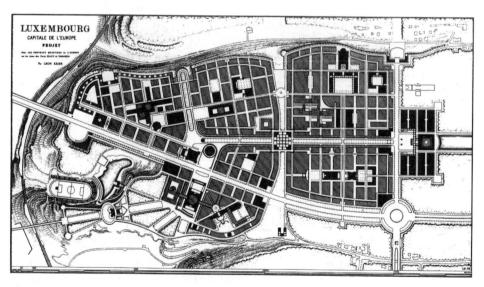

Figure 55   Leon Krier: Luxembourg Project.
Source: L. Krier, 'The Cities Within the City II', *Architectural Design* 49, 1979, 18–32.

necessary due to the distorted sense of history that has prevailed throughout the twentieth century. He points to Le Corbusier's rejection of the Academie as a courageous but nonetheless artistic falsehood, since

> he abandoned the tradition, current until then, that art supported by the ruling classes enjoyed the stamp of legitimacy and, being at an advanced stage of development, materially shaped the periods which followed. It was a revolt at one remove, so as to speak, for the *Academie* lived on, and indeed, came itself to share the same confused historical sense as the followers of the revolution.
>
> (Krier 1979a: 2)

In order to redefine the concept of urban space, Krier resorts to two basic formal elements, namely the street and the square, which have their counterparts within buildings, i.e. the corridor and the room. Reinforcing an approach to urban form qua an anti-aesthetic, Krier warns against the confusion of aesthetic and symbolic categories, on the basis that both categories can transcend the immediate functionality of spatial forms, and that these are retranslated and adapted from one historical period to another. His classification is therefore as value-free as possible, concentrating on elementary forms, their relationships and transformations (Cuthbert 1985: 95–8). Krier then demonstrates in great detail how basic spatial types originating from the square, rectangle and circle are combined, the diversity of forms of intersection of street and square, morphological series of urban spaces, the modulation of spatial types, and the complex effect of these when incorporated with building sections (figure 56). While Krier's typology is the most extensive of its kind, focusing entirely on form deprived of any social, symbolic or other meaning, this of itself generates problems across a fairly wide field. For example, no matter what the typology, architecture is subject to ideological appropriation and intervention, and cannot of itself solve societal problems. A return to a rational architecture will not change this fact, nor will it be able to reconstruct the city in the form of *quartiers* or districts, which such rationalism demands. Similarly, it is unlikely that any architectural ideology could have the desired effect. Because of the tendency of rationalism to emphasise order, structure and clarity of classical forms, rationalist or neoclassical architecture has in the past lent itself to fascist politics, surfacing predominantly in Italy and Germany during the 1930s and early 1940s. The paradox here is that the rationalists, particularly those whose recent history incorporated fascist states, are forced either to accept the use of rational architecture or to resemanticise its imagery, the first being historically unacceptable, the second ideologically unacceptable in architectural terms.

Christopher Alexander

At one level, it is impossible to separate Alexander's theories of urban growth and change from the idea of typologies in general, since his work is replete with examples. From his earliest work, *Notes on a Synthesis of Form*, we are faced with typologies of an enormous range of content. In *Notes*, he is first and

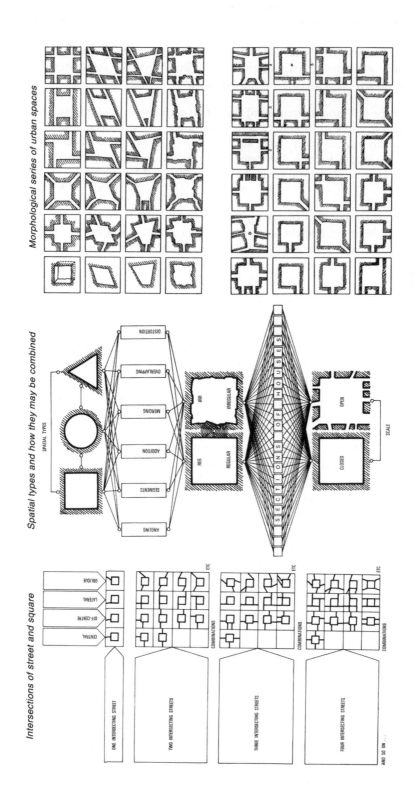

Figure 56 Rob Krier: morphological analysis of urban spatial types.
Source: R. Krier, *Urban Space*. London, 1979. © Rob Krier.

foremost concerned with the design process whereby human settlements develop, and defines design as 'the process of inventing physical things which display new physical order, organization, form, in response to function' (Alexander 1964: 1). His analysis of an Indian village is a classic of its kind, working through the thirteen central typologies that structure the village and demonstrating the complexity of the social structure that results – a taxonomy of 141 basic needs that are to be met in its reorganisation. The advanced mathematics deployed in *Notes* was the last time that Alexander used his mathematical background to deal with complexity. In 'The city as a mechanism for sustaining human contact' (1966), Alexander enunciates his typology for generating those relationships necessary to avoid the alienation that results from urban life, a paper that was closely followed by 'Major changes in environmental form required by social and psychological demands' (1969).

Both these papers owe a significant debt to George Simmel, Lewis Wirth, Abraham Maslow, Eric Erikson, Alexander Leighton and others who have been directly concerned in some manner with the socio-psychological dynamic of urban life. The latter paper is in response to the ideological position he adopts in regard to architecture and planning: 'While architects dream of utterly unimaginable futures, the planners talk about piecemeal incremental planning. The visionary architect is imaginative, daring, but completely mad. The planner's plans are utterly and boringly sane; though based on facts, they offer no comprehensive vision of a better future' (Alexander 1969: 1). This existential position does not seem to have changed over time, and in a recent interview Alexander states 'I have never had a rule in my mind telling me that I must participate in the psychotic process we call architecture today...and what architects now claim is simply being laid aside as the nonsense it really is' (Salingaros 2004). Alexander's ideas of patterns, later to become fully realised in *A Pattern Language* (1977), are also present in the 1969 paper, where he describes a typology of twenty patterns that are central to maintaining psychological health, and defines a pattern as 'a new cultural institution, together with the physical and spatial changes needed to provide a setting for this institution' (Alexander 1969: 82).

In other words the concept of 'pattern' is much more than a simple building block, and accounts for its social context as well. Alexander's basic utopianism and disregard for social reality is also inherent to his patterns, for example there is no central business district in his anticipated city: 'The city consists of hundreds of small residential islands, each with a different subculture. Density is at the edge of these islands and falls off towards the center of each one' (Alexander 1969: 84). But central business districts are not established by planning but by market forces, so unless one gets rid of the market it is unlikely that cities will ever be planned without a hierarchy of centres, which Doxiadis proposed. Given the effects of electronic communication, the intensity of these centres might radically shrink from their present form. Not only this, but a new moral order also needs to be set in place for Alexander's strategies to work. It has not happened over the last forty years of his work, and it would be an unlikely occurrence in the next forty. As I have indicated in chapter 1, this utopianism is a feature of Alexander's work up until the present time. While only the first two volumes of his most recent work, *The Nature of Order* (2003a–d), have appeared in Australia, it is still imbued with the same idealism. This is not to say that his critique is not accurate, his motivation laudable and his sentiments humane. But if we take a look at the world around us, it is not about to undergo a Copernican revolution in the way it goes about doing business.

Implications from Spatial Political Economy

In this final section I will cover a few of the more significant typologies that emerge from considerations in critical theory and spatial political economy (although Foucault might be considered a category in his own right). Here we see attempts to relate forms of space to the processes through which it becomes configured, with a need in some cases to evolve new vocabularies to describe them.

Peter Saunders

A basic typology of theoretical forms of urbanism has been given in Saunders (1986: 245; table 11). These are not typologies of cities but typologies of thinking about urbanism, each of which has its own history and analytical tension. Such conceptualisations are extremely useful for urban designers as a basic reference point for substantial urban theory. Implicit here are the ideological choices one might use in analysis, a point that enunciates a chosen vision of what urban actually means. However, these conceptualisations do not include more recent developments in postmodern theory, where altogether different perspectives might add value, albeit from an altogether different perspective (see sections on Soja and Appadurai below). Saunders also points to the fact that in the search for an 'urban' object of analysis in order to support the idea of a scientific urban sociology, none of the above approaches was successful, and he provides a significant critique of each one, delineating its strengths and weaknesses: 'what was needed, and what was to prove so illusive, was the specification of some social process or phenomenon which could be related to a physically bounded area within the confines of the nation state' (Saunders 1986: 243). This is precisely what Manuel Castells attempted to do.

Manuel Castells

Manuel Castells is one of the greatest social scientists of our time, someone who remains at the forefront of critical thinking about urban development. His trilogy, *The Rise of the Network Society*, *The Power of Identity* and *End of Millennium*, provided a synoptic and critical assessment of urbanisation at the end of the twentieth century, with significant and grounded implications for the twenty-first. While I have commented on aspects of his work elsewhere

Table 11 Sociological conceptualisation of urbanism.

Definition of urban	Analytical tension	Legacy
Ecological system	1. Theory of the city (observable processes) versus 2. Theory of adaptation (non-observable biotic forces)	1. Community studies, ethnographies 2. Functionalist sociology
Cultural form	1. Sociology of number (Simmel) versus 2. Sociology of modernity 1. Demographic analysis (Wirth) versus 2. Class/life cycle analysis	1. Theories of moral density 2. Cultural theories of capitalism
Socio-spatial system	1. Sociology of spatial inequality (Pahl) versus sociology of the state 2. Sociology of the city versus analysis of social stratification	1. Corporatist state theory/ studies of bureaucratic and professional domination 2. Focus on consumption cleavages
Spatial unit of collective consumption	1. Theory of capitalist urbanisation versus 2. Analysis of state functions in reproducing labour-power	1. Political economy of space 2. Sociology of consumption (non-spatial 'urban' sociology)

Source: P. Saunders, *Social Theory and the Urban Question.* London: Unwin Hyman, 1989, p. 245.

(Cuthbert 1985, 1995a,b) and also in this text, I only wish to illustrate a single aspect of his thinking here, namely the relationship between urban functions and the political dimension of urban space. Most of the methods of accounting for land use by planners and urban designers have resorted to abstract taxonomies of functions, disembodied from any economic or political context. Land use can then be discussed in terms of 'zoning', a wonderfully neutral device that permits planners and others to stand outside the reality of what Scott (1980) calls the 'urban land nexus'. One of the most exhaustive of such systems, and the best of its kind despite the fact that it is now over forty years old, is that of Guttenberg (1959). Guttenberg made several major contributions in this paper, challenging the assumed concept of 'use' and the semantic nature of the planners' basic terminology, particularly 'land use', one still used by planners on a daily basis and one which has no clear meaning. Guttenberg proposed his own typology of activity characteristics and an extensive typology of functions, but his main idea was much simpler. He proposed breaking down the term 'land use' into five distinct dimensions, which should be used to delineate the concept of 'use':

Table 12   Manuel Castells' relationship between social reproduction and land-use function.

P	Production: spatial expression of the means of production
C	Consumption: spatial expression of labour power
E	Exchange: derived from transfers between P and C, within P, or within C
I	Ideological: specification
S	Symbolic: content

(1) Consumption (C)

The consumption element refers to the process of the reproduction of labour power:

Simple reproduction	C1, e.g. housing
Economic extension	C2, e.g. open space
Institutional extension	C3, e.g. schools
Ideological extension	C4, e.g. socio-cultural amenity

(2) Production (P)

In this category a fundamental distinction is made 'between instruments of labour and the object of labour (in particular, raw material, on the one hand, and on the other hand, the articulation of production with other instances)'

Labour process (internal) (instr.)	P1, e.g. factories
Labour process (internal) (object)	P2, e.g. raw materials
Labour process; economy	P3, e.g. industrial environment
Labour process; other	P4, e.g. administration offices

(3) Exchange (C)

This category may possess as many transfers as the main elements will allow. Only four are given here:

Production/consumption	E1, e.g. commerce and distribution
Production/production	E2, e.g. urban transportation
Production/production	E3, e.g. goods transportation
Consumption/consumption	E4, e.g. residential mobility

(4) Administration

This category enunciates the relationship between political strategies and the articulation of the urban system. Four articulations are possible:

		Political system	
		Global	**Local**
Urban system	Totality	A1	A2
	Element	A3	A4
(5) Symbolic: not specified			

Source: M. Castells, *The Urban Question.* London: Arnold, 1977, pp. 238–40.

1 general site development;
2 site adaptation (building type/site facility);
3 actual use (the type of activity taking place);
4 economic over-use;
5 activity characteristics.

Castells' approach to land-use functions was to relate them to the concrete system of practices, which derive within capitalism from the interaction between three major components, the economic, the political and the ideological. Each of these devolves into subsystems of interdependent elements and the relations produced by them. The full explanation is given in Castells (1977, chapter 10), and I will give a much-truncated version below. In addition, we must remember that Castells at the time was defining urban functions, not in terms of urban and rural, nor in terms of centre and periphery, but according to which functions were urban and which were non-urban. He comments that 'For it < generalised urbanisation > already presupposes the distinction, and even the contradiction between rural and urban, an opposition and a contradiction that have little meaning in capitalism' (Castells 1997: 446). Hence in Castells' terms, the urban was confined to 'the processes relating to labour power other than its direct application to the production process (but not without relation to it, since its entire reproduction is marked by them!)' (Castells 1997: 236). Urban therefore meant the space of social reproduction, which was physically connected to a specific geography of daily life, the raising of children and the sphere of domesticity. In précis, this was his basic rationale in defining the urban system. He notes that the economic system has two principal elements, and one that is a product of the transferences which occur between them. In addition to these three principal elements of the urban system, there are two others that deal with the general processes of government, and the ideological and symbolic specification of spatial forms. These five elements can be briefly set out as the governing typology of the urban system (table 12).

Castells is somewhat vague about the exact meaning of the symbolic in detail. It would appear that what is required is an appropriate semiotic classification of urban spatial structure as it intersects with specific ideological processes. This lack of clarity may be due to Castells' mode of enquiry itself, that is, not treating the semiotic aspect with sufficient deference and assuming that political–economic factors are sufficient to explain the necessary, as opposed to contingent, urban relations.

Ed Soja

While Castells was concerned with a definition of the urban based on a spatial unit of collective consumption, others such as Soja and Appadurai have focused on the conceptual frameworks of postmodern urbanism and their geographic arraignment. In opposition to Castells' forthright structuralist economism in *The Urban Question*, more recent attempts to grapple with the emerging geography of the third millennium clearly demonstrate that there is, as yet, no coincidence between new spatial typologies and accepted vocabularies to describe them. The coincidence between the materiality of the industrial age and the cybercities being constructed on the old infrastructure generate the need for entirely new conceptual systems, relating new patterns of human and informational activity to nostalgic conceptions of place (Graham 2004). Digital highways are now reconfiguring urban space as canal, rail and road systems delineated the industrial city. Shifting patterns of neocorporate urban governance result in a complex and alienating restructuring. In 'Excavating the material geographies of cybercities', Graham notes that new forms of uneven development so produced result in

> a complex fracturing of urban space as premium and privileged financial, media, corporate and tele-communications nodes extend their connectivity to distant elsewheres whilst stronger efforts are made to control or filter their relationships with the streets and metropolitan spaces in which they locate (through defensive urban design, closed circuit surveillance, the privatization of space, intensive security practices, and even road closures).
>
> (Graham 2004: 139)

In *Postmetropolis*, Soja grapples with the complexity of discourses, models and vocabularies where he enunciates a typology of discourse/practice for the postmodern city in part two of his text, 'Six discourses on the postmetropolis'. Drawing on Iain Chambers' *Border Dialogues: Journeys in Postmodernity* (1990), Soja points out that his term 'postmetropolis' includes many 'posts', postmodern representing only one: 'Of all the "posts" that can be applied to the contemporary metropolis, the least applicable are post-urban, post-industrial, and post-capitalist... but at the same time, the postmodern, postfordist, post-keynesian metropolis does represent something significantly new and different' (Soja 2000: 147–8). Soja maintains that Los Angeles represents a paradigmatic form and incorporates his six discourses, interacting on a multiplicity of levels. While this indeed could be seriously debated, since the basic assumption seems to be that the rest of the world will necessarily follow in its wake, Los Angeles is no doubt what he terms a 'synekistic milieu' within which new urban processes, and hence spatial arrangements, are manifest. The six discourses outline a typology of form that deals with separate and discrete forms of urban phenomena and analysis.

1 The post-Fordist industrial metropolis: restructuring the geopolitical economy of urbanism.
2 Cosmopolis: the globalisation of cityspace.
3 Exopolis: the restructuring of urban form.
4 Fractal city: metropolarities and the restructured social mosaic.
5 The Carceral Archipelago: governing space in the postmetropolis.
6 Simcities: restructuring the urban imagery.

Postmetropolis is an intellectual tour de force, and urban designers will wish to concentrate on chapter 8, which deals with the restructuring of urban form.

Arjun Appadurai

Finally, after looking at the idea of themed landscapes, and of heterotopic landscapes in the previous chapter, we can now look at the associated typologies of morphed landscapes. By *morphed* I mean landscapes that are fundamentally produced from changes in social development that have matured to a point where naming becomes appropriate, reflecting the coincidence between development and urban forms not previously encountered. At the same time, these are simultaneously aesthetic statements in that they will exhibit specific formal, textual and physical properties. The most obvious representation of this process is in the work of Appadurai (2000). As Appadurai comments, 'The world we now live in seems rhizomic, even schizophrenic, calling for theories of rootlessness, alienation, and psychological distance between individuals and groups on the one hand, and fantasies (or nightmares) of electronic propinquity on the other' (Appadurai 2000: 95). As in Foucault's 'other' heterotopias, disorganised capitalism produces fault lines between place, economy and culture, generating landscapes that do not lend themselves to traditional geographic descriptors. Rhizomatic forms then arise, as in nature, where plant forms do not merely burst through the surface from a single seed, and are similarly reproduced, rather they surface sporadically and uncontrollably from an extended root system that generates random surface features, as does bamboo. Appadurai denotes a basic typology consisting in five dimensions of global cultural flows: ethnoscapes, mediascapes, technoscapes, financescapes and ideoscapes. The term 'scape', most usually associated with 'landscape', also denotes an analogy to form and place. These environments emerge as much from individually projected values and needs more than they do from historic places. Appadurai defines these terms as follows.

Ethnoscape: the landscape of persons who constitute the shifting world in which we live, tourists, refugees, exiles, guest workers, and other moving groups and individuals.

Technoscape: the global configuration, also fluid, of technology, and the fact that technology, both high and low, both mechanical and informational, now moves at high speeds across previously impervious boundaries.

Financescape: the disposition of global capital is now a more mysterious, rapid and difficult landscape to follow than ever before, as currency markets, national stock exchanges, and commodity speculations move 'megamonies' through national turnstiles at blinding speed.

Mediascapes: these refer both to the distribution of the electronic capabilities to produce and disseminate information (newspapers, magazines, television stations, film studios) which are now available to a growing number of public and private interests throughout the world, and to the images of the world created by these media.

Ideoscapes: concatenations of images, but they are often directly political and frequently have to do with the ideologies of states and the counter-ideologies of movements explicitly oriented to capturing state power or a piece of it. These ideoscapes are composed of elements of the Enlightenment worldview, which consists in a chain of ideas, terms and images, including freedom, welfare, rights, sovereignty, representation, and the master term, democracy.

(Appadurai 2000: 95–7)

Foucault

One of the more interesting typologies applicable to today's society is that of heterotopias, a concept derived from Michel Foucault, first expressed in *Les Mots et Les Choses* (translated as *The Order of Things*) in 1966. This idea was extended into various typologies in his lecture 'Of other spaces' that is reproduced in Jane Ockman's edited collection *Architecture Culture* (1993). Sarah Chaplin's article 'Heterotopia deserta' researches the concept in some depth in relation to Las Vegas (*DC 26*, see also Rothman 2003). She also notes that Los Angeles is now the dominant case study, due to the intense interest initiated by the novelist Tom Wolfe in 1965, one which has continued over the last forty years in the work of Reyner Banham, Edward Soja, Edward Relph and Mike Davis. The term 'Heteropolis' has also been used by Charles Jencks as the title of his book about Los Angeles (Jencks 1993). While this would appear to be a direct reference to Foucault who first used the terms 'heterotopia' and 'heterotopology', Jencks only makes one passing reference to Foucault in his final chapter, and there is little relationship between the one and the other. Like most concepts originating from contemporary French philosophy, the concept of heterotopia is by no means straightforward, and one has to struggle with its meaning. Chaplin actually argues that Foucault left the concept deliberately fuzzy: 'a productive fuzzy field ... makes his glossing of the heterotopia not necessarily definitive' (*DC 26*: 342). Ross King clarifies the idea in relation to Foucault's work:

> The middle ages, argued Michel Foucault, were characterized by an hierarchic 'ensemble of places' – the Heavenly Jerusalem, the earthly counterpart, church, square, lane, house and so forth. With Galileo ... there is the presentation of a new, enveloping 'space of emplacement' – space better described by grid references than by hierarchies of places. With modernity, this opens to the endlessly unfolding 'space of extension' of material progress and the appropriation of nature. The characteristic spaces of present experience, by contrast are 'heterotopias', the actually lived and socially created spaces of life at its most intense and 'real'.
>
> (King 1996: 123)

The kinds of spaces alluded to by Foucault are museums, gardens, prisons, theatres, cemeteries, sanatoria, hospitals, libraries, etc., each of which is defined by particular social relations and a particular aesthetic, and is capable of transformation in relation to its environment. Chaplin suggests that since the end of the 1960s, there has been a radical shift from utopias to heterotopias as the appropriate paradigm for postmodernity. She draws meaning from the term and elucidates its content in regard to Las Vegas, which possesses real banality, and as such becomes aesthetically 'other' to conventional architectural discourse, and socio-spatial structures: 'Las Vegas is heterotopian either by virtue of its everyday qualities, or by virtue of its ability to exist outside the everyday' (*DC 26*: 347).

Foucault's article has its usual density and his argument is, as one would expect, rooted to historical referents. He points to the fact that concepts of space in the Middle Ages were dissolved by Gallileo's discoveries, and since the seventeenth century, localised medieval space was replaced by the space of extension. Whereas the nineteenth century was obsessed by history, and found 'its mythological resources in the second law of thermodynamics', the era within which Foucault found himself had its parallel in questions relating to space. The sequence he denotes is from localisation to extension to what he calls 'arrangement', which 'is defined by relationships of neighborhood, which can be formally described as series, trees and networks' (Foucault 1993: 421). He describes his interest not in arrangements of transition – how we get from one place to another via transport systems of some kind – nor through related places of temporality (restaurants, theatres, beaches, airports, stations, cafes, etc.), nor even in arranged spaces of rest in the domestic sphere: 'I am only interested in a few of these arrangements: to be precise, those which are endowed with the curious property of being in relation with all the others, but in such a way as to suspend, neutralize, or invert the set of relationships designed, reflected, or mirrored by themselves' (Foucault 1993: 422). He describes these as utopias and heterotopias. The difference between them is that while utopias may be defined as being in opposition to lived space, i.e. spaces of otherness, heterotopias are spaces of otherness defined by society itself. In consequence, Foucault maintains that all societies are constituted on the basis of heterotopias that vary from culture to culture, but equally within so-called primitive societies as they do to life in the third millennium. These he calls *heterotopias of deviance* 'occupied by individuals whose behaviour deviates from the current average or standard. They are the rest homes, psychiatric clinics, and let us be clear, prisons, in a list that must be extended to cover old people's homes, in a way on the border between the heterotopias of crisis and that of deviance' (Foucault 1993: 423). He also includes such institutional structures as cemeteries, theatres, gardens, holiday villages, brothels, colonies, spaces of purification, etc. In 'Of other spaces', Foucault describes his six principles of heterotopology, the last characteristic being that

> they have, in relation to the rest of space, a function that takes place within two opposite poles. On the one hand they perform the task of creating a space of illusion that reveals how all of real space is more illusory, all of the locations within which life is fragmented. On the other they have the function of forming another space, another real space, as perfect, meticulous, and well arranged, as ours is disordered, ill conceived and in a sketchy state.
>
> (Foucault 1993: 425)

As we have seen, typologies have been an integral part of designing cities for many years. They have been applied in a whole diversity of ways, from the practical and the metaphysical in Patrick Geddes' Wheel of Life, through Rob Krier's typologies of architecture and urban space, to Foucault's heterotopias. Of the few examples that have been illustrated, it is clear also that they have been used as thinking tools, as methods of analysis, as ways of classifying and ordering phenomena and of generating vocabularies for the evolving urban spaces of the third millennium. No doubt their use will be extended as new phenomena are investigated, and designers grapple to understand not only their own rationality but also the nature of the urban prospect. I now move from this general principle of how we can think about the problems of urban design and some of the tools that have been used to do this, to the pragmatics of what we should know about the production of urban designers and urban design knowledge, the non-heterotopic spaces of professionalism and education.

Chapter Ten
Pragmatics

Professionalism is one of the public ideologies of the New Class. Professionalism silently installs the New Class as the paradigm of virtuous and legitimate authority... The New Class is a cultural bourgeoisie who appropriates privately the advantages of an historically and collectively produced cultural capital.

Gouldner (1979: 19)

Introduction: Cultural Capital

In this final chapter I will limit my discussion to the two most important factors in the production of cultural capital (knowledge) within the field of urban design. Here I refer to the triadic relationship between the professions, universities, and urban design as a socially sanctioned activity, now enshrined within tertiary education, usually at postgraduate (Master's) level. Rather than simply discussing the education of urban designers on the basis of existing programmes, the opinions of practitioners or the outcomes of individual urban design projects, I will continue with my basic theme that in order for urban design to move forward it should be sourced from the larger socio-political context within which it finds itself. So instead of trying to be prescriptive about urban design education, I will concentrate on this larger context, leaving the detailed content of individual programmes to be worked through on the basis of more elementary considerations (see Cuthbert 1994a,b, 2001). In order to do this, four sets of relations need to be explored in some depth. First, we should understand something of the political economy of professional intervention within the social formation. Second, we should consider the monopolistic role of professions in capturing knowledge systems. Third, we need to investigate the position of the built environment professions in the production of social space. Finally, there are the pragmatic consequences of this general environment for the training of urban designers.

Professional Intervention

The sociology of professions is now a well-established region of social science, and interested parties might wish to refer to some of the major theorists in this area (Young 1958, Etzioni 1969, Elliot 1972, Johnson 1972, Illich 1977, Larson 1977, Derber 1982, Dingwall and Lewis 1983, Abbott 1988, Freidson 1994). Professions do not simply act as an apolitical homeostatic device within society, maintaining the general good on the basis of altruistic and benevolent motives, creating stability and social cohesion within the relative anarchy of the urban land nexus. Instead, they can be seen to form part of the social construction of reality. They are responsible for the formation of specific domains within this totality, along with other agencies such as the church, the state and socialised education. The territorial constructs so manufactured constitute politicised domains whose existence is ideologically reinforced by secular knowledge, monopolistic and mystical practices, self-legitimation and, in many cases, the subversion of democratic processes. Consequently, autonomous action by individuals becomes attenuated, certain liberties are extinguished, and participatory politics are frequently reduced to an unacceptable level of involvement. The liberalist view situates professionalism as a benign contribution to the market system, where services are sold instead of commodities, but as Dunleavy suggests, 'many urban professions have historically sought to minimise or resist "political" control or public "participation" in decision-making' (Dunleavy 1980: 112).

The emergence of modern professions and the entry of capitalism into its corporate phase were synonymous events. The constitution of modern professional markets was the result of a collective effort by the producers of particular forms of expertise to insert them at a critical conjuncture of the production/consumption process within society. This was a unique event within the capitalist system, since it saw the introduction of what Polanyi (1952) referred to as a 'fictitious' as opposed to a real commodity. He first used the term in regard to land, labour and money, elements of market exchange that have not actually been produced for sale. These relations are clearly demonstrated in table 13. The table also demonstrates the position of professions in relationship to the production of surplus value and to the reproduction of a class-based society. Within the system of capitalist social relations, the citizen is both enhanced and disabled by professional dominance and its attendant ideological position, which provides technical services but usually on the basis of a significant subordination of individual autonomy (which also deepens their position as an interpellated subject in Althusserian terms). Deprived of their rights to self-determination, their world turns into 'an echo-chamber of needs' (Illich 1977: 17). This process not only alienates the individual from their own sense of responsibility and motivation, but the concept of need is inexorably translated into a deficiency.

In this overall process, the commodification of artefacts is extended to all other needs, a principle that encompasses not only land and social relations but

Table 13 Relationship between professional service and the capitalist system of production.

Use-value of services	Services exchanged for capital	Services exchanged for revenue
Directly incorporated into production of surplus value	Expert services included within the corporation: professional and managerial (including freelance consulting)	Expert for professional services which contribute to the production of constant capital (in non-profit research and development)
Incorporated only indirectly (contribute to the reproduction of the labour force)	Contribute to the reproduction of the workforce within the corporation or (rarely) in privately owned service firms (e.g. health professions, instruction of different kinds)	(a) Market situation: classic personal professions (b) Non-market situation: welfare professions in the service of the state
Not incorporated	Supervisory or controlling services	Services related to 'law and order', containment and ideological production, including 'free professions'

Source: M. S. Larson, *The Rise of Professionalism*. Berkeley: University of California Press, 1977, p. 215. Reprinted by permission of the University of California Press.

also the material forms which are reproduced in the built environment. In the transference of autonomy from the individual to professional management, a symbolic structure is established by professional–technocratic elites that retranslates concepts of need, autonomy, competence, right, use-value, legality, responsibility and ownership, all of which have the same basic object – the transformation of the individual from an active to a passive subject. I hasten to correct the idea that this is necessarily a conscious process or the outcome of a vast conspiracy. Nonetheless it is deeply ideological in the Gramscian sense of a 'lived system of values'. While professionals themselves are class-divided into those who hire intellectual labour and those who work for a wage, the idea of professionalism as a situated monopoly practice guarantees living standards for its members across the board.

Professions therefore occupy a complex relationship to society, modifying our perspectives on social class, particularly the middle class, the division of labour, state legitimation, capital and ideology. They constitute a new class of intellectual labour in opposition to the proletariat, but 'Ideal typically, professional autonomy is the antithesis of proletarianisation: the workers themselves determine what work they do and how they do it' (Freidson 1994: 164). They are connected to the coordination of labour within management on the basis of knowledge rather than position within the administrative system. They are involved in politics to the extent that the state or even a royal charter accords them privilege, and continuous political lobbying is essential to their survival.

Professions also bear a particular relationship to capital in that they monopolise knowledge markets over traditional commodity markets and develop a relatively inaccessible knowledge base using esoteric linguistic and technical codes. In some cases, their activities, as in the relationship between the medical profession and multinational pharmaceutical companies or between the legal profession and big capital, are so interlinked that their independence is seriously compromised. Professions also act in a quasi-legal sense by establishing their own conditions of existence, determining the standards by which they operate. This situation spills over into ideological beliefs and practices – inherent support for the market system on the basis of monopolistic and hegemonic control over one region by demonising others, for example the medical profession and its relationship to chiropractic and alternative medicine. Overall, however, Freidson (1994: 44) is wary of all totalising descriptors: 'The larger reality of which both are but part is too complex to be reduced to such simple and sweeping characteristics as "dominant", "hegemonic", "proletarianised", "corporatised", "bureaucratized", "rationalised", or "deprofessionalised" '.

On the other hand, we could argue that all these features are, or have been, generally true at particular stages of history, specifically over the last 200 years. Professions, like every other social construct, are continually evolving. Not only this, but as in other aspects of the economy, uneven development characterises professional organisations across the globe. Over this period different professions have appeared erratically in different countries, and even today, in many societies, various professions have yet to attain a unified organisational existence. Former socialist countries such as Russia, China and North Vietnam, operating on entirely different ideologies and with no private sector, have only recently started to consider association with Western professional institutions as a method of legitimising social practice (e.g. the Royal Institute of British Architects). Professionalising the socialists represents a burgeoning new market. As Western democracies have emerged from the Industrial Revolution into service economies and informational capitalism, so professions have also shifted ground in their economic, organisational and political goals. As markets for services, professions have moved with the market system, and over the last 25 years have made a rapid transition from the corporate ideology of the industrialised world into a neocorporate phase of development in line with today's economic and political climate.

The influence of corporations as the infrastructure of business within national economies began to accelerate at the beginning of the twentieth century, and the term 'corporatism' at its most elementary level simply means control of the state (public sector) or capital (private sector) by large interest groups that can influence decision-making in line with their own needs. Corporatism is therefore an ideology that applies equally within both sectors, the corporation representing the organisational framework that promotes the material interests of the stakeholders. The relationships between corporatism, neocorporatism and professionalism have only been marginally addressed.

A landmark study by Marshall (2000) recently investigated the relationship between neocorporatism and professional interest in Canada, using the Canadian Institute of Planners (CIP) as a case study. Marshall notes the hierarchic ordering of corporate strategies:

> Intervention into society at the level of political and economic systems has been labeled *macrocorporatism*. Intervention into specific sectors or markets, often as a means of dividing labour sectorally (such as trade and professional associations and labour unions) is known as *mesocorporatism*. Intervention at the level of the individual firm or corporate entity, such as a municipality is called microcorporatism.
>
> (Marshall 2000: 68)

Marshall also notes the elementary difference between corporatism and neocorporatism as follows:

> Neocorporatism shifts away from corporatism's 'earlier preoccupation with the structure of organized interest intermediation, to a collateral emphasis on the process of policy-making and implementation' (Schmitter 1982: 259). It thus moves away from defining distinctive properties of corporatism and speculation about its origins. Instead it has an empirical focus on the measurement of its presence and the assessment of its influence in policy and decision-making, that is, its power and effect.
>
> (Marshall 2000: 71)

Alternatively one could say that the move to neocorporatism represents a significant deepening of corporate ideology. Corporations are no longer merely interested in organisational efficiency, narrow sectarian interests and profit-seeking strategies. They now seek to become embedded in the political process, influencing and controlling the relations of production at a much deeper level. This lends a whole new meaning to the idea of monopolies, and John Ralston Saul (1997) argues that the legitimate basis for social democracies is being undermined. The extension of corporate influence into the realm of urban politics conflates corporate interests to that of society as a whole. In the case of professional organisations this implies a move away from the somewhat principled, independent, ethical position of the past, to being an active partner in the operations of the state, from carrying out state policy to forming it, from lobbying for contracts to defining what those contracts will be. State power, supposedly representing the power of the people and previously independent to private interest, gradually becomes the legitimating agent for capital in all its forms.

In the Canadian case, the Canadian Federal Government has had its own fiscal crisis to deal with, and like most Western democracies has wholeheartedly embraced the private sector as a means of reducing the costs of urban administration. Marshall (2000: 116–21) notes ten ways in which the Canadian state is being reconstructed, including Flexible Federalism, the Social Union Framework Agreement (SUFA, designed to harmonise government administration, social programmes and diverse underlying attitudes), new federal regulatory policy consultation requirements, alternative delivery systems to non-state actors and other mechanisms. The underlying theme in all of this seems to be a wholesale reconstruction of the state in order to facilitate and lubricate entry to the mechanisms of government for the private sector. While it is a relatively small organisation compared with other professions, the CIP represents this process in microcosm, and I will paraphrase the more important features of this from Marshall (2000: 162–78).

Marshall argues that the move to Flexible Federalism by the Canadian government has afforded opportunities for the CIP to establish a neocorporatist position, similar to those in the business and professional world. The central avenue of approach after 1996 was to establish the CIP as the government's advisor on public policy. This included participation in policy formulation, as well as the exercise of power and influence over government as to the overall trajectory of development in Canada. Marshall quotes CIP President Couture as stating that the role of the CIP Council was 'to focus on national issues and to establish a stronger presence in national policy and decision making. In the fall we addressed the allocation of <the CIP's> resources, both human and financial, to that goal'. This and other statements led Marshall to observe, 'Thus a neo-corporatist ideology took hold in the organisation as a result of the sociopolitical situation in Canada, the influence of the state's neocorporatist ideology, and the thrust taken by the two consecutive councils of the CIP' (Marshall 2000: 165).

She goes on to note that neocorporatist strategies were by no means unconscious or superficial, and were deliberately embedded into the very structure and ideology of the CIP. This was done by hiring top staff for their experience with government, adopting a communications plan in 1999–2000 to deepen the relationship to government, a strategic plan 1999–2001 which emphasised government relations, and a one-year action plan that had the same objectives. In the short space of fifteen years since 1986, the stated goals of the CIP moved rapidly from simply establishing a 'planning' identity through a national association, decentralising tasks to its affiliates (i.e. down the hierarchy) to the opposite position of direct influence over national policy. She then illustrates the mechanisms through which these goals were achieved, with directives at international, national, regional, urban and local levels, providing policy statements, position papers, advising government in international conferences, working on CIP–government policy directives, and exerting influence on national committees on the environment, infrastructure, housing, urban management and international development. Marshall concludes with the observation that 'Because professions have the quintessential corporatist interest mediation structure, they are also ideal neocorporatist actors...If it maintains its present trajectory, it is only a matter of time until the CIP will be able to ensure that its organization is integrated with the state' (Marshall 2000: 202). The overall inference here is that if such intense strategic intervention is taking place in a relatively innocuous profession such as urban planning, it seems reasonable to assume that, collectively, professions are significantly intervening in the management of social life. While neocorporate ideology deepens professional engagement within the overall political economy, moving from a provider of services to deciding what these services should be, professions must also protect, maintain, defend and, if possible, expand their sphere of influence. In order to accomplish this, capturing knowledge systems is essential, and I now briefly investigate what is involved in this process.

Professions and Knowledge Systems

Professional networks derive their authority from three key sources, namely from the state, from connections to capital and from their command over institutions of higher learning. Within tertiary education, professions expropriate, monopolise and mystify knowledge in order to protect their position of privilege within the general schema of capitalist enterprises. Monopolistic practices associated with the development of capital have enshrined knowledge systems qua cultural capital as an intrinsic part of the overall system of capital accumulation. Over historical time, the ruling elites of most societies have monopolised knowledge (mystical or otherwise) in the interests of social control, from Sumeria to Egypt, China, Mexico and Peru. However, the evolution of modern liberal democracies concomitantly with capitalist development, the conscious reproduction of labour that began with the Industrial Revolution, also demanded new institutional forms whereby knowledge systems could be similarly reproduced and extended. New horizons in capital accumulation could not take place without social housing, health care, education and technological advances that maximised the capacity of physical and cultural capital to establish new thresholds in social development. In turn, these social processes induced transformations which demanded that traditional ideas of social class be interrogated – social control was no longer limited to those who had command over inherited wealth, social status, mystical power or religious authority. The twentieth century was to incur two major processes that would force a rethinking of orthodox class analyses. The first involved the two greatest social revolutions that the world had ever witnessed, namely the Communist revolutions in Russia and China, where the concept of social class was entirely abolished. The second of these was the burgeoning of universities and the creation of a new knowledge class within Western societies, which rapidly cut across traditional class barriers.

However, this knowledge class was not new, since the idea had already been enshrined within the idea of the 'new class', a phrase coined by Mikhail Bakunin around 1870 in order to conceptualise the potential division of labour within socialist states. At the same time, the idea contained much relevance for the rise of the meritocracy within capitalism, and a new class of intellectual labour organised round the idea of professional organisations. Since then, the existence of such a class, with its division into technocrats, bureaucrats and intellectuals, as well as its relation to orthodox class distinctions has been the subject of considerable debate (Bruce-Briggs 1979, Gouldner 1979, Wrong 1979, Carter 1985). In his classic text *The Future of Intellectuals and the Rise of the New Class*, Gouldner draws the analogy between money capital and cultural capital (knowledge), arguing that capital may be defined as any produced object used to make saleable utilities, which in turn provides its possessor with income. The possession of cultural capital does not necessarily result in increased economic productivity, but as in the case of other forms of capital its intrinsic function is to increase both the income and the social leverage of those who control it.

Monopolistic practices are part and parcel of capitalist development and the formation of monopolies in business and finance is paralleled in monopolies over knowledge (and therefore of forms of power) that constitute the essential ingredient in this new class formation. However, the type of society within which Gouldner's new class attains political and economic power remains problematic. Also, the political conditions within which cultural capital may replace or reinforce money capital as the power base for new forms of domination remain unspecified: 'The essence of the teleocratic project is to gain power by constructing or reconstructing meaning systems, pre-empting the democratic discourse by monopolising meanings' (Gouldner 1979: 7). Furthermore, the particular forms of power/knowledge, its specific mechanisms or agencies, and its congruence with societal forms such as professional organisations and state apparatuses remain relatively unexplored, although Marshall's work suggests some new directions that this might take.

Professional intervention in capturing knowledge systems is not only political in nature, at its core it is profoundly semiological: it constitutes a process through which a particular matrix of signifiers and therefore a system of meanings is adopted within society. Central to this process of colonising and monopolising a region of knowledge is the establishment of a specialised language unique to the discipline. Specialised languages are as necessary to professional monopolies as stock is to companies. Gouldner has termed this the 'culture of critical discourse' (CCD):

> An historically evolved set of rules, a grammar of discourse...which is the deep structure of the common ideology shared by the new class. The shared ideology of the intellectuals and the intelligentsia is thus an ideology about discourse. Apart from and underlying the various technical languages (or sociolects) spoken by specialised professions, they are commonly committed to a culture of critical discourse. CCD is the latent but mobilisable infrastructure of modern 'technical' languages.
>
> (Gouldner 1979: 28, see also Edelman 1977)

While specialised professional languages are a necessary part of professional life, their use transcends the material relations that they organise. Within the overall development process, for example, entry to debate is controlled by the expropriation of power structures, specialised knowledge, techniques and practices as the rightful domain of the expert. Conversely, the absence of mastery over such arcane practices, of an appropriate knowledge of 'right' or of decoding processes, effectively eliminates any but the most proficient from entering into a profoundly political process. The nature of debate is similarly limited: firstly, to areas which have been agreed upon by experts as problematic in relation to economic and political exigencies; secondly, through control over the rules by which debate is organised; thirdly, according to what is legally permissible in any given situation; fourthly, in the deliberate cultivation of ambiguous, poorly defined or non-existent legislation and the exclusion of participatory rights (Clark and Dear 1984); and fifthly, because of the complex semiotic nature of critical discourse (legal and technical codes, graphic systems and systems of representation, conceptual frameworks, specialised means of communication, etc.), which is consciously or otherwise rendered inaccessible to the average citizen. It is evident within this context that the judgement of political outcomes is conditioned by a near-professional monopoly over all significant variables, particularly when the entire matrix of professional engagement is subsumed to the discourses of commodity-producing society. Scott for example supports this position and points to the embedded nature of urban planning action that 'acquires and changes its specific targets and emphases as well its supportive ideologies (planning theory, planning education, professional codes of practice, etc.) in relation to definite urban manifestations of that same necessity' (Scott 1980: 187).

Professions and Space

Directly involved in this crafting of space are the environmental professions of architecture, urban design and urban planning, but others, including building, real estate, civil and structural engineering, surveying and landscape architecture, also make significant contributions. Because all professional activity takes place either within the private sector or in support of state policy, it can be argued that 'professionalism' is by its very nature a profoundly political and ideological event. Professions have a direct role in the production of ideological forms and stereotypes throughout the entire range of technico-bureaucratic structures erected within society. Their activities are enshrined in legal statutes. In the case of the environmental professions, such laws define the objects and interests of the state (and by extension, the various capitals): in the extraction of surplus value and profit from the development of space, from land in the second dimension, to building in the third, and from the transformation of the organic composition of capital in the fourth.

In the general process of urbanisation within Western societies, language, discourse and the law are inseparable elements in the framework whereby social relations and spatial structures are created. They are central components in the construction of an extensive ideological matrix through which the reproduction of the relations of production are secured. Every revolution in the process of capital accumulation is accompanied by a corresponding ideological revolution, which covertly restructures the beliefs and discourses underlying any new horizon in the development of capitalist social relations. The organisation of both activities, the ideological and the economic, are managed to a significant degree through the state apparatus as it tries to deliver optimal conditions for the production, circulation and exchange of commodities. The organisation and construction of a spatial matrix that can efficiently accommodate these activities in addition to the containment of urban populations has been allocated to a loose coalition of 'environmental' professions.

State legitimating is at the core of all professional activities, which in order to survive must be enshrined in law. In some disciplines, for example urban planning (the process through which the state maximises the reproduction of capital from space), it has no other existence. Without the law, urban planning as a profession, unlike architecture, is wholly deprived of authority since its prime function is state regulation. Within the neocorporatist state, such legal sanction has been enhanced by the increasing coincidence between professional intervention and state control, particularly in the realm of policy formation. In regard to capital, urban planning as a professional activity had been limited historically to implementing state policy or, within the private sector, in generating surplus value from labour on the basis of selling professional services for a fee. Urban planning in the private sector gave up any pretence to independence, for example in the UK, when the law was changed to allow professional firms to become developers as well as offering services. In other words to extend their profits from extracting surplus value from hiring intellectual labour into speculation on land and buildings as well. At that point any claim to neutrality in serving society's needs went hand in hand with profit maximisation for shareholders. Nonetheless, this allowed the built environment professions to extend both their influence and profits by integrating professional services with big capital (construction firms, developers, banks, insurance companies, etc.).

Collectively, the environmental professions manipulate the physical matrix within which the social and property relations of capitalism achieve a concrete form (see Knox *DC* 27). In their professional symbiosis, architecture, urban design and urban planning constitute exacting ideologies of form, both social and physical, which underwrite the prevailing ideology of power. As the requirements of the capitalist system are transformed over time, professional organisations and their supporting structures are modified to mirror necessary changes in the forces and relations of production. The singular failure of the environmental professions to make any significant ongoing contribution to a general theory of urban spatial structure (despite their intervention in tertiary education) may be traced directly to a constellation of factors. First, their primary collective objective (like all political parties) is to stay in power, and to retain political and monopoly control over a specified region of knowledge. The focus is primarily ideological rather than intellectual. Second, they form part of a specific fraction of finance capital whose fundamental brief is not to explain but to exploit the urban system in terms of profit maximisation. Third, all professionals are compromised by their training (indoctrination) into the various monopolies of competence whose economic benefits they enjoy. The cognitive basis of their training therefore inclines them to support rather than to critique the substance of what they do. Fourth, the traditional histories, theories and technologies deployed by professions are constructs whose existence is required for the purposes of legitimising professional training and action, and not to explain the product of their combined endeavours. Finally, their prime purpose is to serve the various capitals and the state within which their political and financial interests are embedded. As we shall see, these qualities play a significant role when they intervene in tertiary education, where the skilling of labour on the basis of market requirements usually takes precedence over society's needs to educate its offspring.

Urban Design Education

Here we have to consider three elements: first, the relationship between urban design and the professions to which it is most closely related, namely architecture and urban planning; second, their collective relationship to tertiary education and, third, to the education of urban designers.

While professions such as law had been established as early as 1739, the first environmental discipline to acquire professional status was architecture, originating in 1834 as the Institute of British Architects, which would later be awarded a royal charter. The first planning legislation was established in 1909, and the town planning profession five years later in 1914. The reason for the delay in legitimising 'planning' might seem rather obvious: architects had for centuries been involved in building and planning cities. The physical organisation of the built environment, to the extent that it was not merely a reflection of geography, land ownership and crude expressions of religious and individual power, did not require any additional knowledge other than that directly connected with building, predominantly engineering. Architecture and urban design have been closely correlated as praxis for millennia. A more satisfying reason, however, might follow the path of political economy – the idea that social practices such as professional organisations surface from structural social requirements, in this case the overwhelming needs of big capital for some form of institution that would take care of the disastrous consequences of the Industrial Revolution, both on the landscape and on the human population. The state as caretaker for this responsibility co-opted the planning profession as an appropriate agency to manage the social wage. For the first seventy-five years of the twentieth century, planning was almost wholly concerned with health, housing and institutional reform.

While architecture and urban planning both constitute social practices, only one can claim to be an academic discipline, namely architecture. As the greatest of the arts, architecture has existed as an academic pursuit for millennia, without the legitimation of any professional organisation. Conversely, one could argue that urban planning as we know it has only ever existed as a profession and not as an academic discipline, since architects and engineers carried out most physical planning. The planning of towns and cities, from the Greek towns of Asia Minor to the Bastide towns of Europe to the British New Towns of the mid-twentieth century, were largely exercises in architectural and urban form. In fact it is also possible to argue that even urban design was a more accurate description of urban planning into the twentieth century, that it was a more conscious process and that it pre-dated urban planning as a necessary social practice. Even Camillo Sitte's great treatise on urban design, *The Art of Building Cities*, was written in 1889, ten years before any similar significant writing about town planning. The laurels here would probably be awarded to Ebeneezer Howard, a government stenographer, who first published his famous treatise *Garden Cities of Tomorrow* in 1898, under the original title of *Tomorrow: A Peaceful Path to Real Reform*. Even then, Howard's plan was fundamentally an exercise in urban design since it relied heavily on a formalised conception of places and spaces.

A more theoretical focus on the actual differences between architecture, planning and urban design therefore reveals some other interesting propositions that have serious implications for education. For a discipline to have any scientific basis at all, it has to possess either a real or a theoretical object of enquiry. While architecture has a real object for theoretical enquiry (the building), planning does not. Architecture can therefore claim status as both an academic discipline and a profession. Planning on the other hand can claim to be a profession only by virtue of its legitimation by the state. The definition given above, that professional action should be based in theory, is difficult to apply to planning in the absence of appropriate objects of enquiry. Hence its claim to professional status is reduced to the legitimation process and not to any internal coherence of its own. Planning is a mongrel discipline, ritually bred from elementary particles derived from social science, economics, architecture, urban geography, law, engineering, etc.

Significantly, the absence of an object of enquiry renders any ideas of planning theory and planning history problematic. The closest planning has come to any internal consistency was in the late 1980s, when it wholeheartedly embraced system theory as its possible salvation. So-called 'planning history' is also a moribund subject for similar reasons. In the absence of a theoretical base, any factual 'planning' history should be limited to the history of the profession and its activities since 1913. Otherwise, planning is seriously constrained in establishing any claim whatever over the history of human settlements, given that dozens of academic disciplines are involved in how economic, political and social processes affected the material production of social space. Even when planning took form as the Royal Town Planning Institute, its members were almost wholly architects and so it stayed for the next half century. In contrast to architecture, the establishment of 'town planning' as a separate project was really dependent on the Institute for its existence. To this day, the architectural profession has significantly more power and authority than does planning. However, our real concern here is not that architecture and planning bear a necessary relationship to each other, but that both claim urban design as their own.

So where does this leave urban design in the legitimation process? My reply to this is simple: it is at least as strong as architecture and significantly superior to urban planning. If we pursue the above argument a bit farther, we can see that urban design came into existence as a general social practice prior to urban planning: the example given by Sitte attests to this. But it also carries greater legitimacy as well, since we can define the theoretical object of urban design as the public domain, a concept embedded within, and inseparable from, the idea of civil society. On this basis urban design is immediately tied into fundamental social processes, theories and practices. It has both a theoretical object (civil society) as well as a real object (the public domain). So, as a point for debate, we could argue that urban design has both a real and a theoretical object, architecture has a real object (the building), and planning has neither. Transparently, the individuals that constitute society are not dimensionless entities. They exist within and through space. The constitution of civil society is therefore intimately tied to the actual concrete manifestation of spaces and places. The central focus of urban design is on how this public domain has evolved, how the space it occupies is transformed, exchanged and designed; what form it takes; and how it materialises as an accretion of signs which embody the meanings of history. There are significant implications in these ideas for the training of urban design professionals, so I will now take a look at the domain of tertiary education as a keystone in the process of professional legitimation.

While I have referred to urban design throughout this text as a professional activity, in fact it has no independent professional identity, retaining a somewhat nefarious relationship to both architecture and urban planning. This raises questions as to whether it should be considered an inherent part of these other professions or whether it has sufficient integrity as a discipline to demand professional status in its own right, and I have suggested above that it does. While architecture, urban design and urban planning have a coterminous existence as praxis, they remain both theoretically and professionally isolated from each other. This position allows several events to take place. First, anybody can lay claim to being an urban designer, thus opening the gate to charlatans of all descriptions. Second, the two professions that colonise urban design can continue to be self-referential when it comes to defining the discipline, whereby urban design becomes politicised rather than theorised. Third, on this basis, urban design education can continue to be anything anybody decides it is. Hence the training of urban designers adopts the format of what teachers know or what professions require. In other words it becomes structured on the basis of personal and professional ideologies. At the root of the problem lies the question of theory, the only unambiguous way to determine the integrity of the discipline and the training of its members, thereby eliminating problems of charlatanism, professional haggling and appropriate educational curricula.

In the education of professionals, production costs are undertaken by the public through the general educational system, and paid for by taxation and the surplus wage of families. But the products (trained professionals) are expropriated by professional organisations in the process of upgrading and reproducing professional services, having taken no material responsibility for their education beyond establishing their own corporate interests. Hence the creation of trained professionals is intimately connected to universities and towards monopolies of competence, which are crucial variables in the development of the professional project. If we believe Wilshire's brilliant *Moral Collapse of the University* (1990), professional bodies have significantly contributed to this decay by alienating knowledge away from its fundamental trajectory of discovery towards a utilitarian, commodified and de-natured process:

> Now [this overview] suggests the danger of professionalising academic fields, and this danger should have drawn some attention. That it has drawn so very little in over one hundred years indicates how tremendously powerful is the urge to professionalise and claim a field for one's own group. A group claims an identity, powers of mimetic engulfment mold the identities of its members, and before one knows it, the group pulls away from others and parochialism disguised as 'science' and 'scholarship' prevails.   (Wilshire 1990: 101)

Paradoxically, state legitimation for professional practice goes to the profession not the university. In turn, professions consolidate their interests and much of their authority, using this derived power to influence professional programmes within institutions of higher learning, trading sanction for control, with no financial commitment of any kind. If universities wish to have their programmes endorsed as legitimate professional activities, the entire structure of degree programmes then falls under the surveillance of professional monopolies: architecture, urban planning, landscape architecture, building, civil engineering, etc. The central problem here, given the relation of professions to the state and big capital, is that society's needs become conflated to professional interests, with the potential editing of educational programmes that this implies.

Urban design fits uneasily into this overall scenario. Several reasons for this have already been given, namely that urban design has traditionally been the province of architects. But the expansion of knowledge systems during the twentieth century, combined with immense societal change over the last twenty-five years, has resulted in urban design problems being diffused across a wide spectrum of disciplines, from law to urban geography. Similarly, the fiscal crisis of the state has forced planning at all levels of government to engage in public–private sector partnerships as part of their neocorporatist agenda. At the urban level, private sector intervention focused on profits from land development has diverted much planning intervention from regulation to deregulation, from policies to plans, and from zoning strategies to project-based design outcomes. As a consequence, urban design has become central rather than marginal to planning, symbolically replacing the tired 'land use planning process' with a more dynamic and strategic urban design approach in order to accelerate capital accumulation from land speculation, profit from building and surplus value from labour. The demand for planners with urban design knowledge is clearly in the ascendancy.

This overall context results in the production of two kinds of urban designers, roughly based in architectural and planning ideologies and their professional agendas, and I have to generalise here due to the global complexity of programmes and degrees. In the first case, architecture programmes within large universities frequently offer postgraduate degrees in urban design that are confined to students with an undergraduate degree in architecture. Urban design is perceived as an extension of architecture (cities are merely larger buildings) and graduates are automatically eligible for professional membership, usually after a year's practice in an architectural office. Secondly, in other universities (e.g. my current domain at the University of New South Wales in Sydney) the urban design programme is also offered at postgraduate level, and to any student who has an undergraduate degree with a direct relationship to the discipline, for example architecture, law, civil engineering, real estate, landscape architecture, urban geography, commerce, etc. This kind of approach to urban design is not recognised by the architectural profession, which usually argues that architects are involved in professional indemnity for the integrity of their work, so only architect urban designers can attain membership (substandard building can kill you but substandard planning only maims). So despite the historical relationship to architecture, the Master in Urban Development and Design at the University of New South Wales is recognised by the Planning Institute of Australia (PIA). Until 2004, when the PIA relinquished its requirement for urban design programmes to be assessed, it was the only programme in Australia with such recognition.

What is certain is that architecture and urban planning still view urban design as an opportunity to colonise another region of knowledge and have very different perspectives on the discipline. People like myself see it as an independent discipline fighting a rearguard action for legitimacy. On the one hand, urban design qua architecture remains wedded to the idea of sectarian knowledge, physical determinism, a renaissance concept of the architect as master builder, and the domain of architectural aesthetics as the proper location for urban design knowledge. On the other hand, and somewhat paradoxically, planning, because of its own diffuse origins and weak theoretical foundations, can afford to see urban design as pluralistic, open to a diversity of disciplines. Similarly, the very power and integrity of architectural ideology and its professional presence has forced it into an extremely limited perspective on urban design, whereas the weaknesses of planning ideology outlined above in this instance offer significant opportunities for an evolving urban design knowledge. This year the PIA added several other chapters to its planning base, which included urban design. In doing so, planning formally recognised urban design as a part of its overall mandate. How all these factors impinge on the actual training of urban designers needs some additional consideration.

Educating urban designers

Overall, the education of urban designers has had comparatively little attention in the academic press, and there is little written on the subject. Of work in print, most exhaustive of these is Anne Vernez Moudon's 'A Catholic approach to organizing what urban designers should know' (1992, *DC* 28) and, more recently, Thomas Schurch's 'Reconsidering urban design' (1999). Jonathan Barnett conflates urban design education to architectural education in 'Architectural education: teaching urban design now that clients want it' (Barnett 1986). Colman (1988) saw urban design as a field in need of broad educational innovation and Hamnett (1988) viewed a renewed interest in urban design as a call to revise planning programmes. Gunder's paper of 2001 is also commendable. The issue of urban design research also has a bearing on urban design education, and two key articles are those of Jacobs (1993) and Heide and Wijnbelt (1996). Significantly, the UK Department of the Environment, Transport and the Regions (DETR) has produced the only state commentary available on urban design education in its report *Training for Urban Design* (2001). Diaz-Moore's article 'The scientist, the social activist, the practitioner and the cleric' is also highly relevant (2001: 14) (see table 14).

Moudon begins by searching for the various fields of knowledge that inform urban design, and notes the significance of individuals such as Lewis Mumford, Christian Norberg-Schulz, Donald Appleyard, Amos Rapoport, Edmund Bacon and Jonathan Barnett, but stressing the collected works of Kevin Lynch as being of primary significance. In order to map the knowledge necessary for urban education, Moudon distinguishes between normative, i.e. prescriptive information as to 'what should be', and substantive descriptive knowledge as to 'what is'. In doing so she separates the principle of understanding cities from the actual process of design. For me this is the fundamental conceptual flaw in the paper. Considering that the substantive dimension is in fact the most important, she concentrates on substantive research and epistemology. Moudon identifies nine concentrations of enquiry (*DC* 28: 367) (see table 15):

1 urban history studies;
2 picturesque studies;
3 image studies;
4 environment–behaviour studies;
5 place studies;
6 material culture studies;
7 typology–morphology studies;
8 space–morphology studies;
9 nature ecology studies.

Moudon introduces three other dimensions that add significantly to the complexity of the task: first, three predominant research strategies in the form of the literary approach, the phenomenological approach and positivism; second, the idea of modes of enquiry (historical-descriptive, empirical-inductive and theoretical-deductive); and third, the specificity of the research focus. She notes that in the USA the favoured approach has been the people/subject orientation, exemplified by the so-called 'man–environment relations' of Amos Rapoport, Gary Moore, David Canter and others. The last part of the process is to screen the research for what she terms its 'ethos', borrowing another two terms from Rapoport, namely 'etic/emic', words which reflect semiological expressions, namely *langue* (written language) and *parole* (spoken language). 'Applied to studies of peoples and cultures, etic and emic relate to the nature of the source of the information gathered – *etic* in the case of the informant being the

Table 14 Ontology, ways of knowing and ways of teaching as exemplified by architectural academics.

Ontological metaphor	Scientist	Social activist	Practitioner	Cleric
Assumptions of human nature	Human beings exist in an interactive relationship with their world	Humans are social actors who operate in a reality of a web of meanings imbued with power and politics	Humans are purposeful social actors interpreting and understanding their milieu, creating a world of significance	Humans are intentional creatures who shape the world within their own experience
Epistemology	Dualist (subject–object duality); objectivist; findings are considered true	Value-mediated findings of a specific context; what can be known is intertwined with a person's perspective, which is shaped by one's values	To take goal-oriented action in an uncertain world; emphasis is placed on resolving problematic situations through negotiation	Phenomenological intuition: transcendental conversion to understanding
Pedagogy	Banking approach: knowledge as a commodity to be deposited	Primarily problem posing; values emphasised	Problem-posing approach: real life-based issues and actions	Journey-guide approach: knowledge seen as being on some distant horizon
Teaching style	Expert and formal authority	Facilitator and personal; instructor and students as co-investigators	Facilitator and expert instructor and students as co-investigators	Personal and formal; mystical master
Teaching method	Lectures; teacher-centred discussion; laboratory	Small group teamwork: problem-based learning; debates; discussion	Case studies; practicum; problem-based learning	Self-discovery activities; coaching; role modelling

Continues

Table 14 *Continued*

Ontological metaphor	Scientist	Social activist	Practitioner	Cleric
Underlying student role	Dependent; individual and competitive	Collaborative; good citizen; participant	Participant; independent; collaborative	Disciple; dependent; individual
Evaluation method	Exams; grades on defined content including basic knowledge; application; critical thinking	Mix of peer, instructor and self-evaluation in relation to expression of social agenda	Based on critical thinking; mix of peer, instructor and self-evaluation in relation to stated goals (social construction)	Instructor prerogative; orthodoxy to the prototype
Major proponents in architecture*	Batchelor (1991)	Dutton (1991, 1996)	Cuff (1989)	Bognar (1985)
	Cohen (1987) Rapoport (1984, 1995)	Mayo (1991, 1996) Weisman (1991, 1998)	Symes (1985) Underwood (1991, 1994)	Graves (1975) Loomis (1991)
	Seidel (1981)	Ward (1996)	Watson (1993, 1994)	Perez-Gomez (1991)

* For further details of references cited here, see Diaz-Moore (2001).

Source: K. D. Diaz-Moore 'The scientist, the social activist, the practitioner and the cleric: pedagogical exploration towards a pedagogy of practice', *The Journal of Architectural and Planning Research*, 18:1, 2001, p. 64.

Table 15 Anne Vernez Moudon's epistemological map for urban design.

Concentration of enquiry	Date	Research focus	Research ethos	Key distributors*	Impact on practice
Urban history studies	1920s–	Object and subject	etic	Dyos (1968) Morris (1972) Mumford (1961) Kostoff (1991)	Critical assessment of post designs and forces
Picturesque studies	1950s–	Object	etic	Cullen (1961) Halprin (1966) Sitte (1889) Unwin (1909)	Visual attributes of cities
Image studies	1960s to 1970s	Subject	emic	Appleyard (1964) Asihara (1983) Higuchi (1983) Lynch (1961)	How people perceive and understand cities
Environment– behaviour studies	1950s–	Subject and object	emic	Altman (1986) Gehl (1987) Moore et al. (1985) Rapoport (1977) etc.	How people perceive, use and interact with the built environment
Place studies	1970s	Object and subject	etic and emic	Hiss (1990) Norberg-Schulz (1983) Relph (1976) Whyte (1988)	How people perceive, feel, use and interact with their surroundings
Material culture studies	1920s	Object	etic	Brunskill (1981) Jackson (1980) Venturi et al. (1977) Wolfe (1965)	The object qualities of the built environment
Typology– morphology studies	1950s	Object	etit	Conzen (1960) Moudon (1986) Rossi (1982) Whitehand (1981)	Urban tissue and analysis and morphology
Space– morphology studies	1950s	Object	etic	Anderson (1977) Gottdiener (1986) Hillier & Hanson (1984)	Urban spatial form and geometry
Nature– ecology studies	1980s	Object and subject	etic	Hough (1984) McHarg (1971) Spirn (1984) Van der Ryn (1986)	Natural processes and the built environment

* For further details of references cited here, see Moudon (1992).
Source: A. Vernez Moudon, 'A Catholic approach to organizing what urban designers should know', *Journal of Planning Literature* 22: 4, 1992, p. 271. Reprinted by permission of Sage Publications, Inc.

researcher, the person who will use the information, and *emic* in the case of the informant being observed' (Moudon *DC* 28: 367). Each of the nine areas is described, and the sources which configure traditional urban design knowledge are laid out in significant detail.

While the article is undoubtedly one of the best of its kind, offering an envelope for urban design knowledge, it is confined to method: 'this first attempt at building an epistemology for urban design emanated from the practical need to introduce students to a large body of literature, to encourage them to focus their readings and to help them relate these readings to actual issues and problems in the field' (Moudon *DC* 28: 378). As a result, there is no cement holding all of the pieces together, and we are left with the feeling that urban design may be defined as the quantum of information read by urban designers. There is no discussion of theory or any substantial explanation of what is essential to urban design, over architecture or urban planning. Similarly, the idea that what urban designers should know is viewed generically and indeed from a singularly American perspective. Nor is there any attempt to suggest that the economic, political and social basis for a resurgent knowledge is influential in how urban design as process actually comes about. Hence the dominant forces structuring the urban realm are excluded from the nine concentrations of enquiry denoted as essential for an urban design education.

Thomas Schurch (1999) concentrates similarly on urban design as a field or profession, defining it as 'form giving to built environments as a primary activity involving the professions of architecture, landscape architecture and planning' and resorts to a hierarchy of physical scale as the appropriate method of encapsulating design intervention. He denotes the most significant aspects of this hierarchy as quality of life, the public realm and something called 'process'. We are informed that 'urban design can be defined as a process should come as no surprise to anyone', that 'urban design has been realized more or less anonymously' and that 'urban design cannot be limited to any one paradigm', thus opening the floodgates to a nefarious and indefinable form of pluralism and ambiguity. The article takes us through a familiar series of prototypical urban design tactics, definitions and homilies that restate the importance of the work of Christopher Alexander, Kevin Lynch and Jane Jacobs, retreads relationships between the professions and arrives at yet another taxonomy of eight essential qualities describing urban design (place, density, mixed and compatible uses, pedestrianisation and human scale, human culture, public realm, built environment and natural environment). The public realm is defined as 'parks, squares, streets and the like, owned by the public' (Schurch 1999: 23). The article is important in that it indicates exactly why any significant theorisation of the subject has been absent to date, why urban design has identity problems and why urban design education remains wholly eclectic, practice oriented and ideological.

More to the point is the DETR publication *Training for Urban Design* (2001), a product of a report by the Department's Urban Taskforce that demanded no less than a national urban design framework defining the core principles of urban design, guidelines showing how good design can support local plans, and three-dimensional spatial master plans showing how a new development will work in its wider urban context. Together with the Urban Design Group, an Urban Design Alliance has been formed, combining five professions with a total membership of 216,000 persons. The report noted four kinds of contemporary urban design practice:

1   urban development design;
2   design policies, guidance and control;
3   public realm design;
4   community urban design.

The report goes on to note that five professional institutes were involved, the Royal Institute of British Architects, the Royal Town Planning Institute, the Royal Institute of Chartered Surveyors, the Landscape Institute and the Institution of Civil Engineers, which are collectively responsible for 166 courses offering professional accreditation in England alone. In addition there are over 30 urban design programmes (DETR 2001: 5). Nine have professional recognition. A list of the knowledge and skills required by urban designers was drawn up, with a template for urban design education enclosed in three basic categories (DETR 2001: 2).

1   Contextual knowledge about cities, development processes and urban design theories and principles.
2   The activities in urban design, from analysis of the physical setting, through formulation of design policies and preparation of the various kinds of design at various scales, to the processes of implementation including development appraisal and development control.
3   The generic skills specific to urban design, including creativity, graphic skills, market awareness and negotiating, and visualisation of outcomes.

Each of these was seen to have significance for training, and is detailed to a fairly precise level of specification. For example, six aspects of implementation are given to suggest the range of urban design intervention (DETR 2001: 11).

1   Design and development briefing: proactive as distinct from reactive forms of guidance prepared in respect of development types (e.g. residential), sites or areas, and capable of coordinating the design requirements of a range of stakeholders and other consultants.
2   Design and development control: the process by which government regulates changes in the use, character, appearance and overall quality of the environment.
3   Development appraisal: assessing the viability of proposals to various degrees of accuracy and specificity and in the context of private and public sector performance requirements.

4   Project funding: concerned with financial instruments and forms and sources of funding.
5   Planning and development law: an essential framework for urban design and development, setting the legal parameters for intervention and change.
6   Project delivery and management: recognised by the Urban Task Force as being of particular relevance in the implementation of projects and programmes for urban development and regeneration.

Finally, the template denotes seven generic skills that are suggested as a foundation for urban design training (DETR 2001: 11):

1   creativity and innovation;
2   design awareness and visual literacy;
3   graphic communication skills;
4   interdisciplinary team working;
5   market awareness and business sense;
6   negotiation skills;
7   ability to interpret plans and visualise intended outcomes in both two and three dimensions.

These three examples offer somewhat different ways of looking at urban design in terms of how the discipline should be conceived and how it should be taught. Moudon concentrates on epistemology, Schurch's paper seeks to establish thresholds of scale and process as a foundation for the discipline, while the DOE is heavily focused on the needs of the professions (all five of them). To a large degree, the hidden message is that it does not matter how urban design is defined, as long as somehow it is wrapped up in particular processes and scalar hierarchies; can been contained in a whole series of methodological interventions; and can be defined, both by what urban designers do and what a diversity of professions require in terms of market strategies. None of this implies that there is not a lot of truth in what is said, and it is undeniable, particularly in Moudon's paper, that traditional urban design may be understood pragmatically in terms of what urban designers do, and her nine concentrations of enquiry give a substantial envelope to urban design knowledge. When all is said and done, however, we are left with the uneasy feeling that the door to what urban design actually is and how it can be theorised is still closed. Without this, urban design knowledge will be endlessly retracked from the same components. So theory in urban design will be condemned to recreate potentially limitless taxonomies of 'essential characteristics' that began with Kevin Lynch's five discrete units of the city (1960), i.e. paths, edges, districts, nodes and landmarks, and his more recent five dimensions of performance (1981), i.e. vitality, sense, fit, access and control; continued with Christopher Alexander's 253 patterns; and progressing right up to date with Schurch's eight jargon-free qualities, goals and principles, i.e. place, density, mixed and compatible uses, pedestrianisation and human scale, human culture, the public realm, built environment and natural environment (1999).

My views on the specificity of urban design and planning education have been published elsewhere, and much of this has been embodied within the Urban Design Program at the University of New South Wales. My basic argument is simple in this regard. Training urban designers should not be an ad hoc process that reflects personal, professional or educational ideologies but should be worked through on the basis of its inherent theoretical project, the public domain. So I will not elaborate unnecessarily on which type of course is appropriate to which context, on the imminent changes to tertiary education in cyberspace, the potential deepening of neocorporatist offerings through web-based education, or whether urban design students should or should not learn about philosophy. Overall this book has been dedicated to a single purpose, that urban design can be informed by substantial theory in the form of spatial political economy. Moreover, its mandate is no less than the custodianship of the public realm and that the greatest concern of urban designers (as opposed to capital or the state) should be the reproduction of urban meaning. On this basis I can see no reason why it should be defined from the outside by an arbitrary collection of professional institutions as seems to be happening in the UK, rather than from its own academic and professional aspirations. As I have argued above, urban design has significantly more integrity in theory and practice than does urban planning, and I look forward to the day when the first professionally sanctioned Institute of Urban Design exists in its own right as a legitimate region of human knowledge and awareness.

Postscript

In my introduction, I clearly stated that this book was not about doing urban design but about knowing it – understanding the concepts and values that inform our actions. So *The Form of Cities* does not have answers and outcomes as its key objective. Nonetheless many important issues have been raised in the course of writing, and I would like now to highlight some of these observations. The purpose here is to provoke discussion and to express somewhat heretical ideas that are frequently more interesting than those that can be reasonably debated. Hence no references or justifications are given (other than my past writing and any inherent logic) to the opinions expressed below.

As each era advances its own material basis for life, it impacts on a pre-existing collage of apparently random three-dimensional forms and spaces. In order to understand the resulting metamorphosis, the concrete institutional frameworks of society must be understood, along with the accompanying ideologies that inform their administration. But evolution cannot be represented by an endless straight-line graph. As in the natural world, our social universe moves in jumps. The terms 'climacteric' or 'paradigm shift' try to capture the cataclysmic change that can take place over relatively short periods of time. We live in such an age. Not only has history been abolished, we have also abolished tomorrow: we live in a permanent state of acceleration in a futile race to retrofit what has already been discovered. Nor is there any apparent purpose to this competition except to increasingly compress the world's storehouse of wealth into the hands of fewer and fewer individuals.

While I consider myself an unrestrained optimist, I retain a deep sense of trepidation about the unenlightened nature of global capitalism, the first process to transcend all historically defined and democratic political processes, situated within or among nation states. Since this process is homologous with the idea of development, a new institutional structure of denationalised global elites supported by emerging institutions, laws and ideologies is being formed outside popular consensus. Until recently, democracy was threatened by only two significant challenges in the twentieth century. These surfaced in the form of

Nazism/Fascism and totalitarian socialism. Today democracy is again threatened by radical forms of Christianity and Islamism, both ideologies playing a significant role in legitimising or resisting the politics of neocorporatism.

Here two major positions appear to dominate. If we adopt a conspiratorial position to development, we assume that some other or others are actually in control of the process. If we do not, then we have to assume that global capitalism is fundamentally out of control, its trajectory dictated by whatever logic remains within Adam Smith's 'invisible hand of the market'. The central institutional form commanding this process is the transnational corporation. It exhibits three primal qualities: first, survival no matter what the price; second, the externalisation of all possible costs; and third, criminality, since the largest corporations such as Exxon, IBM and Pfizer all have criminal records. In the corporate universe, breaking the law is viewed merely as a function of transaction costs, not morality. Corporate power, which is the key generator of gross domestic product (GDP), has also set in place powerful ideologies through its ability to manipulate the mass media. In so doing it has also acquired the capacity to absorb various forms of resistance by usurping their vocabulary and philosophical underpinnings. There is no better example of this today than the terms 'postmodernism' or 'sustainable development'.

The recent important documentary *The Corporation* suggested with some force that transnational corporations do indeed rule the world, that they are getting bigger and bigger, that they rule invisibly and that they exhibit psychopathic tendencies that would be unacceptable in individuals. The only thesis one can extract from this is that the public good will invariably be sacrificed to corporate profit. For example, the unjustified war in Iraq simply offered an appropriate and timely vehicle for converting the surplus wage of all Americans in the form of tax dollars into massive profits for American companies. Overall, the spiralling wealth of developed nations reflects the fact that needs as a signifier of progress have been satisfied. We now live in a world where the infinite space of desire fuels commodity production. In this regard John Gray's book *Straw Dogs* poses a serious challenge to ideas of development, when he suggests that progress is alien to our position in nature. The philosophical and religious foundations underlying the concept of progress have brought us to the point where continuous expansion of GDP based on a parallel exploitation and exhaustion of nature and labour has become the predominant yardstick by which nations are judged. He postulates that progress is a myth upon which human development has been predicated, a proposition that warrants serious consideration.

Paradoxically, transnational neocorporatism reifies the idea of imperialism, albeit in a vastly different form. Thus the concept of imperialism, and the twin concepts of empire and sovereignty it contains, remain significant. Each is being reinvented in a new form, with global implications for the design process. The old-style Western imperialism attacked by Lenin was an ideology for the subjugation and oppression of people of colour everywhere, with the single exception of Japan. This time round, however, governance will be corporate and planetary, and everyone will be granted citizenhood whether they welcome it or not. While the new imperialism may indeed, as many argue, be a force for liberty, equality and humanity, the early warning signs are not good.

The dark vectors of cloning, nanotechnology and the genetic engineering of all living organisms progress faster than society is capable of absorbing and controlling them. Consequently, the product of billions of years of evolution, the human genetic code, is now in the hands of the private sector. One day in the not too distant future, we may all be branded and patented. Added to this we have the destruction of biodiversity, the rise of religious fundamentalism, corporate intervention into national politics, vast urban decay, and an increasing disparity between rich and poor, representing only a few of the issues we confront at the start of the third millennium. All of this exists on a bed of quicksand, where the USA, the 'richest' country in the entire world, could bankrupt the planet. It pays for its standard of living by borrowing on the savings of other nations, a sum now close to its own judicial limit of $US700 billion. In the face of such excess, the developed world as a whole donates less than 0.7% of GDP to the developing world, which now generates a significant portion of the developed world's wealth and where a high percentage of nations are continuously in default.

The implications for the development and design of cities are indeed profound. As corporate power builds more sophisticated target markets using concepts of difference and deconstruction hijacked from postmodernist theory, spaces of meaning represented in prevailing communities are being transformed into Castells' new tribal microterritories, reflecting ever new forms of consumption. In between, traditional societies and communities are disappearing, as the new imperialism gradually transforms the historical process by reorienting concepts of conquest from the body to the mind, as Foucault predicted. In a borderless planet, bodyspace becomes the essential geographic unit, monitored by sophisticated data gathering and processing systems of surveillance and control. Much of our autonomy as reasoning, free-thinking individuals may yet be compromised by globalised production.

In parallel to this scenario, space is also being transformed to accommodate a new political, social and moral order. In this context urban design has a central role to play, since the public realm remains a theatre for class politics. Urban design has the capacity to resist dominant ideologies by creating new forms of space which restate the trajectory of political and cultural development. As outcomes, two architectures are likely to evolve, one of profusion and one of despair, as the economic differences of the society of the spectacle become magnified in a new global empire of increasing competition and inequality. As image, the experience will not be far from what Umberto Eco calls the New Middle Ages. Competition between cities at all levels in the hierarchy implies that there will be both winners and losers in the process. Capitalism has always exhibited an extreme capacity for uneven development, and there is no reason to view this any differently today. Burgeoning populations and depleting resources suggest that this polarisation will accelerate rather than slow down, and that urbanisation will increasingly be characterised by diverging environments of abundance and deprivation at all levels of the urban hierarchy.

The third millennium postmetropolis is likely to dissipate all medieval and modernist concepts of the city by eroding historically defined signifiers and rendering invisible prevailing systems of power. In contrast to prior historical periods, where the power of monarchy or the state offered concrete manifestations of wealth and authority, new power structures contain the ability to remain multivalent and hidden. Visible symbols of the new political order will be in short supply, making their presence felt instead within neo-Benthamite structures of surveillance and control. While it is likely that urban densities will continue to reduce, the 'densification' of cities remains an arena of serious disagreement and debate. Themed environments designed to accommodate specific consumption processes will reflect the increasing complexity of commodity space in the market. Cities which attempt to project a unique image and opportunities, either real or symbolic, will do so on the basis of their capacity to commodify history, simulate authenticity, provide sites for spectacles or conserve exotic natural settings. Reconstructed centres for desire, spectacle and commodity fetishism are already nascent around the world, in Winnipeg, Dubai, Los Angeles and Las Vegas.

Even traditional modes of transport are being reconstituted in the face of global tourism, both literally, in transformations of use, and figuratively, through virtual reality. Airports and other major points of transfer will gradually morph into themeports, destinations rather than points of transfer, capable of providing all the surrogate experiences tourists require. At the moment, old-style cruise ships are being reconceived as floating towns that are designed to go nowhere at all. So the post-tourist simulacrum built on the disposable wages of the developed world may actually negate travel, as simulation transcends reality. Why should one go anywhere? As Alain de Botton (2002: 27) suggests, 'the imagination can provide a more than adequate substitute for the vulgar reality of actual experience'. In the light of global terrorism, epidemics such as SARS and AIDS, and catastrophes such as earthquakes, volcanic eruptions and the South-east Asian tsunami, post-tourism opens up a parallel universe, a metaverse of non-threatening travel. Overall, prevailing institutional structures that organise capital and labour will be radically transformed, and hence the socio-spatial environment which results, the object of urban designers, will change in concert with them.

In this process, urban designers may choose to abandon any attempt to understand what is going on and simply design to briefs. For those who wish to engage in any serious debate about urban form and urban design, many other issues need to be considered. Over the nineteenth century and into the twentieth, the study of urban development was dominated by investigation where only socio-economic processes mattered. Early in the twentieth century, the fact that space matters received increasing recognition. Today, urban design qua professional practice springs from the nature of globalised production, where the importance of form has now become significant. The wasting away of the nation state, the rise of regionalism and public–private sector global partnerships has resulted in a project-based foundation for development, all of which implies an urban design approach.

In turn, this has seen the authority of urban planning practice diminish in favour of urban design. But due to the absence of an urban design profession built upon substantial theory, the discipline has been swallowed by the architectural and planning professions. Arguably, urban design already constitutes one half of urban planning practice, with policy planning and regulation forming the other. If we extract urban design from the agenda, planning is left with only one honest leg to stand on, namely the legitimation process.

In the preceding text I sketched out an encompassing theoretical framework for those who wish to be informed about the design of cities. Each chapter could be expanded into a single book, so I have only been able to touch on the conceptual scaffolding of a significantly larger edifice. Prime among these is the principle that the vast array of social, political and economic forms that structure our lives generate the form of cities and the design that is imprinted on the environment. Urban design and the consciousness that informs it are both social products. They are born within society and emerge from a historically specific political economy and its contingent social relations.

Hence an urban design knowledge should involve nothing less than the study of how the global built environment achieves its physical form and how it materialises through design. Significantly, we must begin with the assumption that all urban space is designed by human action of some kind, and does not emerge as a totality from the drawing boards and computer software of architects and planners. If this single observation were to be generally adopted by urban design programmes internationally, they would necessarily commit themselves to serious educational restructuring. Indeed, depending on whom one quotes, architects and urban designers are only involved in the actual design and construction of 15 percent of all building in first-world economies, decreasing to zero in some developing nations. So over historical time, designers have actually played a rather small part, however significant, in dictating the form of cities.

In approaching this problem I have chosen to adopt nine elements that constitute the building blocks of necessary theory. While I would maintain that these elements are irreducible, there is no reason why other methods could not satisfactorily accomplish the same task. Since the overall text adopts one of two major approaches to economics, a separate chapter on economics is not included. That approach is political economy, one which does not separate economic decisions from political decisions. Chapters are also subject to their own form of uneven development. Spatial political economy has more relevance in some areas than others. Most significant of these is undoubtedly the chapter on environment, where I searched in vain for some light at the end of the tunnel. Historically, social control, morality and ethics were exercised through church and state, with business left to generate wealth however it wished. The weakening of the nation state has meant that significant stewardship over these regions of human behaviour has been diverted to the private sector, where profits dominate over principle. Scarcity and deprivation are social constructs.

Problematic is the fact that none of the arguments about natural capitalism, sustainable development or technology are convincing. The very concept of sustainability has been colonised by big capital and turned into another huge marketing operation to guarantee the reproduction of corporate profits. The idea of a sustainable urban design is locked into this paradigm, where solutions are constrained to areas where big business can make money, almost exclusively limited to technical fixes in the form of photovoltaic cells, solar energy hot water systems, double glazing panels, light rail systems and recycling materials of value. Unfortunately there is no technical fix to the problems we now confront in designing cities, which are primarily about sustainable value systems in the face of enormous problems of equity and environment worldwide.

The relationships between history, theory and philosophy have significant overlap, and it might have been better to write one huge chapter rather than three. If we are to learn about the values and value systems underlying our actions as I have suggested, this is probably the best place to start making choices. The marriage of philosophy and history has generated a vast array of ideological perspectives that condition any understanding of urban design. Urban design is imbued with problems of theory, identity, ownership and legitimation. There is still no precision to the term 'urban' or whether design is homologous with professional activity. I have indicated a preference for the phrase 'the production of urban form' rather than 'the production of urban design' but, once again, questions as to what is actually being formed or designed are legion.

Many answers come from philosophy, where semiotics, phenomenology and political economy provide a significant framework for analysing the production of urban form and design. While the task would be enormous, it should first be attempted at a global scale, to include the processes of imperialism indicated above. No text on the history of urban form in post-colonial environments would be complete without this inclusion, as attested by our annual international projects in the Master's Program at the University of New South Wales to Jakarta, Beijing, Hanoi, Taipei, Jakarta, Cebu, Mumbai and other locations. The politics of imperialism also need to be understood in order to comprehend why many Asian cities ended up being designed as they are today. Mike Davis' *Late Victorian Holocausts* is a psychologically harrowing entry to part of this process, one of the few texts I have ever read that made me ashamed to be human.

Urban space, culture and design are inseparable concepts. The canvas for urban design practice is the public realm, and once again urban designers should not avoid knowing how this public realm has been reproduced, how it is legitimated and how it is represented. I have written elsewhere that my first impression of Hong Kong was that it had almost managed to eliminate the public realm in its entirety. The only way business could extract any more profit from space was to produce dimensionless human beings. Either that or to improve commodity circulation to the point where people no longer had to move about, with massive savings in sidewalks and transport infrastructure. Fortunately this is unlikely to happen, and local culture still permeates both the public and domestic spheres of social life. So urban designers must be conscious of how culture is transformed at the global, national and local levels, without assuming that their own personal experience will suffice.

From a design perspective, it is all too easy to see culture as monolithic rather than composed of myriads of diffuse interests and alliances. Culture is a dynamic phenomenon, and as some cultures die, others are reborn in forms that are likely to be alien to popular consciousness. But we cannot forget that such transformations can occur in one or more dimensions and remain static in others. The most obvious example of this hiatus is the position of women in society, and the gendering of space remains an altogether ignored consideration in designing cities. As in most theatres of human experience, men have historically dominated decision-making processes, and the time to set the record straight has long since passed: 10,000 years with patriarchy in the driving seat is perhaps excessive. As a matter of some urgency, urban designers need to address the problems of urban space in relation to equality of control, access and design, indicated in the text. It is also well within the bounds of reason that if more women were involved directly in senior positions of power across the entire spectrum of decision-making, then the life-saving shift in values indicated above might have a significantly higher possibility of success.

Finally, at the level of pragmatics, designers do not exist in a social vacuum. They operate from a perspective of highly persuasive educational and professional processes and rule systems. The training of urban designers must escape from an accretion of outdated and obsolete ideologies with a new consciousness of what they do, how they understand what they do, and how they may influence development and design to generate more humane outcomes. In *The Form of Cities* I have tried to suggest how our knowledge needs to change, and how the substance of this process of critical self-reflection might be structured. The outset of the third millennium seems like a reasonable place to begin.

References

Abbott, A. 1988: *The System of Professions: An Essay on the Division of Expert Labour.* Chicago: University of Chicago Press.

Abel, C. 1969: Ditching the dinosaur sanctuary. *Architectural Design*, 39, 419–24.

Abel, C. 1988: Analogical models in architecture and urban design. *METU JFA*, 8(2), 161–88.

Abel, C. 2000: *Architecture and Identity: Responses to Cultural and Technological Change.* London: Oxford.

Abel, C. 2004: *Sky High: Vertical Architecture.* London: Royal Academy Publications.

Adams, W.H. 1991: *Nature Perfected: Gardens Throughout History.* New York: Abbeyville Press.

Adler, S. and Brenner, J. 1992: Gender and space: lesbians and gays in the city. *International Journal of Urban and Regional Research*, 16, 24–34.

Adorno, T. 1991a: The culture industry reconsidered. In *The Culture Industry*. London: Routledge, 85–92.

Adorno, T. 1991b: How to look at television. In *The Culture Industry*. London: Routledge, 136–53.

Agger, B. 1992: *Cultural Studies as Critical Theory.* London: Falmer Press.

Agnew, J. 1989: *Place and Politics: The Geographical Mediation of State and Society.* London: Allen and Unwin.

Agrest, D., Conway, P. and Weisman, L. (eds) 1996: *The Sex of Architecture.* New York: Harry N. Abrams.

Ainley, R. (ed.) 1998: *New Frontiers of Space, Bodies and Gender.* London: Routledge.

Alberti, L.B. 1966: *De Re Aedificatoria.* Milano: II Polifilo.

Alexander, C. 1964: *Notes on a Synthesis of Form.* Cambridge, MA: Harvard University Press.

Alexander, C. 1966: The city as a mechanism for sustaining human contact. Working Paper No. 50. Centre for Planning and Development Research, University of California, Berkeley.

Alexander, C. 1969: Major changes in environmental form required by social and psychological demands. *Ekistics*, 28(165), 78–86.

Alexander, C. 1973: A city is not a tree. In J. Thackara (ed.), *Design After Modernism*. London: Thames and Hudson, 67–84.

Alexander, C. 1977: *A Pattern Language*. New York: Oxford University Press.

Alexander, C. 1979: *The Timeless Way of Building*. London: Oxford University Press.

Alexander, C. 1987: *A New Theory of Urban Design*. New York: Oxford University Press.

Alexander, C. 2003a: *The Nature of Order. Book 1: The Phenomenon of Life*. Berkeley: Centre for Environmental Structure.

Alexander, C. 2003b: *The Nature of Order. Book 2: The Process of Creating Life*. Berkeley: Centre for Environmental Structure.

Alexander, C. 2003c: *The Nature of Order. Book 3: A Vision of a Living World*. Berkeley: Centre for Environmental Structure.

Alexander, C. 2003d: *The Nature of Order. Book 4: The Luminous Ground*. Berkeley: Centre for Environmental Structure.

Al-Hindi, K.F. and Staddon, C. 1997: The hidden histories and geographies of neotraditional town planning: the case of seaside, Florida. *Environment and Planning D: Society and Space*, 15, 349–372.

Althusser, L. 1984: *Essays on Ideology*. London: Verso.

Althusser, L. and Balibar, E. 1970: *Reading 'Capital'*. London: New Left Books.

Amin, S. 1997: *Capitalism in the Age of Globalisation*. London: Zed Books.

Anderson, S. 1978: *On Streets*. Cambridge, MA: MIT Press.

Andrews, M. 1989: *The Search for the Picturesque: Landscape, Aesthetics and Tourism 1760–1800*. Aldershot: Gower Press.

Anscombe, G.E.M. and Wright, G.H. 1970: *Ludwig Wittgenstein: Zettel*. Berkeley: University of California Press.

Appadurai, A. 1996: *Modernity at Large: The Cultural Dimension of Globalisation*. Minneapolis: University of Minnesota Press.

Appadurai, A. 2000: Disjuncture and difference in the global cultural economy. In J. Beynon and D. Dunkerley (eds), *Globalisation: The Reader*, part B1, 93–100.

Appleyard, D. 1979: The environment as a social symbol: within a theory of environmental action and perception. *Journal of the American Planning Association*, 45(2), 143–53.

Appleyard, D. 1981: *Liveable Streets*. Berkeley: University of California Press.

Arato, A. and Gebhardt, E. (eds) 1982: *The Essential Frankfurt School Reader*. New York: Continuum Publishing Company.

Aravot, I. 2002: Back to phenomenological placemaking. *Journal of Urban Design*, 7(2), 201–12.

Ardener, S. 1981: *Women and Space: Ground Rules and Social Maps*. London: Croom Hill.

Arendt, H. 1959: *The Human Condition*. New York: Doubleday.

Arrighi, G. (1994) *The Long Twentieth Century*. London: Verso.

Ashcroft, B., Griffiths, G. and Tiffin, H. (eds) 1998: *Key Concepts in Post Colonial Studies*. London: Routledge.

Audirac, I. and Shermyen, A. 1994: An evaluation of neotraditional design's social prescription: postmodern placebo or remedy for suburban malaise? *Journal of Planning Education and Research*, 13(3), 161–73.

Bachelard, G. 1969: *The Poetics of Space*. Boston, MA: Beacon Press.

Bacon, E. 1967: *Design of Cities*. New York: Viking.

Bacon, F. and Verulam, L. 1900: *The New Atlantis*. Cambridge: Cambridge University Press; edited with introduction, notes, glossary and an excursus on Bacon's grammar by G.C. Moore Smith.

Bagguley, P. 1990: *Restructuring: Place, Class and Gender*. London: Sage.

Balaben, O. 1995: *Politics and Ideology: A Philosophical Approach*. London: Avebury Press.

Banaji, J. 1977: Modes of production in a materialist conception of history. *Capital and Class*, 2, 34–52.

Banham, R. 1960: *Theory and Design in the First Machine Age*. London: Architectural Press.

Banham, R. 1973: *Los Angeles: The Architecture of Four Ecologies*. Harmondsworth: Penguin.

Barnett, J. 1986: Architectural education: teaching urban design now that clients want it. *Architectural Record*, 174(12), 49.

Barnett, J. 1982: *An Introduction to Urban Design*. New York: Harper and Row.

Barthes, R. 1964: *Elements of Semiology*. Seuil: Paris.

Bassett, K. 1993: Urban cultural strategies and urban regeneration: a case study critique. *Environment and Planning A*, 25, 1773–88.

Bateson, G. 1972: *Steps to an Ecology of the Mind*. San Francisco: Chandler.

Baudrillard, J. 1981: *For a Critique of the Political Economy of the Sign*. St Louis: Telos Press.

Baudrillard, J. 1986: *America*. London: Verso.

Baudrillard, J. 1990: *Cool Memories I*. London: Verso.

Baudrillard, J. 1996: *Cool Memories II*. Cambridge: Polity Press.

Baudrillard, J. 1997: *Cool Memories III*. London: Verso.

Beardsley, J. 1996: The haunting of Federal Plaza. *Landscape Architecture Magazine*, May, 159.

Benevolo L. 1967: *The Origins of Modern Town Planning*. London: Routledge and Kegan Paul.

Benevolo, L. 1980: *History of Cities*. Cambridge, MA: MIT Press.

Benevolo, L. 1993: *The European City*. Oxford: Blackwell.

Benjamin, W. 1968: *Illuminations*. New York: Harcourt, Brace and World.

Benjamin, W. 1978: *Reflections*. New York: Schocken.

Benton, T. (ed.) 1996: *The Greening of Marxism*. London: Guilford.

Berke, D. 1982: *Rob Krier: Urban Projects 1968–82*. New York: Rizzoli.

Berman, M. 1982: *All That is Solid Melts into Air*. Harmondsworth: Penguin.

Bertalanffy, L.V. 1968: *A General Theory of Systems*. London: Allen Lane, The Penguin Press.

Bhabha, H.K. 1994: *The Location of Culture*. London: Routledge.

Bierman, V. (ed.) 2003: *Architectural Theory from the Renaissance to the Present*. Cologne: Taschen.

Birkstead, J. (ed.) 2000: *Landscape of Memory*. London: Spon.

Blaikie, N. 1993: *Approaches to Social Enquiry*. Oxford: Blackwell.

Blau, J. 1998: *The Shape of Culture*. Cambridge: Cambridge University Press.

Boardman, D. 1978: *The Worlds of Patrick Geddes*. London: Routledge and Kegan Paul.

Bober M. 1950: *Karl Marx Interpretation of History*. Cambridge, MA: MIT Press.

Bogard, W. 1996: *The Simulacra of Surveillance*. Cambridge: Cambridge University Press.

Bondi, L. 1990: Progress in geography and gender: feminism and difference. *Progress in Human Geography*, 14, 438–45.

Bookchin, M. 1980: *Towards an Ecological Society*. Montreal: Black Rose Books.

Bookchin, M. 1982: *The Ecology of Freedom*. Palo Alto, CA: Stanford University Press.

Borden, I. 1995: Gender and the city. In I. Borden and D. Dunster (eds), *Architecture and the Sites of History*. London: Butterworth, 317–32.

Bottomore, T. 1983: *A Dictionary of Marxist Thought*. Oxford: Blackwell.

Boudin, L. 1907: *The Theoretical System of Karl Marx, in the Light of Recent Criticism*. Chicago: Kerr.

Bourassa, S.T. 1991: *The Aesthetics of Landscape*. London: Belhaven.

Bourdieu, P. 1977: *Outline of a Theory of Practice*. Cambridge: Cambridge University Press. (Translated by R. Nice)

Bourdieu, P. 2000: *Pascalian Meditations*. Cambridge: Polity Press.

Bowlby, S. (ed.) 1984: Women and the built environment. *Built Environment*, 10 (special issue).

Bowlby, S. (ed.) 1990: Women and the designed environment. *Built Environment*, 16 (special issue).

Bowman, C.G. 1993: Street harassment and the informal ghettoisation of women. *Harvard Law Review*, 106, 517–80.

Boyer, M.C. 1983: *Dreaming the Rational City*. Cambridge, MA: MIT Press.

Boyer, M.C. 1993: The city of illusion: New York's public places. In P.L. Knox (ed.), *The Restless Urban Landscape*. Englewood Cliffs, NJ: Prentice Hall, 111–26.

Boyer, M.C. 1994: *The City of Collective Memory*. Cambridge, MA: MIT Press.

Boys, J. 1984: Is there a feminist analysis of architecture? *Built Environment*, 10(1), 25–34.

Boys, J. 1985: Women and public space. In Matrix (ed.), *Making Space: Women and the Man-made Environment*. London: Pluto Press, 37–54.

Boys, J. 1990: Women and the designed environment: dealing with the difference. *Built Environment*, 16, 249–56.

Boys, J. 1998: Beyond maps and metaphors. Rethinking the relationships between architecture and gender. In R. Ainsley (ed.), *New Frontiers of Space, Bodies and Gender*. London: Routledge, 201–17.

Breen, M. 1994: The commodity logic of contemporary culture in Australia. *Media Information Australia*, 72 (May).

Breheny, M.J. 1992: *Sustainable Development and Urban Form*. London: Pion.

Brienes, S. 1974: *The Pedestrian Revolution: Streets without Cars*. New York: Vintage.

Britton, S. 1991: Tourism, capital and place: towards a critical geography of tourism. *Environment and Planning C: Society and Space*, 9, 451–78.

Broadbent, G. 1977: A plain man's guide to the theory of signs in architecture. In K. Nesbitt (ed.), *Theorising a New Agenda for Architecture*. New York: Princeton Architectural Press, 122–40.

Broadbent, G. 1990: *Emerging Concepts in Urban Space Design*. New York: Van Nostrand.

Brown, N.O. 1959: *Life against Death*. New York: Vintage.

Bruce Briggs, B. 1979: *The New Class?* New Brunswick, NJ: Transaction Books.

Bryant, G.A. and Jary, D. (eds) 1991: *Giddens Theory of Structuration*. London: Routledge.

Brydon, L. and Chant, S. (eds.) 1989: *Women in the Third World: Gender Issues in Rural and Urban Areas*. London: Edward Elgar.

Buchanan, C. 1963: *Traffic in Towns*. London: HMSO.

Bunker, R. 1983: *Urban Consolidation: The Experience of Melbourne, Sydney and Adelaide*. Canberra: Australian Institute of Urban Studies.

Burkett, P. 1999: *Marx and Nature: A Red and Green Perspective*. New York: St Martin's Press.

Burnett, J. 1986: *A Social History of Housing*. London: Methuen.

Burnett, P. 1973: Social change, the status of women and models of city form and development. *Antipode*, 5, 57–61.

Burns, R. and Rayment-Pickard, H. 2000: *Philosophies of History*. Oxford: Blackwell.

Cabet, E. 1848: *Voyage en Icarie*. Paris: Bureau du Populaire.

Calicott, J.B. and Ames, R.T. (eds) 1989: *Nature in Asian Traditions of Thought*. Albany: State University of New York Press.

Calvino, I. 1986: *Travels in Hyper-reality*. London: Pan.

Campbell, S. 1999: Capital reconstruction and capital accumulation in Berlin: a reply to Peter Marcuse. *International Journal of Urban and Regional Research*, 23(1), 173–9.

Carmona, M. 1996: Controlling urban design: a possible renaissance? *Journal of Urban Design*, 1(1), 47–74.

Carr, E.H. 1987: *What is History?* Hardmondsworth: Penguin.

Carson, R. 1962: *Silent Spring*. London: Hamish Hamilton.

Carter, B. 1985: *Capitalism, Class Conflict and the New Middle Class*. London: Routledge and Kegan Paul.

Carter, E., Donald, J. and Squires, J. (eds) 1993: *Space and Place, Theories of Identity and Location*. London: Lawrence and Wishart.

Cartier, C. 1999: The state, property development and symbolic landscape in high rise Hong Kong. *Landscape Research*, 24(2), 185–208.

Castells, M. 1977: *The Urban Question: A Marxist Approach*. London: Edward Arnold.

Castells, M. 1978: *City, Class and Power*. London: Macmillan.

Castells, M. 1983: *The City and the Grassroots: A Cross-cultural Theory of Urban Social Movements*. Berkeley: University of California Press.

Castells, M. 1989: *The Informational City*. Oxford: Blackwell.

Castells, M. 1996: *The Rise of the Network Society*. Oxford: Blackwell.

Castells, M. 1997: *The Power of Identity*. Oxford: Blackwell.

Castells, M. 1998: *End of Millennium*. Oxford: Blackwell.

Castoriadis, C. 1987: *The Imaginary Constitution of Society*. Cambridge: Polity Press.

Castree, N. and Braun, B. 1998: *Nature at the End of the Millennium: Remaking Reality at the End of the Twentieth Century*. London: Routledge.

Castro, C. 2004: Sustainable development: mainstream and critical perspectives. *Organisation and Environment*, 17(2), 195–226.

Celik, Z., Favro, D. and Ingersoll, R. (eds.) 1994: *Streets: A Critical Perspective on Urban Space*. Berkeley: University of California Press.

Chambers, E. (ed.) 1997: *Tourism and Culture: An Applied Perspective*. Albany: State University of New York Press.

Chambers, I. 1990: *Border Dialogues: Journeys in Postmodernity*. London: Routledge.

Chermayeff, S. and Alexander, C. 1960: *Community and Privacy: Toward a New Architecture of Humanism*. New York: Doubleday.

Childe, V.G. 1935: *Man Makes Himself*. London: Watts.

Chossudofsky, M. 1998: *The Globalisation of Poverty*. Sydney: Pluto Press.

Clark, G. and Dear, M. 1984: *State Apparatus: Structures and Language of Legitimacy*. London: Allen and Unwin.

Clark, G., Forbes, D. and Francis, R. 1993: *Multiculturalism, Difference and Postmodernism*. Melbourne: Longman.

Clark, J. 2001: Contributions to the critique of political ecology. *Capital, Nature, Socialism: a Journal of Socialist Ecology*, 12(3), 29–38.

Clarke, D. (ed.) 1997: *The Cinematic City*. London: Routledge.

Cohen, G.A. 1978: *Karl Marx's Theory of History*. Oxford: Clarendon Press.

Collins, G.R. and Collins, C.C. 1986: *Camillo Sitte: The Birth of Modern City Planning*. New York: Rizzolli.

Colman, J. 1988: Urban design, a field in need of broad educational innovation. *Ekistics*, 55, 106–9.

Colomina, B. (ed.) 1992: *Sexuality and Space*. New York: Princeton Architectural Press.

Connor, S. 1996: Cultural sociology and cultural sciences. In B.S. Turner (ed.), *The Blackwell Companion to Social Theory*. Oxford: Blackwell, 340–68.

Cooke, P. 1983: *Theories of Planning and Spatial Development*. London: Hutchison.

Cooper-Marcus, C. 1996: Statement vs. design. *Landscape Architecture Magazine*, November, 24–31.

Cosgrove, D. 1984: *Social Formation and Symbolic Landscape*. Madison: University of Wisconsin Press.

Cosgrove, D. 1997: Spectacle and society: landscape as theatre in premodern and postmodern societies. In P. Groth and T. Bressi (eds), *Understanding Ordinary Landscapes*. New Haven, CT: Yale University Press, 99–110.

Cosgrove, D. and Daniels, S. (eds.) 1988: *The Iconography of Landscape: Essays on the Symbolic Representation, Design and Use of Past Environment*. Cambridge: Cambridge University Press.

Costanza, R. (ed.) 1991: *Ecological Economics: The Science and Management of Sustainability*. New York: Columbia University Press.

Craik, J. 1996: The potential and limits of cultural policy strategies. *Culture and Policy*, 7(1), 46–63.

Craik, J. 1997: The culture of tourism. In C. Rojek and J. Urry (eds), *Touring Cultures*. London: Routledge, 113–36.

Cullen, G. 1961: *Townscape*. London: Architectural Press.

Cuthbert, A.R. 1984: Conservation and capital accumulation in Hong Kong. *Third World Planning Review*, 6(1), 95–115.

Cuthbert, A.R. 1985: Architecture, society and space: the high-density question re-examined. *Progress in Planning*, 24(2), 72–160.

Cuthbert, A.R. 1987: The transition to socialism: ideology discourse and urban spatial structure. *Environment and Planning D: Society and Space*, 5, 123–50.

Cuthbert, A.R. 1989: Between two worlds: the future of the environmental professions in Hong Kong. *Habitat International*, 13(4), 137–46.

Cuthbert, A.R. 1991: A fistful of dollars: legitimation and development in Hong Kong. *International Journal of Urban and Regional Research*, 13(2), 234–49.

Cuthbert, A.R. 1992a: In search of the miraculous. *International Journal of Urban and Regional Research*, 16(2), 325–29.

Cuthbert, A.R. 1992b: For a few dollars more: urban planning and the legitimation process in Hong Kong. *International Journal of Urban and Regional Research*, 15(4), 575–93.

Cuthbert, A.R. 1994a: An agenda for planning education in the nineties (Part 1). *The Australian Planner*, 31(4), 206–11.

Cuthbert, A.R. 1994b: An agenda for planning education in the nineties (Part 2). *The Australian Planner*, 32(1), 49–55.

Cuthbert, A.R. 1995a: An interview with Manuel Castells. *Polis*, 3, 22–9.

Cuthbert, A.R. 1995b: The right to the city: surveillance, private interest and the public domain in Hong Kong. *Cities*, 12(5), 293–310.

Cuthbert, A.R. 1997: *MUDD yearbook 1997–1998*. Sydney: Faculty of the Built Environment, University of New South Wales.

Cuthbert, A.R. 2001: Going global: reflexivity and contextualism in urban design education. *Journal of Urban Design*, 6(3), 297–316.

Cuthbert, A.R. (ed.) 2003: *Designing Cities*. Oxford: Blackwell.

Cuthbert, A.R. and McKinnell, K. 1997: Ambiguous space, ambiguous rights? Corporate power and social control in Hong Kong. *Cities*, 14(5), 295–312.

Dandeneker, C. 1990: *Surveillance, Power and Modernity*. New York: St Martin's Press.

Davis, M. 1990: *The City of Quartz*. London: Verso.

Davis, M. 1998: *The Ecology of Fear*. New York: Random House.

Davis, M. 2002: *Dead Cities*. New York: The New Press.

Day, K. 1997: Better safe than sorry? Consequences of sexual assault prevention for women in urban space. *Perspectives on Social Problems*, 9, 83–101.

Day, K. 1999a: Introducing gender to the critique of privatized public space. *Journal of Urban Design*, 4(2), 155–78.

Day, K. 1999b: Embassies and sanctuaries: women's experiences of race and fear in public space. *Environment and Planning D: Society and Space*, 17, 307–28.

Dear, M. 1986: Postmodernism and planning. *Environment and Planning D: Society and Space*, 4, 367–84.

Dear, M.J. 2000: *The Postmodern Urban Condition*. Oxford: Blackwell.

Dear, M.J. 2001: *From Chicago to LA: Making Sense of Urban Theory*. London: Sage.

Debord, G. 1967: *Society of the Spectacle*. London: Practical Paradise Publications.

De Botton, A. 2002: *The Art of Travel*. London: Hamilton.

De Certeau, M. 1993: Walking in the city. In S. During (ed.), *The Cultural Studies Reader*. London: Routledge.

Delfries, A. 1924: *The Interpreter Geddes*. London: Routledge.

Delphy, C. 1988: Patriarchy, domestic mode of production, gender and class. In G. Nelson and L. Grossberg (eds), *Marxism and the Interpretation of Culture*. London: Macmillan, 259–69.

Department of the Environment, Transport and the Regions (DETR) 2001: *Training for Urban Design*. http://www.planning.detr.gov.uk/urbandesign. Accessed on 25 July 2001.

Derber, C. 1982: *Professionals as Workers: Mental Labour in Advanced Capitalism*. Boston, MA: Hall.

Derrida, J. 1976: *Of Grammatology*. Boston, MA: Johns Hopkins University Press.

Derrida, J. 1978: *Writing and Difference*. London: Routledge and Kegan Paul.

Deutsche, R. 1991: Boy's town. *Environment and Planning D: Society and Space*, 9(1), 5–30.

Deutsche, R. 1996: *Evictions: Art and Spatial Politics*. Cambridge, MA: MIT Press.

Diaz-Moore, K.D. 2001: The scientist, the social activist, the practitioner and the cleric. Pedagogical exploration towards a pedagogy of practice. *Journal of Architectural and Planning Research*, 18(1), 59–75.

Dickens, P. 1979: Marxism and architectural theory: a critique. *Environment and Planning D: Society and Space*, 6, 105–16.

Dickens, P. 1980: Social science and design theory. *Environment and Planning D: Society and Space*, 17, 353–60.

Dickens, P. 1981: The hut and the machine: towards a social theory of architecture. *Architectural Design*, 51(1), 32–45.

Dingwall, R. and Lewis, P. 1983: *The Sociology of Professions*. London: Macmillan.

Dordoy, A. and Mellor, M. 2000: Ecological socialism. *Capital, Nature, Socialism: a Journal of Socialist Ecology*, 11(3), 41–63.

Dovey, K. 1992: Corporate towers and symbolic capital. *Environment and Planning B: Planning and Design*, 1, 173–88.

Dovey, K. 1999: *Framing Places: Mediating Power in Built Form*. London: Routledge.

Dovey, K. 2001: Memory, democracy and urban space: Bangkok's path to democracy. *Journal of Urban Design*, 6(3), 265–82.

Downs, R. and Stea, P. 1978: *Maps in Minds*. New York: Harper and Row.

Doxiadis, C.A. 1963: *Architecture in Transition*. London: Oxford University Press.

Doxiadis, C.A. 1968: *Ekistics, an Introduction to the Science of Human Settlements*. New York: Oxford University Press.

Doxiadis, C.A. 1972: *Architectural Space in Ancient Greece*. Cambridge, MA: MIT Press.

Doxiadis, C.A. 1974: *Anthropolis: City for Human Development*. New York: W.W. Norton.

Doxiadis, C.A. 1975: *Building Eutopia*. Athens: Athens Publishing Centre.

Doxiadis, C.A. with Papaoanniou, J. 1974: *Ecumenopolis: the Inevitable City of the Future*. Athens: Athens Centre of Ekistics.

Droste, M. 1998: *Bauhaus 1919–1933*. Berlin: Bauhaus Archive Museum.

Drucker, S.J. and Gumbert, G. (eds) 1997: *Voices in the Street: Explorations in Gender, Media, and Public Space*. Cresskill, NJ: Hampton Press.

Duany, A. and Talen, E. (eds.) 2002: The transect. *Journal of Urban Design*, 7 (special issue).

Duncan, N. (ed.) 1996: *Bodyspace: Destabilising Geographies of Gender and Sexuality*. London: Routledge.

Duncan, O.D. 1964: Human ecology and population studies. In P.M. Hauser and O.D. Duncan (eds), *The Study of Population*. Chicago: Chicago University Press.

Dunleavy, P. 1980: *Urban Political Analysis*. London: Macmillan.

Dunleavy, P. 1981: *The Politics of Mass Housing in Britain 1945–75*. Oxford: Clarendon.

Earle, W. 1999: Bourdieu nouveau. In R. Schusterman (ed.), *Bourdieu, a Critical Reader*. Oxford: Blackwell, 175–91.

Eaton, R. 2001: *Ideal Cities*. New York: Thames and Hudson

Eco, U. 1976: *A Theory of Semiotics*. Bloomington: Indiana University Press.

Eco, U. 1984: *Semiotics and the Philosophy of Language*. London: Macmillan.

Edelman, M. 1977: *Political Language: Words that Succeed, Policies that Fail*. New York: Academic Press.

Eder, K. 1996: *The Social Construction of Nature*. London: Sage.

Edquist, H. and Bird, V. (eds) 1994: *The Culture of Landscape Architecture*. Melbourne: Edge.

Ehrlich, P.R. and Ehrlich, A.H. 1990: *The Population Explosion*. New York: Simon and Schuster.

Ehrlich, P.R. and Ehrlich, A.H. 1992: *Healing the Planet: Strategies for Resolving the Environmental Crisis*. Chipping Norton, NSW: Beatty & Sons.

Eichler, M. 1995: *Change of Plans: Towards a Non-sexist, Sustainable City*. Toronto: Garamond.

El Khoury, R. and Robbins E. 2002: *Shaping the City: Studies in Theory, History and Urban Design*. New York: Routledge.

Ellin, N. 1996: *Postmodern Urbanism*. Oxford: Blackwell.

Elliot, P. 1972: *The Sociology of the Professions*. London: Macmillan.

Elster, J. 1985: *Making Sense of Marx*. Cambridge: Cambridge University Press.

England, K. 1991: Gender relations and the spatial structure of the city. *Geoforum*, 22, 135–47.

Escobar, A. 1995: *Encountering Development. The Making and Unmaking of the Third World*. New York: St Martin's Press.

Etzioni, A. 1969: *The Semi-professionals*. New York: The Free Press.

Evans, R. 1997: *In Defense of History*. London: Granta.

Faludi, A. (ed.) 1973: *A Reader in Planning Theory*. Oxford: Pergamon.

Fanon, F. 1986: *Black Skin, White Masks*. London: Pluto Press.

Featherstone, M. 1990: *Global Culture: Nationalism, Globalisation and Modernity*. London: Sage.

Featherstone, M. 1991: *Consumer Culture and Postmodernism*. London: Sage.

Featherstone, M. 1993: Global and local cultures. In J. Bird, B. Curtis, T. Putnam, G. Robertson and L. Tickner (eds), *Making the Futures: Local Cultures, Global Change*. London: Routledge, 169–87.

Fenster, T. 1999: Space for gender: cultural roles of the forbidden and the permitted. *Environment and Planning D: Society and Space*, 17, 227–46.

Finkelpearl, T. 2000: Interview: Douglas Crimp on Tilted Arc. In T. Finkelpearl (ed.), *Dialogues in Public Art*. Cambridge, MA: MIT Press, 132–8.

Fishman, R. 1987: *Bourgeois Utopias: The Rise and Fall of Suburbia*. New York: Basic Books.

Fletcher, B. 1961: *A History of Architecture on the Comparative Method*. London: Athlone Press.

Fogelson, R.E. 1986: *Planning the Capitalist City: The Colonial Era to the 1920s*. Princeton, NJ: Princeton University Press.

Foster, J.B. 2000: *Marx's Ecology: Materialism and Nature*. New York: Monthly Review Press.

Foucault, M. 1977: *The Archaeology of Knowledge*. London: Tavistock.

Foucault, M. 1993: Of other spaces. In J. Ockman (ed.), *Architecture Culture, 1943–1968*. New York: Rizzoli, 419–26.

Fox, W. 1995: *Towards a Transpersonal Ecology*. Boston, MA: Shamballa.

Fraad, H., Resnick, S. and Wolff, R. 1994: *Bringing it All Back Home: Class, Gender and Power in the Modern Household*. London: Pluto Press.

Frampton, K. 1980: *Modern Architecture: A Critical History*. London: Thames and Hudson.

Frampton, K. 1983: Towards a critical regionalism: six points for an architecture of resistance. In H. Foster (ed.), *Postmodern Culture*. London: Pluto Press, 16–30.

Frampton, K. 1988: Place, form and cultural identity. In J. Thackara (ed.), *Design after Modernism: Beyond the Object*. London: Thames and Hudson, 51–66.

Frampton, K. 2002: *Labour, Work and Architecture*. London: Phaedon.

Frankel, B. 1983: *Beyond the State*. London: Macmillan.

Freidson, E. 1994: *Professionalism Reborn: Theory, Prophecy and Policy*. Cambridge: Polity Press.

Freud, S. 1930: Civilisation and its discontents. In J. Strachey (ed.), *The Standard Edition of the Complete Psychological Works of Sigmund Freud*. Hogarth: London, vol. 21.

Frey, H. 1999: *Designing the City: Towards a More Sustainable Urban Form*. London: Spon.

Frow, J. 1997: Class, education, culture. *Culture and Policy*, 8(1), 73–87.

Fuery, P. and Mansfield, N. 1997: *Cultural Studies and Critical Theory*. Oxford: Oxford University Press.

Fukuyama, F. 1992: *The End of History and the Last Man*. New York: The Free Press.

Fulbrook, M. 2002: *Historical Theory*. London: Routledge.

Gaffkind, F. and Morrissey, M. 1999: Sustainable cities. In F. Gafkin and M. Morrissey (eds), *City Visions: Imagining Place, Enfranchising People*. London: Pluto Press, 90–103.

Gans, H. 1962: *The Urban Villagers*. New York: The Free Press.

Gardner, C.B. 1989: Analysing gender in public places. *American Sociologist*, 20(1), 42–56.

Gardner, C.B. 1995: *Passing By: Gender and Public Harassment*. Berkeley: University of California Press.

Garreau, J. 1992: *Edge City: Life on the New Frontier*. New York: Anchor.

Geddes, P. 1915: *Cities in Evolution*. London: Williams Press.

Gehl, J. 1987: *Life between Buildings: Using Public Space*. New York: Van Nostrand Reinhold.

Gehl, J. and Gemzoe, L. 1996: *Public Space–Public Life*. Copenhagen: Danish Architectural Press.

Geist, J.F. 1985: *Arcades: The History of a Building Type*. New York: Oxford University Press.

Gibberd, F. 1953: *Town Design*. New York: Praeger.

Gibson-Graham, J.K. 1996: *The End of Capitalism (As We Knew It): A Feminist Critique of Political Economy*. Oxford: Blackwell.

Giddens, A. 1979: *Central Problems in Social Theory*. London: Macmillan.

Gilbert, G., Stevenson, D., Girardet, H. and Stren, R. 1996: *Making Cities Work*. London: Earthscan.

Gilbert, S. 1963: *James Joyce's Ulysses*. Harmondsworth: Penguin Books, 38.

Goode, T. 1992: Typological theory in the United States: the consumption of architectural 'authenticity'. *Journal of Architectural Education*, 6(1), 2–13.

Gordon, C. 1980: *Michel Foucault: Power/Knowledge*. Brighton: Harvester.

Gordon, P. and Richardson, H.W. 1990: Gasoline consumption in cities: a reply. *Journal of the American Planning Association*, 55, 342–5.

Gosling, D. 1984: Definitions of urban design. *Architectural Design*, 54 (1/2), 16–25.

Gosling, D. and Gosling, M.C. 2003: *The Evolution of American Urban Design: A Chronological Anthology*. London: Wiley–Academy.

Gosling, D. and Maitland, B. 1984: *Concepts of Urban Design*. London: Academy.

Gospodini, A. 2002: European cities in competition and the new 'uses' of urban design. *Journal of Urban Design*, 7(1), 59–74.

Gottdiener, M. 1986: Recapturing the center: a semiotic analysis of shopping malls. In M. Gottdiener and A. Lagopoulos (eds), *The City and the Sign: An Introduction to Urban Semiotics*. New York: Columbia University Press, 288–302.

Gottdiener, M. 1997: *The Theming of America: Dreams, Visions and Commercial Spaces*. Oxford: Westview Press.

Gouldner, A. 1979: *The Future of Intellectuals and the Rise of the New Class*. New York: Seabury Press.

Graham, S. (ed.) 2004: *The Cybercities Reader*. London: Routledge.

Gramsci, A. 1971: *Selections from the Prison Notebooks*. London: Lawrence and Wishart.

Gray, J. 2002: *Straw Dogs*. London. Granta.

Gregory, D. 1994: *Geographical Imaginations*. Oxford: Blackwell.

Griffiths, R. 1993: The politics of cultural policy in urban regeneration. *Policy and Politics*, 21(1), 39–46.

Grundmann, R. 1991: *Marxism and Ecology*. Oxford: Clarendon.

Guiraud, P. 1973: *La Semiologie*. Paris: Paris Presses Universitaires de France.

Gunder, M. 2001: A story from Auckland. In R. Freestone and S. Thompson (eds), *Bridging Theory and Practice in Planning Education*, Proceedings of the 2001 ANZAPS Conference held at the University of New South Wales. Kensington: University of New South Wales Press, 21–32.

Gutkind, E.A. 1964: *The International History of City Development*. New York: The Free Press of Glencoe.

Guttenberg, A.Z. 1959: A multiple land use classification system. *American Institute of Planners Journal*, 25(2), 143–50.

Habermas, J. 1976: *Legitimation Crisis*. London: Heinemann.

Habermas, J. 1987: *The Philosophical Discourse of Modernity*. Cambridge, MA: MIT Press.

Hajer, M. 1995: *The Politics of Environmental Discourse*. Oxford: Clarendon.

Hall, E.T. 1959: *The Silent Language*. New York: Doubleday.

Hall, E.T. 1969: *The Hidden Dimension*. New York: Doubleday

Hall, E.T. 1976: *Beyond Culture*. New York: Doubleday.

Hall, P. 1982: *Great Planning Disasters*. Harmondsworth: Penguin.

Hall, P. 1988: *Cities of Tomorrow*. Oxford: Blackwell.

Hall, P. 1998: *Cities in Civilisation*. London: Weidenfeld and Nicolson.

Halprin, L. 1963: *Cities*. New York: Reinhold.

Halprin, L. 1969: *The RSVP Cycles: Creative Processes in the Human Environment*. New York: Braziller.

Hamnett, S. 1988: The current interest in urban design: implications for planning education in Australia. *Ekistics*, 55, 101–5.

Hanson, S and Johnson, I. 1985: Gender difference in work length trip: explanations and implications. *Urban Geography*, 6, 193–219.

Hardt, M. and Negri, A. 2000: *Empire*. Cambridge, MA: Harvard University Press.

Hargrove, E.C. 1989: *Foundations of Environmental Ethics*. Englewood Cliffs, NJ: Prentice-Hall.

Harvey, D. 1973: *Explanation in Geography*. London: Edward Arnold.

Harvey, D. 1979a: Monument and myth. *Annals of the Association of American Geographers*, 68(3), 362–81.

Harvey, D. 1979b: *Social Justice and the City*. London: Edward Arnold.

Harvey, D. 1982: *The Limits to Capital*. Oxford: Blackwell.

Harvey, D. 1985: *The Urbanization of Capital*. Oxford: Blackwell.

Harvey, D. 1989: *The Condition of Postmodernity*. Baltimore, MD: Johns Hopkins University Press.

Harvey, D. 1993: From place to space and back again: reflections on the condition of postmodernity. In J. Bird, B. Curtis, T. Putnam, T. Robertson and G.L. Tickner (eds), *Making the Futures: Local Cultures and Global Change*. London: Routledge, 3–29.

Harvey, D. 1996: *Justice, Nature and the Geography of Difference*. Oxford: Blackwell.

Harvey, D. 2000: *Spaces of Hope*. Edinburgh: Edinburgh University Press.

Harvey, D. 2003: *The New Imperialism*. Oxford: Oxford University Press.

Haug, W.F. 1986: *A Critique of Commodity Aesthetics*. Oxford: Polity Press.

Haug, W.F. 1987: *Commodity Aesthetics, Ideology and Culture*. New York: International General.

Haughton, G. and Hunter, C. 1994: *Sustainable Cities*. London: Jessica Kingsley.

Hawken, P., Lovins, A. and Lovins, H. 1999: *Natural Capitalism*. London: Earthscan.

Hawley, A. 1950: *Human Ecology*. New York: Ronald Press.

Hawley, A. 1956: *The Changing Shape of Metropolitan America*. Glencoe: The Free Press.

Hayden, D. 1976: *Seven American Utopias: The Architecture of Communitarian Socialism 1790–1975*. Cambridge, MA: MIT Press.

Hayden, D. 1980: What would a non-sexist city be like? Speculations on housing, urban design and human work. In C. Stimpson, E. Dixler, M. Nelson and K. Yatrakis (eds), *Women and the American City*. Chicago: Chicago University Press, 266–81.

Hayden, D. 1981: *The Grand Domestic Revolution: A History of Feminist Designs for American Homes, Neighborhoods and Cities*. Cambridge, MA: MIT Press.

Hayden, D. 1995: *The Power of Place: Urban Landscapes as Public History*. Cambridge, MA: MIT Press.

Hays, K.M. (ed.) 1998: *Architectural Theory Since 1968*. Cambridge, MA: MIT Press.

Hays, M.K. 1992: *Modernism and the Posthumanist Subject: The Architecture of Hannes Meyer and Ludwig Hilberseimer*. Cambridge, MA: MIT Press.

Hearn, J. 1987: *The Gender of Oppression: Men, Masculinity and the Critique of Marxism*. New York: St Martin's Press.

Heide, H. and Wijnbelt, D. 1996: To know and to make: the link between research and urban design. *Journal of Urban Design*, 1(1), 75–90.

Heidegger, M. 1962: *Being and Time*. Evanston, IL: Northwestern University Press.

Held, D. 1980: *Introduction to Critical Theory: Horkheimer to Habermas*. Berkeley: University of California Press.

Heller, A. 1993: *A Philosophy of History in Fragments*. Oxford. Blackwell.

Hester, R.T., Blazej, N.J. and Moore, I.S. 1999: Whose wild? Resolving cultural and biological diversity conflicts in urban wilderness. *Landscape Journal*, 18(2), 137–46.

Hilberseimer, L. 1955: *The Nature of Cities*. Chicago: Paul Theobald.

Hillier, W. 1973: In defence of space. *RIBA Journal*, 80(11), 539–44.

Hillier, W. 1989: The architecture of the urban object. *Ekistics*, 334, 5–21.

Hillier, W. 1996: *Space is the Machine*. Cambridge: Cambridge University Press.

Hillier, W. and Hanson, J. 1984: *The Social Logic of Space*. Cambridge: Cambridge University Press.

Hobsbawm, E.J. 1986: Labour and human rights. In J. Donald and S. Hall (eds), *Politics and Ideology*. Milton Keynes: Open University Press, 77–87.

Hobsbawm, E. 1997: *On History*. London: Weidenfeld and Nicolson.

Hoggart, R. 1958: *The Uses of Literacy*. London: Penguin.

Hollahan, J. 1982: *Environmental Psychology*. New York: Random House.

Hoogveldt, A. 1982: *The Third World in Global Development*. London: Macmillan.

Hopkins, P.D. 1998: *Sex/Machine*. Bloomington: Indiana University Press.

Horkheimer, M. and Adorno, T. 1972: *The Dialectic of Enlightenment*. New York: Seabury Press. (Original 1944)

Hough, M. 1984: *City Form and Natural Process: Towards a New Urban Vernacular*. London: Croom Helm.

Howard, E. 1946: *Garden Cities of Tomorrow*. London: Faber and Faber.

Huet, B. 2000: Formalism–realism. In K.M. Hays (ed.), *Architecture Theory Since 1968*. Cambridge, MA: MIT Press, 149–73.

Hunt, J.D. 1992: *Gardens and the Picturesque*. Cambridge, MA: MIT Press.

Husserl, E. 1931: *Ideas: General Introduction to Pure Phenomenology*. New York: Macmillan.

Huxley, A. 1960: *Brave New World*. London: Chatto and Windus.

Huxley, A. 1962: *Island*. London: Chatto and Windus.

Huxley, M. 1988: Feminist urban theory: gender, class and the built environment. *Transition*, (winter), 39–43.

Huxley, M. 1997: 'Necessary but by no means sufficient'. Spatial political economy, town planning and the possibility of better cities: a commentary on Brian McLoughlin's last paper. *European Planning Studies*, 5(6), 741–51.

Illich, I. 1977: *Disabling Professions*. London: Marion Boyars.

Inam, A. 2002: Meaningful urban design: teleological, catalytic, relevant. *Journal of Urban Design*, 7(1), 35–58.

Irvine, S. and Ponton, A. 1988: *A Green Manifesto: Policies for a Green Future*. London: Optima.

Jacobs, J. 1961: *The Death and Life of Great American Cities*. New York: Random House.

Jacobs, J.M. 1993: The city unbound: qualitative approaches to the city. *Urban Studies*, 30(4/5), 827–48.

Jameson, F. 1991: *Postmodernism, or the Cultural Logic of Late Capitalism*. Durham, NC: Duke University Press.

Jayasuriya, L. 1990: Rethinking Australian multiculturalism: towards a new paradigm. *Australian Quarterly*, 26(62), 50–63.

Jencks, C. 1993: *Heteropolis*. London: Academy.

Jencks, C. 1977: *The Language of Post-modern Architecture*. New York: Rizzoli.

Jencks, C. and Baird, G. (eds) 1969: *Meaning in Architecture*. London: Crescent Press.

Jencks, C. and Valentine, M. 1987: The architecture of democracy: the hidden tradition. *Architectural Design*, 57(9/10), 8–25.

Jenkins, K. 1991: *Rethinking History*. London: Routledge.

Jenks, M. and Burgess, R. (eds) 2000: *Compact Cities: Sustainable Urban Form for Developing Countries*. London: Spon.

Jenks, M., Burton, E. and Williams, K. (eds) 1996: *The Compact City: A Sustainable Urban Form?* London: Spon.

Jessop, B. 1977: *The Capitalist State*. Oxford: Robertson.

Jiven, J. and Larkham, P.J. 2003: Sense of place, authenticity and character: a commentary. *Journal of Urban Design*, 8(1), 67–82.

Johnson, N. 1995: Cast in stone: monuments, geography and nationalism. *Environment and Planning D: Society and Space*, 13, 51–65.

Johnson, T.J. 1972: *Professions and Power*. London: Macmillan.

Joyce, J. 1993: *Ulysses*. Oxford, New York: Oxford University Press.

Kallus, R. 2001: From abstract to concrete: subjective reading of urban space. *Journal of Urban Design*, 6(2), 129–50.

Katz, P. 1994: *The New Urbanism*. New York: McGraw-Hill.

Kayden, J.S. 2000: *Privately Owned Public Space*. New York: Wiley.

Keller, S. (ed.) 1981: *Building for Women*. Lexington, MA: Lexington Books.

Kellner, D. 1984: *Herbert Marcuse and the Crisis of Marxism*. London: Macmillan.

Kiernan, M.J. 1983: Ideology, politics and planning: reflections on the theory and practice of urban planning. *Environment and Planning B: Planning and Design*, 10, 71–87.

Kimmel, M.S. 2000: *The Gendered Society*. New York: Oxford.

Kincheloe, J. and Steinberg, R. 1997: *Changing Multiculturalism*. Bristol: Open University Press.

King, A.D. 1984: The social production of building form: theory and research. *Environment and Planning D: Society and Space*, 2, 367–492.

King R.J. 1988: Urban design in capitalist society. *Environment and Planning D: Society and Space*, 6, 445–74.

King, R.J. 1996: *Emancipating Space: Geography, Architecture and Urban Design*. New York: Guilford Press.

Kirby, A.M. 1983: On society without space: a critique of Saunder's nonspatial urban sociology. *Environment and Planning D: Society and Space*, 1, 226–33.

Kitchen, P. 1975: *A Most Unsettling Person*. London: Gollancz.

Knesl, J.A. 1984: The powers of architecture. *Environment and Planning D: Society and Space*, 1, 3–22.

Knopp, L. 1990: Some theoretical implications of gay involvement in an urban land market. *Political Geography Quarterly*, 9, 337–52.

Knopp, L. 1992: Sexuality and the spatial dynamics of capitalism. *Environment and Planning D: Society and Space*, 10, 651–69.

Knopp, L. 1995: Sexuality and urban space: a framework for analysis. In D. Bell and G. Valentine (eds.), *Mapping Desire: Geographies of Sexualities*. London: Routledge, 149–61.

Knox, P.L. 1982: The social production of the built environment. *Ekistics*, 295, July/August, 23–37.

Korilos, T.S. 1979: Sociology of architecture: an emerging perspective. *Ekistics*, 12(15), 24–34.

Korn, A. 1953: *History Builds the Town*. [Publisher unknown]

Kostoff, S. 1991: *The City Shaped*. London: Thames and Hudson.

Kostoff, S. 1992: *The City Assembled*. London. Thames and Hudson.

Krampen, M.K. 1979: *Meaning in the Urban Environment*. London: Pion.

Krier, L. 1975: *The Reconstruction of the City*. Brussels: Archives D'Architecture Moderne.

Krier, R. 1979a. Typological and morphological elements of the concept of urban space. *Architectural Design*, 49(1), 1–8.

Krier, R. 1979b: *Urban Space*. New York: Rizzoli.

Krier, R. 1988: *Architectural Composition*. New York: Rizzoli.

Kruft, H.W. 1994: *A History of Architectural Theory: From Vitruvius to the Present*. London: Zwemmer.

Laclau, E. and Mouffe, C. 1985: *Hegemony and Socialist Strategy*. London: Verso.

Lang, J. 1994: *Urban Design: The American Experience*. New York: Van Nostrand.

Larson, M.S. 1977: *The Rise of Professionalism*. Berkeley: University of California Press.

Lash, S. and Urry, J. 1994: *Economies of Signs and Space*. London: Sage.

Lauria, M. and Knopp, L. 1985: Towards an analysis of the role of gay communities in the urban renaissance. *Urban Geography*, 6, 152–69.

Leach, R. 1993: *Political Ideologies*. Melbourne: Macmillan.

Lechte, J. 1994: *Fifty Key Contemporary Thinkers*. London: Routledge.

Lefebvre, H. 1968: *The Right to the City*. Paris: Anthropos.

Lefebvre, H. 1970: *La Révolution Urbaine*. Paris: Gallimard.

Lefebvre, H. 1991: *The Production of Space*. Oxford: Blackwell.

Lehan, R. 1998: *The City in Literature*. Berkeley: University of California Press.

Lévi-Strauss, C. 1962: *Totemism*. Harmondsworth, Middlesex: Penguin.

Lévi-Strauss, C. 1978: *Structural Anthropology*. London: Allen Lane.

Lewis, J. 2002: *Cultural Studies: The Basics*. London: Sage.

Ley, D. and Olds, K. 1988: Landscape as spectacle: worlds fairs and the culture of heroic consumption. *Environment and Planning D: Society and Space*, 6, 191–212.

Liggett, H. and Perry, D. 1995: *Spatial Practices*. London: Sage.

Little, J., Peake, L. and Richardson, P. 1988: *Women in Cities: Gender and the Urban Environment*. London: Macmillan.

Lofland, L. 1984: Women and urban public space. *Women and Environments*, 6(2), 12–14.

Longhurst, R. 2002: Geography and gender: a 'critical' time? *Progress in Human Geography*, 26(4), 544–52.

Lorenz, K. 1963: *Man and Aggression*. Oxford: Oxford University Press.

Lorenz, K. 1981: *The Foundation of Ethology*. New York: Springer-Verlag.

Lovejoy, D. 1979: *Land Use and Landscape Planning*. Glasgow: Leonard Hill.

Lovell, T. 1996: Feminist social theory. In B.S. Turner (ed.), *Social Theory*. Oxford: Blackwell, 307–39.

Luke, T.W. 1988: The dreams of deep ecology. *Telos*, 76, 65–92.

Lukes, S. 1986: *Power*. Oxford: Blackwell.

Lundahl, G. and Sangregorio, I.L. 1992: *Kemton Kollektivhus, an idé förverkligas (Fifteen Collective Houses, an Idea put into Practice)*. Stockholm: Council for Building Research.

Lynch, K. 1960: *The Image of the City*. Cambridge, MA: MIT Press.

Lynch, K. 1971: *Site Planning*. Cambridge, MA: MIT Press.

Lynch, K. 1981: *A Theory of Good City Form*. Cambridge, MA: MIT Press.

Lyon, D. 2002: Editorial. Surveillance studies: understanding visibility, mobility and the phenetic fix. *Surveillance and Society*, 1(1), 1–7.

Lyotard, J.P. 1985: *The Postmodern Condition*. Minneapolis: University of Minnesota Press.

McAuslan, P. 1980: *The Ideologies of Planning Law*. Oxford: Pergamon Press.

MacCannell, D. 1989: *The Tourist: A New Theory of the Leisure Class*. London: Macmillan.

McCarthy, T. 1982: *The Critical Theory of Jurgen Habermas*. Cambridge, MA: MIT Press.

McDowell, L. 1983: Towards an understanding of the gender division of urban space. *Environment and Planning D: Society and Space*, 1, 59–72.

McDowell, L. 1989: Women, gender and the organization of space. In D. Gregory and R. Walford (eds), *Horizons in Human Geography*. London: Macmillan, 136–51.

McDowell, L. 1993: Space, place and gender relations. Part 1: feminist empiricism and the geography of social relations. *Progress in Human Geography*, 17(2), 157–79.

McHarg, I. 1969: *Design with Nature*. Garden City, NY: Natural History Press.

McKenzie, R. 1967: The ecological approach to the study of the human community. In R. Park and E. Burgess (eds), *The City*. Chicago: University of Chicago Press.

MacKenzie, S. 1988: Building women, building cities: towards gender sensitive theory in environmental disciplines. In C. Andrew and B. Moore Milroy (eds), *Life Spaces: Gender, Household, Employment*. Vancouver: University of British Columbia Press.

MacKenzie, S. 1989: Women in the city. In R. Peet and N. Thrift (eds), *New Models in Geography: The Political Economy Perspective*. London: Unwin Hyman, 109–26.

McLoughlin, J.B. 1970: *Urban and Regional Planning: A Systems Approach*. London: Faber and Faber.

McLoughlin, J.B. 1991: Urban consolidation and urban sprawl: a question of density. *Urban Policy and Research*, 9(3), 148–56.

McLoughlin, J.B. 1992: *Shaping Melbourne's Future*. Melbourne: Cambridge University Press.

McLoughlin, J.B. 1994: Centre or periphery? Town planning and spatial political economy. *Environment and Planning A: Society and Space*, 26, 1111–22.

McLuhan, M. 1964: *Understanding Media*. London: Routledge and Kegan Paul.

Madanipour, A. 1996a: *Design of Urban Space*. Chichester: John Wiley.

Madanipour, A. 1996b: Urban design and the dilemmas of space. *Environment and Planning D: Society and Space*, 14, 331–55.

Madanipour, A. 1999: Why are the design and development of public spaces significant for cities? *Environment and Planning B: Planning and Design*, 26(6), 879–91.

March, L. and Steadman, P. 1971: *The Geometry of Environment*. London: Methuen.

Marco, G., Hollingworth, M. and Durham, W. (eds) 1987: *Silent Spring Revisited*. Washington, DC: American Chemical Society.

Marcuse, H. 1964: *One Dimensional Man*. Boston, MA: Beacon Press.

Marcuse, H. 1968: *Negations*. Boston, MA: Beacon Press.

Marcuse, H. 1985: *Eros and Civilisation*. Boston, MA: Beacon Press.

Marcuse, P. 1998: Reflections on Berlin: the meaning of construction and the construction of meaning. *International Journal of Urban and Regional Research*, 22(2), 331–8.

Marshall, N.G. 2000: *Into the Third Millennium: Neocorporatism, the State and the Urban Planning Profession*. Doctoral thesis, Faculty of the Built Environment, University of New South Wales.

Martinez Alier, J. 2003: Scale, environmental justice and unsustainable cities. *Capital, Nature, Socialism: a Journal of Socialist Ecology*, 14(4), 43–57.

Marx, K. 1959: *Capital, Volume 3: A Critique of Political Economy*. London: Lawrence and Wishart. (Original 1894.)

Marx, K. 1981: *The German Ideology*. New York: International Publishers.

Massey, D. 1991: Flexible sexism. *Environment and Planning D: Society and Space*, 9, 5–31.

Massey, D. 1994: *Space, Place and Gender*. Cambridge: Polity Press.

Maxwell, R. 1977: Tafuri, Culot and Krier, the role of ideology. *Architectural Design*, 3(9), 23–32.

Maynard, M. 1990: The re-shaping of sociology: trends in the study of gender. *Sociology*, 24, 269–90.

Meadows, D. 1972: *The Limits to Growth*. New York: Universe Books.

Meller, H.E. 1994: *Patrick Geddes, Social Evolutionary and City Planner*. London: Routledge.

Mellor, M. 1999: *Feminism and Ecology*. New York: New York University Press.

Merchant, C. 1989: *The Death of Nature: Women, Ecology, and the Scientific Revolution*. New York: Harper and Row.

Merleau-Ponty, M. 1962: *Phenomenology of Perception*. London: Routledge.

Merrifield, A. 2000: Flexible Marxism and the metropolis. In G. Bridge and S. Watson (eds), *A Companion to the City*. Oxford: Blackwell, chapter 12.

Mies, M. and Shiva, V. 1993: *Ecofeminism*. London: Zed Books.

Miles, M. and Hall, T. (eds) 2000: *The City Cultures Reader*. London: Routledge.

Miller, K. 2001: The politics of defining public space. Obtainable from the author, Department of Sociology, University of Minnesota, Minneapolis, MN, USA.

Minca, C. (ed.) 2001: *Postmodern Geography*. Oxford: Blackwell.

Mingione, E. 1981: *Social Conflict and the City*. Oxford: Blackwell.

Mitchel, W.J. 1995: *City of Bits: Place, Space and the Infobahn*. Cambridge, MA: MIT Press.

Mitchell, D. 1996: Introduction: public space and the city. *Urban Geography*, 17(2), 127–31.

Moholy-Nagy, S. 1968: *The Matrix of Man*. London: Pall Mall.

Molotch, H. 1996: LA as design product: how art works in a regional economy. In A.J. Scott and E.W. Soja (eds.), *The City: Los Angeles and Urban Theory at the End of the Twentieth Century*. Berkeley: University of California Press, 225–75.

Momsen, J. and Townsend, J. (eds) 1987: *Geography and Gender in the Third World*. London: Hutchison.

Morgan, J. 2003: Getting the story right. *Sydney Morning Herald*, 19/20 July, 23.

Morris, A.E.J. 1979: *History of Urban Form: Before the Industrial Revolutions*. London: Godwin.

Morris, W. 1891: *News from Nowhere*. London: Longmans Green.

Moudon, A.V. 1992: A Catholic approach to organizing what urban designers should know. *Journal of Planning Literature*, 6(4), 331–49.

Moughtin, C. 1992: *Urban Design: Street and Square*. Oxford: Butterworth.

Moughtin, J.C. 1996: *Urban Design: Green Dimensions*. London: Architectural Press.

Mumford, L. 1922: *The Story of Utopias*. New York: Viking Press.

Mumford, L. 1938: *The Culture of Cities*. London: Macmillan.

Mumford, L. 1961: *The City in History*. New York: Harcourt, Brace, Jovanovich.

Mumford, L. 1968: *The Urban Prospect*. London: Secker & Warburg.

Murphy, P. and Watson, S. 1997: *Surface City*. Sydney: Pluto Press.

Naess, A. 1986: The deep ecological movement: some philosophical aspects. *Philosophical Enquiry*, 8, 10–31.

Naess, A. 1989: *Ecology, Community and Lifestyle: Outline of an Ecosophy*. Cambridge: Cambridge University Press.

Namaste, K. 1996: Genderbashing: sexuality, gender and the regulation of public space. *Environment and Planning D: Society and Space*, 14, 221–40.

Nash, R.F. 1989: *The Rights of Nature: a History of Environmental Ethics*. Madison: University of Wisconsin Press.

Newman, O. 1971: *Crime Prevention through Architectural Design*. Washington, DC: US Department of Justice, Law Enforcement Assistance Administration.

Newman, O. 1972: *Defensible Space: People and Design in the Violent City*. New York: Macmillan.

Newman, O. 1973: *Defensible Space*. London: Architectural Press.

Newman, O. 1976: *Design Guidelines for Creating Defensible Space*. Washington, DC: US Justice Department.

Newman, O. 1980: *Community of Interest*. Garden City, NY: Anchor Press.

Newman, O. 1995: Defensible space: a new physical planning tool for urban revitalization. *Journal of the American Planning Association*, 61(2), 149–55.

Newman, P. 1994: Urban design, transportation and the greenhouse effect. In R. Samuels and D. Prasad (eds), *Global Warming and the Built Environment*. London: E. and F.N. Spon, 69–84.

Newman, P. and Kenworthy, J. 1999: *Sustainability and Cities*. Washington, DC: Island Press.

Norberg-Schulz, C. 1964: *Intentions in Architecture*. Oslo: Universitetsforlaget.

Norberg-Schulz, C. 1971: *Existence, Space and Architecture*. London: Studio Vista.

Norberg-Schulz, C. 1976: The phenomenon of place. *Architecture Association Quarterly*, 8(4), 3–10.

Norberg-Schulz, C. 1979: *Genius Loci: Towards a Phenomenology of Architecture*. New York: Rizzoli.

Nowell-Smith, G. 2001: Cities: real and imagined. In M. Shield and T. Fitzmaurice (eds), *Cinema and the City*. Oxford: Blackwell, 99–108.

Ockman, J. (ed.) 1993: *Architecture Culture*. New York: Rizzoli.

O'Connor, M. 1996: The second contradiction of capitalism. In T. Benton (ed.), *The Greening of Marxism*. New York: Guilford, 197–221.

Odum, E.P. 1971: *Fundamentals of Ecology*. Philadelphia: Saunders.

Oliver, P. 1977: *Shelter, Sign and Symbol*. Woodstock, NJ: Overlook Press.

Olsen, D.J. 1986: *The City as a Work of Art*. New Haven, CT: Yale University Press.

O'Riordan, T. 1976: *Environmentalism*. London: Pion.

Orwell, G. 1992: *Nineteen Eighty Four*. New York: Alfred A. Knopf. (Original 1948.)

Ostergaard, L. (ed.) 1992: *Gender and Development*. London: Routledge.

Ouf, A.M.S. 2001: Authenticity and the sense of place in urban design. *Journal of Urban Design*, 6(1), 73–86.

Outhwaite, W. 1994: *Habermas: A Critical Introduction*. Cambridge: Polity Press.

Padovan, R. 1999: *Proportion*. London and New York: Spon.

Pahl, R. 1970: *Patterns of Urban Life*. London: Longmans.

Pahl, R. 1975: *Whose City?* Harmondsworth: Penguin.

Pahl, R. 1983: Whatever happened to urban sociology? Critical reflections on social theory and the urban question. *Environment and Planning D*, 1, 217–39.

Pain, R. 1991: Space, sexual violence and social control: integrating geographical and feminist analyses of women's fear of crime. *Progress in Human Geography*, 15, 415–31.

Palladio, A. 1965: *The Four Books of Architecture*. New York: Dover. (Original 1570.)

Panayotakis, C. 2003: Capitalism's 'dialectic of scarcity' and the emancipatory project. *Capital, Nature, Socialism: a Journal of Socialist Ecology*, 14(1), 88–94.

Parker, J. 2000: *Total Surveillance*. London: Piatkus Press.

Peet, R. and Watts, M. (eds.) 1996: *Liberation Ecologies: Environment, Development, Social Movements*. London: Routledge.

Perez de Arce, R. 1978: Urban transformations. *The Architectural Design*, 4, 26–32.

Perez-Gomez, A. 1983: *Architecture and the Crisis of Modern Science*. Cambridge, MA: MIT Press.

Perez-Gomez, A. 2000: Introduction to architecture and the crisis of modern science. In K.M. Hays (ed.), *Architecture Theory Since 1968*. Cambridge, MA: MIT Press, 462–75.

Perrin, C. 1970: *With Man in Mind*. Cambridge, MA: MIT Press.

Petersen, S. 1979: Urban design tactics. *Architectural Design*, 49, 3–4.

Piaget, J. 1955: *The Child's Construction of Reality*. London: Routledge and Kegan Paul. Translated from the French by Margaret Cook.

Piaget, J. 1971: *Structuralism*. London: Routledge and Kegan Paul.

Pile, S. 1996: *The Body and the City: Psychoanalysis, Space and Subjectivity*. London: Routledge.

Platt, R.H., Rowentree, R.A. and Muick, P.C. 1994: *The Ecological City: Preserving and Restoring Urban Biodiversity*. Amherst: University of Massachusetts Press.

Polanyi, K. 1952: *The Great Transformation*. New York: Octagon Books.

Pollock, G. 2000: Excerpts from 'modernity and the spaces of femininity'. In J. Rendell, B. Penner and I. Borden (eds), *Gender, Space and Architecture*. London: Routledge, 154–67.

Popper, K. 1986: *The Poverty of Historicism*. London: Ark.

Poster, M. 1984: *Foucault, Marxism and Critique*. Cambridge: Polity Press.

Poster, M. 1990: *The Mode of Information: Post Structuralism and Social Content*. Cambridge: Polity Press.

Preteceille, E. 1982: Urban planning: the contradictions of capitalist urbanisation. In C. Paris (ed.), *Critical Readings in Planning Theory*. Oxford: Pergamon, 129–46.

Preziosi, M. 1979: *Architecture, Language and Meaning*. The Hague: Mouton.

Pritchard, A. and Morgan, N.J. 2000: Constructing tourism landscapes: gender, sexuality, space. *Tourism Geographies*, 2(2), 115–39.

Proshansky, H.M., Ittelson, W.H. and Rivlin, L.G. 1970: *Environmental Psychology: Man and His Physical Setting*. New York: Holt, Rinehart and Winston.

Punter, J. 1996: Urban design theory in planning practice: the British perspective. *Built Environment*, 22(4), 263–77.

Quatremère de Quincy 1999: *The True, the Fictive and the Real: The Historical Dictionary of Quatremère De Quincy*. London: Papadakis.

Randall, T. 2002: *Sustainable Urban Design*. London: Spon.

Rapoport, A. 1969: *House, Form and Culture*. Englewood Cliffs, NJ: Prentice-Hall.

Rapoport, A. 1977: *The Human Aspects of Urban Form*. Oxford: Pergamon.

Rapoport, A. 1982: *The Meaning of the Built Environment*. Beverley Hills: Sage.

Ravetz, J. 2000: Urban form and the sustainability of urban systems: theory and practice in a northern conurbation. In K. Williams, E. Burton and M. Jenks (eds), *Achieving Sustainable Urban Form*. London: Spon, 215–28.

Rawls, J. 1999: *A Theory of Justice*. Oxford: Oxford University Press.

Regan, T. 1983: *The Case for Animal Rights*. Berkeley: University of California Press.

Regulska, J. 1991: Changing gender relations in urban space. *Geoforum*, 22 (special issue).

Relph, E. 1976: *Place and Placelessness*. London: Pion.

Relph, E. 1987: *Modern Urban Landscapes*. London: Croom Helm.

Rendell, J., Penner, B. and Borden, I. (eds.) 2000: *Gender, Space and Architecture: An Interdisciplinary Introduction*. London: Routledge.

Reolofs, J. 2000: Eco-cities and green politics. *Capital, Nature, Socialism: A Journal of Socialist Ecology*, 11(1), 139–49.

Reps, J.W. 1965: *The Making of Urban America: A History of City Planning in the United States*. Princeton, NJ: Princeton University Press.

Rizdoff, M. 1994: A feminist analysis of gender and residential zoning in the United States. In I. Altman and A. Churchman (eds), *Women and the Environment*. New York: Plenum, 255–79.

Roberts, M. 1998: Urban design, gender and the future of cities. *Journal of Urban Design*, 3(2), 133–5.

Rojek, C. and Urry, J. 1997: *Touring Cultures: Transformations of Travel and Theory*. London: Routledge.

Roseneau, H. 1983: *The Ideal City*. London: Methuen.

Rothenberg, D. 1993: *Is it Too Painful to Think?* Minneapolis: University of Minnesota Press.

Rothman, H. 2003: *Neon Metropolis*. London: Routledge.

Rowe, C. and Koetter, F. 1978: *Collage City*. Cambridge, MA: MIT Press.

Rowley, A. 1994: Definitions of urban design. *Planning Practice and Research*, 9(3), 179–97.

Rubin, B. 1979: Aesthetic ideology and urban design. *Annals of the Association of American Geographers*, 69(3), 339–61.

Ruddick, S. 1996: Constructing difference in public spaces: race, class and gender as interlocking systems. *Urban Geography*, 17(2), 132–51.

Rudofsky, B. 1964: *Architecture without Architects: An Introduction to Nonpedigreed Architecture*. New York: Moma.

Rudofsky, B. 1969: *Streets for People*. Garden City, NY: Doubleday.

Ryan, M. 1982: *Marxism and Deconstruction*. Baltimore, MD: Johns Hopkins University Press.

Rykwert, J. 2000: *The Seduction of Place: The City in the Twenty-First Century*. London: Weidenfeld and Nicolson.

Sachs, W. 1993: *Global Ecology*. London: Zed Books.

Saegert, S. 1980: Masculine cities and feminine suburbs: polarised ideas, contradictory realities. *Signs*, 5(3), 93–108.

Said, E. 1978: *Orientalism*. London: Penguin.

Said, E. 1994: *Culture and Imperialism*. New York: Vintage.

Salingaros, N. 2004: 'The Nature of Order': Christopher Alexander and the New Architecture. Book review and interview of Christopher Alexander. http://www.math.utsa.edu/sphere /salingar/nature-interview.html. Accessed on 22 July 2001.

Samuels, R. and Prasad, D. (eds.) 1994: *Global Warming and the Built Environment*. London: E. and F.N. Spon.

Sandercock, L. 1990: *Property, Politics and Urban Planning*. New Brunswick, NJ: Transaction Press.

Sandercock, L. and Forsyth, A. 1992: A gender agenda: new directions for planning theory. *APA Journal*, 49(winter), 49–59.

Sapir, E. 1921: *Language*. New York: Harcourt, Brace, and World.

Sartre, J.P. 1992: *Being and Nothingness*. New York: Washington Square Press.

Sassen, S. 1991: *The Global City*. Princeton, NJ: Princeton University Press.

Saul, J.R. 1997: *The Unconscious Civilisation*. Ringwood: Penguin.

Saunders, P. 1979: *Urban Politics: A Sociological Interpretation*. London: Hutchison.

Saunders, P. 1986: *Social Theory and the Urban Question*. London: Routledge.

Sayer, A. 1976: A critique of urban modelling. *Progress in Planning*, 6(3), 187–254.

Sayer, A. 1984: *Method in Social Science: A Realist Approach*. London: Hutchison.

Schmitter, P. 1982: Reflections on where the theory of neocorporatism has gone and where the praxis of neocorporatism may be going. In P. Lehmbruch and P.C. Schmitter (eds), *Trends towards Corporatist Intermediation*. London: Sage, 55–73.

Schorske, C.E. 1981: *Fin-de-Siècle Vienna*. New York: Random House.

Schumacher, E.F. 1973: *Small is Beautiful: Economics as if People Mattered*. New York: Harper and Row.

Schurch, T.W. 1999: Reconsidering urban design: thoughts about its definition and status as a field or profession. *Journal of Urban Design*, 4(1), 5–28.

Schusterman, R. 1999: *Bourdieu: A Critical Reader*. Oxford: Blackwell.

Scott, A.J. 1980: *The Urban Land Nexus and the State*. London: Pion.

Scott, A.J. 1988: *Metropolis*. Los Angeles: University of California Press.

Scott, A.J. 1997: The cultural economy of cities. *International Journal of Urban and Regional Research*, 21(2), 323–39.

Scott, A.J. 2000a: *The Cultural Economy of Cities*. London: Sage.

Scott, A.J. 2000b: Globalisation and (late-/post-) modernity. In J. Beynon and D. Dunkerley (eds), *Globalisation: The Reader*. London: Athlone, 55–7.

Scott, A.J. and Roweis, S.T. 1977: Urban planning in theory and practice: a reappraisal. *Environment and Planning A: Society and Space*, 9, 1097–1119.

Scruton, R. 1974: *Art and Imagination*. London: Methuen.

Scruton, R. 1979: *The Aesthetics of Architecture*. London: Methuen.

Seife, C. 2000: *Zero: The Biography of a Dangerous Idea*. London: Souvenir Press.

Serlio, S. 1982: *Five Books on Architecture*. New York: Dover. (Original 1611.)

Shane, G. 1976: Contextualism. *The Architectural Design*, June/July, 11.

Sharpe, D. (ed.) 1978: *The Rationalists*. London: Architectural Press.

Shiel, M. and Fitzmaurice, T. (eds) 2001: *Cinema and the City*. Oxford: Blackwell.

Shiel, M. and Fitzmaurice, T. (eds) 2003: *Screening the City*. London: Verso.

Simmel, G. 1990: *The Philosophy of Money*. London: Routledge. (Original 1900.)

Simon, H. 1969: *The Sciences of the Artificial*. Cambridge, MA: MIT Press.

Sitte, C. 1945: *The Art of Building Cities: City Building According to its Artistic Fundamentals*. New York: Reinhold. (Original 1889.)

Skinner, B.F. 1962: *Walden Two*. New York: Macmillan. (Original 1948.)

Slater, P. 1977: *Origin and Significance of the Frankfurt School*. London: Routledge and Kegan Paul.

Smart, B. 1983: *Foucault, Marxism and Critique*. London: Routledge and Kegan Paul.

Smart, B. 1996: Postmodern social theory. In B.S. Turner (ed.), *The Blackwell Companion to Social Theory*. Blackwell: Oxford, 396–428.

Smith, A.D. 1990: Towards a global culture. *Theory Culture and Society*, 7, 2–3.

Smith, N. 1984: *Uneven Development: Nature, Capital and the Production of Space*. Oxford: Basil Blackwell.

Smith, N. 2001: Rescaling politics: geography, globalism, and the new urbanism. In C. Minca (ed.), *Postmodern Geography*. Oxford: Blackwell, 147–68.

Smith, P. 1974: *The Dynamics of Urbanism*. London: Hutchison.

Smith, P. 1976: *The Syntax of Cities*. London: Hutchison.

Smith, P.M. 2001: *Transnational Urbanism*. Oxford: Blackwell.

Soja, E. 1989: *Postmodern Geographies*. London: Verso.

Soja, E. 2000: *Postmetropolis*. Oxford: Blackwell.

Soltan, M. 1996: Deconstruction and architecture. In T. Dutton and L. Mann (eds), *Reconstructing Architecture*. Minneapolis: University of Minnesota Press, 234–58.

Sommer, R. 1969: *Personal Space: The Behavioural Basis for Design*. Englewood Cliffs, NJ: Prentice Hall.

Soule, M.E. 1991: Land use planning and wildlife maintenance: guidelines for conserving wildlife in an urban landscape. *Journal of the American Planning Association*, 57, 313–23.

Soule, M.E. and Lease, G. (eds) 1995: *Reinventing Nature?* Washington, DC: Island Press.

Sprieregen, P. 1965: *Urban Design: The Architecture of Towns and Cities*. New York: McGraw-Hill.

Squire, S.J. 1994: Accounting for cultural meanings: the interface between geography and tourism studies re-examined. *Progress in Human Geography*, 18(1), 1–16.

Stephenson, G. 1992: *On a Human Scale*. Fremantle: Fremantle Arts Centre Press.

Stevenson, N. 1992: *Snow Crash*. London: Penguin.

Stilwell, F. 2002: *Political Economy: The Contest of Economic Ideas*. Melbourne: Oxford.

Stone, B. and Rodgers, M. 2001: Urban form and thermal efficiency: how the design of cities influences the urban heat island effect. *APA Journal*, 67(2), 186–98.

Suartika, G.A.M. 2005: *Vanishing Paradise. Planning and Conflict in Bali*. PhD thesis, Faculty of the Built Environment, University of New South Wales, Australia.

Swaffield, S. 2002: *Theory in Landscape Architecture*. Boston, MA: University of Pennsylvania Press.

Szelenyi, I. 1983: *Urban Inequalities under State Socialism*. Oxford: Oxford University Press.

Tafuri, M. 1974: L'architecture dans le boudoir: the language of criticism and the criticism of language. In K.M. Hays (ed.), *Architecture Theory Since 1968*. Cambridge, MA: MIT Press, 149–73.

Tafuri, M. 1976: *Architecture and Utopia: Design and Capitalist Development*. Cambridge, MA: MIT Press.

Tafuri, M. 1980: *Theories and History of Architecture*. New York: Harper and Rowe.

Tafuri, M. 1987: *The Sphere and the Labyrinth*. Cambridge, MA: MIT Press.

Tarkofsky, A. 1986: *Sculpting in Time*. Austin: University of Texas Press.

Taylor, N. 1999: The elements of townscape and the art of urban design. *Journal of Urban Design*, 4(2), 195–209.

Taylor, N. 2002: State surveillance and the right to privacy. *Surveillance and Society*, 1(1), 66–85.

Thiel, P. 1961: A sequence–experience notation for architectural and urban spaces. *Town Planning Review*, 32, 33–52.

Thompson, E.P. 1963: *The Making of the English Working Class*. London: Gollancz.

Thompson E.P. 1995: *The Poverty of Theory*. London: Merlin.

Throsby, D. 1997: The relationship between cultural and economic policy. *Culture and Policy*, 8(1), 25–35.

Toledo, V.M. 1996: The ecological crisis: a second contradiction of capitalism. In T. Benton (ed.), *The Greening of Marxism*. London: Guilford, 222–8.

Touraine, A. 1995: *A Critique of Modernity*. Blackwell: Oxford.

Trancik, R. 1986: *Finding Lost Space: Theories of Urban Design*. New York: Van Nostrand Reinhold.

Trepl, L. 1996: City and ecology. *Capital, Nature, Socialism: A Journal of Socialist Ecology*, 7(2), 85–94.

Troy, P. 1996: *The Perils of Urban Consolidation*. Sydney: Federation Press.

Tschumi, B. 1996: *Architecture and Disjunction*. Cambridge, MA: MIT Press.

Tunnard, C. 1953: *The City of Man*. New York: Charles Scribner's Sons.

Turner, T. 1996: *City as Landscape: A Postmodern View of Design and Planning*. London: Spon.

United Nations Conference on Environment and Development 1992: Agenda 21, Chapter 2 'Promoting sustainable development'.

Unwin, R. 1994: *Town Planning in Practice: An Introduction to the Art of Designing Cities and Suburbs*. New York: Princeton Architectural Press. (Original 1909.)

Urry, J. 1981: *The Anatomy of Capitalist Societies*. London: Macmillan.

Urry, J. 1990: *The Tourist Gaze*. London: Sage.

Urry, J. 1995: *Consuming Places*. London: Routledge.

Valentine, G. 1990: Women's fear and the design of public space. *Built Environment*, 16, 288–303.

Valentine, G. 1993: (Hetero)sexing space: lesbian perceptions and experiences of everyday spaces. *Environment and Planning D: Society and Space*, 11, 395–448.

Valentine, G. 1995: Out and about: geographies of lesbian landscapes. *International Journal of Urban and Regional Research*, 19(1), 96–111.

Vance, M. 1981: *Plazas: A Bibliography*. Urbana, IL: Montecello.

Vazquez, A.S. 1973: *Art and Society: Essays in Marxist Aesthetics*. London: Monthly Review Press.

Venturi, R., Scott-Brown, D. and Izenour, S. 1977: *Learning from Las Vegas*. Cambridge, MA: MIT Press.

Vidler, A. 1978: The third typology. In *Architecture Rationelle: The Reconstruction of the European City*. Brussels: Editions Archives d'Architecture, 28–32.

Vincent, A. 1992: *Modern Political Ideologies*. Oxford: Blackwell.

Vitruvius, M.P. 1988: *The Ten Books of Architecture*. London: R. Alfray (1775 Leoni Edition).

Wachs, M. and Crawford, M. (eds) 1992: *The Car and the City: The Automobile, the Built Environment and Daily Life*. Ann Arbor: University of Michigan Press.

Wagner, B., Pacifini, R. and Schwartz, B. 1991: The Vietnam Veterans' Memorial: commemorating a difficult past. *American Journal of Sociology*, 97, 376–420.

Wagner, O. 1988: *Modern Architecture: A Guide for his Students to this Field of Art*. Los Angeles: Getty Research Institute.

Walby, S. 1990: *Theorising Patriarchy*. Oxford: Blackwell.

Walker, L. 1998: Home and away: the feminist remapping of public and private space in Victorian London. In R. Ainsley (ed.), *New Frontiers of Space, Bodies and Gender*. London: Routledge, 66–75.

Wallerstein, I. 2000: The world system. In J. Beynon and D. Dunkerley (eds), *Globalization: The Reader*. London: Athlone Press, 233–8.

Wansborough, M. and Magean, A. 2000: The role of urban design in cultural regeneration. *Journal of Urban Design*, 5(2), 187–97.

Ward, A. 1996: The suppression of the social in design: architecture as war. In T.A. Dutton and L.H. Mann (eds), *Reconstructing Architecture*. Minneapolis: University of Minnesota Press, 27–70.

Warren, B. 1980: *Imperialism, Pioneer of Capitalism*. London: Verso.

Watkin, D. 1982: *The English Vision: The Picturesque in Architecture, Landscape Architecture and Garden Design*. London: Breslich and Foss.

Watson, P. 2000: *A Terrible Beauty: A History of the People and Ideas that Shaped the Modern Mind*. London: Weidenfeld and Nicolson.

Watson, S. 1986: *Accommodating Inequality: Gender and Housing*. Sydney: Allen and Unwin.

Webb, M. 1990: *The City Square*. London: Thames and Hudson.

Webber M. 1963: The urban place and the non-place urban realm. In M. Webber (ed.), *Explorations into Urban Structure*. Philadelphia: University of Pennsylvania Press, 6–31.

Weber, M. 1968: *Economy and Society*. New York: Bedminster Press.

Weisman, L.K. 1992: *Discrimination by Design: A Feminist Critique of the Man-made Environment*. Urbana: University of Illinois Press.

White, W. 1980: *The Social Life of Small Urban Spaces*. Washington, DC: The Conservation Foundation.

Whitehead, M 2003: (Re)-analysing the sustainable city: nature, urbanisation and the regulation of socio-environmental relations in the U.K. *Urban Studies*, 7(11), 1183–1206.

Wicherley, R.E. 1967: *How The Greeks Built Cities*. London: Macmillan.

Wiener, N. 1948: *Cybernetics*. Cambridge, MA: MIT Press.

Willett, J. 1978: *Art and Politics in the Weimar Period. The New Sobriety 1917–1933*. New York: Pantheon.

Williams, K., Burton, E. and Jenks, M (eds) 2000: *Achieving Sustainable Urban Form*. London: Spon.

Williams, R. 1958: *Culture and Society*. London: Chatto and Windus

Williams, R. 1965: *The Long Revolution*. London: Penguin.

Williams, R. 1981: *Culture*. London: Fontana.

Willis, K. and Yeoh, B. (eds) 2000: *Gender and Migration*. Cheltenham: Edward Elgar.

Wilshire, B. 1990: *The Moral Collapse of the University: Professionalism, Purity and Alienation*. Albany: State University of New York Press.

Wirth, L. 1938: Urbanism as a way of life. *American Journal of Sociology*, 44, 1–24.

Wittgenstein, L. 1974: *Philosophical Grammar*. Oxford: Blackwell.

Wolch, J. 1996: Zoopolis. *Capital, Nature, Socialism: A Journal of Socialist Ecology*, 7(2), 21–47.

Woodward, R. 1982: Urban symbolism. *Ekistics*, 295, 35–42.

World Commission on Environment and Development 1987: *Our Common Future*. Oxford: Oxford University Press.

Worskett, R. 1969: *The Character of Towns*. London: Architectural Press.

Wrong, D.H. 1979: *Power: Its Forms, Bases and Uses*. Oxford: Blackwell.

Yiftachel, O. 1989: Towards a new typology of urban planning theories. *Environment and Planning B: Society and Space*, 7, 63–82.

Yiftachel, O. and Alexander, I. 1995: The state of metropolitan planning: decline or restructuring? *Environment and Planning C: Government and Policy*, 13(2), 273–96.

Young, J. 1990: *Post-environmentalism*. London: Belhaven.

Young, M. 1958: *The Rise of the Meritocracy*. Harmondsworth: Penguin.

Zimmerman, M.E. 1987: Feminism, deep ecology, and environmental ethics. *Environmental Ethics*, 9, 21–44.

Zucker, P. 1959: *Town and Square: From the Agora to the Village*. Cambridge, MA: MIT Press.

Zukin, S. 1991: *Landscapes of Power: From Detroit to Disney World*. Berkeley: University of California Press.

Index

Page numbers in *italics* denotes an illustration/table